WITHDRAWN

THE UNITED STATES AND DECOLONIZATION IN WEST AFRICA, 1950–1960

**ROCHESTER STUDIES in
AFRICAN HISTORY and the DIASPORA**
Toyin Falola, Senior Editor
University of Texas at Austin

(ISSN: 1092-5228)

1. *Power Relations in Nigeria: Ilorin Slaves and Their Successors*
Ann O'Hear

2. *Dilemmas of Democracy in Nigeria*
Edited by Paul Beckett and Crawford Young
(ISSN: 1092-5228)

3. *Science and Power in Colonial Mauritius*
William Kelleher Storey

4. *Namibia's Post-Apartheid Regional Institutions: The Founding Year*
Joshua Bernard Forrest

5. *A Saro Community in the Niger Delta, 1912–1984:
The Potts-Johnsons of Port Harcourt and Their Heirs*
Mac Dixon-Fyle

6. *Contested Power in Angola: 1840s to the Present*
Linda Heywood

7. *Nigerian Chiefs: Traditional Power in Modern Politics, 1890s–1990s*
Olufemi Vaughan

8. *West Indians in West Africa, 1808–1880: The African Diaspora in Reverse*
Nemata Blyden

9. *The United States and Decolonization in West Africa, 1950–1960*
Ebere Nwaubani

THE UNITED STATES AND DECOLONIZATION IN WEST AFRICA, 1950–1960

Ebere Nwaubani

UNIVERSITY OF ROCHESTER PRESS

Copyright © 2001 Ebere Nwaubani

All Rights Reserved. Except as permitted under current legislation, no part of this work may be photocopied, stored in a retrieval system, published, performed in public, adapted, broadcast, transmitted, recorded or reproduced in any form or by any means, without the prior permission of the copyright owner.

First published 2001
by the University of Rochester Press

The University of Rochester Press is an imprint of Boydell & Brewer, Inc.
668 Mt. Hope Avenue, Rochester, NY 14620, USA
and of Boydell & Brewer, Ltd.
P.O. Box 9, Woodbridge, Suffolk 1P12 3DF, UK

ISBN 1-58046-076-3
ISSN-1092-5228
RSAHD 9

Library of Congress Cataloging-in-Publication Data
Nwaubani, Ebere, 1956–
    The United States and decolonizationin West Africa, 1950–1960 / Ebere Nwaubani.
       p. cm. — (Rochester studies in African history and the diaspora, ISSN 1092-5228 ; v. 9)
    Includes bibliographical references and index.
    ISBN 1-58046-076-3
    1. Africa, West—Politics and government—1884–1960. 2. Decolonization—Africa, West—History—20th century. 3. Africa, West—Relations—United States. 4. United States—Relations—Africa, West. I. Title. II. Series.

DT476.2.N88 2001
966.03—dc21   00-049445

British Library Cataloguing-in-Publication Data
A catalogue record for this book is available from the British Library

Designed and typeset by ISIS-1 Corporation
Printed in the United States of America
This publication is printed on acid-free paper

To my parents
Joseph Nwachukwu and Rose Nwankakwa,
my first teachers,
for their abiding interest

CONTENTS

	Illustrations	ix
	Table	x
	Acknowledgments	xiii
	Introduction	xv
	Abbreviations	xx
1	Decolonization in West Africa	1
2	The Archaeology of Policy	28
3	Truman's Dual Mandate	56
4	Minimalism as Policy	86
5	Ghana: Honeymoon and Estrangement	119
6	The Political Economy of the Volta Project	163
7	Guinea: The Weight of Residual Interests	205
8	Summing Up	228
	Notes	246
	Bibliography	311
	Index	328

ILLUSTRATIONS

1   Map of West Africa   xi
2   Map of Ghana: The Volta River Project   167

TABLE

Table of United States Aid to West Africa, 1953–60   100

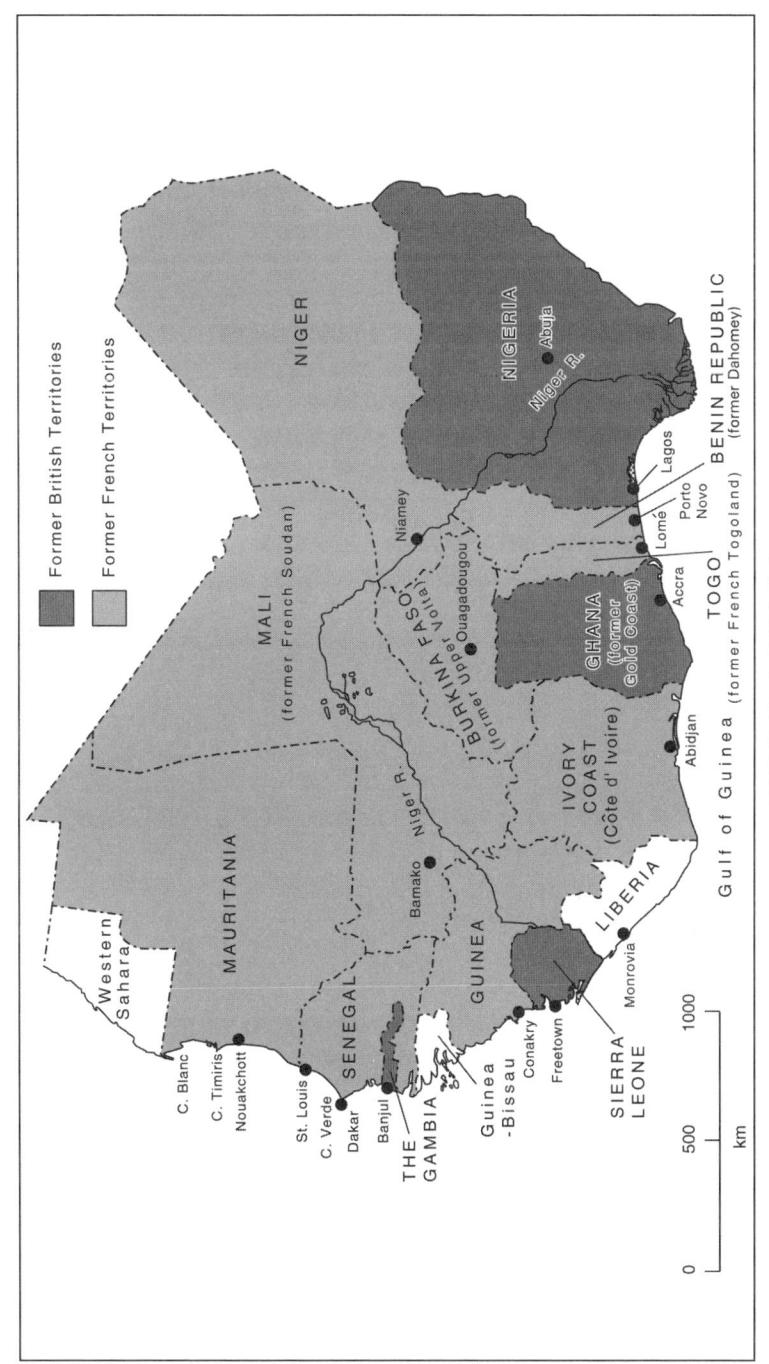

ACKNOWLEDGMENTS

I have long been interested in understanding and explaining the causal background of independence, that is, the transfer of political power from Europeans to Africans. In spring 1992, Martin Klein of the University of Toronto suggested that I explore the United States dimension of this subject. Since then, from the research phase and the many drafts this work has gone through, so many people and institutions have been of tremendous assistance and support to me that it is difficult to remember all or even acknowledge them adequately.

Research funding came from the Associates of the University of Toronto Travel Grant Fund; the Stacey Graduate Travel Fund of the History Department, University of Toronto; the John F. Kennedy Library Foundation Research Grant; the Abilene Travel Grant of the Eisenhower World Affairs Institute; and the Truman Library Institute. A two-year residential fellowship at the Frederick Douglass Institute for African and African-American Studies, University of Rochester, New York, afforded me the time to write the initial drafts. To all these institutions, I owe a deep debt of gratitude. In the various archives and communities in which I did my research, I met many good-natured men and women who went beyond the call of duty to help me. Like others, I found the Truman Library, Independence, Missouri, to be the most hospitable of all repositories. Abilene, Kansas—the home of the Eisenhower Library—has as its motto, "History. Heroes. Hospitality." I went to Abilene in search of history, but I also met some of the friendliest people I have ever known. In this regard, I must mention Mr. John Zutavern and Attorney Robert H. "Hank" Royer, Jr., who went to unusually great lengths to make my stay in Abilene as comfortable as possible.

Robert Accinelli, Cranford Pratt, Ronald Pruessen, and Jean Smith, all of the University of Toronto; Robert McMahon of the University of Florida at Gainesville; Thomas Noer of Carthage College, Kenosha, Wisconsin; and Richard Rathbone of the School of Oriental and African Studies, London, all read at least one draft of the entire manuscript. My colleagues at Boulder, Robert Schulzinger and Thomas Zeiler, read the first and second drafts. Another Boulder colleague, Jim Jankowski, read the second draft. I cannot thank them enough for being so generous with their time. I must add that this book gained a lot from their insightful comments, suggestions, and encouragement.

A number of friends—especially Adeleke Adeeko, Ademola Adeleke, Robert Hanks, and Onaiwu Ogbomo—have been very supportive and helpful in manifold ways. I am no less indebted to Joseph Inikori of the University of Rochester and Toyin Falola of the University of Texas at Austin, both of whom have been very helpful in this and other endeavors. Pat Murphy, our in-house technical consultant in the History Department, University of Colorado at Boulder, helped me out with the more arcane aspects of computer word processing. I would also like to mention Timothy Madigan and Louise Goldberg of the University of Rochester Press: their enthusiasm, sense of urgency, and professional guidance were important in seeing this book through.

In all, Martin Klein stands out for particular mention. Since fall 1990, he has been my counselor, mentor, guardian, and much more. He suggested this book, persuaded me of its relevance to those interested in the decolonization process in Africa, and has remained very interested and encouraging through the various phases of its gestation.

Ebere Nwaubani
Boulder, Colorado
July 2000

INTRODUCTION

In a 1981 essay, Thomas Noer lamented the "non-benign neglect" of sub-Saharan Africa by historians of American foreign policy.[1] Since then, a number of historical texts—virtually all focused on South Africa, the Congo crisis, and the period after 1960—have appeared. Nevertheless, it is still the case that relative to other parts of the world, the history of United States involvement in Africa remains very much understudied. There is therefore a pressing need for books such as this, which—drawing on the pertinent primary sources—explores the nature, basis, and objectives of United States presence in West Africa in 1950–60.

From a purely Africanist perspective—and this is what attracted me to this study—there is an additional justification for this book. In the existing literature as well as the popular mythology dealing with Africa's transition from European domination to independence, the United States appears as the anticolonial power par excellence. Writing in 1947, Obafemi Awolowo, who went on to become a leading Nigerian politician in the period 1952–83, asserted that the issue of whether independence or self-government was the ultimate goal of British colonies "never received the attention it deserved until the people of the United States forced it into prominence."[2] This perception remains very influential in texts on West African—indeed, African—history.

In a standard text on West African history, Olajide Aluko describes the influence of the United States on Britain's decolonization program as "profound." He believes that after World War II, "it seemed as though the disappearance of the British Empire was the first objective of American policy." West Africa is excluded from any Cold War entanglements in this regard, for "there were no defense problems of any significance to complicate United States. policy. The area was physically distant from the communist world, and the Sino-Soviet political and economic influence there was insignificant." Aluko is thus able to insist that "U.S. policy was directed towards accelerating the process of decolonization which the British Government had decisively begun in 1951 with the introduction of representative governments in all its colonial territories in West Africa except the Gambia."[3]

Focusing on how the United States affected the end of the British Empire in tropical Africa, Wm. Roger Louis and Ronald Robinson argue that while the United States "tended to act more often than not as a guarantor of Europe's remaining colonies," it also insisted on "liberal advances toward independence." On this basis, they conclude that "[i]n the shadow of their powerful American ally, the British followed certain golden rules more warily than ever: handle the colonies with kid gloves, concede to subjects rather than risk confrontations with them; and above all avoid all the dangers of possible uprisings, armed repressions, and colonial wars. Only thus could the possibility of American intervention in the African empire be averted."[4]

The anticolonial image of the United States is not confined to Africanist circles. Jeffrey Frieden, for example, has argued that the evolution of United States policies towards the underdeveloped countries (UDCs) after World War II were "crucially affected by the rapidity of the changes in America's international economic position," best evidenced in its dramatic transformation from the world's largest borrower to its largest lender. The changes ensured a structural shift from investment in primary production to "[a] new set of overseas American economic interests: direct investors interested primarily in local markets, and portfolio investors lending to strong national governments." These "new investment interests were far less prone to lobbying for home-country direct intervention" in the political affairs of the countries where they were operating. At the same time, the preeminent economic strength of the United States "reduced the need for exclusive access to markets." On the other hand, local economic, political, and social conditions in the UDCs had, by 1945, attained a degree of sophistication that made United States military intervention "both less feasible and less necessary," a far cry from the conditions prevalent between 1890 and 1920. Consequently, "American policy became far more willing to compromise with local leaders and was insistent that the European powers follow suit and decolonize."[5]

These claims for United States anticolonialism are not based on any study of the primary records. Consequently, the nature of United States involvement in Africa's transition to independence features prominently in this book. This is particularly necessary, for as Louis and Robinson pointed out, the subject matter is a "cardinally important aspect" of the Africanist discourse on the decolonization process.[6]

A word on usages: in this book, "Africa" is used in reference to "Africa south of the Sahara." In its West African coverage, this book excludes Liberia, which was granted independence by the United States in 1847. It also excludes the Portuguese colonies (Guinea-Bissau and the Cape Verde Islands) since Portugal was not decolonizing during the period covered here. For convenience, the "United States" and "Washington" will be used interchangeably in reference to the "official mind" of the United States, particularly the segment that was involved in the formulation and execution of foreign policy. "Western Europe" (or Europe) refers to the European powers that had colonies in (West) Africa, especially Britain and France.

In the 1950s, the foreign policy establishment in Washington split continental Africa into four categories: Egypt, which was considered as part of the Near East; North Africa (Libya, Morocco, and Tunisia; for all practical purposes, Algeria was regarded as an integral part of France); the white settler enclaves, especially South Africa; and the rest—West Africa, Central Africa, and East Africa (including the Horn)—which were collectively referred to as "Africa South of the Sahara." The United States had a uniform policy for the latter. There was thus no distinct policy statement on West Africa until 1960. The implication, and this needs to be emphasized, is that *the general lines of policy discussed in this book are of equal relevance to all of sub-Saharan Africa.* The methodological approach here has been to extract West Africa from this general picture and to make a conscious effort to distinguish those strands of policy that had a distinctly West African flavor.

All through this book, "communist/communism" appear in quotation marks. In Western (including the United States) discourse, "communism" and "communist" refer to the Soviet system and society (as well as its look-alikes, such as China). My own conceptualization of communism is derived from Karl Marx himself. And as is well known, the communism envisioned by Marx bears no relationship to the now defunct Soviet model of organizing a society—with its Leninist "vanguard" political party as well as the brutal, totalitarian regime of Joseph Stalin with its gulags, convict farm labor, repression, and purges. It is thus very misleading to refer to Stalinism as "communism"; it does not matter that the former masqueraded itself under an ideology of proletarian internationalism.

There is, in this study, a total absence of nongovernmental agents and agencies of any sort. The reason is that I did not find any domestic constituency or lobby group (with the possible exception of Kaiser in chapter 6) involved in shaping United States policy and presence in Africa during the period covered by this book. There were, admittedly, a number of congressional reports on Africa, but I found no evidence that any of them had a bearing on policy formulation. Indeed, except for its drastic cuts in foreign aid appropriations, Congress followed the executive branch on matters relating to Africa. Policy formulation was thus entirely a bureaucratic affair. I will return to this matter in the concluding chapter, but it is worth raising at this point in order to head off any criticism that the book is too much in the "what one clerk said to another" mold and therefore mechanical in its description and analysis.

In the State Department itself, until the creation of the Bureau of African Affairs in 1958, Africa south of the Sahara fell under the jurisdiction of the Bureau of Near Eastern, South Asian, and African Affairs. One would imagine that in this cluster, there must have been very little time for Africa. The first national intelligence estimate (NIE) on Africa was issued in December 1953[7] while the first National Security Council (NSC) paper on the region appeared in August 1957.[8] Yet, it seems that as far as Africa was concerned, the assistant secretaries who headed those bureaus were in charge of policy formulation and execution. The secretaries of state and their undersecretaries injected Africa only into the wider discourse on the United States position on the so-called colonial question. With the exception of Ghana, which achieved its independence in March 1957, the president had nothing whatsoever to do with Africa until 1960.[9]

In spite of the creation of the Bureau of African Affairs and even the end of European rule, the underlying factor in policy making remained unchanged: the "European-oriented perspective," as Gabriel Kolko points out, "defined Washington's policies [towards Africa] completely [in the 1950s], and while a small group that saw Africa as a problem in its own right emerged towards the end of the decade to create relatively minor internal differences in its discussions, policy itself remained firmly in the hands of the Europeanists in the State Department." Consequently, at "the end of 1960 it [Africa] was firmly assigned to Europe's sphere of influence as ever."[10]

Decolonization as an Analytical Framework

As chapter 3 shows, the beginning of post–World War II United States involvement in Africa can be traced to the activities of the Economic Cooperation Administration (ECA), which went into operation in 1948. By coincidence, 1948 was also a key turning point in the "decolonization" process in Africa. On the heels of the February 1948 riots in the Gold Coast (now Ghana), far-reaching constitutional changes were put in place in the territory in 1950. In a general sense, the developments in the Gold Coast set the stage for the transfer of political power to Africans. From then, the "wind of change" blew so hard and fast that 1960 became Africa's " year of independence": that year, seventeen countries achieved independence from European colonial rule.[11] It was against this background that United States presence and interest in Africa were expanding, albeit, rather cautiously. In the circumstance, "decolonization" seems appropriate as the analytical backdrop for a discussion of Washington's policy in Africa in the 1950s.

Chapter 1 discusses the decolonization process in West Africa and offers a redefinition of what the process involves. In this regard, a clear distinction is made between decolonization and independence: the former includes, but goes beyond, independence (the transfer of political power to Africans). This conceptual clarification serves two purposes: first, it allows decolonization to accommodate the colonial continuities in the postcolonial state; and second, it enables one to use decolonization as a useful analytical tool in the study of Africa's location in contemporary international relations. This framework is particularly relevant here because from the mid-1950s, the translation of decolonization into neocolonialism was the thrust of United States policy in Africa.

To recapitulate: central to the analytical usage of decolonization in this book is an understanding that it involved a redefinition of center-periphery relations to allow for the integration of the "independent" African states (and their political elite) into a European-constructed neocolonial network. This book is about the United States response as this political reconfiguration unfolded in West Africa. Much of the serious study of United States involvement in sub-Saharan Africa has focused on the Congo crisis, South Africa, Southern Rhodesia, and Portuguese-controlled Africa—all of which had one obvious residual entanglement or the other with the potential to complicate United States policy. West Africa affords the platform for a study of United States conduct in Africa in the absence of any such entanglements.

The country case studies in this book are Ghana and Guinea, the only countries that achieved their independence in the 1950s. The archival sources on Guinea are rather thin because the United States had practically no relationship with that country, and this is reflected in the study here. Nonetheless, the chapter on Guinea, like chapter 5 which deals with Ghana, furnishes an empirical study of Washington's response to the decolonization process in West Africa. Guinea, in addition, serves as the litmus test for Washington's response to the "communist" advance into West Africa in the period 1950–60.

ABBREVIATIONS

ACUA	Advisory Committee on Underdeveloped Areas (ECA Dependent Areas Branch)
AID	Agency for International Development
ALCAN	Aluminum of Canada Limited
ALCOA	Aluminum Company of America
AmCongen	United States consulate general
AmConsulate	United States consulate
AmEmbassy	United States embassy
AWF	Ann Whitman File (Eisenhower Library, Abilene, Kansas)
BAC	British Aluminum Company
CIA	Central Intelligence Agency
CPP	Convention Peoples' Party (of Ghana)
DDE	Dwight David Eisenhower
DDEL	Dwight David Eisenhower Library (Abilene, Kansas)
Desp.	Despatch
DLF	Development Loan Fund
DOTs	Dependent Overseas Territories
ECA	Economic Cooperation Administration
ERP	European Recovery Program
ExCo	Executive Council
FOA	Foreign Operations Administration
FRUS	*Foreign Relations of the United States* (State Department publication)
FWA	French West Africa
FY	financial year
HSTL	Harry S. Truman Library (Independence, Missouri)
ICA	International Cooperation Administration
IR	Intelligence Report (produced by State Department Office of Intelligence Research)
JCS	Joint Chiefs of Staff
Leg Co	Legislative Council
MSA	Mutual Security Agency
MSP	Mutual Security Program

NA	National Archives, Washington, D.C.
NIE	National Intelligence Estimate
NSC	National Security Council
OCB	(NSC) Operations Coordinating Board
OIR	State Department Office of Intelligence Research
OSS	Office of Strategic Services
OTs	Overseas Territories
PSF	President's Secretary Office (Truman Library, Independence, Missouri)
RG	Record Group (of National Archives documents)
TC	United Nations Trusteeship Council
TCOR	*UN Trusteeship Council Official Records*
UDCs	underdeveloped countries
UGCC	United Gold Coast Convention
USIA	United States Information Agency
USIS	United States Information Service
USOM	United States Operations Mission
USUN	United States Mission at the United Nations, New York
VALCO	Volta Aluminum Company
VRP	Volta River Project
WFM	Washington Foreign Ministers' Meeting

1
DECOLONIZATION IN WEST AFRICA

Many equate decolonization with independence and will therefore agree with Aguibou Yansane that decolonization in Africa "refers to the formal transfer of political authority and sovereignty from a colonial state to indigenous leaders who hold autonomous power to decide on political, economic, cultural and social policies affecting the lives of all the nationals."[1] Much of the explanation of the process leading up to this transfer of power is built upon the epistemological foundation of modernization theory. The central concept in modernization is change, tremendous changes in many aspects of the society, which enable the forces of transition to be channeled through a wider network of circulation. The agents of these changes are middle-class elites who are themselves products of the modernization process: it is these elements who challenge and reshape the preexisting order.

The starting point in applying the concept of modernization to the discourse on decolonization is that the colonial presence was, by definition, the harbinger of Western forces of social change such as expanded lines of physical and social communication, Western education, wage labor, a money economy, urbanization, and above all, a Westernized African class. By the very fact of its internalization of the values of the percolating European culture, this class was better placed to mediate social change for the rest of the African population, patterning, in the process, the growth and diffusion of political, economic, and social "modernization." Martin Kilson, for example, asserts that "[i]t is evident that the source of modernization in Africa was the establishment of colonial rule—or more precisely, the colonial situation." He argues that "Africans caught up" in the modernization process "were to one degree or another, modernized, which meant that they in turn would become modernizers. It is here that the social and political aspects of change meet, and in a colonial situation this often leads to conflict," which "affects power relationships, and which is often resolved in favor of one group of modernizers or the other."[2]

The literature shows how the upper segment of the Westernized or "modernized" class organized the anticolonial political movements and "demanded" or "struggled" for and "won" independence.[3] Anthony Hopkins, for example, holds that in the post-1945 era, African anticolonial movements "assumed a more organized and a more overt political form." This development, according to him, had its antecedents in the 1930s, but "[t]he years between 1945 and 1950 saw an upsurge of militant, anticolonial activities in the West African territories—in the Press, in mass demonstrations and in confrontation between African leaders and colonial officials." After 1950, the character of African opposition to colonialism changed "from that of bitterness and militancy" to "a more conciliatory and cooperative mood." As an explanation for this switch, Hopkins says that "the colonial powers had started to make substantial concessions to African demands by promoting a greater degree of self-government."[4] Given the stress placed on the centrality of the nationalist endeavor, I regard the perspective offered by works in this genre as the "nationalist" interpretation of the decolonization process.

The Transfer of Power in British and French West Africa: An Overview

Since space constraints here do not permit a discussion of the decolonization process in every West African state, I will focus on Ghana.[5] This choice has been dictated by two reasons: first, Ghana is widely accepted as the pacesetter of African independence; and second, it is the primary country case study in this book.

There is an eternal aptness in Andrew Cohen's evaluation of British policy in Africa in the pre-1940 era.[6] Constitutional development, he says, was "cautious . . . , more important for the future than for what it was at the time, important in fact for the form and pattern which it created." Cohen recalls that indirect rule "figured so large in this whole period" because the British assumed that they had "indefinite time ahead during which the system could grow" under their guidance.[7]

Elsewhere, I have shown that British policy in Africa continued to be shackled by the dogma of indirect rule until 1948.[8] In the Gold Coast, for example, the chiefs were assigned six out of the fourteen unofficial seats in the Legislative Council (LegCo) created by the 1925 constitution. The 1946 constitution increased the chiefs' representation: out of the eighteen unofficial seats in the new LegCo, the Joint Provincial Council of Chiefs had nine and four were allotted to the Ashanti Confederacy Council.[9] But these figures still do not convey the real significance of the chiefs, the fact that by the mid-1940s, indirect rule had been enhanced to provide the structural basis of the entire colonial political process.

Under the constitutions framed for Nigeria and the Gold Coast in 1946, the native authorities (the chiefs) were no longer mere local government agencies: they were fused together into regional groupings and the groupings in turn joined into something of a central "native authority council"; a direct link was thus formed between the regional and central legislatures. Members of the regional assemblies were selected from the native authorities, and the assemblies in turn served as electoral colleges for the legislative councils.[10] This meant that to be associated at all with the political system, one had to relate to the chiefs.[11]

Utilizing the native authorities as the agencies of political recruitment, the constitutions gave an appearance of unofficial majorities in the LegCos by increasing African representation. Beyond this, the territories were in no way set on the path of self-government. The governors remained, as before, the instruments of policy, responsible for initiating bills and with the power to veto any legislation that did not receive their approval. It was the February 1948 Gold Coast "riots" that finally forced the issue and made the transfer of power to Africans a matter of serious politics in London.

On 28 February 1948, ex-servicemen demonstrating in Accra against nonpayment of discharge benefits and unemployment were fired upon by the police: two were killed, five wounded. Three days of rioting engulfed not only Accra but most other towns as well. In the end, 29 people were killed, and 237 injured. The riots were a spontaneous mass revolt, which occurred against a background of widespread discontent and tension arising largely from economic causes.[12] Politics intruded into this discontent in the sense that the difficulties were, or were believed to have been, caused by a colonial administration that did not seem to be doing anything to alleviate the situation.

By 1947, the major concern in the Gold Coast arose from "swollen shoot" disease, which attacked cocoa trees. The only known remedy at the time was to cut down infected trees. But the farmers, resentful of an approach that threatened their livelihood, were not enthusiastic about cutting their trees down. As a consequence, the Agriculture Department became more directly involved in the process: from January 1947, it sent its own men to destroy infected trees. By the end of the year, 2.5 million trees had been destroyed, and it was calculated that 50 million trees, a quarter of the total, were still infected.[13]

Since the late 1920s, when it constituted 78 percent of Ghana's total exports,[14] cocoa has been the mainstay of the country's economy and society. Swollen shoot disease was thus a national disaster. It was particularly so for the farmers, especially the Akan. Commenting on the atmosphere prevailing in the affected areas, one official assessment observed that "[i]t is a widespread economic depression which has affected the social and moral life of the community. . . .It has created a sensation. The disaster is felt appallingly."[15]

Even more widespread and problematic than swollen shoot was inflation. In the years following the end of World War II, the prices of local staples in the Gold Coast were "probably about two and a half times the prewar level" and many imported foodstuffs were hard to come by.[16] Worse, wages lagged behind inflation: the real wage index (for unskilled labor in Accra) fell from 100 in 1939 to 66 by November 1941; and even after the wage increases of December 1941, the index still stood at 81. A second wage increase in July 1947 raised the index to 91, but the impact was erased by rising inflation. Consequently, the purchasing power of the laborer's wage dropped to 86 by November 1947.[17]

These difficulties coalesced into a groundswell of mass discontent, which was canalized by Nii Kwabena Bonne, a Ga chief and highly successful Accra-based businessman. In December 1947, he issued an ultimatum: unless the European and Syrian stores reduced their prices, he would call for a mass boycott of imported goods from 24 January 1948.[18] It took the Gold Coast government until 20 February 1948 to convene a meeting that brought Nii Bonne together with the council of chiefs, the chamber of commerce, and the umbrella platform of the European trading companies known as the Association of West African Merchants (AWAM).[19] Meanwhile, the boycott had started as Bonne proposed, and held on well. At the meeting, the companies agreed to reduce their gross overall profit margin (of noncontrolled commodities) from 75 to 50 percent for a three-month trial period. In return, Nii Bonne agreed to call the boycott off on Saturday, 28 February.[20]

Incidentally, the boycott was ending on the day ex-servicemen had planned a procession to present a petition to the governor. "These two events," Kwame Nkrumah was later to recall, "were entirely disconnected and it was mere coincidence that they should have happened on the same day."[21] No sooner had the ex-servicemen started their procession than they abandoned their approved route (in the direction of the government secretariat) and made for Christiansborg Castle (the governor's residence). Almost immediately, they ran into a police barricade; with little hesitancy, the police fired at them. Elsewhere in the town, another major crisis was fast gathering steam: the undertaking by the foreign trading companies to cut prices had been widely misinterpreted as implying an across-the-board 50 percent reduction in prices.[22] Following the police confrontation, the rump of the ex-servicemen turned back and merged with crowds already infuriated because prices had not been reduced as much as had been generally expected. The news of the police shooting was thus the fire on a gunpowder trail: violence erupted immediately. European and Syrian stores and offices were looted, cars were burnt, the prison at Ussher Fort was broken into, and prisoners were released.[23]

A three-man commission headed by Aiken Watson, recorder of Bury, St. Edmunds,[24] was promptly constituted by the British government to "inquire into and report" on the riots "and their underlying causes, and to make recommendations on any matter arising from their inquiry." The commission gave the broadest interpretation to its brief and peeped inquisitively into every cupboard: Africanization of the public service, native administration and the chiefs, tardiness in constitutional reform, trading discrimination against Africans, immigration, housing, land tenure, agriculture, industrial development, law reform, and education. In each case, it uncovered and commented on a skeleton. The commission identified "deeper-lying political, economic and social grievances" as the background cause of the riots. Among the political grievances, it mentioned the discontent of the ex-servicemen who "by the reason of their contact with other peoples" had developed a "political and national consciousness" and now felt disappointed with conditions at home; "a universal feeling" that Africanization was "merely a promise and not a driving force" in government policy; the frustration of the Westernized Africans who saw "no prospect of ever exercising political power under existing conditions"; and a failure to realize that the "star of rule through the chiefs was on the wane."[25]

Finding the 1946 constitution "outmoded at birth," the commission went ahead not just to recommend but to write a new constitution. In the main, the commission proposed an enlarged "Board of Ministers" or executive council (ExCo) and an enlarged LegCo (to be known as the House of Assembly), both with an African majority. The ExCo was to consist of nine full-time, salaried ministers, five of whom were to be African members of the Assembly. The governor was to retain his reserve powers and chairmanship of the ExCo. But the ExCo was to become "a Board of Ministers" with powers to initiate policy and with collective responsibility to the legislature. The governor was excised from the LegCo which, it was proposed, would consist of forty-five elected and five nominated members, "as well as ex officio members, chosen for four years (unless dissolved earlier on the advice of the "Board of Ministers.")[26]

Reacting to the commission's report, which was submitted in August 1948, the British government rejected the criticisms of the 1946 constitution, which, it said, was "framed in consultation with the representatives of the people of the Gold Coast" and was "accepted with enthusiasm by the press and public." The government further recalled that in the two years the constitution had been operational, no demands had been received from the Gold Coast for further constitutional reform. Nonetheless, London committed itself to the Watson proposals, provided they were "acceptable to local opinion."[27] To gauge that opinion, the government appointed an all-Gold Coast committee of forty men, under the chairmanship of Mr. Justice J. Henley Coussey, specifically to examine the Watson Commission's constitutional proposals.

The Coussey Committee commenced sitting on 20 January 1949 and reported to the Gold Coast governor on 17 August of the same year. By twenty votes to nineteen, the committee favored a bicameral legislature, which was to include a House of Assembly consisting of seventy-eight elected members. The House was to elect its speaker from among its members. Besides, it provided for a leader of the House "elected as such by the Assembly and appointed by the Governor." Legislation was to be enacted by the governor "with the advice and consent" of the legislature. In place of the existing ExCo with its merely advisory powers and predominantly official membership, the committee proposed one that would be collectively responsible to the legislature and would have full executive functions and the power of originating policy. The governor, who was to preside over all meetings of the ExCo, was vested with reserve powers to veto or enforce legislation as he deemed fit. In addition, the executive was to consist of not more than three ex-officio members and eight members of the House of Assembly; all eight would have the status of ministers in the ExCo although only six were to have portfolios. The leader of the House, who was to be in the latter category, was also to lead the elected segment of the ExCo in the House, and so be the equivalent of a prime minister.[28]

In October 1949, Secretary of State Arthur Creech Jones published the report of the Coussey Committee together with his comments on it.

He gave a general welcome to the committee's recommendations as the groundwork on which further constitutional progress in the territory could be based. He endorsed the proposal for an ExCo with a majority of Africans who had executive responsibility for departments, and he suggested that the council should be the principal instrument of policy; that it should not meet only when summoned by the governor, as under the 1946 constitution, but also on the request of two-thirds of its members; and that the council should take its decisions by a simple majority vote, the governor having only a casting vote. In addition, Creech Jones suggested that the governor should have the right to act against the majority of the council on matters within the scope of his reserve powers. However, he added that it would be necessary for the exercise of this right (except in emergencies) to be subject to the prior approval of the secretary of state.[29]

On the provision for a leader of the House, Creech Jones felt that in the absence of a party system, the leader would not be sure of retaining the support of a majority in the legislature and that without such a majority, continuity in the conduct of public business could not be maintained. He suggested instead that the ExCo should elect one of its own members to perform the function of the leader of the government side in the legislature. On the proposal for collective executive responsibility to the legislature, the secretary of state observed that while the committee opposed the ExCo being responsible to the governor, it did not recommend the granting of full responsibility to the ministers. The committee had recommended that the governor should remain as the council's chairman and with reserve powers, and that the council itself should include official members. Creech Jones explained that since the governor had such reserve powers, he, rather than the legislature, must retain ultimate responsibility. Although the Coussey Committee had opted for a bicameral legislature, it also presented alternative proposals for a unicameral body. The British government chose the latter.[30]

The 1950 Gold Coast constitution that followed embodied the recommendations of the Coussey Committee as amended by the views of the secretary of state. Given that the governor and the Colonial Office still retained ultimate responsibility for the administration of the territory through overriding reserve powers, the constitution granted an advanced form of colony government rather than a semi-responsible one. Nevertheless, the constitution was a watershed in the Gold Coast's constitutional history and, indeed, in contemporary African history. First, it "conferred on the Gold Coast a greater measure of responsibility for her own internal affairs than had hitherto been conceded to any non-white colonial government on the African continent."[31] The representative element preponderated in the House of Assembly, which had three officials, six nominees representing mining and commercial interests, and seventy-five elected Africans of whom only one-third were chiefs. The governor lost his place in the Assembly. The ExCo, now the major instrument of policy, had a total membership of eleven, which included eight African members of the Assembly; six of the Africans held portfolios.

The constitution had wider implications. Historically, there was "little genuine enthusiasm" on the part of the British "for exporting the 'Westminster model' to countries which lacked the presence of British settlers."[32] The 1950 Gold Coast constitution was therefore revolutionary as it meant a total shift away from indirect rule; with it, the application of the Westminster model to Africa finally became the definitive, irrevocable British policy. And by ending the preeminence of rule through the chiefs, the constitution laid the foundation for self-government,[33] not just in the Gold Coast but in all of British Africa, and even in the French colonies.[34] The white settlers in Kenya saw the constitution as the beginning of the end of "the white man's control throughout the continent."[35]

Nigeria was the immediate beneficiary of the political advance of the Gold Coast. The Colonial Office felt that the Watson report, when published, would "arouse public interest in Nigeria" especially because of the "constitutional chapter with its rather radical recommendations." On this account, a copy of the report was sent—before its publication—to John Macpherson, governor of Nigeria, for "any comments" that occurred to him "on the probable reactions in Nigeria." London clearly prodded the governor: "It is pretty certain," the Colonial Office added, "that Zik will want to make capital out of the report and no doubt you will be considering this aspect of the matter."[36] In his response, Macpherson acknowledged that "[t]here will certainly be lively reactions in Nigeria to the report." He therefore accepted that "[w]e *may* have to alter our timetable for the revision of the Constitution."[37] On 17 August 1948, he announced that the 1947 constitution was due for revision. The 1951 Nigerian constitution that followed was closely patterned after the 1950 Gold Coast constitution. Nigeria's was a federal constitution providing for regional legislatures and ExCos under lieutenant governors in the Northern, Eastern, and Western Regions, as well as a legislature and council of ministers under the chairmanship of the governor at the center. The council of ministers consisted of twelve African ministers and six ex-officio members. The central legislature, the House of Representatives, consisted of a president, appointed by the governor from outside the House; 6 ex-officios, 6 special members and 136 elected members (68 from the North and 34 each from the East and the West).

The question one must address has to do with the role of the "nationalist" elements, especially, Nkrumah, in the achievement of the 1950 Gold Coast constitution. To begin with, the 1946 constitution was warmly received by the nationalist elements;[38] and from 23 July 1946 when it was inaugurated until the short-lived "Positive Action" of 1950, when the details of the 1950 constitution had already been worked out, there were no political protests or pressure for a constitutional revision.

At the time of the February 1948 riots, the United Gold Coast Convention (UGCC) which had come into existence in August 1947, was virtually the only nationalist movement in the Gold Coast. The Watson Commission held the UGCC Working Committee responsible for the riots. There is, however, abundant evidence that the "nationalist" politicians neither organized nor inspired these events (that is, Nii Bonne's boycott, the demonstration by the ex-servicemen, and the riots). "Nii Bonne and his supporters in this boycott," Nkrumah attested, "had never been members of the United Gold Coast Convention and I was therefore quite certain that the campaign had nothing whatever to do with the UGCC." Nkrumah—who had just returned from Britain[39] and was staying with his mother at Tarkwa at the material moment—readily confessed that he "had no time to take part in the boycott" being organized by Nii Bonne. He did not even attend a rally held at Tarkwa at which Nii Bonne spoke, canvassing support.[40] At the time of the riots in Accra, Nkrumah and the UGCC Working Committee were in Saltpond, sixty miles away. Nkrumah readily admitted that he neither had any part in the riots nor any influence on the participants. On the ex-servicemen, he said that he was "certainly aware of their general dissatisfaction" and that "it had been my intention to organize them in due course as an arm of our movement."[41]

By holding the UGCC leadership liable for the riots, the Watson report inadvertently but instantly turned them into nationalist heroes. Nkrumah was the major beneficiary. As John Hargreaves has put it: "Nkrumah had not made the Accra riots; but the government's response helped to make Nkrumah."[42] In the aftermath of the riots, the police had found a (British) Communist Party card on him. Nkrumah, in his own words, explained "in all honesty that the card was of no consequence," that when he was in England, he "had associated [himself] with all parties ranging from the extreme right to the extreme left in order to gain as much knowledge as I could to help me in organizing my own nationalist party on the best possible lines when I eventually returned to my country."[43] Yet, the

Watson report dwelt at length with Nkrumah's "communist affiliations"; asserted his "avowed aim for a Union of West African Soviet Socialist Republics"; and held that he "boldly proposes a program which is all too familiar to those which have fallen the victims of Communist enslavement" and that the UGCC "Working Committee, fired by Mr. Nkrumah's enthusiasm and drive, were eager to seize political power and for the time being were indifferent to the means adopted to attain it."[44] Perhaps of greater significance was the fact that all the leading Gold Coast politicians, except Nkrumah, were appointed to the Coussey commission. By thus isolating him, the colonial regime built up Nkrumah's stature as the leading anti-British antagonist.

The UGCC leadership, meeting at Saltpond, learnt of the riots at about 5.30 p.m., by telephone, and left immediately, arriving in Accra around 8.30 p.m. After assessing the situation, they met again, after which J. B. Danquah, as the party's leader, despatched an 8000–word cablegram alerting the secretary of state that "Civil Government Gold Coast broken down" and that "the Working Committee United Gold Coast Convention declare they are prepared and ready to take over interim government." Nkrumah, the UGCC secretary, sent out a condensed version demanding the recall of the governor and the institution of a commission to supervise the establishment of a constituent assembly. He chose as his outlets the UN, the *New York Times,* and the *Moscow New Times.*[45]

In retrospect, those two cablegrams served as a signal of the differences between Nkrumah and the rest of the UGCC leadership. By August 1948, the differences had become so serious that Nkrumah was demoted from his post as the party's secretary to the post of treasurer. From then onward, he virtually went his own way, even as he remained in the UGCC fold. By September, he and Komla Gbedemah had established a nation wide movement called the Committee on Youth Organization (CYO); this was quickly built up as the basis of a new political party. On 12 June 1949, the breach became final: Nkrumah announced the formation of the Convention Peoples' Party (CPP). The new party immediately committed itself "[t]o fight relentlessly by all constitutional means for the achievement of 'Self-Government NOW' for the Chiefs and people of the Gold Coast."[46] For Nkrumah, this was the dividing line with the UGCC: "The actual conflict, if one existed at all," he later recollected, "was between the CYO and the Working Committee of the UGCC owing to the demand of the former for 'full Self-Government NOW' as opposed to the latter's—'full Self-Government within the shortest possible time.'"[47]

It is easy to read much into Nkrumah's distinction between the two political parties. Certainly, the CPP did not intend to subvert the colonial status quo; and like the UGCC leadership, Nkrumah did not intend to confront Britain on the issue of self-government. Like the UGCC, the CPP's approach was constitutional "nationalism," that is anticolonial journalism as well as petitions and deputations to London to protest specific grievances against the colonial administration. From the onset, Nkrumah worked on the assumption that the achievement of self-government would require the close cooperation of the authorities in London. He had persuaded the CPP to adopt "Self-Government NOW," he said, "as the Labour Government . . . then in power in the United Kingdom . . . would be more favorably disposed towards our demand. If the Conservatives were returned to power the following year our struggle for independence might be suppressed."[48]

The Coussey report was published at the end of October 1949. The UGCC members who had served on the committee had, in their minority report, opposed the continuance of the "reserve powers" and the presence of ex-officio members in the executive.[49] In spite of these reservations, the UGCC accepted the report and undertook "to try and work it despite its shortcomings."[50] Nkrumah's response came on 20 November 1949 when he convened the Ghana People's Representative Assembly. He intended the assembly as a forum "to coalesce public opinion against the Coussey Report and to urge the people into effective action." Representatives from "over fifty" organizations attended; the UGCC was a notable exception. The assembly resolved "that the Coussey report and His Majesty's Government's statement thereto are unacceptable to the country as a whole" and declared "that the people of the Gold Coast be granted immediate self-government, that is, full Dominion status with the Commonwealth of Nations based on the Statute of Westminster." On 15 December, Nkrumah communicated these resolutions to the governor and threatened "Positive Action" if they were ignored. The same day, he published a front-page article entitled "The Era of Positive Action Draws Nigh" in *Evening News*; and addressed a rally in Accra, where he issued an ultimatum: "If nothing was done by the British Government concerning our request for a constituent assembly within two weeks from that date . . . Positive Action would take place any time thereafter."[51]

The ultimatum prompted Gold Coast Colonial Secretary Reginald Saloway to meet with Nkrumah. "All we are asking for," Nkrumah remembers telling Saloway, "is a constituent assembly which necessitates dividing the country into constituencies, calling a general election and letting the people decide for themselves whether they will adopt the Coussey Report or not." By Nkrumah's account, the colonial secretary was not willing to accommodate the demand, and so the meeting did not head off the imminence of "Positive Action."[52] Saloway, on the other hand, recalls telling Nkrumah "that if he put his plan for 'Positive Action' into operation he would do great harm to the country and would impede constitutional reform. . . . The people did not want violence and would welcome its suppression by the government." Nkrumah was therefore advised that "if he followed the constitutional road which would be opened by the forthcoming reforms [the 1950 constitution] he would win at the elections." According to Saloway's recollection, this argument had the desired effect: "After some hours of discussion the CPP [executive] Committee agreed to follow constitutional methods. Nkrumah publicly called off 'Positive Action.'"[53] It seems that Nkrumah did actually back down: *Evening News*, the CPP newspaper, twice announced the postponement of "Positive Action."[54]

Meanwhile, the CPP threat was occurring against the background of simmering tension between labor and government. On 13 November, the Trade Union Congress (TUC) threatened a general strike as a response to the dismissal of sixty Meteorological Department workers charged with staging an illegal strike in October 1949. Nkrumah concedes that although it was happening independently of him, the TUC strike threat "at this particular time increased the popularity of Positive Action."[55] Playing the role of mediators, the Joint Provincial Council of Chiefs met with the labor leaders on 6 January 1950. However, labor was in no mood to soften its stand; instead, they expanded their demands at the meeting to include "(a) the withdrawal of the government circular concerning the political activities of civil servants," and "(b) the immediate granting of Dominion status." That same day, the TUC announced a general strike to start at midnight.[56]

The question as to whether or not the CPP wanted "Positive Action" became academic once labor went on strike. Richard Jeffries learnt that Nkrumah would have "backed down" from the 1950 "Positive Action" strike had the leaders of the railway workers, especially Pobee Biney, not "forced his hand."[57] Nkrumah himself acknowledged that what finally decided the matter for the CPP was that "[t]he TUC had already declared a strike which had been in action since midnight on 6th January, two days earlier." But even with the TUC strike well under way, Nkrumah remained very undecided. According to Saloway, Nkrumah had "tried hard to get the Trade Union Congress to call off the general strike but the TUC no longer had any control over the wild men." In addition, "Danquah taunted Nkrumah with having sold himself to the Colonial Secretary and thus infuriated the rank and file of the CPP who forced Nkrumah to retract."[58]

The strike and "Positive Action" affected the railroads, electricity, communications, and other key public services; in addition, there were demonstrations and rallies. As these unfolded, *West Africa* (14 January 1950) found Nkrumah "the most worried man in the Gold Coast" and that he "has been sincere in not wanting violence or a 'show-down.'" Since it merely merged with and was indeed driven by a strike that had its own distinct dynamic, it is difficult to assess the causal significance of "Positive Action." Clearly, it seems to have given the strike a political coloration.

On 10 January, the colonial regime imposed a state of emergency on the entire Gold Coast; the CPP and labor leaders were arrested, later arraigned and convicted on charges ranging from sedition to coercing the government and promoting an illegal strike. At the trials, "[t]he spirit of courageous defiance was clearly absent." CPP leaders either denied knowing what "Positive Action" meant or maintained that they did not like it; the treasurer even denied being a member of the party. "Only Nkrumah admitted having anything to do with the 'Positive Action' campaign." But he "denied having called on anybody to strike: he maintained that he even tried to stop the strike when he heard of it. Furthermore, Nkrumah said that he did not know of any section of the people which had struck because of the CPP."[59]

With most of the CPP leadership in prison, it fell to Gbedemah to hold the party together and prepare it for the general elections that were around the corner. In the event, he did a superb job of setting up a formidable party network all over the Gold Coast. He also had an important asset: the imprisonment of CPP leaders strengthened its nationalist credentials and therefore helped its cause.[60] In the elections, which took place on 8 February 1951, the CPP won 34 of the 38 seats in the LegCo. Four days later, Governor Charles Arden-Clarke released Nkrumah from prison and immediately invited him to form a government.[61] Nkrumah accepted the offer and became the leader of government business. At his first press conference after leaving prison, he substituted "Tactical action" for "Positive Action": like the UGCC, he was now prepared to give the Coussey constitution a chance. With that, Nkrumah jettisoned his own dictum, announced at the birth of the CPP, that "[a] policy of collaboration and appeasement would get us nowhere in our struggle for immediate self-government."[62]

Once in power, Nkrumah and his party cooperated with the British and their schedule for independence. This was in marked contrast to the attitude of the labor leaders who still "felt that further 'Positive Action' was required to force the government's hand," and who were therefore until August 1951 "pursuing a course of escalating opposition to the Colonial

Government."[63] By the time of the CPP's third annual conference in August 1952, there was much internal criticism of the party leadership. The critics "thought the compromise had gone too far, the pace of movement towards self-government too slow."[64] In the event, the achievement of Nkrumah's "Tactical Action" was that it enabled the Gold Coast to make steady political "progress" through a nonviolent, constitutional path mutually charted by the British and the CPP governments.

When Secretary of State Oliver Lyttleton visited the Gold Coast in June 1952, Nkrumah reminded him that the Gold Coast "desired full self-government" and that "certain constitutional changes were [therefore] necessary." Lyttleton indicated a willingness to consider any proposals that the Gold Coast government, after consultation with the chiefs, submitted for a revision of the 1950 constitution. At this signal, the Gold Coast government drew up a proposal for a new constitution and solicited public opinion on it. The entire process formed the basis of the government's paper on constitutional reform which, was published in June 1953. The paper proposed the assignment of the police to an African minister; the establishment in other countries, such as the United States and Canada, of offices similar to the one the Gold Coast had in London, to promote interest in and trade with the territory; the entrusting of responsibility for the Gold Coast to the secretary of state for Commonwealth affairs before the attainment of independence; and that as soon as the necessary constitutional and administrative arrangements had been concluded, the British government should make an explicit commitment to grant the Gold Coast self-government within the Commonwealth (as distinct from becoming "a full and independent member of the Commonwealth"). Except for the proposal that responsibility for the Gold Coast be transferred to the secretary of state for Commonwealth affairs, the British accepted the proposals that came from Accra and stated that an appropriate declaration on self-government would be made "probably early in 1954."[65]

In June 1954, the CPP won a second general election and retained power. Thereafter, the 1950 constitution was amended, along the lines endorsed by the British, to provide full internal self-government.[66] The 1954 constitution provided for an all-African cabinet presided over by a prime minister; the cabinet was to be advised by an economic and financial adviser, and an attorney general, both Europeans. Election to the legislature was to be direct and based on universal adult suffrage; the governor's reserve powers were to be retained and, through a deputy governor acting as secretary of defense, he was to exercise responsibility for the police and defense.[67]

The 1954 CPP victory generated a major complication: by the end of the year, an amalgam of diverse groups, consisting mainly of the Ashanti and the people of the Northern Territories, pressed for a revision of the constitution along federal lines.[68] The situation was saved by the CPP's broad political base, which cut across ethnic boundaries. Thus in the July 1956 election, the CPP won 72 of the 104 seats in Parliament, even though it lost in Ashanti and in the North. The size of its victory and British intervention persuaded its opponents to drop the demand for a federation. The constitution was amended again: legislative and executive control were retained at the center, but interim regional assemblies were introduced, and provisions for constitutional and minority safeguards were entrenched.[69] On 6 March 1957, the Gold Coast "emerged from its colonial status as the independent state of Ghana, and in doing so started a chain reaction among the still dependent states of Africa."[70]

Of great significance here is Basil Davidson's observation that from the moment he was co-opted into the colonial regime, Nkrumah made a "Swing to the Right." The result, Davidson explains, was that Nkrumah "worked for [the] fruits" of his compromise with Arden-Clarke "with the 'tactical action' which, he joked a little defensively, might also be called 'tactful action.' He was tremendously tactful. He was moderate. He was flexible. He was willing to listen to the most orthodox advice."[71] The overall result was that Nkrumah and Arden-Clarke "worked closely together to achieve the goal of independence, but few outside a very small circle of colleagues realized how complete was their cooperation."[72]

Arden-Clarke does indeed provide a splendid example of the role of the colonial governors in the transfer of power to Africans. On Sunday, 16 September 1956, he wrote to his wife: "The Secretary of State was doing a wobble and wanting to defer announcing a firm date for independence, while I was insisting that the announcement must be made before the Assembly rises on Tuesday next [18 September]. Yesterday the S[ecretary] of S[tate] surrendered with the words 'I feel you have left me no alternative'—he was right, I hadn't!" Later that same day (16 September), London sent a despatch to Accra announcing its intention that independence should come on or about 6 March 1957.[73] The following day, Arden-Clarke informed Nkrumah of the despatch and congratulated him: "This is a great day for you. It is the end of what you have struggled for." Recognizing that the governor had also been part of the "struggle," Nkrumah corrected Arden-Clarke: "It is the end of what *we* have been struggling for, Sir Charles. You have contributed a great deal towards this; in fact, I might not have succeeded without your help and cooperation."[74]

The chronology of events in Ghana clearly shows that the 1950 constitution that was the watershed in Ghana's political evolution came about in spite of the "nationalist" elements. And as Dennis Austin has pointed out, the 1951 election that brought Nkrumah and his party to power would have been held whether Nkrumah and the CPP existed or not. Besides, the 1954 constitution—introduced following Nkrumah's July 1953 "motion of destiny"—which replaced that of 1950, "was much like the minority report drawn up by the UGCC leaders on the Coussey Committee."[75] It is also worth recalling that from the time he went into government, Nkrumah's major struggle was not against the British, his partners in power, but against the domestic ethnic chauvinists who formulated their manifesto in federalist terms.

The Ghanaian case raises serious questions about the causal significance of African nationalism as an anticolonial movement. Such questions apply with even greater force to other case studies. According to Michael Crowder and Donal Cruise O'Brien, "French West African politicians . . . differed fundamentally from their English-speaking neighbors in that the French-speaking African leaders formally rejected independence in favor of a greater participation in the political process of a French Union or Community of which Africa would be a constituent part."[76] The result was that "the independence of the African territories in 1960 came more as a result of French 'goodwill' and 'magnanimity' than under the pressure of African nationalist movements."[77] Like francophone African politicians, the Sierra Leonean "nationalists" hardly pressed for independence. As Hargreaves has pointed out, the transfer of political power occurred in Sierra Leone "despite a notable lack of urgency on the part of Prime Minister Sir Milton Margai."[78]

In the case of Nigeria, the "nationalist" literature itself clearly shows that what passed for Nigerian "nationalism" or "anticolonial" movement was essentially the fragmented politics of debilitating intraelite hostility that was projected in primeval terms. For example, James Coleman noted that between 1948 and 1950, less was heard of "British autocracy" and "rapacious colonial exploitation" than of Fulani threats either to continue their "interrupted" march to the sea or to withdraw to the Western Sudan and Yoruba allegations of threatened Igbo domination.[79] This feuding ensured that Nigeria's independence was delayed, not by Britain but by the Nigerian political elite. In his memoir, Dennis Osadebay—one of Nigeria's "nationalist" politicians—confessed that the bickering within the Nigerian "nationalist" camp was not "conducive to winning independence."[80]

For those who evaluate the significance of an anticolonial movement by the magnitude of its ferocity and physical confrontation with the colonial authority, the nationalism of anglophone and francophone West Africa proves very disappointing indeed. At the best of times, the anticolonial effort consisted of writings in newspapers, petitions and delegations to the metropolitan capitals, and the attendance at constitutional conferences. There was nothing like the protest marches that characterized the African-American civil rights struggle in the United States Nor was there much of a civic education program aimed at the construction of a popular-democratic social order. The conflation of this "pen and paper" nationalism into a heroic anticolonial struggle that ousted the colonial powers presumes an astonishing degree of cause and effect, which has not and cannot be convincingly demonstrated. Yet as circumscribed as it was, there is no denying that this "pen and paper" nationalism represented pressure of a kind on the colonial authorities.

It is nearer the truth to argue that even in the late 1940s, Nigeria still had an incipient anticolonial movement with the potential of spiraling towards a fullblown counterhegemonic challenge to imperialism. The Zikist Movement, formed in 1946, was a signal of this possibility. The movement drew its membership from angry young men, without higher education and thus less wedded to Western ways, who were itching to seize the initiative and force the pace of Nigeria's political development through "positive action," consisting of outright defiance of colonial authority, militant demonstrations, strikes, and boycott of European goods.[81]

An essential element of what Gary Wasserman calls "consensual decolonization" is the integration by the metropolitan power of "a potentially disruptive nationalist movement into the structures and requisites of the colonial political-economic system."[82] Confronted with the Zikist challenge, the British effected this integration by dislocating the militant mass consciousness of the Zikists and co-opting the more pliant segment of the Nigerian political elite—the Nnamdi Azikiwes, Obafemi Awolowos, and Ahmadu Bellos—into a collaborative endeavor. The first objective was achieved in 1950 when the Zikist Movement was decapitated. The second was actualized by the 1951 constitution. Obafemi Awolowo, a major beneficiary of the power reallocation, was later to concede that the extremism of the younger elements "must have brought home vividly to the British government that if the apostles of constructive nationalism were discredited by undue delay on Britain's part to accede to the wishes of the people of Nigeria, political extremism would be enthroned and the friendship of Nigeria would be forfeited for good."[83]

The co-optation of Nkrumah was the test run of this strategy of "buying off" or "integrating" incipient African nationalism before it gathered momentum. In his discussion of the transition process in Ghana, Austin says that in 1950–51, Britain suddenly found itself "caught in the difficulty of trying to maintain the balance at the middle of a seesaw which was beginning to tilt quite unexpectedly and sharply downwards on the populist side" of Nkrumah and his CPP. Austin added that the British effort to grapple with the situation "produced policies of collaboration, notionally defined as 'diarchy,' which enabled the colonial government to retain control until the final ceremony of independence."[84]

Austin will readily concede that metropolitan control survived independence. The result was an independence that was strong in form and vacuous in content. "The process of decolonization," in Ghana, Judith Marshall explains, "was designed to protect the institutions of colonial domination, the state and foreign companies, from any radical challenge, and to bring the commercial and bureaucratic bourgeoisies into alliance with imperialism." Thus, after the 1948 riots and the brief general strike of 1950, the nationalist movement was

> skillfully channeled, via the conciliatory posture of the colonial administration, into narrow political solutions. The right to determination was affirmed, leading to a gradual transfer of power. This kept the levers of power in British hands as effective bargaining tools against nationalist demands. Everything in the shared power arrangement of 1951–57 militated against any radicalization of the national movement and the genuine decolonization of the state. Imperialism could accede the "political kingdom" in order to maintain the substance of economic domination.[85]

In general, the British strategy in (West) Africa was analogous to its approach in the Middle East: Wm. Roger Louis talks of a British "grand strategy" in the Middle East, an "attempt to transform the system of domination . . . into a relationship of equal partners . . . to prevent the initiative from passing to 'anti-British extremists,' and to sustain British influence by economic and social reform, in order to maintain Britain's influence as a 'world power' with a predominant place in the Middle East."[86]

France reached the same goal as Britain, but from a different route, which stretches back to the French Revolution. The Revolution espoused a republican creed that promised to integrate all humanity into a supranational French community. This tradition was carried over into colonial administration, in the form of "assimilation." In a fundamental sense, assimilation assumed that the colonials were potential French men, women, and children, who would all be integrated into the supranational French nation; there was to be no self-government for the colonies, just as there was none for the departments. Thus, "assimilation defined decolonization as total integration and equality of status." Another tradition inspired by the Revolution was the concept of "the one and indivisible Republic." In the 1920s, this concept was commonplace as a definition of the relationship between France and its colonies. The two concepts provided the basis for the French Community put forward in 1958 by Charles de Gaulle. Unlike the British Commonwealth, the Community was not a loose, informal partnership; it was, instead, an expression of the organic, indissoluble unity of Greater France, a France that included both the metropolis and the colonies as its constituent units. Self-government within the Community meant "freedom," not for a sociopolitical aggregate but for the individual.[87]

Independence for African territories in 1960 was not intended as a departure from the underlying ideology of integration into Greater France.[88] This continuity found formal expression in the "cooperation agreements" that heralded the transfer of power to Africans: France and the African states "agreed" to work in tandem before taking major decisions on foreign policy; there was provision for common defense arrangements; the creation of individual currencies was permitted, but the states were to adhere to the franc zone; the preexisting principle of reciprocal preferential trade arrangements was retained; France was to continue providing economic and financial assistance and was also to help the African states to maintain their administrative services. In return, the states undertook to turn to France first for their personnel needs, and French firms were to be treated as the domestic ones.[89] For France, the two notions of independence and "cooperation" may have been genetically linked, but "[t]hrough the linkages established between the accession to international sovereignty and the signing of the cooperation agreements, France managed to institutionalize her political, economic, monetary, and cultural preeminence over a number of African states, which thereby remained almost totally dependent on her."[90]

In fairness, it is worth emphasizing that the African political elite actively supported France in the realization of its neocolonial designs. To begin with, one recurring theme in the literature is that there was no pressure for independence by francophone African politicians. Even by early 1958, such a demand seemed heretical to them. Thus the Parti Africaine d'Indépendence (PAI) was promptly expelled from a conference of all French West African political parties that met in Paris in February 1958. The party offended the sensibilities of the more elderly politicians for intransigently demanding that the conferees embrace the principle of immediate and unconditional independence. It is instructive that Sekou Toure, who led Guinea to vote against the French Community in 1958, was among those who tried to limit the demands put forth by the PAI: while asking that Africa be given the right to determine its form of association with France, he upheld the necessity of maintaining close links with the metropole.[91]

As late as May 1958, Toure had not really moved from his desire for some form of partnership with France rather than independence for Guinea. On 18 May 1958, the Parti Démocratique de Guinée (PDG) met in Conakry and demanded a new constitution that would provide for (a) autonomous African states, each with a legislative assembly and an executive; (b) a federal state that all the constituent units of the French Union would join on a contractual basis, a federation that would have a common parliament and an executive with responsibility for foreign affairs, defense, justice, general economy and currency, and higher education; (c) the transformation of the federal Grand Conseil into a real legislative assembly; (d) federal executives in West and Equatorial Africa who would take over the functions of the high commissioner and the French Overseas Ministry (which would be abolished); and (e) end the representation of the colonial territories in the organs of the French metropolitan government, including the National Assembly.[92] At the time, the PDG position was the most radical in West Africa, but it still envisaged that these changes would take place within the framework of the French Community. "The motive for the creation of Federal Executives" according to *West Africa* (2 August 1958), "was to give Africa greater strength vis-à-vis France in any Franco-African Community."

It was not until July 1958 that Toure finally embraced independence as distinct from defining Africa's place within the Franco-African Community. On 28 July 1958, he told a PDG assembly that his government had informed Paris that any constitution that did not provide for the right of independence of the colonies would be unacceptable to Guinea.[93] This demand did not mean that Toure wished to burn his bridges with Paris. Even on that fateful 25 August 1958, when he addressed de Gaulle in Conakry and rejected the French Community, Toure took pains to explain: "Our heart, our reason, as well as our most obvious interests, make us choose . . . . interdependence and liberty in this union, rather than defining ourselves without France and against France."[94]

In the referendum of 29 September 1958 on the French Community, the proportion of "Yes" votes was well over 90 percent in all territories except Niger and Guinea where it was 75 and less than 5 percent respectively.[95] The surprise was not Guinea's vote against the Community; by September 1958, that was a settled issue. The surprise was the massive support for the French Community, given that far more "No" votes had been expected from Senegal, Niger, and Dahomey. Several factors worked in favor of de Gaulle. Elliot Berg has discussed the economic considerations, showing that in the post-1945 period, economic activity in the French territories derived overwhelmingly from the infusion of French capital. He estimates that French public investment in West Africa in 1947–56 was close to $1 billion. The extent of the dependence on France was greater than this figure suggests. France underwrote many of the administrative costs of its colonies and cushioned primary exports with subsidies. Senegal, for example, depended on France to maintain the artificially high price of its groundnuts. In view of this degree of dependence on France, many must have calculated that a sudden rupture would be calamitous.[96]

Economics alone does not explain the massive endorsement of the French Community. The Ivory Coast, for example, could well have stood on its own. It is therefore worthy of note that in October 1957, Felix Houphouet-Boigny, the doyen of Ivorien politics, pointed out that "[i]f we had been colonized by the Anglo-Saxons, there is no doubt that we would have chosen independence even at the cost of economic disadvantages. But in France we think we catch a note of human fraternity."[97] A month earlier, Senegal's Leopold Senghor told the French National Assembly that "[i]n Africa, when children have grown up, they leave the parents' hut, and build a hut of their own by its side and in the same compound. Believe me, we don't want to leave the French compound. We have grown up in it and it is good to be alive in it. We want simply to build our own huts."[98] This explicit expression of a deep sentimental attachment to France and the implied negation of independence were shared by most French African politicians.

According to Crowder, part of the explanation for this disinclination for independence was that "[t]he concept of a French Union, of a Greater France, of a Franco-African community" in which peoples of "different races and color were drawn together by French culture . . . had a very great appeal for the African leaders."[99] The fundamental explanation for this inclination lies in the nature of the French colonial socialization process of "assimilation." Way back in 1942, the United States State Department Intelligence Unit reported that

> [t]he French have consciously cultivated a native elite for use as auxiliaries in the administration of the French colonial domain. This select native group, well educated, and employed in the service of the government, is composed of the French assimiles—natives who are given French citizenship and who approach the status of equality with metropolitan Frenchmen. The special privilege and prestige given such French natives has induced them to orientate their thinking and loyalties within the French rather than the native orbit.[100]

It is true that assimilation was never applied systematically in Africa, but it remained a real possibility for the elite. It is therefore not surprising that from Blaise Diagne in the 1920s to Senghor and Houphouët-Boigny in the 1940s and 1950s, one sees a genuine desire, among the African elite, to be assimilated into Greater France. Thus "assimilation" ensured that France meant much to the African political and middle-class elites and that at the critical moment, there was a solid captive audience quite willing to defend the system.

Neocolonialism: The Reality of Decolonization

In comparison with the French, Britain was subtle in creating an institutional framework for Africa's postcolonial dependency; but in both cases, independence turned out to be a transition to neocolonialism. This reality was already perceptible by January 1960: at the All African Peoples' conference held in Tunis that month, Kojo Botsio of Ghana drew attention to how the European powers were willing to "concede political independence so long as they are sure that they will dominate the African countries afterwards through economic and other controls." Kojo characterized this phenomenon as "neocolonialism," and many at the conference agreed with him.[101]

Neocolonialism was a bigger irritation at the 1961 All African Peoples' conference held in Cairo. The conference defined it as "the survival of the colonial system in spite of the formal recognition of political independence in emerging countries which become victims of an indirect and subtle form of domination by political, economic, social, military or technical means."[102] Independent African states were warned to be on guard against this phenomenon, which was associated with Britain, the United States, France, West Germany, Israel, Belgium, the Netherlands, and South Africa.[103]

The pervasive nature of the imperialistic continuities in postcolonial Africa has spawned a revisionist perspective of the decolonization sequence. The basic proposition is that "the national movements headed mainly by the petty bourgeoisie were given control of the superstructure, while imperialism controlled the economic base, namely the key sectors of the economy. Imperialism granted political independence, therefore, confident that the superstructure would serve its interests and that the change would be only one of personnel and not of structure."[104] The emerging pattern has been to develop this general line and explore the underlying dynamics, that ensured that what glittered at independence was far less than gold.

Wasserman argues that decolonization was predicated on the *co-optation* of the nationalist elite "into the leadership or policy-determining structure of the system as a means of averting threats" to the "stability or existence" of the colonial system. He considers co-optation in terms of the political socialization of the nationalist elements into the colonial apparatus, and he shows that this socialization took various forms. One was their induction into the processes directly related with "the recruitment into, and performance of, specialized political roles in the bureaucracy and leadership positions." It also involved "the ostensibly non-political learning which nevertheless ultimately affects political behavior. This would include the learning of politically relevant social attitudes and personality characteristics." Another aspect of the socialization process was "constitutional participation," which not only sucked the nationalists into "the colonial political norms but also deflected nationalist agitation into governmental cooperation and, indeed, created a counter interest to mass rebellion." Wasserman points out that these varieties of co-optation had an "essentially conservative character with regard to existing political arrangements." This leads him to stress that "[t]he result of the decolonization process, then, was the integration of an indigenous leadership into colonial political, social and economic patterns." The objective of the acculturation process, he says, was to alter

> political authority (while perhaps changing the methods of social control), in order to preserve the essential features of the colonial political economy. . . .Independence for the new state marked not so much a moving out of the colonial relationship as an enlarging and enhancing of that dependent relationship, with the colonial patterns emerging relatively unscathed.[105]

Operating from the same standpoint as Wasserman, Colin Leys demonstrates that the essence of imperialism, "with or without direct rule," is the expropriation of resources from the periphery to the metropolis. He accepts the "nationalist" interpretation that colonial rule saw to the emergence of a new indigenous African social class. For Leys, however, this class was only too willing to sustain rather than challenge or subvert the status quo. He adds that as the African elite acquired more political relevance and, more particularly, as "primitive accumulation gave way to capitalist accumulation (in which the apparently 'natural' forces of the market for labor are sufficient to ensure that the surplus is appropriated by the capitalist)," the need for continued direct control became unnecessary. This, Leys insists, "facilitated the replacement of direct colonial administration by 'independent' governments representing the local strata and classes with an interest in sustaining the colonial economic relationships."[106]

It will be readily observed that the pedigree of this revisionism is dependency theory (*dependencia*). The application of this theory in the explanation of decolonization has been necessitated by the search for the historical basis of Africa's worsening destitution and enduring dependence on the West. In this sense, *dependencia* derives its relevance from its postulation of a theory of peripheral state formation, and particularly from its basic thesis that once established, economic domination by the West is self-reinforcing, and therefore that while imperialism may change its form, its basic nature remains constant. By the logic of this argument, independence appears not as Africa's liberation but as the new bottle for the old wine of imperialism.

According to *dependencia*, the translation of imperialistic forces and features into internal effects is mediated by local (African) agents. In this matrix, the "nationalists" appear not as *anti*colonialists but as compradors, willing collaborators, in the transmutation of Africa's march to freedom: for them, the prospect of office and its perquisites—power, privilege, and patronage—and the fascination with the rituals surrounding a new flag and anthem were sufficiently alluring.[107]

It remains to be said that the view that decolonization essentially meant a maximizing process for the colonial powers is not unique to dependency theorists (*dependencistas*). In an essay published in 1953, John Gallagher and Ronald Robinson abandoned the equation of imperialism with direct, political control and insisted on the underlying unity between "formal" and "informal" empire in British policy formulation. According to them, Britain had habitually followed the principle of extending control informally if possible and formally only if necessary; the establishment of formal control arising only where the informal approach failed to provide sufficient security for British interests. What matters to Britain in any given case, they held, is "the combination of commercial penetration and political influence . . . to command those economies which could be made to fit best into her own." From this observation, Gallagher and Robinson charted a cyclical pattern in British imperial policy: informal imperialism yields formal control, which in turn reverts to informal control. "The difference between formal and informal empire," they explained,

> has not been one of fundamental nature but of degree. The ease with which a region has slipped from one status to the other helps to confirm this. Within the last two hundred years, for example, India has passed from informal to

formal association with the United Kingdom and, since World War II, back to an informal connection. Similarly, British West Africa has passed through the first two stages and seems to-day likely to follow India into the third.

Against this background, they offered an explanation of the real essence and implication of the transfer of power to the colonized. The affinity of their explanation with the *dependencia* proposition is striking. As Gallagher and Robinson put it,

> In other words, responsible government [independence], far from being a separatist device, was simply a change from direct to indirect methods of maintaining British interests. By slackening the formal political bond at the appropriate time, it was possible to rely on economic dependence and mutual good-feeling to keep the colonies bound to Britain while still using them as agents for further British expansion.

Like the *dependencistas,* Gallagher and Robinson acknowledged the critical role of local comprador regimes in sustaining informal imperialism: "once their economies had become sufficiently dependent on foreign trade the classes whose prosperity was drawn from that trade normally worked themselves in local politics to preserve the local political conditions needed for it."[108]

Redefining Decolonization

Decolonization, as noted early in this chapter, is usually conceptualized as synonymous with independence, and therefore as the transfer of political power from the colonial power to the indigenous political elite within the framework of state sovereignty. There is, however, a growing realization that in spite of the personnel substitution—that is, the transfer of power from Europeans to Africans—the remarkable thing about independence was its superficiality, the fact that it did not subvert the substance of the colonial relationship. This reality, as demonstrated in this chapter, has led to a fresh perspective on what independence was all about. Frantz Fanon, for example, characterized independence as "false decolonization" and the successor African governments as "Western business agents."[109] In a similar vein, Bade Onimode sneers at the end result of the decolonization process as "flag independence."[110]

The realization that European interests remained paramount behind the facade of African rule has also induced a rethink of the definition of decolonization. For example, Wasserman has pointed out that the equation of decolonization with the transfer of political power to the ex-colonials "deals only with the formal transfer of 'authority,' referring to the capacity to legitimate political decisions, and not with political 'power,' which may be taken to mean the ability to influence those decisions. . . .Decolonization or the 'attainment of independence' as such do not necessarily say anything about what is an empirical question of influence."[111] Consequently, *decolonization is now increasingly seen as a process embracing but also going beyond independence (the transfer of political power)*. This reconceptualization addresses the need for "decolonization" to accommodate the subsistence of colonial continuities in the postcolonial state. Thus, while conceding that the equation of decolonization with independence has "the merit of precision," John Darwin simultaneously emphasizes that it is very narrow, and so not only robs decolonization of "much of its value as an organizing concept" but also conceals "deep-rooted continuities." To remedy this lapse, he proposes that decolonization be defined as "a partial retraction, redeployment and redistribution of European influences in the regions of the extra-European world whose economic, political and cultural life had previously seemed destined to flow into Western molds."[112] The strength of this definition is that it enables one to use decolonization as an analytical tool in the study of power politics and, especially, in locating Africa in contemporary international relations.

To be sure, I am not suggesting that decolonization had no disjunctive effects; it certainly ruptured some linkages. The point is that it concealed much: as Wasserman has explained, decolonization "reaffirmed and enhanced" substantial linkages between the "independent states" and the metropolitan powers "in the form of economic dependency, development assistance, foreign investment, and the political, social and economic compatibility of objectives among the involved elites." The construction of these linkages was an essential part of the co-optation process, and the overall objective, he says, was "to constrain the new states to remain in the appointed orbit."[113]

In sum, there is now hardly any quarrel with the view that in spite of the externals (the personnel substitution, the bogus titles, the flag, the anthem, the twenty-one gun salutes, membership in the UN and other international bodies), independence or the transfer of power to Africans occurred within the unchanged framework of colonial rule. Consequently, independence did not entail the inversion of the hegemonic relationship instituted by colonialism; it did not, in other words, reintroduce as subjects of history peoples who as colonials had been merely its objects. This outcome is hardly surprising since independence itself is a constituent of decolonization. The latter concept, as already explained, refers to the broader redefinition of center-periphery relations to allow for the integration of the African political elite into neocolonial political, social, and economic networks. Meanwhile, this redefinition of the Euro-African relationship coincided with a fundamental restructuring of the world stage—given that World War II had simultaneously seen to the geopolitical shrinkage of Western Europe and the dawn of what Henry Luce had, in 1941, called the "American Century."[114] This redistribution of power at the global level meant that the redefinition of the Euro-African relationship was occurring within a world system dominated by Washington. The chapters that follow will confront the question: How did the United States perceive or respond to this redefinition?

2

THE ARCHAEOLOGY OF POLICY

There is a consensus that sub-Saharan Africa has traditionally been "a foreign policy backwater" and of the "lowest priority" in United States foreign policy.[1] This point was succinctly made by George Ball, United States undersecretary of state during the presidency of John F. Kennedy. Meeting with Antonio de Oliveira Salazar, president of the Council of Ministers of Portugal, in August 1963, he emphasized that "of all the areas in the world Africa was the least important from the point of view of American national interests"[2] These first sentences are intended as a caution against any high expectations about United States involvement in West Africa. Indeed, over and over again, this book shows that relative to its involvement in other parts of the "Third World," Washington's interest and presence in West Africa (and sub-Saharan Africa generally) in the 1950s was particularly minuscule.

It is nonetheless true that during World War II, West Africa was of geostrategic importance to the United States. This derived partly from the Takoradi-Chad air route to North Africa, but particularly from the strategic location of Dakar. From July 1940, when Italy assaulted North Africa, United States war planes were flown to Takoradi (in what was then the Gold Coast) and from there to Egypt and the theater of war in the Eastern Mediterranean. This route grew in importance for the Allied forces in 1941 and 1942, after the United States had helped to modernize the facilities at Takoradi.[3] As Lord Swinton, Britain's wartime resident in West Africa, told the Royal Empire Society in 1945: "West Africa became literally the lifeline of our Air Force and of the American Air Force also. It was the only way by which aircraft could be brought to Egypt and to the battle front in Libya, and by which aircraft could pass to India, the Middle East, Russia and China."[4]

Dakar, at the westernmost tip of Africa, assumed particular importance for Washington after the fall of France to Nazi forces in 1940. This stemmed, above all else, from the fact that Dakar is separated from Natal in Brazil by only a 1,500–mile stretch of ocean. There was thus the worry that the Germans could seize and use it as a raider and submarine base against Brazil, thereby directly threatening the United States itself.[5] Franklin Roosevelt (United States president, 1933–45) never disguised his conviction that "Dakar in unsure hands was a direct threat to the Americas."[6] In May 1941, he proposed sending a message to Congress declaring all of West Africa north of the equator, as well as the Atlantic islands of the Azores, Cape Verde, Madeira, and the Canaries "as thenceforth falling under the protective provisions of the Monroe Doctrine." He was restrained by Cordell Hull, his secretary of state, who argued that the threat from a German occupation of the islands or Dakar "could be better stated nakedly without raising a technical Monroe Doctrine issue."[7] The following month, Roosevelt announced that in order to neutralize the possibility of Hitler invading the Western Hemisphere, the United States "must and will take military action without further notice to prevent Germany from acquiring bases in Greenland, Iceland, Dakar, the Azores and Cape Verde Islands."[8]

Roosevelt dropped no hint as to how he intended to take the wind out of Hitler's sails. But given the circumstances, it is possible to trace a direct linkage from the White House to a plan drawn up by the Office of Strategic Services (OSS), the precursor of the Central Intelligence Agency (CIA). Issued in December 1941, the OSS paper asserted that West Africa was threatened by the possibility of a German attack. The paper ruled out equipping France and Britain to counter this German menace: France because of the "general objection of most Frenchmen to [Charles] de Gaulle, caused by previous deep misunderstandings. Full military aid and recognition of de Gaulle would mean extension to the United States of French objections to de Gaulle"; and Britain because of "fear of British conquest and existing psychological antipathies between the French and British." A United States expedition was thus considered to be the most viable option.[9]

The expedition did not materialize and Roosevelt never ceased worrying that "the Germans had in their power to take over Dakar and use it as a raider and submarine base. It's a direct threat against Brazil and this continent, the West Indies, and so forth." He therefore proposed that at the end of the war, West Africa would be demilitarized "all the way down," and there should be "a strong point in either Dakar or Bathurst, where we will have sufficient air strength, sufficient Navy, and sufficient airfields, and so forth, to prevent any aggressor Nation in the future from reestablishing a threat against this continent."[10] When de Gaulle visited Washington in July 1944, Roosevelt "raised one of the questions that absorbed him, the need for some strategic bases such as Dakar to safeguard American security."[11]

The Policy Framework

After World War II, and with the German threat eliminated, West Africa—and the rest of Africa—instantly became a strategic superfluity in Washington. Up till the early 1950s, there were still indications of a United States commitment "to assure the security of the 'bulge' area near Dakar."[12] It is, however, truer that during the presidency of Harry Truman, West Africa lost the prominence Roosevelt had accorded it in United States strategic architecture. Top on the list of a 1947 ranking by the CIA of areas important to United States security was Western Europe, followed by the Near and Middle East, the Far East, South Asia, and finally, North Africa.[13] Sub-Saharan Africa was not mentioned in that ranking nor in that of the Joint Chiefs of Staff (JCS), which listed Western Europe (including Britain), North America (including Greenland and Alaska), the Middle East, Northwest Africa, Latin America, and the Far East, in this order, as the regions of "importance to the national security of the United States."[14]

George Kennan, probably the first high official in post-World War II Washington to give any thought to Africa, did so in the context of how the exploitation of Africa's resources could help the United States to rehabilitate the European political economy. In February 1948, Kennan, counselor and director of the State Department Policy Planning Staff, defined the basic issue for United States national security in terms of the constitution of some "form of political, military and economic union in Western Europe if the free nations of Europe are to hold their own" against the Soviet Union. For him, Britain's participation in such a union was necessary to guarantee its viability. He, however, acknowledged that "Britain's long term economic problem . . . can scarcely be solved just by closer association with the other Western European countries, since these countries do not have, by and large, the food and raw material surpluses she needs." But de-linking Britain from Western Europe might "have the ultimate effect of rendering the continental nations more vulnerable to Russian pressures." As a way out of the difficulty, Kennan recommended that all of Western Europe, rather than Britain alone, be brought into "a closer economic association" with the United States and Canada. However, the real solution to the puzzle was Africa: "a union of Western European nations" should, Kennan urged, "undertake jointly the economic development and exploitation of the colonial and dependent areas of the African Continent." The "idea itself," he emphasized,

> has much to recommend it. The African Continent is relatively little exposed to communist pressures; and most of it is not today a subject of great power rivalries. It lies easily accessible to the maritime nations of Western Europe, and politically they control or influence most of it. Its resources are still relatively undeveloped. It could absorb great numbers of people and a great deal of Europe's surplus technical and administrative energy. Finally, it would lend to the idea of Western European union that tangible objective for which everyone has been rather unsuccessfully groping in recent months.[15]

It is apparent that in Kennan's calculations, Africa had no intrinsic value in the context of United States diplomacy; the region's relevance was, instead, a derivative of Washington's European concerns. As it turned out, this thinking and its policy implications—expressed through the exploitation of Africa's raw materials—constituted the cornerstone of United States involvement in the region in the 1950s. And as a result, United States policy in Africa necessarily subserved a larger interest in Europe.

There is no denying that Washington's post-1945 diplomacy was partly concerned with maneuvering for power in the international system. This meant that the strategic value of any country or region to the United States was calculated in terms of the degree to which it expanded the overall correlations of global power. The fact that Africa possessed so little, if any, strategic value for Washington raises questions regarding United States geopolitical interest in the region.

The point has been made, in the preceding chapter, that the transfer of power to Africans involved a reformulation of power relationships between the West and the ex-colonials in a manner that sustained, rather than subverted, the established global distribution of power. This political reconfiguration of Africa coincided with the emergence of the United States as a superpower with far-flung global interests. These interests, however defined, acquired added significance as the United States and the Soviet Union confronted each other for the dominance of the world. By definition, the resulting imperial bifurcation made every happening in every far-off corner of the globe strategically and urgently relevant in United States, as in Soviet, calculations. More particularly, there was the realization in Washington that with the "gradual disintegration of the colonial systems and the emergence of young, nationalistic states," a new power configuration was emerging in the "Third World" and that "unless the Western European nations, and with them the U.S., can secure the goodwill of these newly liberated and as yet dependent areas, they may be aligned with the USSR."[16] Thus, in maneuvering for power in the international system, the United States was anxious to influence the process of political change in Africa. This broad rubric included ensuring that the "emerging states" were acculturated into a global setting conducive to United States national security interests, by ensuring a pro-Western orientation by Africans and therefore warding off countervailing influences such as "communism" and nonalignment.

Washington, Colonialism, and Nationalism

Exploiting Africa's raw materials for the benefit of Europe and influencing the pattern and content of political change were clearly the key planks of United States policy in Africa. On the other hand, African opinion evaluated that policy primarily in terms of Washington's role in the liquidation of European colonial rule. Senators Frank Church, Gale W. McGhee, and Frank E. Moss visited a number of African countries at the end of 1960 and found that "American policies toward African causes, particularly as manifested at the United Nations, have tended to draw down our reservoir of good will and understanding in Africa. This is especially true with respect to our policy positions on Algeria, and as to a number of our votes on 'colonial questions.'"[17]

In the early 1940s, Roosevelt voiced a strong anticolonial position. High hopes were thus raised that the United States was against colonial empires and would, indeed, facilitate their liquidation. "An important phase of the foreign policy of Franklin D. Roosevelt," according to one early assessment, "was a vigorous and persistent opposition to colonialism."[18] More recent scholarship reveals neither vigor nor persistence in his anticolonialism, whether it was in connection with the Atlantic Charter, India, the question of French positions in the Far East and North Africa, or the attempt to create an international superintendency over the colonies.[19]

In a radio broadcast on 23 July 1942, Secretary of State Hull explained the United States position on independence for European colonies. "We have always believed," he said, "that all peoples, without distinction of race, color, or religion, who are prepared and willing to accept the responsibilities of liberty, are entitled to its enjoyment."After pointing out that the United States had "striven to meet squarely our own responsibility in this respect" in Cuba and the Philippines, he balanced the demand for independence against the capacity for responsibility, emphasizing that it would always be the administration's goal "to use the full measure of our influence to support the attainment of freedom by all peoples who, by their acts, show themselves worthy of it and ready for it."[20] Roosevelt himself pointed to the United States experience in the Philippines to support the view that independence should be preceded by a long period of institution building.[21]

Wm. Roger Louis asked himself the question: "To what extent did anti-colonial sentiment in the United States contribute to the decolonization of the British Empire?" His response, based on a painstaking study, was that "from about 1943 into the period of the cold war the general policy of the American government, in pursuit of security, tended to support rather than break up the British Imperial system."[22] Hull was later to recall that "[a]t no time did we press Britain, France, or The Netherlands for an immediate grant of self-government to their colonies." The United States, he concedes, had "frequent conversations" with those countries but "could not press them too far . . . in view of the fact that we were seeking the closest possible cooperation with them in Europe. We could not alienate them in the Orient and expect to work with them in Europe."[23]

Hull most certainly had World War II in mind. But even before the end of that war, Washington's suspicions and perceptions of Soviet strength and intentions were already beginning to define the United States position on the "colonial question." On 12 April 1945 (just ten days before Roosevelt's death), the OSS issued a policy paper that projected a grim picture of the postwar international balance of power. The paper recalled that the United States had joined World War II to prevent Germany and Japan from dominating Europe and Asia respectively. It prophesied that at the cessation of hostilities, the United States "will be confronted with a situation potentially more dangerous than any preceding one" for in the long run, the Soviet Union alone, given its human and natural resources, was in a position "to dominate Europe and at the same time to establish her hegemony over Asia." Such an outcome, it was felt, would greatly upset the global balance of power to Washington's disadvantage.[24]

The OSS insisted that the United States should not "wait until Russia's policy is fully revealed" before taking security measures. It recommended "a clear, firm, and thoroughly non-provocative policy" in restraining the

Soviets. In addition, the paper suggested that the United States should construct an anti-Soviet alliance, with Britain and France as the cornerstones, and that this would involve doing "everything possible to restore France to the rank of a great power." The OSS linked the European colonies with the preservation of an international balance of power that would be favorable to the United States. Emphasizing that the imperial ties would enhance United States national security, the paper urged that Washington "should realize its interest in the maintenance of the British, French, and Dutch colonial empires. . . . We have at present no interest in weakening or liquidating these empires or in championing schemes of international trusteeship which may provoke unrest and result in colonial disintegration, and may at the same time alienate from us the European states whose help we need to balance the Soviet power."[25]

Early in May 1945, this OSS paper was forwarded to Truman, the new president. There is no indication of his initial reaction to the paper. But as Scott Bills has aptly observed, "the attitudes and priorities discussed in the OSS paper . . . became, by 1947, the basis for American foreign policy: a Eurocentric focus, a global struggle to contain Soviet influence, a retreat from advocacy of anticolonial views which might interfere with consolidation of a Euro-American security system."[26]

In his memoirs, Truman asserted: "I had always been opposed to colonialism. Whatever justification may be cited at any stage, colonialism in any form is hateful to Americans. America fought her own war of liberation against colonialism, and we shall always regard with sympathy and understanding the desire of people everywhere to be free of colonial bondage." Citing the Philippines as proof of this commitment, he reemphasized Washington's traditional endorsement of the "undeniable rights of a people to determine its own political destiny. . . . There could be no 'ifs' attached to this right, unless we were to backslide on our political creed."[27] The Truman administration attached very serious qualifications to this "undeniable right," especially with respect to Africans and Africa.

In general, the administration regarded the "colonial question" as an integral component of United States national security interests. A major policy statement recognized that the "problems that arise because a very large segment of the world's population continues to reside in territories which have not yet become fully self-governing have assumed wide significance in the development of American foreign policy." It further explained that "[i]n the formulation of United States policy on colonial questions considerations relating to the security of the United States and to general international security are clearly of great importance." These interests were broadly conceived to include "such remote elements" as an adequate landing strip "on an obscure Pacific atoll or a friendly administration in a little known territory of Central Africa." On this basis, Washington believed that "[i]n most dependent areas of the world the security interests of the United States at the present time will best be served by a policy of support for the Western Colonial Powers."[28]

At the October 1945 San Francisco Conference which led to the formation of the United Nations, China and the Soviet Union proposed "independence" as an objective of the trusteeship system. The United States joined Britain and France in favoring "progressive development toward self-government."[29] The United States preference was conditioned by the emerging Cold War entanglements. Isaiah Bowman, who was a member of the United States delegation to the conference, wondered: "When perhaps the inevitable struggle came between Russia and ourselves the question would be who are our friends. Would we have as friends those we had weakened in the struggle. . . .Would we have the support of Great Britain if we had undermined her position?"[30] Against this background, many in Washington agreed with the CIA that independence for European colonies was "no longer a purely domestic issue between the European colonial powers and their dependencies." It was related to the complications in United States-Soviet diplomacy. And in this regard, independence worried Washington, for "[i]n contrast to the ever closer integration of the Satellites into the Soviet system, there is an increasing fragmentation of the non-Soviet world."[31] There was also the fear that independence might result in a "situation of weakness" (in the new states), creating an opening for Soviet penetration.[32]

By 1948, United States anticolonialism had so mellowed that Arthur Creech Jones, Britain's secretary of state for the colonies, told his cabinet colleagues that "the United States have largely come round to our point of view . . . [and] are at present too much preoccupied with communism to spare much time for 'British imperialism.' "[33] Two years later, the British ambassador in Washington confirmed that "Anti-colonialism in the United States today is a traditional attitude rather than an active crusading force. . . .the broad masses of the American people, including the liberals, are convinced that the supreme danger confronting their civilization is not old-fashioned colonialism but modern communism. They therefore regard the democracies of Western Europe, among whom the chief colonial powers are numbered, as their natural and indispensable allies."[34]

As the ambassador observed, the Cold War helped mute United States anticolonialism. This, in policy terms, translated into an endorsement of the colonial status quo. Thus in respect of French West and Equatorial Africa, the stated "primary objective" of the United States was to keep them under "friendly and effective administration," and this meant the recognition of the "legitimacy and desirability of French political control." As a consequence, Washington approved what it called "the liberal measures" of the 1946 French constitution and committed itself to the "orderly development of democracy in both territories within the structure of the French Union."[35]

At the July 1950 Anglo-American colonial policy talks, John Hickerson, the United States assistant secretary for UN Affairs, assured the British that the United States "was not out to break up the [British] Empire. We consider it as a great force for stability."[36] Using exactly the same words, he gave a similar assurance to the French at the Franco-American colonial policy talks that followed a few days later. This time, George McGhee, assistant secretary of state for Near Eastern, South Asian, and African Affairs, pointed out the inconsistency "if the United States followed a policy of encouraging European unity and at the same time fragmentation in Africa."[37]

The preoccupation with establishing a common front with the Europeans over Africa was indeed an important theme of the Truman presidency. At Northwestern University on 27 June 1951, McGhee spoke on how the European colonial presence served as a bulwark against the "communist" threat to Africa. He acknowledged that European colonial rule had ensured Africa's automatic orientation towards the West: "Since three-fourths of the Continent's inhabitants are under European control, and the sovereign countries of Africa are allied both economically and politically with Europe and the United States, Africa is firmly associated with the free world." At the same time, he indicated that Africa's value for the West lay in its strategic importance to the Europeans. "The Europeans," McGhee emphasized, "regard their African territories as essential to their economic well-being, their military security, and their political position in the world community. Since the Second World War, Africa's importance to them has been greatly enhanced."[38]

Given that Africa's linkage with the West, and thus insurance against "communism," derived from the European colonial presence, and given that Africa was so important to Europe, McGhee's logic implied that the United States should not be expected to support the anticolonial crusade. It is therefore not surprising that he was impressed by the European colonial record, pointing out that since 1945, "countries containing 550 millions of people have become independent . . . and others are moving forward toward independence." Afraid that independence would undermine European influence in Africa, Asia, and the Middle East and thus open up these areas to "communist" expansion, the assistant secretary hinted that the United States did not welcome the political transformation of the colonies. He therefore found it imperative to caution that "[i]mmediate independence is . . . not a cure for all colonial problems." The United States, he added, "has always maintained that premature independence for primitive, uneducated peoples can do them more harm than good and subject them to an exploitation by indigenous leaders, unrestrained by the civil standards that come with widespread education, that can be just as ruthless as that of aliens. Also, giving full independence to peoples unprepared to meet aggression or subversion can endanger not only the people themselves but the security of the free world."[39]

The basic strategy of the Truman administration was Eurocentric, defending European interests and power, which, for the administration, included the colonial empires. Influential in this regard was Secretary of State Dean Acheson. In 1952, he reported that he "flew via Africa and was interested and impressed by the work done by the French in that area."[40]

By all accounts, Acheson was Truman's alter ego and epitomized the mind-set of the administration's diplomacy. Gaddis Smith has pointed out that he "gave only glancing attention to the mass of the world's population who did not have white skins, advanced industrial economies, and homes in Western Europe or the United States."[41] Lucius Battle, Acheson's former special assistant, recalls that as secretary of state, Acheson "considered the core relationship that the United States had in the world was with Europe. . . .This point of view assumed the preservation, as much as possible, of the status quo of the various empires or near-empires that existed at the time."[42] Acheson was therefore "antipathetic and condescending to the European colonies struggling to become independent states."[43] He was, in addition, "downright belligerent to Americans" who supported anticolonial aspirations.[44] No wonder then that in 1952, Acheson strongly resisted entreaties by Senator Francis Green that "the sympathy of the American people for those who were trying to get self-government should be broadcast even if all we can do is to put this sympathy into words." He would not relent even when the senator suggested that "some words or phrases should be inserted in the appropriation bills" instead.[45]

"The Eurocentric Acheson," Douglas Brinkley observed, "never, whether in office or after, recognized the strength of the currents running against the old European imperial tradition."[46] In the particular case of Africa, a "colonialist view toward the peoples of the region, an attitude of white and Western superiority, became more pronounced in his postsecretarial years."[47] "Whatever may be said about colonialism," Acheson wrote in 1964, "one thing must be said about our attitude toward it, an attitude which we have had for nearly a hundred and fifty years, and that is that anti-colonialism is not a policy. It is merely an attitude of mind and not a very sensible one at that."[48] In his view,

> colonialism ended not because the colonial people became able to govern themselves and not because they had the strength to gain their own independence, but because rule fell from the enfeebled hands of the imperial powers of Europe and left the dependent people, unable to govern themselves in a most precarious and difficult situation.[49]

Until his death in October 1971, Acheson was never converted to the idea of black African self-determination, whether in the Portuguese territories, in Zimbabwe (former Southern Rhodesia), or in South Africa.[50] Indeed, he devoted a good portion of his last years advocating that the UN "had no right to interfere in the 'domestic jurisdiction' of the white-ruled African states—Angola, Mozambique, Rhodesia, and South Africa—even if their racial policies posed a threat not only to their indigenous populations but to neighboring states."[51]

By the time Dwight David Eisenhower became president in January 1953, Washington was well aware that "Third World" nationalism had acquired a distinctive prominence in international relations. In October 1953, Henry Byroade, assistant secretary of state for Near Eastern, South Asian, and African Affairs, observed that "[t]hroughout parts of Africa, the Near East, South Asia, and the Far East, human interests and emotions are focused primarily on such questions as 'imperialism,' 'colonialism,' and 'nationalism.' In many of these areas, the principal motivating force is the desire of dependent peoples to end foreign domination and achieve political and economic self-determination." He described this "movement toward self-determination" as "one of the most powerful forces in 20th century affairs" and added: "When the history of our era is finally written it may prove to have been the most significant of all."[52]

Against this background, it was only logical that Eisenhower should pay more personal attention to the "colonial question" than his predecessor had. And he did. In a personal letter to British Prime Minister Winston Churchill in July 1954, Eisenhower insisted that "[c]olonialism is on the way out as a relationship among peoples. The sole question is one of time and method." He was not advocating independence for the colonies, as he also agreed with Churchill that "in a number of areas the people are not yet ready for self-rule and that any attempt to make them now responsible for their own governing would be to condemn them to lowered standards of life and probably to communistic domination." He only wanted the colonial powers to recognize that "there is abroad in the world a fierce and growing spirit of nationalism. Should we try to damn it up completely, it would, like a mighty river, burst through the barriers and create havoc." This recognition, he hoped, would lead to a change of strategy in colonial policy: "if we are intelligent enough to make use of this force," he continued, "then the result, far from being disastrous, could redound greatly to our advantage, particularly in our struggle against the Kremlin's power."[53]

Eisenhower thought that a resolution could be achieved by canalizing the anticolonial movement, "so as to win adherents to Western aims." In order to achieve this objective, he suggested to Churchill "a thoughtful speech [on] the rights to self-government," to include "the economic requirements of independent existence," and "the burdensome responsibilities of self-rule; internal and external security; proper systems for the administration of justice; the promotion of health and general welfare." Eisenhower assured Churchill that by emphasizing the problems of nation-building, the proposed speech would dampen the demand for independence: "Each [of the colonies]," he added, "would cling more tightly to the mother country and be a more valuable part thereof."[54]

On 30 November 1954, Eisenhower wrote a similar letter to his friend, Alfred Grunther, the supreme commander of the Allied Forces in Europe. This time, he remarked that "[French Prime Minister] Pierre Mendes-France is Churchillian in his attitude toward 'dependent peoples.' He has the same obsession . . . that his prestige is lowered if he should lose one iota of the area of function over which he exercises some degree of influence or control. . . .Consequently he may feel that unless he makes certain of continued French domination of North Africa, he would immediately become an 'ex.'" Eisenhower dismissed such an attitude as "short-sightedness" and emphasized that "[i]n this day and time no so-called 'dependent people' can, by force, be kept indefinitely in that position."[55]

Eisenhower's letter to Grunther reiterated the issues he had raised in his letter to Churchill. Again, he emphasized that Churchill "is absolutely right in his contention that a number of these peoples who are screaming for independence are not yet equipped to support it, and that by now laying down British responsibility in this regard, he would be merely contributing to further unrest and possibly the spread of communism in the world." So more as a propaganda stunt, Eisenhower advocated that the colonial powers "should insist upon the independence of all these peoples and announce in glowing language a great program of preparing these people to support independence, *with all its obligations and costs,* as well as its satisfaction of the spirit of nationalism." As in his letter to Churchill, he made it clear that he did not expect such a move to scuttle colonialism: "My own belief," he stated, "is that [the colonial powers'] experience would be much like ours in Puerto Rico—in most cases, faced with such prospects of responsibilities and increased costs, these peoples would insist upon retaining their connections with the mother country."[56]

The letters to Churchill and Grunther reveal Eisenhower's inner and unfiltered thoughts on the "Third World" anticolonial movement. Quite obvious is his ambivalence on the issue of independence for European colonies. This ambivalence stemmed from his conviction that nationalism lacked the innate capacity to withstand "communist" advances, and therefore that independence had the potential of opening up the "Third World" to Soviet expansion. Thus the letters show an Eisenhower who burdened himself with how to disentangle nationalism from the perceived grip of Soviet influence.[57]

More significantly, the letters show that Eisenhower's inclination was towards the sustenance, not the subversion, of colonialism. He gave expression to this inclination on other occasions. In 1951, he stated that he considered Morocco a part of France.[58] And when the Republican congressional caucus informed him on 2 July 1957 that Senator John Kennedy intended to propose a resolution in favor of Algerian independence, Eisenhower maintained that the "people of Algeria still lacked sufficient education and training to run their own government in the most efficient way."[59] Thus, beyond the contradiction and ambivalence that pervaded his response to nationalism, Eisenhower desired that the Europeans should retain their "stabilizing" influence in their colonies and former colonies. Consequently, he wanted France to grant Algeria independence with a treaty establishing economic relationships;[60] and he applauded the French Community, which sustained colonial linkages in postcolonial francophone Africa.[61] In the circumstances, Eisenhower's acknowledgment of nationalism was merely a grudging acceptance of a reality that could hardly be ignored in 1950s. His position, it must be said, was quite representative of the administration's general stand on the "colonial question."

Perhaps the basic tenor of the administration's position on the "colonial question" was best represented by Secretary of State John Foster Dulles. His official involvement with the matter goes back to the 1945 San Francisco Conference: as a member of the United States delegation, he opposed "independence" as the objective of UN trusteeship.[62] At the same forum, he held that Algeria was an integral part of metropolitan France and should therefore be excluded from the purview of chapter 12 of the UN Charter.[63] Like Acheson, Dulles was concerned, above all else, with the dynamics of a favorable global balance of power. On this score, Dulles, like his predecessor, also worried that independence would weaken the colonial powers and for this reason, he, like Acheson, preferred French control over Indochina.[64] Dulles had not shifted from these positions by the time he came into office as secretary of state.

In November 1952—two months before his assumption of office as secretary of state—Dulles proposed to Anthony Eden, Britain's foreign secretary, that "when Western nations had to face such non-Western problems as those of Colonial Africa . . . it was of the utmost importance" that Britain, France and the United States "should first . . . create a united position."[65] Given this predisposition, he was unwilling to diverge from, and alienate, the colonial powers. In 1953, Indian Prime Minister Jawaharlal Nehru urged that the United States should use its influence to get the colonial powers to adopt more liberal policies in Africa. The response from Dulles was: "we did not (repeat not) feel we could afford [an] open break with the British and French in this matter."[66] On one occasion, Dulles also reminded Eden that "the U.S. held back when charged with imperialism and colonialism, in order to protect the UK and France."[67]

In his speech of 18 November 1953, which set out the administration's "general policy in the colonial field,"[68] Dulles placed the "colonial question" within the wider context of United States foreign policy. He identified three main theaters in the global struggle between "liberty and despotism": the home front, the "free-world" front, and the "Third World" front. "On the free-world front the colonial and dependent areas are the field of dramatic contest. Here the policies of the West and those of Soviet imperialism come into headlong collision." Dulles held that while the ruthless nineteenth-century brand of Western colonialism was "transitory and self-liquidating," "international communism" had, as part of its drive for world domination, "hit on nationalism as a device for absorbing the colonial peoples." The Western powers, including the United States, were thus faced with "a task of indefinite difficulty and delicacy" in responding to the demands by the colonial peoples for independence. He was concerned that "[t]here are some who, having just gained political independence, already stand close to losing it in the way the communists planned." Therefore to those who felt that the United States was being too cautious on the "colonial question," he counseled that "[z]eal needs to be balanced by patience."[69]

In "balancing zeal by patience," the Eisenhower administration advocated an "evolutionary development"of "eventual self-determination for all peoples" as opposed to "premature independence" (or "immediate sovereignty" for all dependent peoples).[70]

Beyond these semantics, a 1954 policy paper declared, quite explicitly, that a "major U.S. interest" in Africa was "[s]upport of the colonial powers' presence in the area and of their responsibility for the security, political and material progress of the African peoples, and the latters' adherence to the free world."[71] It is therefore not surprising to find a delighted (British) Colonial Office observe in June 1954 that

> It is the case that, especially since the advent of the Republican Administration, the State Department has been markedly more sympathetic towards the colonial policies and activities of H.M. Government. . . .We believe that this has been the result of an increasing American realization that the grant of premature self-government to colonial peoples, and attempts to apply in practice such catchwords as "self-determination," would merely increase the areas of political instability in the world and expose any newly independent but economically and socially unstable countries which might emerge from it to infiltration by communism.[72]

Just a month earlier, the State Department had enumerated a number of policies required to counter the "the aggressive strategy and techniques of Soviet communism." One of them was "[v]italizing liberty and freedom within the free world so that it becomes a dynamic force countering the revolutionary spirit with which communism imbues its followers." The department regretted that this objective had been "stifled by U.S. identification with the 'colonialism' of UK, France and Belgium. . . .By defending our allies at the UN and at international conferences and failing to play our historic role as an apostle of political liberty, we have enabled communist propaganda plausibly to brand us as today's leading 'imperialist.' "[73] In spite of this diplomatic liability, there was hardly any change in Washington's position, including its voting behavior at the UN. In June 1956, Henry Lodge, United States representative at the UN, wrote to Eisenhower reporting that the United States "was not appealing to young people worldwide because of its sympathy with colonial powers." Lodge suggested that "we go much harder on the anticolonial side than we are now going," especially by setting a timetable for an end to colonial rule, including in United States dependencies. Dulles simply replied: "The President and I have frequently discussed a change in our public attitude on this subject. My feeling has been that conditions are not yet ripe for such a change."[74]

In the same 1956, Douglas Dillon (the United States ambassador to France) made a long speech in Paris, to clear up the "increasing misunderstanding in France of United States policy toward North Africa." After pointing out that the United States recognized France's achievements in North Africa, he recalled how Washington had

> loyally supported the French Government in its search for solutions to North African problems, solutions that will make possible long-term close cooperation between France and the Moslem communities of Tunisia, Morocco and Algeria. The United States has consistently supported France when North African subjects have been discussed in the United Nations. The most recent instance was our strong support last fall of the position that Algeria is an internal French problem and therefore not appropriate for discussion by the UN.[75]

Not only was the administration "loyally" supporting the European colonial powers, it was also lining up Latin American votes in the UN General Assembly for them. *New York Times* (13 April 1956) reported that "[o]ne area of world policy where South Americans are growing particularly restless is the question of colonialism. Though their natural sympathy lies mainly with the colonial peoples, they often vote in the United Nations with the so-called colonial Powers because of United States pressure."

In June 1959, George Allen, director of the United States Information Agency, journeyed to Paris to reassure Charles de Gaulle, especially on Algeria. By then, the Muslim Algerians had engaged France in a bloody four-and-a-half-year-old war of independence. "In Algeria," Allen assured his hosts, "we recognize that France faces a problem of greater difficulty and complexity than that which burdens any other free world nation." He approved de Gaulle's "Constantine plan" to raise the standard of living in Algeria, his recognition of Algeria's "special personality" and his offer of a "peace of the brave," all of which the Muslims had rejected. "We sincerely hope, as do the friends of France everywhere," Allen continued, "that an equitable and liberal solution—one that will maintain French ties to Algeria—will be found." He assured de Gaulle that he had "the wholehearted support of the United States Government" in his efforts to find such a solution.[76] As the New York *Herald Tribune* observed, Algeria was at the time the most emotionally charged political issue in France, "and it was obvious that it was a policy decision for Mr. Allen to speak so favorably on France's actions and intentions" there. The newspaper added that the speech "would be interpreted and welcomed by the French government as moral support from Washington for its Algerian policy."[77]

In 1960, Washington voted in the UN Political Committee against a resolution calling for independence for Algeria.[78] Later in the same year, the Fourth Committee of the UN General Assembly adopted a resolution holding that the Portuguese colonies were in fact not self-governing, and that Lisbon was therefore obliged to submit information about them to the UN as required by Article 73e of the organization's charter. The United States abstained from voting on this important resolution,[79] important because Lisbon had, in 1951, incorporated its colonies into the Portuguese state. From then on, Portugal had regarded any issue relating to its colonies as an "internal" affair, not subject to any external meddling.

In this sequence, the Eisenhower administration ended on a melodramatic note: along with Australia, Belgium, Britain, the Dominican Republic, France, Portugal, Spain, and South Africa, the United States abstained from voting on the UN General Assembly's "Declaration on the Granting of Independence to Colonial Countries and Peoples." The declaration, adopted in December 1960, by a vote of eighty-nine to zero (with nine abstentions), held that the subjection of peoples to alien domination constituted a denial of fundamental human rights and was contrary to the UN Charter and an impediment to the promotion of world peace and cooperation. The assembly asserted that all peoples had the right to self-determination and that inadequacy of political, economic, social, or educational preparedness should never be a pretext for delaying their independence. It therefore urged that immediate steps be taken in all territories that had not yet attained independence to "transfer all powers to peoples of those Territories, without any conditions or reservations."[80]

The United States explained that it abstained because "there are difficulties in the language and thought of this resolution . . . which made it impossible for us to support it, because they seem to negate certain provisions of the Charter." Four "difficulties" were specified: (1) the silence of the resolution on the contribution of the colonial powers towards the advancement of colonial peoples to "self-government or independence"; (2) "the interpretation that the question of preparation for independence is wholly irrelevant"; (3) the preclusion of "even legitimate measures for the maintenance of law and order"; and (4) the "very strong statement that only complete independence and freedom is the acceptable goal for dependent peoples."[81] In a statement that castigated the administration's attitude on the colonial question, United States delegation member Senator Wayne Morse showed that the declaration accommodated all the reservations. He therefore dismissed the objections as "very unsubstantial."[82]

The United States delegation had the prior approval of the State Department to vote for the declaration. Eisenhower personally ordered the

United States abstention following a request by British Prime Minister Harold Macmillan. When the instruction arrived from the White House, James Wadsworth, the United States representative at the UN, "tried to reach Eisenhower to argue the case. Eisenhower declined to accept his call."[83]

The entire trajectory of the Eisenhower administration's policy put the United States on the side of the colonial powers and elicited sharp criticisms from Africans. In April 1959, Tom Mboya, member of the Kenyan Legislative Council, told a New York audience that Africans "have great expectations" of the United States because of its background and history [as a former colony] and consequently "are sometimes depressed and disappointed" to see Washington "take steps which betray these expectations and hopes." He specifically charged that the United States was "giving priority to the interests of its allies rather than the human struggle taking place in Africa."[84]

George Padmore, the Liberian ambassador to the United States, put the matter even more pointedly: in June 1959, he told State Department officials that "the general feeling in Monrovia is that the United States is unwilling to take any position on Africa which is unfavorable to either France or Great Britain."[85] A month later, Sekou Toure of Guinea stressed that the United States must change its attitude on the question of the termination of European colonial rule if it wanted to make friends in Africa. "There can be no middle way," he insisted; "no compromise policy between colonial interest and African interest, which are contradictory by nature and definition. The United States cannot rightly hope that relations with Africa will be erected on a foundation of contradictions brought about by [zones of] influence and colonial interests."[86] When he paid an official visit to Washington later in the year, Toure emphasized the need for "a dynamic American policy," one adapted to "the new realities in Africa." He explained that he did not imply that the United States should declare war on the colonial powers but that the "consideration of African problems [should] not be subordinated to the views of colonial powers since colonialism is outdated."[87] On another occasion, Toure had to urge that the United States should "deal directly with Africa, in terms of African needs and aspirations, and not through Paris and London."[88] In 1960, Nkrumah implored the United States "to appreciate the African point of view and speak out truthfully and boldly against colonialism and the forces that are militating against nationalism and emancipation."[89]

Explaining Policy Behavior

A major determinant of policy for the Truman administration was that "[t]he principal colonial powers are Western European democratic nations whose security and recovery of political and economic strengths are fundamental objectives of [the] United States."⁹⁰ European recovery was an equally critical factor for the Eisenhower administration. Enunciating an "evolutionary development" of "eventual self-determination for all peoples," as the "basic policy" of the Eisenhower administration, Assistant Secretary Byroade admitted that Washington "must approach colonial questions in terms of the enlightened self-interest of the United States." Against this background, he urged: "let us be frank in recognizing our stake in the strength and stability of certain European nations which exercise influence in the dependent areas. These European nations are our allies. They share many common interests with us. They will probably represent, for many years to come, the major source of free-world defensive power outside our own." The administration also appreciated what it regarded as "the legitimate economic interests which European nations possess" in the colonial territories, and the "importance of these interests to the European economy which we have contributed so much to support."⁹¹

More than its predecessor, the Eisenhower administration understood the reality and force of "Third World" nationalism. However, from Byroade's rhetoric, it is clear that this appreciation clashed with a long-standing Washington culture: its underlying Eurocentric priorities, chief of which was the preservation of a favorable balance of power in Europe. This, in general, required the United States to safeguard Western European interests and power, which certainly included the colonial status quo. Washington's strategic interests were also predicated upon an economically healthy Western Europe. Africa's raw materials, it was clear, played a large part in ensuring a prosperous Europe. And this, by its very logic, translated into a commitment to the colonial status quo.

It is equally apparent that the Eisenhower administration shared the wider strategic concerns and presumptions of its predecessor, in terms of a favorable global balance of power. In early 1960, the Navy Department prepared a position paper as part of a broader NSC study of possible changes in the global distribution of power. The paper estimated that "[w]ithin the next 5 to 10 years virtually all of Africa," as well as some Middle Eastern and Far Eastern territories "presently under Western control will gain either complete independence or a high degree of autonomy, often associated with an increased drift from Western influence." The department envisaged that independence would entail "the withdrawal of Western military and naval forces from, and the denial or restriction of Western military base facilities in, many of these areas." The West's loss, it was believed, would be the Soviet's gain. The department anticipated that "[i]n some of these areas significant indigenous military forces . . . are likely to be developed only with the direct or indirect assistance of the Soviet bloc." It was also calculated that independence would lead to the "strengthening of anti-Western voting strength in the UN"; but worse, independence promised to provide a pool that the Soviet bloc could, "under the guise of 'peace' and 'anti-imperialism,'" mobilize to further its interests at the UN.[92] This kind of reasoning counted for much in policy formulation and thereby heavily compromised the United States position on the liquidation of colonial rule in Africa.

Much of the argument here has been that, in its various manifestations, Washington's attitude to colonialism and nationalism—as well as its commitment to exploit Africa's resources for the rehabilitation of Europe—were conditioned by strategic considerations revolving around the international balance of power (which included Cold War dictates). Eisenhower himself gave personal testimony that his administration was not enthusiastic about Africa's transition to independence because "with a position of leadership in the Free World, we . . . could not afford to see turmoil in an area where the communists would be only too delighted to take an advantage."[93] In spite of this kind of official rhetoric, which is very much in evidence in the archival records, there is ample evidence that anti-Sovietism was not the only reason for Washington's Eurocentric agenda in Africa.

At a general level, one may argue that Washington's newfound status and role as a global hegemon after World War II clashed with those of the old Great Powers, the Europeans, seeking to negotiate their transition to the status of lesser powers with as much dignity as the circumstances could afford them. In this sense, their colonial empires gave the Europeans a sense of continuing self-importance on the post-World War II international stage, thereby blunting their resentment of United States preeminence. The fact is that Britain and France, in particular, were never totally reconciled to playing second fiddle in world affairs in the aftermath of World War II. Yet, it was only too apparent that any claim on their part to world power status after the war was legitimized by the colonies, especially Africa (the region where they were still firmly in the saddle after 1945). This reality was well understood in Washington: in 1951, Elmer Bourgerie, director, State Department Office of African Affairs, acknowledged that "[t]he European Colonial Governments . . . regard their African territories as essential to their military security, economic well-being and political position in the world community. Since these Governments have lost most of their Asiatic possessions, Africa is more important to them than ever before."[94]

There is therefore a great deal of merit in arguing that Africa's strategic importance to Europe was a key element in shaping the nature of

Washington's behavior. Closely related to this recognition was the fact that both the Truman and Eisenhower administrations operated on the assumption that Africa was a European sphere of influence. This notion found explicit expression in various forms, such as that of Vernon McKay of the State Department in 1953: "The direct responsibility for Africa," he explained, "belongs to other [that is, Western European] governments."[95] This geopolitical division of labor had a number of broad policy implications, including the Eurocentric bias of United States policy in Africa. More fundamentally, it committed the United States to accept the European position and perspective as the governing bases of its policy in Africa.

To policymakers in Washington, Western Europe has traditionally been of the utmost importance in foreign policy.[96] Although often expressed in geopolitical idioms, the Eurocentric dimension of United States diplomacy has its own distinct institutional autonomy. This assertion proceeds from the fact that the top echelons of both the Truman and Eisenhower administrations were occupied by Europhiles, men whose primary point of reference in international affairs was, by instinct, Western Europe (and Britain in particular). Much of this instinctive attitude derived from "a shared heritage and kindred institutions."[97] The "most striking characteristic" of those high policymakers, according to Robert Divine,

> was their homogeneity. Virtually all were old-stock Protestant Americans. Descendants of English and Scottish settlers, they were Anglophiles who believed that the United States had inherited England's role as arbiter of world affairs. As representatives of a social class that had taken on many characteristics of a caste, they showed little sympathy for the colonial peoples. The world they wanted to save was limited to Europe . . . ; they took Latin America for granted and neglected the Orient.[98]

In this worldview, Africa was definitely nonexistent, except as an overseas province of Western Europe.

This intersection of the sociocultural milieu of the policymaker and his strategic worldview—and, especially, the fact that this convergence translated into a Eurocentric bias in Washington—points to what Michael Hunt has identified as the ideological underpinning of United States foreign policy. In spite of the Marxist view that it is a cognitive distortion, many will agree with the definition of ideology as "a syndrome of functionally interrelated beliefs and values that encourages particular behavior."[99] In *Ideology and U.S. Foreign Policy,* Hunt identified three underlying ideas, all rooted in the eighteenth and nineteenth centuries, which have traditionally defined United

States foreign policy (and therefore behavior towards other nations). These ideological underpinnings are a vision of national greatness, a hierarchical construction of race, and a distaste for revolutionary change ("the perils of revolution," in Hunt's words). The last two are pertinent to the discussion here.

Hunt shows that "[i]n the structure of American race thinking, Anglo-Saxonism—the belief that Americans and the British were one people united by uncommon qualities and common interests—occupied a central position. By the first half of the nineteenth century Americans had begun to claim with pride their place in a trans-Atlantic community of English-speaking peoples." This hierarchical structuring was transplanted "into the fabric of thinking on world affairs." Africans were at the other extreme: "Predictably, farthest back were the peoples of Africa. . . .the 'dark continent' . . . the fascinating home of 'savage beasts and beastly savages.' Above all other places Africa invited white dominion."[100] Racial postures derived from the enslavement of Africans and the resulting Jim Crow domestic black-white race relations reinforced this perception and shaped official United States attitudes towards Africa.[101] Thus in August 1943, Henry Villard, assistant chief of the State Department Division of Near Eastern Affairs, referred to Africa as a land with "a relatively primitive population."[102]

With the likes of Acheson at the helm, there is no doubt that this mind-set and its policy implications pervaded the Truman administration. In the administration's estimation, Africans fell into the category of "primitive, uneducated peoples" for whom "premature independence" would have been an illwind. At the May 1950 tripartite foreign ministers' (of France, Britain, the United States) meeting in London, Washington excluded Africa from its belief in the "progressive development of all dependent people towards self-government and where conditions are suitable towards independence." The excuse was that "the peoples of 'Black Africa' have not yet achieved full understanding of modern political, social and economic institutions." Consequently, Washington proposed a paternalistic mission for the colonial powers: "we believe that there must be an orderly, guided development of these people towards political maturity which only time and patience can provide."[103] In part, Acheson himself resented anticolonialism and independence for the European colonies in Africa because, as he put it: "For simple and largely illiterate people, people in an agricultural or sometimes pre-agricultural state, as in the Congo, to establish a government and attain the cultural development necessary both to maintain that government and to emerge from a purely agricultural society is a very great task indeed."[104]

It is safe to contend that Eisenhower and his entourage subscribed to the notion that Africans were "primitive, uneducated peoples" who deserved to be excluded from the "progressive development of all dependent people towards self-government." At an NSC meeting on 14 January 1960, Vice President Richard Nixon, the administration's leading in-house "Africanist,"[105] claimed that the British anticipated that, in many African countries, a South American-type dictatorship would emerge. He therefore urged, "We must recognize, although we cannot say it publicly, that we need the strong men of Africa on our side . . . it would be naive of the United States to hope that Africa will be democratic." Nixon's premise was that the problems confronting African political leadership were overwhelming, especially because "[s]ome of the peoples of Africa have been out of the trees for only about fifty years."[106]

Intertwined with the racial stereotyping of Africa and Africans was Washington's perception of Africa. In general, there was (and still is) an otherness in the American worldview about "Third World" peoples: they are non-European; they live in unfamiliar lands, and are therefore unfamiliar and exotic peoples and cultures; they are, in addition, largely nonindustrialized; materially destitute, or "backward," and "fickle and malleable." In this context, it should be emphasized that although foreign policy elites behave like rational realpolitik actors, it is now well established that psychological attitudes (that is, worldviews, belief systems, and perceptions) function as mental maps that help agents to coordinate their behavior.[107] Gary Hess, for example, has argued that "American images of India help [us] to understand the assumptions not only of foreign policy, but also of informational, educational, and economic programs. . . .Attitudes about the country reflected distorted, stereotypical images of the Indian people and their culture."[108]

Historically, the "image" of Africa in the West has largely been a literary, fictive one.[109] In this provenance must be included not only imaginative literature but also supposedly nonfictional disciplines like anthropology and history.[110] According to Elliot Skinner, down to the 1940s, Americans "showed little interest in Africa and Africans." To them, Africans "were cruel, cannibalistic savages. . . .Africa was the place where one went on safari, where missionaries braved all sorts of unknown dangers to raise the heathen from their darkness, and where Tarzan, the noble white savage, ruled as 'king of the jungle.'"[111] In 1956, the State Department confessed that "[t]he incomplete comprehension of Africa is to some extent the result of our own disinterest. If the American public thinks of Africa at all, it looks upon it as a place where lions roam, missionaries preach, or natives are exploited."[112] Even today, the American "image" or perception of Africa and Africans has shifted very little from this fictive stereotype.[113]

As would be expected, this fictive image contributed (and continues to contribute) to shackling United States initiative in Africa. In the words of Rupert Emerson and Martin Kilson, "The assumption that Africa was inhabited by primitive peoples who had barely made a start toward civilization rendered all the more tempting the inclination to abstain from concern with the continent."[114]

By the "perils of revolution," Hunt refers to America's distaste for revolutionary change. Although Americans had dislodged their British overlords in the eighteenth century, that experience did not, according to Hunt, prepare them to accommodate revolutionary change. Instead, it taught them that "[r]evolution was a solemn affair, to be conducted with a minimum of disorder, led by respectable citizens, harnessed to moderate political goals, and happily concluded only after a balanced constitution, essential to safeguarding human and property rights, was securely in place." Put simply, they believed that "[p]olitical change was possible but had to occur slowly and within the existing system."[115] This was particularly true of the years immediately after World War II when the United States dominated the world in every realm. By the very fact of this dominance, Washington was heavily invested in the status quo.

Against this background, the policymakers in Washington viewed the radical political changes of the twentieth century—from the Bolshevik Revolution in 1917 through Mao Tse-tung's triumph in China in 1949 and the militancy of the Vietminh in Indochina—as unacceptable conducts. Even the more sedate anticolonial stirrings in Africa and Asia were not perceived in a better light: they too held out the prospect of subverting the status quo. This aversion was reinforced by the fact that notwithstanding any historical and ideological differences, the "Third World" nationalist manifesto consisted of four unifying elements: "political independence; freedom from external economic control; social revolution aimed at removing indigenous oppression based on tradition and/or that stemming from the implantation of structures of exploitation by the colonial power; and, finally, cultural regeneration with a view to restoring the dignity and self-respect" of the ex-colonials. As a matter of course, Washington opposed this manifesto because it was "far more closely compatible with the Soviet than it is with the Western conception of political and social development."[116]

There was another side to these "perils of revolution." Washington, according to Hunt, believed that the "modernization" of the colonial societies was a precondition for their political development.[117] This belief can easily be detected among the United States administrations considered above, from Roosevelt to Eisenhower. In his October 1953 speech, Byroade held that "[c]onditions of life in a large part [of Africa] are still primitive, and advancement toward complete self-determination of the local population will require political, economic, social, and cultural development. All these factors are inseparable."[118]

As late as October 1958, Secretary of State Dulles assured Belgian Foreign Minister Pierre Wigny that the United States understood that the process of preparing colonies for self-government was "a slow and difficult one" and regretted that most of "the new independent countries," which had not undergone such a long tutoring, "had become targets for international communism." His sensitivities were thus offended because "the admission of these newly independent, but unprepared nations into the UN with the same vote as older and greater powers debased the concept of independent nations exercising self-responsibility in international affairs." In particular, he scoffed at Guinea's independence, saying that it "could only be described as 'premature.' " In language reminiscent of Cordell Hull in 1942, Dulles insisted that as an essential precondition for independence, "the governing elements should be educated, moral and self-disciplined and . . . much time is required to achieve this degree of preparation." Drawing on the United States experience in the Philippines, he volunteered what he considered an adequate period to groom a colony for independence: the United States, he recalled, had "spent 50 years preparing the Philippines for independence and there were times we believed that had perhaps not been long enough."[119]

There were other factors that contributed to inhibit a bold United States policy in Africa, a policy with its own internal momentum. In general, there is no disputing that although United States interest in Africa expanded in the 1950s, concrete and identifiable interests remained sparse; by 1960, there were still no deep commitments, no vested interests, whether one talks in economic or strategic terms. These, along with the geographical distance between the two regions, effectively put Africa in the outer realms of United States diplomacy.

Africa is rich in primary resources, some of which the United States has needed since the 1950s. But the region has also been traditionally of little economic value to Americans. This is illustrated by the flow of private United States investments. In 1950, the value of United States direct private investment in Africa was $297 million out of a global total of $11,788 million. By 1960, investments in Africa stood at $925 million out of a global total of $32,778 million. It must be pointed out that much of this investment was in white-dominated South Africa and the Federation of

Rhodesia and Nyasaland. For example, in 1950, half ($140 million out of $287 million) of the total figure for Africa was invested in South Africa.[120]

Significantly, this neglect of Africa by private United States capital was not a reflection of market signals such as the rate of return on investment: in 1950, the rate of return on all United States overseas investment before foreign income taxes was about 26 percent; for continental Africa, it was about 30 percent.[121] Nor can the limited presence of private United States capital in Africa be blamed on the colonial policies of the Europeans. Well after African states achieved their independence, the bulk of private United States investment in Africa continued to be directed to South Africa. In 1975, for example, the global value of private United States investment was $124,212 million. Of this, Africa's share was only $3,996 million, out of which South Africa alone took $1,582 million.[122] Like the public officials in Washington, the United States business community regarded Africa as a European reserve.[123]

In terms of strategic considerations, the index that counted most was what the CIA called "industrial-military power," which consisted of military power and installations, an advanced industrial base, and a skilled workforce.[124] In the JCS ranking of areas vital to United States security (which has already been mentioned in this chapter), the importance of Northwest Africa—which appeared on the list—derived from its constituting "an important buttress to Western defense positions in Europe and the Middle East, a major element in Western control of the Mediterranean, and potentially a vital base for assembly of troops and supplies and a staging area for counterattack in the event of Soviet invasion of Europe or the Middle East."[125] Sub-Saharan Africa was of the least consequence precisely because it lacked these elements so essential to United States national security imperatives.

True, Washington often couched the rhetoric of its interest in Africa in Cold War vocabulary, that is, in terms of heading off Soviet expansion into the region. There was, however, also a realization that the real possibility of such a development was minimal, if not nonexistent. In the first place, unlike Southeast Asia, Africa was not a Cold War danger zone. Second, for most of the 1950s, Africa was still very much under Western European political control and this shielded the region from any real Soviet penetration. Third, even at the twilight of European rule by the late 1950s, it was obvious that African political leaders were oriented to the West. At any rate, in spite of all the sound and fury, the Soviets made no aggressive push into Africa, even at the end of colonial rule; like the United States, they were content with modest aid programs. Although Moscow strongly supported the termination of colonialism, its efforts were generally no more than symbolic gestures, not threatening enough to warrant countermeasures by Washington.

Conclusion

At a fundamental level, there was little, if anything, to differentiate the policies of the Truman and Eisenhower administrations towards Africa. The former believed that "the attainment of United States objectives in the colonial field—economic and social, as well as political—is dependent upon the active support and cooperation" of the colonial powers.[126] Consequently, "cooperation" between the United States and the colonial powers became the guidepost of policy in Africa. At the May 1950 tripartite foreign ministers' meeting in London, the United States began from the premise that it was in the common interest of the Western powers to have short, and long-range conditions of political, economic, and social stability in Africa, resilient enough to enable the region to resist domination by "unfriendly" movements or powers either through aggression or subversion. Starting from this premise, the United States favored institution-building by the colonial powers, in Africa. In addition, Washington announced its support for the "advancement of the economic and, where suitable, the strategic advantages to France and the UK of their colonies and trust territories" and the "strengthening of the relationship between the metropolitan powers and the colonial territories so long as the people therein desire such development."[127] Under Eisenhower, these policy positions were elaborated.

In 1956, the State Department pointed out that the United States did not "have an infinite capacity to influence" the European colonial powers in Africa to take actions that accorded with its own policies. This limitation, it explained, went beyond the Europeans being merely unable to agree with the United States "because of their internal political situation. It is also a question of their being unwilling to jeopardize arrangements which we [the United States] consider of utmost significance if pressed too far. This fact has a particular significance for Africa, since much of what we would like to see done in the continent must be accomplished through the European administering countries."[128] Like the Truman administration, the department was, in effect, saying that the European colonial presence in Africa facilitated, rather than complicated, United States policy in the region and that this counted for much in policy making. European political control facilitated the exploitation of Africa's resources for Europe's benefit, a pivotal Washington objective. The European colonial presence was also helpful for Washington in a number of other important ways, notably, shielding Africa from "evil" influences such as Soviet penetration. In October 1956, the United States Operations Mission (USOM) in London defined United States interest in Africa as "primarily political" and "dependent on [the] continuing control of metropolitan powers on the Continent and their ability to maintain stability in the territories." United States strategic interest in Africa was also considered "secondary so long as the metropolitan powers are firmly in the saddle."[129]

From Truman to Eisenhower, the one constant in United States policy was a continuing, strong European presence in Africa. This was based on the calculation that the European presence and influence in Africa saved the United States the costs of a more active and direct involvement in the region. It is therefore no surprise that as the transfer of political power from the Europeans to Africans became a reality, the Eisenhower administration still desired the continuance of European influence and therefore advocated a strong neocolonial relationship between Africa and Europe. NSC 6005, adopted as a policy statement on 9 April 1960, urged that the United States should impress upon Western European countries "the continuing importance to them of a stable and prosperous West Africa and conduct all United States activities with a realization that a continued close Euro-African relationship is important to the United States itself." In turn, West Africans were to be impressed with the "fact that their national well-being depends in large part on a continued close economic and cultural relationship with Western Europe." It was therefore recommended that the Western Europeans be urged "to expand their efforts to influence and support their respective dependent and recently independent areas."[130]

Finally, it is instructive that United States leaders—from Roosevelt and Hull, through Truman and Acheson, to Eisenhower and Dulles—routinely held up their country's experience in the Philippines as the model for the decolonization of European colonies. The United States granted independence to the Philippines on 4 July 1946; but this was circumscribed by the Philippine Trade Act. Section 341 of this act, which was passed by the United States Congress, required the Philippines to grant American businessmen the same rights as their indigenous counterparts. The Philippine constitutional provision that prevented foreigners from owning more than 40 percent in any local business venture was amended so that Americans would, for its purposes, be regarded as Filipinos. The act tied the Philippine currency to the dollar until 1974 and allocated export quotas to both American and local firms.[131] By substituting trade and investment relationships for political control, this act ensured that United States economic and even strategic interests were well secured in the independent Philippines.

3

TRUMAN'S DUAL MANDATE[1]

The year 1950 has an undeniable significance in the history of post-1945 United States involvement in Africa. In his memoir, George McGhee, assistant secretary of state for Near Eastern, South Asian, and African Affairs, recalled that "in 1950, no comprehensive U.S. policy had been formulated for Africa south of the Sahara."[2] An effort in this direction was initiated with a panel discussion on Africa, organized by the State Department on 6 February 1950 and chaired by McGhee. In addition to officers of the department, the participants were drawn from academia, foundations, and various commercial and religious organizations involved with Africa.[3]

The panelists considered Africa to be clay waiting to be molded by external agents. It was acknowledged that the Europeans, United States allies, were already doing the job, but they seemed ill-equipped. The panel therefore proposed that in addition to supplying vital construction materials, the United States would be the site supervisor, providing some leadership for the Europeans. According to their final report:

> Africa is a relatively malleable area, more susceptible at present and for some time to come to outside determinism than any other large area of the world. Accordingly, it is the last large region in which outsiders can continue for a time to do very much as they please, because of the limited economic and political powers of the African peoples, their lack of cohesion and solidarity on a continental scale, and their helplessness except through the medium of world public opinion.

This alleged helplessness, they held, imposed a great responsibility on Western powers, particularly, the United States. As the panel put it:

> The U.S. is in a position of great influence to determine the actions of the Western nations with regard to Africa, because Africa contains no resident powers possessing sufficient strength and historical and ideological acceptability to gain pan-African predominance; because we are effectively allied with all of the governing powers except Spain, which are in high degree dependent upon us; because many Africans look upon American institutions, influence, and support as desirable; and because of their recognition of our sympathy towards and contribution to the rapid indigenous development of all peoples. Accordingly, of all the nations having access to Africa, the U.S. is in the best position to influence for good the entire continent....

Essentially, the panel recommended that the United States should seek the accomplishment of its objectives and policy in Africa through the operations of the Economic Cooperation Administration (ECA) and Point IV,[4] and in "cooperation with the European colonial countries" and Africans themselves.[5]

The panel was part of the groundwork for the West and East African Regional Conference held in Lourenço Marques, Mozambique, from 27 February to 2 March 1950. The conference was chaired by McGhee and attended by United States consular officials stationed in sub-Saharan Africa. It was, according to one official report, the first United States consular conference exclusively concerned with the region. Its objective, the report added, "was to develop information which would assist the [State] Department in formulating a U.S. policy for Africa—a policy that would recognize our long-range interests in the area without prejudicing our relations with the European powers."[6]

McGhee later explained that the Lourenço Marques conference "developed a preliminary statement regarding our attitudes, objectives and policy towards Africa."[7] In the main, the policy was to be a balancing act, accommodating United States interests without undermining the European position. The conference recommended that in the "political sphere" (possibly meaning in matters of colonial administration), the United States should not "inject itself into the situation"; the initiative was to be left to the colonial powers. On the other hand, the United States would seek economic returns from Africa: while acknowledging that the entrenched positions of European business interests militated against the penetration of United States private capital, the conference discussed the possibilities of increasing African commodity exports to the United States and ensuring that United States access to the region's economic resources equaled that of the Europeans.[8]

The Lourenço Marques conference was clearly reflected in the policy that followed. McGhee's address to the Foreign Policy Association of Oklahoma City on 8 May 1950 was possibly the first official enunciation of United States policy for Africa. He described Africa as "a region in which we have few direct responsibilities" and pointed out that "[o]ther nations, chiefly those with whom we are associated under the North Atlantic Treaty, are directly responsible for solution of the day-to-day problems of Africa." Not only did the United States consider Africa to be Europe's responsibility, but McGhee gave a clear indication that policy would be based on this perception. "We must keep in mind," he added, "the fact that we are not in a position to exercise direct responsibility with respect to Africa. We have no desire to assume the responsibilities borne by other powers and, indeed, our principles, our existing commitments, and our lack of experience all militate against our assumption of such obligations." By highlighting these limitations, the speech sent a clear signal that the United States intended to work in Africa in cooperation with, not in opposition to, the Europeans. Continuing, McGhee observed that "communism" had not made any significant inroad into Africa, thus providing the United States and its European allies with the opportunity to develop "healthy political, economic, and social institutions" in Africa; "to create an understanding on the part of Africans of the forces of communism . . . and to inspire a determination to resist those forces."[9]

It was against this background that McGhee outlined the objectives of United States policy for Africa. The United States favored "the progressive development" of African territories "toward the goal of self-government or, where conditions are suitable, toward independence." Second there was a desire for the development of mutually advantageous economic relations between Western Europe and Africa, "in the interests of contributing to the restoration of a sound European economy and in the interests of furthering the aspirations of the African peoples." At the same time, the United States wished to "preserve its rights of equal economic treatment in the territories of Africa" and to participate "both commercially and financially" in Africa's development "along with other nations of the world." In the same vein, the United States "must continue to have access to Africa's vital reservoir of minerals which are critical stockpile items in the United States—manganese, chrome ore, rubber, industrial diamonds essential to our machine tool industry, asbestos, and many other important minerals."

Finally, it was "a major" United States objective to assist in the establishment of an environment in which Africans "will feel that their aspirations can best be served by continued association and cooperation with the nations of the free world, both in their present status and as they advance towards self-government or independence and in accordance with the UN Charter." He added that these objectives were to be promoted through the ECA, the United States Information Service (USIS), the Educational Exchange program, and Point IV.[10]

The Quest for Raw Materials and Europe's Economic Health

As McGhee had proposed, the ECA, Point IV and, later, the Mutual Security Agency (MSA) programs were the basic mechanisms for United States involvement in Africa during the Truman presidency. In enacting the Foreign Assistance Act of 1948, the United States Congress established the ECA and authorized it to provide material and financial assistance to any country that had adhered to the report of the Committee of European Cooperation at Paris on 22 September 1947, "together with dependent areas under its administration." From 1948, this provision enabled the United States to extend "assistance" to European colonies, including those in Africa, as part of the United States assistance to the metropolitan countries.[11]

Under its procurement authorization procedure, requests for ECA programs in Africa could only emanate from the metropolitan countries and for such projects as they designated.[12] Consequently, the programs were integrated into existing colonial development schemes.[13] Essentially, the ECA limited itself to using United States dollars to obtain capital equipment or technical personnel not available in the participating countries. This meant that apart from providing United States personnel, ECA funds were used to purchase American capital goods (especially tractors, scrappers, graders, and other types of earth-moving equipment and agricultural machinery). Such funds did not cover expenses in local currency or equipment available in the participating countries.[14]

Point IV, which followed in 1950, was exclusively focused on "technical assistance." As passed by Congress in September 1950, the legislation that established Point IV provided for furnishing technical assistance to governments of underdeveloped countries (UDCs) and territories. Technical assistance, according to the legislation, could take the form of providing experts to advise a government, conduct demonstration projects, or "impart techniques by other means in the fields of agriculture, power development, mining, health, education, etc." It also included training the nationals of a cooperating country in the United States or other country agreed upon with the United States. It did not include the provision of capital for a development project. Point IV funds could therefore be used to assist a government if it required expert advice or a survey in connection with land reclamation, but not for the reclamation itself. Congress also ruled that technical assistance in this sense did not constitute a further obligation by the United States to provide loans or grants.[15]

By its very nature (in terms of the animating impulses, the degree of financial involvement, the scope and objectives), United States involvement in Africa was very conservative and minuscule. To begin with, the financial input of the ECA and Point IV, even as "technical assistance" programs, was miserly. By the end of 1950, the maximum ECA dollar expenditure per project was pegged at 2 percent of total cost (down from 10 to 15 percent at the beginning of the Marshall Plan). The bulk of the expenditures for programs involving the ECA were in local currencies provided by the metropolitan and local governments.[16] In its turn, Point IV, according to Gabriel Kolko, was "a program with inflated pretensions but very little money."[17] Truman had requested $45 million as the total funds for the first year of Point IV, but Congress approved only $34.5 million,[18] and that was for all of Africa, Asia, the Middle East, the Far East, and Latin America. Of course, it was made quite explicit that the United States was not taking on a "principal role" in the "development" of Western Europe's colonies; that responsibility, according to the ECA, was "already being met, in substantial measure, by the European countries and the territories themselves."[19]

On account of their financial limitations, neither the ECA nor the Point IV programs made any provision for capital development. Indeed, Robert Pollard has shown that the Truman administration had no real development or foreign aid program for the UDCs. Instead, it believed that recovery in Europe would trickle down, through the intermediation of private capital, to spur economic activity in the UDCs.[20] Of greater significance, however, was the realization in Washington that the economic problems of the UDCs were more deeply rooted than those of Europe. In this sense, the solution to the UDCs' problems was perceived as a long-drawn-out, daunting exercise, which would have required more financial input than the United States could possibly afford. This thinking and its policy implications were put in perspective by the policy planning staff of the State Department in July 1947. While acknowledging that "[t]here are, and will continue to be areas outside of Europe which will have need of U.S. cooperation in their development," they noted that "Europe's needs are, in their aggregate, clear in outline, readily susceptible of short-term solution." Comparing the European situation with that of the UDCs, the planning staff felt that "[t]he problem in Europe is basically one of releasing the capacity for self-help already present in certain highly advanced countries. This is a short-term problem. In the case of many non-European areas, what is needed is not the release of existing energies but the creation of new ones. This is a long-term problem."[21]

The United States programs were rendered even more conservative by their objectives and underlying impulses. Kolko says that after World War II, the United States had hoped that Western Europe's economic health would be fully restored after a "short period of loans and grants." When it became clear that this was not to be, the Truman administration embraced the idea that the solution lay in Europe earning "far more dollars through increased exports to the United States from its present and former colonies." This, according to Kolko, was the background to Point IV.[22]

Numerous official records confirm that the involvement of both the ECA and Point IV in the UDCs were animated and focused on increased supplies of raw materials. Western Europe was intended to be the primary beneficiary, with Africa as the major source of the raw materials. In July 1950, John Orchard, chairman of the ECA Advisory Committee on Overseas Territories recounted the two "original reasons" for the ECA overseas development program: (1) to support European recovery, and (2) the possibilities of increasing raw material production, including "strategic materials" for the United States stockpile. "Recent developments," he added, "have given us a selfish interest in carrying forward the program . . . the possibilities of finding and developing sources of industrial and strategic materials in defensible areas, particularly Africa."[23] A year later, Allan Smith, acting director of ECA Overseas Territories Division, spoke in a similar vein and criticized this disingenuous pattern of "economic assistance" to Africa. "We specifically feel," he emphasized, "that we must not repeat not continue to regard aid to African territories as merely supplementary to and part of aid to Europe." He recalled that economic aid to Europe was "oriented to maintaining and building up economic conditions required for a strong rearmament effort," but when applied to Africa, which had "no direct rearmament facilities," the objective "would indicate support [for] only increased production [of] strategic materials and financing collateral development required in this regard such as port and rail facilities, possibly power."[24]

In May 1950, McGhee graphically illustrated the significance of Africa's contribution to Europe's well-being. He pointed out that the volume of Africa's exports to Western Europe in 1948 "totaled about 2.5 billion dollars, or approximately half as much as the United States itself exported to Europe," so that "a relatively small increase in Africa's production will go far toward improving the present dollar deficit position of the Western European countries."[25] Another report described the ECA program in Africa as "closely related to the economic recovery of Europe, inasmuch as resource development in Africa could contribute (a) to reduce the dollar import requirements of the colonial powers, and (b) to provide those powers with additional sources of dollar earnings." In 1950, the calculation was that ECA activities would enable African territories "by F[inancial]Y[ear] 1953, to increase their dollar earnings and savings" by half a billion dollars as compared with their pre-ECA performance. This increased earning was intended to make a significant "annual contribution to the balance-of-payments positions of the metropolitan countries."[26]

It is worth emphasizing that the United States itself also had a great need for Africa's raw materials. So great was this need that in January 1951, Truman established the International Materials Policy Commission, chaired by William Paley, to examine the overall position of the United States with regard to the supply of raw materials necessary for its national security purposes. In June 1952, the commission submitted the first volume of its report, which emphasized that on account of the speed with which they were being utilized by the industrial nations, raw materials were in such high demand and were thus rising so rapidly in price that the resulting crisis could "undermine our rising standard of living, impair the dynamic quality of American capitalism, and weaken the economic foundations of national security." To avert this threat, the commission recommended that the United States "must principally look for an expansion of its mineral imports" in Canada, Latin America, Africa, the Near East, and South and Southeast Asia.[27] In this way, the Paley Commission reminded United States policymakers of the long-term economic importance of the UDCs to United States prosperity. The ECA itself did not disguise the fact that it also devoted "a major share of its effort" in Africa to the "procurement of strategic materials for the U.S. stockpile."[28] It explained that "[m]ost contracts are written to provide for repayment of ECA's investment in a portion of the materials being developed."[29]

In the early 1950s, Africa was the principal source of a number of strategic minerals which the United States needed: 97 percent of United States columbium ore requirements came from Nigeria and the Belgian

Congo; 81 percent of its palm oil, 68 percent of its cobalt, and 52 percent of its industrial diamonds came from the Belgian Congo; while 23 percent of its manganese ore came from the Gold Coast and Morocco. In addition, Africa provided the United States with appreciable quantities of corundum, tantalite, copper, lead, zinc, graphite mica, tin, quartz, platinum, sisal, ivory, cocoa, palm products, tropical hardwoods, and cinchona and its derivatives.[30] All these were very important since the degree of their substitutability by United States domestic production was low or even nonexistent.

The ECA attributed United States strategic interest in raw materials to the outbreak of the Korean War in June 1950 and the vast defense program which it occasioned. "It was quickly apparent," the ECA observed,

> that if steadily mounting rearmament programs in the United States and Western Europe were to be carried out without precipitating disastrous declines in living standards throughout the free world, it would be necessary to bring about a swift and substantial expansion in the supply of strategic and other basic materials. For many of these primary commodities required in both military and civilian production, the United States, as well as Western Europe, must rely heavily and in some cases almost entirely, upon production in the overseas territories—chiefly in Africa and the Far East.[31]

The centrality of raw materials in United States operations in Africa was amply reflected in the nature of the projects in which the ECA was involved. ECA funds were, for example, used for the procurement of diesel-electric locomotives for the Dakar-Niger railroad; the Dakar-based Bureau Minier de la France d'Outre-Mer (a government corporation engaged in mineral exploration and prospecting) obtained $8,000 for its laboratories, $3,000 for a large pickup truck, and $26,000 for a pilot mill to be used in ore concentration; Péchiney, a private French concern, which was working on a phosphate deposit, received ECA compressed air equipment, a conveyor, and a mechanical shovel worth about $160,000.[32] In addition, there was a road construction from Douala, a major port of the Cameroons, into the hinterland, "tapping the diamond and tin producing areas, among others"; the development of the "iron mine and mineral port" at Conakry, Guinea; the modernization of the Congo-Ocean railroad, "which taps French Equatorial Africa and the Belgian Congo"; expansion of the port, power, and water supply facilities of Brazzaville, "the key processing and transport center" for French Equatorial Africa; and geological mapping and research.[33] There was the construction of hydroelectric power stations in Léopoldville,

Stanleyville, and Albertville, all in the Belgian Congo, to "facilitate production and export of palm oil, rubber, as well as other essential raw materials found in the Congo."[34]

The ECA explained that it became involved in these projects because of the realization that "[p]roduction cannot be sharply expanded in underdeveloped areas simply by increasing the capital equipment employed for directly productive purposes. Provision must also be made for essential supporting facilities—railways, roads, and ports for importing equipment and supplies and evacuating the output; power and other utilities at the site of production and at transportation and processing centers; housing and health facilities for workers; etc."[35]

From the ECA, France secured equipment for an irrigation and land reclamation project for rice cultivation, involving some 50,000 acres of land in Markala, on the central Niger River.[36] This too was tied in to increasing raw material production. "During the last war," the ECA explained, "the production of peanuts in French West Africa, which provide a major share of Europe's supply of edible fats, fell to a fraction of normal, for one reason only: When imports of Far Eastern rice to FWA [French West Africa] were largely cut off the peasant producers of peanuts overwhelmingly reverted to growing millet for their own food."[37] Elsewhere, the ECA had stated: "Experience during World War II had shown that the bringing of new labor into an area or the diversion of local labor from production for domestic consumption often tended to create shortages in housing, food, and other basic necessities. If output of materials exported from the territories was to be expanded to any large degree, local food production would have to be increased."[38]

On 24 May 1951, Truman sent a message on foreign aid to Congress, asserting that "[t]he condition of the people in the underdeveloped areas would be a matter of humanitarian concern even if our national security were not involved." Nonetheless, national security—defined in terms of securing raw materials—was his primary consideration: he stressed that Africa, Asia, and South America "produce strategic materials which are essential to the defense and economic health of the free world. Production of these materials must be increased" as they helped "the whole free world by increasing the supply of raw materials essential to defense and to an expanding world economy."[39] In the same year, the MSA absorbed both the ECA and Point IV, inheriting their functions, objectives, and traditions.

As with its predecessors, the MSA's programs in Africa were "on a modest scale, supplementing at certain key points the much larger programs financed by the European countries themselves." The programs were specifically designed to serve three purposes: raw materials production and support projects; military support projects, and technical assistance. Technical assistance, provided in response to requests from European governments, consisted principally of providing the services of American experts to help local administrators and technicians; scientific data on special problems; opportunities for advanced training and observation in the United States or elsewhere for selected specialists from the territories; and limited equipment and supplies essential to the effective execution of the technical assistance provided.[40]

As with the ECA and Point IV, the MSA continued to define the relevance of the UDCs in terms of their role as sources of raw materials: "The overseas territories," it was stated, "are important producers of mineral and other raw materials now required, in increasing volume, for the defense program. Together they constitute the free world's largest reservoir of untapped natural resources." Again as with the ECA and Point IV, Europe continued to be the MSA's major concern. As the agency put it, "The European metropolitan countries are heavily dependent upon a constant inflow of the raw materials without which their highly industrialized economies cannot function. An expansion in the production and export of basic resources is imperative in order to meet minimum industrial requirements in Europe, to check the inflation of production costs in the rearmament program, to reduce dependence upon United States sources, and to earn as well as save dollars." These concerns meant that the MSA mission was primarily focused on raw material extraction. Thus the agency favored "the development or improvement of transport and port facilities, power installation and other auxiliary services vital to expansion in the production and export of basic materials required in both Europe and the United States."[41]

The MSA's technical assistance program involved "the surveying of mineral resources; the adoption of technological improvements in mineral production; increased agricultural efficiency to expand available supplies of foods and also as a means of releasing local manpower for other productive work; the improvement of health conditions in Africa, an important obstacle to production increases; the prevention of plant and animal diseases; and the training of local workers."[42] For West Africa in particular, the agency emphasized that transportation, notably roads, was "especially important to open up new mineral areas and enable the product to be evacuated, and to permit more efficient production and exchange of food and other agricultural output."[43]

Africa's importance to Washington was thus essentially defined in terms of the raw materials it furnished to the United States and its Western European allies. A 1950 CIA report considered British West Africa important to the United States, not only because of its strategic minerals but also because it afforded Britain a major opportunity "for reducing its dependence on non-sterling areas for the necessities of life": dollar exchange, foodstuffs, and vital raw materials.[44] This focus, by its very logic, subordinated African interests to Europe's well-being.

Strangers in Paradise

In large part, the drive by the ECA, Point IV, and the MSA for Africa's raw materials reflected the United States post-1945 commitment to rebuild Western Europe, especially Britain and France. In turn, this commitment should be seen within the context of the asymmetrical post-World War II partnership in which the United States emerged as a hegemon and undertook to defend Western Europe while the latter agreed to follow United States diplomatic lead. Since, however, no great power is without self-serving objectives and policies, it is difficult to draw a line between where a hegemonic or collective interest ends and a more limited national one begins. It is therefore hardly surprising that in spite of Washington's repeated affirmations of a common goal with them in Africa, the colonial powers were highly suspicious of its motives.

In June 1950, the United States diplomatic mission in Dakar reported that the "attitude of officials of the French West African Government toward the United States remains one of suspicion and mistrust." The French were reported to have believed that the United States intended to push for the early development of self-government and independence in Africa, a development which would have undermined the French scheme to develop its African colonies as "integral parts of the French Union." The United States was also suspected of wanting to use the Marshall Plan and the Point IV program as "stalking horses for the economic penetration of Africa." Finally, it was reported that "[t]he strategic concern of the United States with the territory of French West Africa," because of its geographical location on the Atlantic, was "fully understood by French officials and further buttressed their suspicion that the United States has ulterior motives in any form of relationship with their territories."[45]

The French concerns reported from Dakar reflected a wider European mood. After eighteen months in Paris as special adviser on overseas development to the special ECA representative in Europe, John Orchard reported in July 1950 that "it had been a difficult job to break down European suspicions of U.S. intentions in Africa."⁴⁶ Writing to McGhee in May 1950, Richard Bissell, Jr., an ECA assistant administrator, enumerated specific European suspicions: a fear that "enamored with thoughts of a bold new program," the United States would "insist upon the launching of far-reaching but impractical schemes in the colonial areas"; "a fear of American economic expansion and influence within the territories which may undercut the authority and influence" of the colonial powers; a suspicion that "unexpressed strategic aims may be primarily responsible" for United States interest in the economic development of Africa; a concern that either directly or through the UN, the United States might exert "increasing pressures toward progressive political independence in the colonies at an unrealistic rate"; a fear that the United States was "thinking too much in terms of rapid exploitation of African resources for the benefit of Europe and the U.S. without sufficient attention to the needs of basic economic development" in the colonies themselves. There was also the apprehension that United States "private investment, burgeoning in an unrestrained fashion, may create new problems and pressures, upsetting vested interests and existing controls." Bissell urged that the European worries be fully taken into account in policy formulation, emphasizing that "[t]he extent to which these apprehensions are real, and the extent to which they are rationalizations of a desire to handle colonial problems without external influence, is immaterial so long as they stand in the way of effective cooperation between the European powers and the U.S. in accelerating economic development in the African colonial territories."⁴⁷

European suspicion of United States intentions was felt outside official circles. In April 1950, *Economist* speculated that the ECA and Point IV were only the harbingers of a more activist United States economic presence in Africa. After observing that "[t]he possibility of bigger and better developments in Africa has caught the imagination of the State Department and of ECA officials," *Economist* cautioned: "The development of Africa, however, is not as simple as some think." It noted that because of African nationalism and "the lack of food and lack of labor," the Europeans had "to move slowly and cautiously with their plans," adding, "If Africa had been a plum simply needing to be picked to be enjoyed, it would have been picked a long time ago." The editorial insisted that "difficulties in the way of the sort of development which the Americans visualize are immense, and they cannot easily be overcome." It then concluded:

> This does not mean to say that American help under Point Four is not needed in Africa; it is as welcome there as it is in Europe. But if quick results are

wanted, they will not be achieved in the Colonies. If, on the other hand, the American Administration—and, what is most doubtful, the private investor—is prepared to look a long way ahead and to help the European colonial powers to lay the foundations for later developments—railways, agricultural schemes and power plants—rather than try at once to tap Africa's hidden wealth, success will be more certain and more lasting.[48]

European discontent was well-founded. As already indicated, Europe's well-being was a major motive in the United States drive for African raw materials. But Washington had its own distinct need for "strategic" minerals, which was aggressively pursued to the point of breaching the colonial cordon by, for example, inflating the market price in the case of Nigeria's columbium.[49] An article in the 18 July 1952 issue of *Mining Journal* of London showed that United States needs for the metal were such that the U.S. Defense Materials Procurement Agency (DMPA) had to introduce a new pricing policy for it in May 1952. Under the new prices, producers were to receive £15. 0. 6d. for ores containing sixty-five percent columbium; and there was, in addition, an incentive bonus of 100 percent on the prices. Before the new pricing policy, the Nigerian producers were receiving approximately £15 per unit, "equivalent to 1,040 pounds per ton consisting of 65 units (of ore) to the ton." Besides, rather than being fixed, the price was related to the quality of the ore per ton, and therefore varied according to whether the ore was high-grade or low-grade. The essence of the DMPA pricing policy, said the article, was to "establish a guaranteed purchase program to encourage the expansion of the production of columbium-tantalum bearing ores and concentrates in countries of the free world."[50] It was, however, also clear that by raising the prices, the United States policy put Britain at a disadvantage.

More worrying for the Europeans must have been what they perceived as the United States commitment to achieve an Open Door in Africa. This was expressed on a number of occasions: at the Lourenço Marques Conference,[51] in McGhee's policy speech in May 1950, and at the May 1950 tripartite foreign ministers' (France, Britain, and the United States) meeting in London. On the last-mentioned occasion, Washington expressed its belief that an increase in Africa's economic activity, including a greater participation in world trade, would benefit Europe, the United States, and the African peoples; it therefore pledged to assist Britain and France in their efforts in this regard. It also gave the assurance that the United States desired "the greatest possible mutual cooperation and understanding with the UK and France on African matters." Side by side with these assurances was the emphasis on the particular interest of the United States: "On our part we desire to develop our trade, transportation and investment interests in Africa whenever and wherever possible; to have access to raw materials, air and sea facilities, air routes and communications points; and to have guaranteed rights of equal treatment in Africa for American capital and nationals."[52]

For Washington there was no contradiction between its simultaneous commitment to ensure the economic integration of Africa with Europe and its pressure for an Open Door in Africa for American business interests. A State Department policy statement observed that the "gradual weakening of the economic ties of the European powers with their Far Eastern possessions and the need for rehabilitating their domestic economy has led these nations to look to the development of Africa as a means of strengthening their overall economic and strategic position in the world." It was stated that the United States "supports this objective through ECA assistance and Point Four aid." Yet, the statement immediately added that "in seeking to attain this objective there is a growing tendency for some European colonial powers to endeavor to monopolize colonial trade to the detriment of United States commercial interests."[53]

In considering how to eliminate this monopoly and advance United States business interests, the department recommended that the United States should (a) continue to seek the removal or liberalization of policies and practices of the colonial governments that discriminated against United States trade and investment; (b) inform the appropriate European authorities that restrictive economic and financial policies might lead to unfavorable public reaction in the United States, "and that a more liberal policy would seem advisable if U.S. financial aid is to be continued"; (c) urge the colonial powers to liberalize their investment and exchange control policies in Africa so as to encourage the flow of United States investment capital to the region; (d) continue the effort to expand the United States market for commodities of which the Africans were actual or potential producers; and (e) continue to take all necessary steps, with the assistance of the ECA, to assure the continued flow of strategic materials from Africa to the United States.[54] It is worthy of note that practical measures were undertaken in pursuit of the Open Door. For example, as a follow-up to the Lourenço Marques conference, the United States had separate discussions with Britain and France in September 1950 to seek ways of eliminating discriminatory trade practices in Africa.[55]

In spite of their irritation, Britain and France allowed, even solicited, United States economic involvement in their African colonies. In April

1949, the United States consulate general in Dakar reported that there were considerable quantities of United States agricultural, road-making and earth-moving machinery (including tractors and trucks) in French West Africa, acquired under the Marshall Plan. It added that a special section, the "Marshall Plan Section," had been created in the Economic Affairs Department of the government of French West Africa.[56] By April 1950, officials in the African Affairs department of the French Foreign Office were canvassing the view that Soviet penetration into Africa could only be restrained through a coordinated large-scale Western economic and social development program for the region; they expected the United States to be actively involved in such an effort.[57]

French officials went to the May 1950 foreign ministers' meeting in London, prepared for an extensive discussion of the economic development of Africa, and they could not conceal their disappointment that the meeting provided no opportunity for such a discussion.[58] At the meeting, the French submitted a paper stressing that for the implementation of their development plans in Africa, "it will be necessary to seek all the available resources of the countries of Western Europe who see therein a means of manifesting solidarity, as well as the United States, who are interested, as in Europe, in African development."[59]

Even after the meeting, the French did not give up their efforts to involve the United States in the economic development of their African colonies. In July 1950, Elmer H. Bourgerie of the State Department Office of African and Near Eastern Affairs had to inform McGhee that "[f]rom previous conversations I have had with members of the French Embassy, I gained the impression that the French Government is very much interested in interesting the U.S. Government in making substantial financial commitments in Africa to assist them in carrying out their development plans." Bourgerie, however, advised that "in view of the present temper of Congress, it would be unwise for us to give the French any encouragement at this time regarding U.S. financial participation in such a plan."[60] On several occasions, British officials also invited United States assistance for their colonies.[61] In 1952, Britain issued a despatch to its colonial administrations, emphasizing its interest in creating conditions that would stimulate the flow of private United States capital into Africa.[62]

Nonetheless, European apprehensions also made them wary of allowing much United States involvement in the colonies. In February 1950, R. E. Vidal, the Gold Coast acting secretary of commerce, told Hyman Bloom, the United States consul in Accra, that he knew of no private or official projects in the territory that would require any form of ECA assistance.[63] A year later, the ECA complained that "[t]he offer of American aid for the DOT's is not received with enthusiasm by the British. Americans who have not had comparable experience with dependent peoples are felt to be too rash in their undertakings. . . .There is also some fear of increased competition from American exports."[64] This lack of enthusiasm may explain why the framework for the injection of United States "aid" programs seemed somewhat chaotic in British colonies. The chaos may well have been a ploy by the British to hedge their colonies against excessive United States penetration. In April 1951, C. W. Michie, Nigeria's acting principal assistant secretary, complained that while his office was "constantly preparing reports, submitting projects, and carrying on discussions" with the ECA, he had very little to show for his efforts. He attributed this to "inadequate coordination of activity between the Nigerian Government and the Colonial Office" in respect of ECA programs, so that ECA officials in London did not get the "complete and exact information concerning the Nigerian side of the picture."[65]

The primary documents reveal that the French also put up subtle but effective barriers to limit United States economic presence in their colonies. A decree issued in December 1949 provided that any equipment and materials manufactured in France could not be imported into French West Africa from any other country. According to the interpretation of the United States consulate general in Dakar, the decree was aimed at excluding the entry of American products under the ECA program.[66] There were also instances of the French refusing to grant licenses for the importation of American products into West Africa, even where no French dollar exchange was involved, as the importers intended to utilize their own dollars in the United States.[67] American technicians (and perhaps other personnel as well) suffered the same restriction. The excuse, as made by Gabriel van Laethem, the second secretary of the French embassy in Washington, was that the French perceived several problems connected with sending technicians to Africa. In his words, "[i]n French Africa there are already many French technicians. To have an influx of American or other technicians might create an unsatisfactory atmosphere."[68]

The French placed limitations not only on United States capital equipment and personnel but also on programs. In January 1950, the United States consulate general in Dakar notified the State Department that the governor-general of French West Africa did not wish to see Point IV programs introduced into his territory. Nor did the federation's director-general of public health, for the "French are very proud of their development of health research and activities in this territory."[69] Another despatch from Dakar shows that the situation had not changed by 1951.[70]

American private capital fared no better as the French were not favorably disposed towards the flow of foreign (and especially United States) private capital into their African colonies. In the early 1950s, the governments of French West and Equatorial Africa assisted the Compagnie Française de Distribution des Pétroles en Afrique (CFDPA) to establish an advantageous marketing position in the areas under their jurisdiction, at the expense of the more established United States companies such as the Texas Company. The measures the governments adopted included the following: (a) impeding plans by the United States companies to expand their bulk storage terminals, (b) putting pressure on local chambers of commerce to allocate to CFDPA import quota percentages that exceeded its capacity; (c) permitting CFDPA to import quantities in excess of those estimated and licensed by the government; (d) increasing the estimate of annual colony consumption and allocating the surplus to CFDPA; (e) waiving official storage regulations to permit CFDPA to store excess imports in the open: such dumps could later be declared public hazards, but at that point, the government purchased the stocks from the company.[71]

The French administrative intervention in the oil business worried the United States consulate general in Dakar since "[t]he commercial operations of the American petroleum companies constitute the largest and most active single element in the trade relations of the United States and these territories."[72] The State Department resented France's discriminatory practices and cartel arrangements, stressing that it would only tolerate practices "confined to accepted competitive devices." The United States embassy in Paris was therefore asked to strongly protest the French regulation of the oil market.[73] The State Department later entered into negotiations with the French, on behalf of the United States oil companies.[74] It does not appear that the French were moved by the department's protests and pressures.

In putting the French regulation of the oil market in its proper context, a starting point is that it was customary for the colonial powers to align the economies of their colonies to the metropole. The result was the predominance of the metropole in the economic life of its colonies, via the roles of principal customer and supplier. France, far more than Britain, pressed this alignment to its extreme. France's overwhelming dominance of its African colonial economies was achieved through a combination of quantitative restrictions and preferential import duties, which worked to the disadvantage of other industrialized countries. Foreign exchange, for example, was generally made available only for foreign goods that the franc zone countries could not supply. On the other hand, since importers of products from the United States were not allocated the dollars necessary to pay for freight, United States shipping lines, for example, had great difficulty finding cargoes to transport to French West Africa. The result was that French goods, even those selling above world prices, remained predominant in the African trade.[75] This all-pervasive French presence in its African colonial economies, the fact that Paris in effect regarded its colonies as a *chasse gardée* (reserved territory), placed a definite limit on the infusion of external capital into its colonies.

There was a strategic dimension to the French regulation of the oil market. Daniel Yergin says that in the 1950s, the West considered Africa to be the "new frontier" in world oil production and that France took the lead in exploring it. According to Yergin, France believed that it should have its own petroleum supplies if it was to remain a great power; to this end, de Gaulle ordered a maximum effort to develop oil sources within the French Empire.[76] This concern must have predisposed France to squeeze all foreign competitors out of its (colonial) market.

Overall, care must be taken not to exaggerate the degree of British and French resentment over United States intentions and presence in Africa. The disagreements were not deep-seated enough to disarticulate the content and form of British, French, and United States approaches towards Africa. The United States certainly desired an Open Door, for the benefit of its private enterprise, in Africa; but the overriding objective at the time "was the restoration of a sound European economy which would then be strong enough and confident enough to cooperate with the larger American design for an integrated world economic order."[77] For this purpose, Washington was quite willing to retreat from its pursuit of a laissez-faire international economic regime. This included tolerating trade and investment restrictions by the European countries, not just in Africa but as a matter of general policy.[78]

More particularly, Washington's commitment to the rehabilitation of Europe went hand in hand with the recognition that African resources (minerals, commodities, foodstuffs, and markets) were critically important for rebuilding and strengthening Western Europe. As a result of this recognition, the United States did not strenuously pursue the Open Door policy in Africa. It is also meant that the United States and Western Europe were locked into a symbiosis that created more grounds for cooperation and amity than for conflict. When he spoke at Oklahoma City on 8 May 1950, McGhee pointed out that "[b]y virtue of the European Recovery Program and the Mutual Defense Assistance Program, the Western European powers, which are also the leading metropolitan powers in Africa, have a closer and more intimate relation with us than at any other time in history. This is a reciprocal relation for defense and for economic recovery which none of these powers wishes to disturb."⁷⁹ This approach—cooperation between the United States and Western Europe—was equally evident on the "colonial question."

Entente Cordiale on Colonialism: The "Ewe Question"

The United States, Britain, and France had various means through which they harmonized political and diplomatic policies on Africa. One means was the annual colonial policy talks, another was the foreign ministers' meetings. For example, at their May 1950 foreign ministers' meeting, it was agreed that consultation between the three countries on colonial territories "with a view to concerting their positions" should precede UN meetings.⁸⁰ One issue which generated a lot of such consultation and cooperation was the "Ewe question," which the State Department described in June 1951 as "among the controversial issues facing [the] U.S. in Trusteeship Council and General Assembly."⁸¹

For the most part, the colonies the Europeans created in Africa were novel political geographies. More often than not, their boundaries fragmented traditional social units (ethnic groups, villages, even families) into territories under different colonial powers. The so-called Ewe question was a result of this arbitrariness of the colonial boundaries. By 1900, when the European partition of West Africa had been practically concluded, the Ewe found themselves partly in Togoland (a German colony) and also partly in the Gold Coast (a British colony). After World War I, Togoland became a League of Nations mandate, split between Britain and France. At the end of World War II (as the League of Nations mandated territories became UN trust territories), the Ewe found themselves split among three colonies: the Gold Coast and the two UN trust territories of Togo (British Togoland and French Togoland).⁸²

The Ewe never reconciled themselves to their fragmentation. They saw the collapse of German rule as an opportunity to finally address the issue. It was to this end that they petitioned the British Colonial Office in September 1919. Next, they laid their case before Warren Harding (United States president, 1921–23) and the Permanent Mandates Commission of the League of Nations. Their petitions complained of the difficulties arising from their fragmentation, especially the separation of people of the same lineage from one another and of villages from their farms. These petitions yielded no results, but the Ewe never relented. It says something for the Ewe's concentration of purpose that their petition was before the UN Trusteeship Council (TC) at its very first session. Dated 2 April 1947, the petition which came from the All-Ewe Conference, notified the TC that "[w]e deplore and protest against the partition of Eweland. Request unification of Eweland under single administration to be chosen by people themselves by plebiscite."[83]

Seven Ewe petitions were examined by the council at its second session, two during the third session, one each at the fourth and fifth sessions. More than 100 Ewe petitions, presented to the UN Visiting Mission that went to Togo in November/December 1949, were considered during the TC's seventh session in 1950. By then, the "Ewe question" had assumed a dominant and enduring presence on the TC agenda. Thus of "the over 188 petitions" before the TC by mid-1950, 105 related to the Ewe question. All the petitions called for the unification of all Ewe under one administration.[84] Before the second session of the TC convened, the All-Ewe Conference—an organization formed in June 1946 to crystallize Ewe opinion—petitioned for the opportunity to send representatives to submit their written petition with an oral statement in accordance with Rule 80 of the council's Rules of Proceedings. This request, which had no precedent, was extensively discussed and approved after the TC opened its second session on 20 November 1947.[85]

Meanwhile, in a joint memorandum dated 17 November 1947, Britain and France presented their views on the Ewe petitions to the TC. They acknowledged that "there are disabilities arising from the present system, and that the Ewes have certain legitimate grievances." Nonetheless, the two administering authorities opposed Ewe unification, as "such a territorial unit based on tribal[86] unity could not, under any circumstances, possess a national character in the modern sense of the word." The gist of their remedial proposals was to instruct local governments to remove any obstacles to the movement of persons and goods across the boundaries, to harmonize tax rates in the British and French territories and ensure that individuals were not subjected to double taxation, and to introduce the teaching of French in the schools in British Togo and English in the schools in French Togo. To coordinate and "give necessary impetus" to these proposals, a standing consultative commission for Togoland affairs was to be established. Jointly chaired by the governor of the Gold Coast and the *commissaire de la République* of French Togoland, the commission consisted of two representatives of the inhabitants of each of the trust territories.[87]

On 8 December 1947, Sylvanus Olympio, representing the All-Ewe Conference, appeared before the TC for the first time to present the Ewe case. He recited the problems the people had to contend with as a result of the arbitrary partitioning of their territory and stressed that theirs was simply the request of an ethnic group "to be allowed to live together under one roof, and one government, so that they could achieve peace and prosperity." He dismissed the reforms proposed by Britain and France as "hopelessly inadequate" to solve the problems involved.[88] Three days of discussions at the TC followed, with Olympio in attendance. In the course of the discussions, the United States representative obtained from the French the clarification that the reform proposals could be regarded as a transitional step towards unification. This paved the way for the council to adopt a resolution. In its preamble, the resolution conceded that the All-Ewe Conference represented the wishes of the majority of the Ewe and that the political boundaries caused many difficulties and much resentment. It also noted that the representative of the All-Ewe Conference was dissatisfied with the remedial measures proposed by the administering authorities. In spite of this tone, the resolution itself welcomed the measures as an earnest and constructive initial effort and recommended that the administering authorities should take steps to ameliorate the problems of which the Ewe complained.[89]

The Joint Anglo-French Consultative Commission was duly set up. It first met on 26–27 May 1948, with the pro-unification Ewe leaders participating: Olympio and Ephraim Amu (secretary general of the All-Ewe Conference) were among its members. But because it was, by definition, an inadequate forum to press Ewe unification, the commission could not assuage the worries of the pro-unification forces.[90] Nor was its legitimacy helped by the TC Visiting Mission of 1949, which reported that the joint effort of the administering authorities was a step in the right direction but an inadequate one, and that the pro-unification movement was assuming "the character of a popular nationalistic movement."[91] Before the TC again on 20 March 1950, Olympio stated that the demand for unification was primarily political and could not be solved by piecemeal economic palliatives. He held that the commission was "utterly inadequate" and called for a body with full powers to deal with all the dimensions of the problem. In addition, he proposed the unification of the Ewe under a five-year plan, with self-government at the end of the period.[92]

From the beginning, Britain and France solicited United States support for the proposals they put before the TC in response to the Ewe petitions.[93] They were thus able to harmonize their position with the United States. The administering authorities were, in the first place, opposed to any change in the political status or boundaries of the territories. Britain, which administered its Togo trust territory as part of the Gold Coast, was not in favor of unification, that would have resulted in the loss of the Ewe from the Gold Coast. D. E. K. Amenumey has offered two explanations for the French hostility to the Ewe unification movement. First, the Ewe showed an open preference for British administration. As a result, France tended to see "the whole business of Ewe unification as a ruse to snatch her trust territory for Britain." Besides, the implications of the Ewe demand went against the underlying goal of French colonial policy. As Amenumey pointed out, "Even though France had placed her mandated territories under the trusteeship system in 1946 and signed trusteeship agreements by which she undertook to promote the progressive development of her trust territories to self-government and independence, she still intended quite clearly to keep the territories of Togo and Cameroun firmly within the French Union."[94]

As the Ewe issue was on the international agenda, both Britain and France also recognized that they occasionally had to yield ground to head off TC pressure for more radical adjustments. Following the observations of the 1949 visiting mission and obviously influenced by Olympio's appearances before the TC, Britain and France jointly proposed to enlarge the competence and composition of the joint commission. The commission was now to have seventeen representatives from British Togoland and twenty-two from French Togoland, all elected by the inhabitants of the respective territories. Besides, it was now to be charged with submitting to the two governments its views as to the practical means of satisfying the wishes of the inhabitants of all parts of the trust territories, "within the framework of British and French administration."[95] An aide mémoire outlining this proposal was submitted to the United States by France in May 1950.[96] (It is safe to assume that a similar submission was made to Washington by London.) A month later, Washington informed London and Paris that it supported their proposal to enlarge the scope of the commission.[97] The proposal was adopted by the TC.

However, appearing again before the TC on 5 July 1950, Olympio announced that the All-Ewe Conference was not going to participate in the enlarged commission because the latter's terms of reference precluded it from dealing with the question of unification. This position was, however, complicated by alternative Ewe proposals presented at the same TC session. There was never a common Ewe position on the unification issue. The Ewe in British Togoland, for example, favored a unification of the two Togo trust territories, without the inclusion of the Ewe of the Gold Coast.[98] This and other viewpoints contradicting the pro-unification elements were vigorously canvassed at the TC. S. G. Asare and F. Y. Antor, on behalf of the Togoland Union, the Natural Rulers of Western Togoland, and the Togoland Farmers Association, made a case for the unification of the two Togolands rather than the Ewe as a whole. Pedro Olympio, cousin of Sylvanus, appeared for the Togoland Progress Party and argued for the territorial integrity of French Togoland. He proposed that the Ewe should cooperate with the French administration so that the Togolese could gradually take over responsibility for the territory. D. Ayeva, representing the chiefs and people of Northern Togoland, agreed with Pedro Olympio, opposed the unification of the two Togolands, and condemned the Ewe unification movement as "subversive."[99]

In the ensuing TC discussion, considerable opposition to the new Anglo–French proposal was expressed. Following this, Britain and France decided to clarify the section referring to a solution "within the framework of the British and French administration" by adding to it the phrase "and not precluding the unification of any parts of the two trust territories." The United States representative held that the consultative commission was, on this account, authorized to make recommendations regarding the unification of the Ewe people and that such unification could take place either under a British or a French administration, or even under an Anglo–French administration. As it turned out, the so-called clarification and interpretation were more of a ruse to get Sylvanus Olympio out of the way. Once he left New York, satisfied with the interpretation, the United States and Argentina submitted a joint draft resolution, which expressed the hope that the administering authorities would proceed along the line they had proposed and would take all appropriate steps to ensure that the consultative commission would equitably represent the different sections and groups in the two trust territories. The Chinese, Iraqi, and Philippine delegations proposed amendments to the United States/Argentine draft: these asked that the fresh Anglo–French scheme be ignored and proposed that the problem could only be solved by the unification of the Ewe under a single administration. The United States/Argentine draft was adopted on 14 July by the council, by eight votes to two (Iraq, the Philippines) and one abstention (China).[100]

The elections to the enlarged consultative commission on Togoland Affairs were held in October 1950. The French went to great lengths to ensure that no seats were won by the Comité de l'Unité (CUT), the party controlled by the All–Ewe Conference. According to a British account, Africans who were not legally qualified to vote were added to the electoral roll, political parties opposed to the CUT were established with government funds, and pro–unification partisans were deported or imprisoned.[101] On 30 September 1950, the Ewe pro–unification group cabled the UN secretary–general, complaining of the corrupt methods employed by the French in the elections.[102] In spite of French protests that the established procedure was for such matters to go to the TC first, the Fourth Committee of the General Assembly took up the petition. India, Indonesia, Iraq, the Philippines, and Yugoslavia later submitted a joint draft resolution, which was adopted by the committee and then by the General Assembly on 2 December 1950. The resolution called for an adequate solution to the Ewe question "as soon as possible," in accordance with the wishes and interests of the people; emphasized the necessity of conducting elections to the consultative commission in a democratic manner; and directed the administering authority to "investigate promptly the practices complained of in the petition with a view to ascertaining whether the methods of election which have been applied ensure that the views of all sections of the population are faithfully reflected." France was asked to report on this investigation at the next session of the TC, and the latter was requested to devote to the Ewe question a special chapter or subchapter of its annual report to the sixth session of the General Assembly.[103]

The CUT had boycotted the elections to the enlarged consultative commission on account of the massive French–orchestrated irregularities that had attended it. This ensured that in 1951, the basic Anglo–French objective was to convince the TC that the elections allowed enough room for all parties to be equitably involved, that the door was still open for the Ewe pro–unification forces to participate in the commission, and therefore that the joint council should urge the Ewe pro–unification groups to join the commission. This was embodied in a joint resolution they proposed to the TC.[104] To entice the pro–unification groups into the deal, Britain and France offered to increase the membership of the commission, allocating eight seats to the CUT and a proportionate five seats to "be selected" for British Togoland "by the existing parties in proportion to their present strength" in the commission. The objective and proposal were discussed at length at a meeting of the TC representatives of Britain, France, Belgium, Australia, New Zealand, and the United States on 16 February 1951.[105] In addition, Britain and France discussed this proposal separately with the United States on several occasions in February 1951.[106]

Washington itself acknowledged that the consideration of the Ewe petition by the Fourth Committee in late 1950 "not only established a precedent but also was evidence of the growing impatience of a number of non–administering countries with the slow progress made by the administering authorities concerned and by the Trusteeship Council toward a solution of the problem." It was felt that this concern "introduces a new element of urgency and gives greater weight to the desirability of making demonstrable progress before the next session of the Assembly."[107] On this account, the United States undertook to help its allies pull their chestnuts from the fire by offering an amendment to the proposed Anglo–French resolution. The amendment adopted the Anglo–French proposal but also provided the alternative of fresh elections in the southern part of French Togoland, where the CUT had not participated.[108] This amendment was stillborn: the French rejected any fresh elections, arguing that in addition to creating "endless recriminations, with no settlement of problem possible," it "would be an admission that [the] original elections [were] not properly conducted, and might give rise to demands for [a] review of electoral results in districts other than those predominantly Ewe."[109] In addition, the French deplored "possible parading of lack of unanimity among North Atlantic powers before [a] Trusteeship Council on [the] Ewe problem."[110]

Confronted with the French intransigence, the United States retreated. United States Acting Secretary of State James Webb promptly telegraphed Paris that "U.S. suggestions were made privately" to France and Britain "in effort be helpful meeting situation with which both confronted in TC." France was assured that the "U.S. does not consider its proposal implies . . . conduct of original elections in any way questionable."[111] At their meeting on 1 March 1951, Webb further assured French Ambassador Henri Bonnet that "[t]he last thing on our minds was to create more difficulties for the French and we thought that by offering the Ewes who refused to participate in the previous election a choice of two alternatives, it would be more difficult for them to reject either one and would, at the same time secure wider support in the Trusteeship Council and perhaps obviate an acrimonious discussion later in the General Assembly."[112]

On 5 March 1951, Alan Burns, the British representative at the TC, suggested to the United States delegation that a way out of the impasse might be for the TC to merely take note of the steps thus far taken by the two administering authorities in regard to the Ewe question, to request them to continue their efforts to set up procedures for consulting all elements of the population of the two Togolands, and to request them further to report back to the next session of the council.[113] The State Department was "impressed" with this and promised to introduce an amended resolution embodying the suggestion, "after having determined that such an amendment is acceptable to the French and British Delegations."[114]

Essentially, the new United States amendment took note of the "statements made by the administering authorities" and "request[d] them to continue their efforts to complete the composition of the Consultative Commission in such a manner as to make it representative of the principal elements in the population."[115] This was discussed in New York on 5 March 1951 with the French delegation,[116] which found it "acceptable." The following day, Alan Burns was given a copy of the amendment, and he thought it was "an excellent one and . . . was acceptable to the United Kingdom Government." At the same time, he suggested that the United States should work to get Iraq as a cosponsor of the amendment,[117] possibly to make it more credible and ensure an easier passage. Assured of Anglo–French support for the amendment, the United States went ahead to do the groundwork necessary to achieve an outcome favorable to the British and the French at the TC. It is useful to quote the State Department itself on this:

> After considerable consultation with French, British and other interested dels fol plan was evolved: that Franco–British res (T/L.140) would be introduced by British rep with appropriate statement; that Iraq–U.S. res (T/L.141) would then be introduced; that President would call for vote on latter first; that France and UK would abstain on this vote; and that adoption of Iraq–U.S. res would render unnecessary vote on Franco–British res. This plan was successfully followed, resulting on March 9, 1951, in adoption by vote of Iraq–U.S. res. . . .Both [Britain and France] expressed their appreciation to U.S. Del for our help in persuading Iraq to cosponsor res which avoided serious clashes on Ewe questions in TC. . . .The French and British Govts will presumably consult this Govt before next session of TC with view to obtaining our support for such substantive proposals as they agree to make.[118]

The council's resolution, adopted by a vote of a nine to zero, with three abstentions (Britain, France, and the Soviet Union), drew the attention of the administering authorities to the necessity of seeking a solution with the utmost expedition; invited them to continue their efforts to solve the problem in the spirit of the council's resolution of 14 July 1950; urged the Ewe pro–unification parties to cooperate with the administering authorities; and recommended that whether or not the composition of the consultative commission was completed, the administering authorities should "as soon as possible" formulate substantive proposals for a practicable solution of the question and inform the council accordingly not later than 1 July 1951.[119]

In order to meet the requirements of the resolution, Britain and France jointly drew up a proposal for a reconstituted consultative commission. The proposal ruled out the possibility of any "alteration in boundaries or political allegiance" on the grounds that no arrangement along such lines would have the support of the "peoples of [the] territories or even agreement of [the] majority." It claimed that the consultative commission had served its purpose and should therefore be supplanted by another forum, which would enable the peoples of the Togolands under British and French administration to exchange and coordinate views and measures on development "in every field harmonized." It was intended that such a body would advise the two administering authorities on "planning and implementation of [a] program of development, economic and social, in [the] light [of] available resources and on all other practical questions relating to [the] preservation [of a] close connection between peoples on each side of [the] frontier." An advance copy of this proposal was forwarded to the United States for its comments.[120]

Although it held that the Anglo–French proposal would be widely seen as too "negative and defensive," the State Department considered it the "minimum" that provided a basis "on which [to] proceed." Nonetheless, the department emphasized the desirability of "changing the impression that the door to political unification was closed, for although this may be [the] fact," the TC would have great difficulty endorsing such a statement.[121] At the same time, the United States delegation to the TC was advised that in order to leave room for negotiation, it would not be fruitful to "push Britain and France into submitting [a] proposal containing [the] maximum to which they can agree."[122]

Britain and France went along with the suggestion that, for purposes of strategy, they should not foreclose the possibility of Ewe unity, and they redrafted the proposal accordingly.[123] The United States itself later produced a draft amendment to the revised Anglo–French proposal. The draft accepted the view that the consultative commission had outlived its usefulness and should therefore be replaced, as proposed by Britain and France. The United States draft proposed that the administering authorities be allowed to establish the new body, which should be able to deal with all questions of common concern to the people of the two trust territories. The United States also proposed that the body should include all sections of the people of the Togolands.[124] Britain and France welcomed the draft, except that the latter wanted the deletion of the paragraph enjoining them to ensure that all major groups in the territories participated in the new body.[125]

On 24 July, the TC adopted the United States amendment, which was sponsored by the Dominican Republic, Thailand, and the United States and then adopted the Anglo–French proposal as amended. The council agreed that a new joint council should be set up in a manner that would secure the participation of all major groups in the two territories, and that the new body should be given a fair and reasonable opportunity to prove its effectiveness as a means for the people to influence developments in which they had a common concern. The resolution recommended that the new body should be implemented in time for the 1952 UN Visiting Mission to West Africa to make an evaluation of its accomplishments.[126]

The new joint council was not set up as quickly as the TC resolution had envisaged. Even a UN General Assembly resolution of 18 January 1952, which urged speed in implementing the TC resolution, had no impact on Britain and France. The two had their reasons for being tardy on the matter. By late 1951, Britain had become committed to the integration of British Togoland with the Gold Coast; it felt that a strengthened joint council of the two Togolands would frustrate this objective. The French, who had opposed unification from the start, were in no hurry either.[127] Since the joint council had not been established, Britain and France were anxious to delay receiving the UN Visiting Mission for as long as they could. For example, France argued that it was undesirable for the mission to arrive during the campaigns for the elections to the Representative Assembly of French Togoland scheduled for 30 March 1952. They proposed early July as a better date for the mission to arrive. On the other hand, the British were thinking of early September.[128]

Britain and France had the support of the United States in delaying the arrival of the visiting mission until September 1952. On 29 February 1952, Alan Burns expressed his appreciation to the United States delegation to the TC for the " 'support and assistance' which the United States had given to the United Kingdom and France in connection with their desire to have the Visiting Mission to West Africa arrive in the Togolands as late as possible." According to the records, Burns

> referred to the fact that, after the British and French delegations had outlined the various reasons why it would be impossible for them to receive a Visiting Mission before September 1, Ambassador [Francis] Sayre [of the United States] had proposed that the Council [TC] decide that the Visiting Mission assemble at [the UN] Headquarters in August, arrive in the Togolands not later than September 1, spend 30 days in investigations in the territory, and prepare their report in time for examination by the Trusteeship Council at a session to convene not later than November 7.[129]

To the end of the Truman administration, Britain and France continued to enjoy the full backing of the United States on the Ewe question. The strategy was the same: harmonizing positions with the Europeans and shielding them from serious scrutiny and indictment by UN bodies. Diplomatic support such as this at the UN was of considerable importance to the Europeans; it shielded them from the huge embarrassment of being isolated in an international arena that was increasingly hostile to colonialism.

Conclusion

In practical terms, United States presence in Africa during the Truman presidency was achieved through the programs of the ECA, Point IV, and the MSA. Those programs, it needs to be restated, were extensions of the Marshall Plan. Recent scholarship shows that beyond rehabilitating Western European economies, this plan was the agency through which the region was retooled to fit into an integrated international political economy designed and controlled by the United States.[130] Given the very strong center–periphery relations existing at the time between Western Europe and its African colonies, the latter could not have escaped the broader implications of the consolidation of United States hegemony over Western Europe. In other words, just as the Marshall Plan facilitated the incorporation of Western Europe into the United States world system, the programs of the ECA, Point IV, and the MSA ensured the accommodation of—or at least, formalized—the United States presence in Africa's relations with the West.

The Europeans were alarmed by this broadening of center–periphery relations since United States involvement had the potential of weakening the structures established by colonial rule. In the event, McGhee has explained that while "there was no endorsement of the views attributed to the colonial powers," there was also "no hint of boldness" on the part of Washington "with respect to the promotion of decolonization." The focus, according to him, "was on stimulating cooperation [with the colonial powers] in the economic field."[131] At the same time, he admits that there were wider strategic considerations that made cooperation with the Europeans more compelling, and thus constrained Washington: "We [the United States]," McGhee recalled, "had few national interests of importance" in Africa, "most of which we recognized was the responsibility of the European 'metropolitan' powers. . . .World–wide we were at that time concerned primarily with our Cold War with the Soviet Union, which had reached crisis proportions with the Korean War. In meeting the communist threat, the cooperation of our European allies was essential."[132]

In its classical form, the "dual mandate" was incompatible with African self–government. In response to African nationalist endeavor, Frederick Lugard wrote: "However strong a sympathy we may feel for the aspirations of these African progressives, sane counselors will advise them to recognize their present limitations. At no time in the world's history has there been so cordial a hand held out to Africa . . . or a keener desire to assist the African in the path of progress."[133] On this score, Truman was reminiscent of Frederick Lugard. According to Kolko, especially for the sake of Europe's recovery, Washington had a vested interest in raw material extraction from the UDCs. This, he says, was partially why "Washington opposed an accelerated decolonization process that [would] cut the economic ties that bound much of the Third World to European imperialism."[134]

4

MINIMALISM AS POLICY

The preceding chapter showed that the Truman administration considered Africa and Africans to be malleable and highly susceptible to external direction and manipulation. As a consequence, a key objective of the administration was to influence the form and content of change in Africa. The belief that the United States could influence political developments in Africa—and especially, pattern the nature and direction of Africa's acculturation in the international system—was an equally ever present theme in policy making during Eisenhower's tenure. In 1954, the State Department proposed a statement of policy on United States objectives and policies in Africa. In addition to securing United States economic interests, the department was primarily occupied with retaining Africa as a Western sphere of influence.

The United States, the statement said, desired the social, political, and economic advancement of African peoples "as rapidly as possible—as an end in itself and also as a means of convincing them that their individual and national aspirations can best be achieved through continued association with the free nations of the world." The United States also desired stable political and economic state systems in Africa that could prevent the domination of the region "in whole or in part by unfriendly movements or powers"; the maintenance of the "strategic interests of the U.S. and its allies, including access to strategic raw materials, as means of strengthening the free world"; and the advancement of United States "business interests, including the securing of non-discriminatory treatment for U.S. nationals."

The department recommended that a major plank of United States policy in Africa should be to "make the most practicable use" of economic, technical, and, where necessary, military assistance, to "influence the process of political change" as a means of promoting Western interests.[1]

In 1955, the United States Operations Mission (USOM) in London held that "most Africans" had not "decided on cooperation with the Soviets, or the Egyptians, or even on an 'Africa for the Africans,' " and so they "can be influenced"; and the circumstances were auspicious enough since they "still look first to Western democracies for help and guidance in the problems of their development." In the context, Washington's role was clearly defined: "In the part of this process which concerns money, materials and technological skills, an adequate United States contribution can be a significant influence."[2] Two years later, the NSC resolved that

> policy must be guided by the fact that in the long run the orientation of Africa South of the Sahara will depend on where the leaders and the peoples feel their best interest lies. To a considerable extent, the African is still immature and unsophisticated with respect to his attitudes towards the issues that divide the world today. The African's mind is not made up and he is being subjected to a number of contradictory forces. This pressure will increase in the future. The African is a target for the advocation of communism, old-fashioned colonialism, xenophobic nationalism, and Egyptian "Islamic" propaganda, as well as for the proponents of an orderly development of the various political entities in the area in question, closely tied to the West.[3]

A briefing paper prepared for Eisenhower when Prime Minister Kwame Nkrumah of Ghana paid an official visit to the United States in July 1958 remarked that "Ghana's policies and institutions are still in a formative state, and their future character can be affected substantially by the attitude and actions of the United States."[4]

The official papers reveal three policy instruments that Washington employed in its effort to influence developments in Africa: (1) the checking of countervailing influences, (2) "hegemonic socialization," and (3) economic assistance. It is worthwhile to discuss the actual implementation of each of these policy instruments, since taken together, they seem to furnish an objective criterion for an understanding and appraisal of overall United States policy in Africa.

Checking Countervailing Influences

Washington's belief that it could affect the process of change in Africa necessarily predisposed it to work towards limiting the range of alternative ideological thinking in Africa, or as stated by a Mutual Security Program paper, "to counter the growth of communist or other influence inimical to political stability and free world orientation."[5] The importance of this objective is indicated by its recurrence in a number of the policy papers. A paper prepared in early 1956 recommended that the United States "should do everything possible to assure the evolution of Africa in a manner that is compatible with our national interest." This specifically involved the prevention of "a growth of inimical foreign influences in Africa, especially those favoring the Soviet Union."[6]

The official documents also mention Egypt, as well as India and the related issue of nonalignment, as secondary "inimical foreign influences." A 1956 national intelligence estimate (NIE) held that "the communists and the Arab-Asian states will be competing with the West for power and influence" in Africa. "Egypt will continue to encourage and support native nationalism and the spread of Islam as part of its effort to become a leader in Africa, particularly at the expense of the colonial powers. India will also continue to give support to African and other movements for independence in a bid for leadership of the Afro-Asian countries."[7] In the same year, the State Department observed that "The anti-white and anti-Western sentiment in Africa may be intensified as it is stimulated by other external pressures. For example, the spread of Islam in Africa South of the Sahara may be merely an obstacle to the Westernization of these peoples, but if it ever becomes effectively controlled by outside Arab states this religious development may have serious political consequences." India's efforts to influence African states and "communism" were mentioned as the second and third "external pressures."[8]

For many in Washington, there was hardly any distinction between "communism," nonalignment, and Egypt's Arab nationalism. At the very least, there was the feeling that the last two were handmaids of Soviet hegemony. At an NSC meeting in August 1957, Vice President Nixon drew attention to what he regarded as the council's tendency to underestimate the seriousness of the "communist" threat in Africa, adding: "After all, we do not have to count only card-carrying communists as a measure of the communist threat. In Africa . . . the communists will clothe themselves in Islamic, racist, anti-racist, or nationalistic clothing." With Secretary of State Christian Herter in agreement, Nixon insisted that "[n]either the Egyptian nor the Indian influence should be overlooked, because both might be used effectively by the communists." Eisenhower explained that Islam should generally be "anti-communist not pro-communist," but General Charles Cabell, the deputy director of the CIA, cited Egypt to show that Islam could be manipulated in favor of "communism."[9]

Washington's resentment of Egyptian influence in Africa has to be put into perspective. Eisenhower recalled that with the accession of Gamal Abdel Nasser in Egypt, the West "tended to look hopefully toward him" in the hope that he would follow "a pro-Western alignment."[10] This expectation evaporated in 1955: the administration saw the first deliveries of Czech arms to Cairo in late 1955 and Egypt's recognition of the People's Republic of China in May 1956 as proofs that Nasser had fallen into the Soviet orbit.[11] Eisenhower immediately convinced himself that "[a] fundamental factor in the problem is the growing ambition of Nasser, the sense of power he has gained out of his association with the Soviets, his belief that he can emerge as a true leader of the entire Arab world—and because of these beliefs, his rejection of every proposition advanced as a measure of conciliation between the Arabs and Israel." He immediately proposed to undercut Nasser by building up "some other individual as a prospective leader of the Arab world." Eisenhower's choice was King Saud, even though he confessed, "I do not know the man, and therefore do not know whether he could be built up into the position I visualize." In spite of these apprehensions, he was not deterred: "Nevertheless Arabia is a country that contains the holy places of the Moslem world. . . .Consequently, the King could be built up."[12]

Washington promptly adjusted its policy towards Egypt to reflect its changed attitude towards Nasser. Among other measures, it was decided that the United States and Britain would deny Egypt export licenses for arms shipments; that both countries would continue to delay conclusion of the negotiations on the Aswan Dam; and that the United States would continue to delay action on Egypt's requests for grains and oil under Public Law 480.[13] On 19 July 1956, the United States withdrew its offer to help finance the Aswan Dam. A week later, Nasser, seeking alternative means of funding the dam project, nationalized the Suez Canal. The Suez crisis that followed was an additional complication in Nasser's relations with Washington. In this setting, the Eisenhower administration became more deeply averse to Nasser and the radical Arab nationalism he represented. The administration, in addition, intensified its effort to limit Nasser's influence by building up a rival leader in the Arab world.[14]

It seems that by the end of 1958, United States policy towards Nasser had undergone another radical revision. NSC 5820/1 acknowledged that "the prevention of further Soviet penetration of the Near East and progress in solving Near Eastern problems depends on the degree to which the United States is able to work more closely with Arab nationalism." More particularly, it was also conceded that "denial of the area to Soviet domination" and "continued availability of sufficient Near Eastern oil to meet vital Western European requirements on reasonable terms" made it imperative that the United States should "deal with Nasser as head of the UAR [United Arab Republic] on specific problems and issues, area-wide as well as local, affecting the UAR's legitimate interests."[15]

Paradoxically, the authors of NSC 58201/1 also believed that Washington faced "the fact that certain aspects of the drive toward Arab unity, particularly as led by Nasser, are strongly inimical to our interests." There was, specifically, the fear that Egyptian influence in Africa could serve as a funnel for Soviet penetration.[16] In July 1960, against the background of the Congo crisis, CIA Director Allen Dulles told the NSC that "[t]he USSR is apparently attempting to use Egypt as a spearhead in the Congo and in Africa generally."[17]

As explained by an internal State Department memorandum, the problem with India arose because it was "making a desperate bid to assert its influence, and even its leadership, throughout Africa." Benjamin Gerig (the director of the Office of Dependent Area Affairs), who raised the issue, traced the origin of this alleged conduct on the part of India partially to the 1955 Bandung Conference but particularly to the 1956 UN General Assembly and Trusteeship Council sessions. His memorandum recalled that it was an "accepted Departmental policy" that India's growing influence in Africa was not "in the interest of the United States or of the Western World." After emphasizing that it was "to the interest of the Western World to keep African orientation westward rather than eastward," Gerig added, "If for historical reasons it should be difficult to continue the close ties which have associated much of Africa with Europe and with the United States, it should certainly be advantageous to Western interests to have African peoples and nations develop on an independent basis rather than to be oriented eastward toward Asia."[18]

Without doubt, the basis of India's "evil influence," as far as Washington was concerned, derived from its adherence to a policy of nonalignment. In July 1954, the State Department sent an alert to United States diplomatic missions in Africa. It claimed that "[s]ufficient information has accumulated on the activities of the Government of India in Africa to indicate beyond a reasonable doubt that India is launched on a propaganda program to attract developing African governments to neutralism and the Asian-African bloc." Worried because a successful Indian effort "would swing these politically developing areas away from cooperation with the United States," the department felt the need to have "the activities of India throughout the continent be fully known." The missions were therefore instructed to monitor the political and cultural activities of Indian government representatives and Indian citizens resident in Africa, as well as "those assigned to India by one or another of the technical agencies of the United Nations" in order "to determine the pattern, and the techniques employed, together with an estimate of the effectiveness of the program."[19]

Beginning with the 1955 Afro-Asian Conference in Bandung, nonalignment and neutralism (with its variant, "positive neutralism") gained wide currency as a descriptive label for the foreign policy orientation of the UDCs that had opted not to be affiliated with either the United States-led Western camp or the Soviet-led Eastern camp. India's adherence to nonalignment antedated Bandung. In December 1947, about five months after independence, Prime Minister Nehru told India's Parliament: "We have sought to avoid foreign entanglements by not joining one bloc or the other. We propose to keep on the closest terms of friendship with all countries unless they themselves create difficulties. We shall be friends with Americans and intend cooperating with them. We intend also to cooperate fully with the Soviet Union."[20]

It was a major United States goal to wean India away from nonalignment. At their August 1951 meeting, the foreign ministers of the United States and Britain agreed that "Mr. Nehru's foreign policy of 'neutralism' militates against the achievement of collective security and therefore, in final analysis, is favorable to the Soviet Union." The conferees resolved to "seek to convince India that neutralism is a danger to India's existence as an independent country, and hinders progress toward a free world order based on law and the peaceful settlement of international disputes; and that collective security and closer association with the non-Soviet countries, far from increasing the possibility of India's becoming involved in war, are the best assurances that it will not."[21] To Washington's chagrin, India remained a leading light in the nonaligned movement.

Early in 1951, *Economist* explained that the "neutrality upon which [Nehru's foreign] policy is based springs from a genuine inability, at this stage, to see world politics in terms of pure black and pure white; and this leads to the decision to attempt to avoid alignments and the taking of sides. That outlook appears unrealistic to many statesmen in the West. In the United States, where the division of the world is often seen in rigid terms of good and evil, there is the added tendency to dismiss it as immoral."[22]

There may have been moments of flexibility,[23] but Washington, and Dulles in particular, considered nonalignment or neutralism "immoral" because it was seen as transitional to "communism."[24] At a press conference on 6 June 1956, Eisenhower attempted to soften Washington's hostility to nonalignment. Recalling that the United States itself had followed a similar policy, especially in connection with European affairs, in its "first hundred years or more," he contended that contemporary neutrality "doesn't necessarily mean what it is so often interpreted to mean, neutral as between right and wrong or decency or indecency." He understood that the concept was being used "with respect to military alliances," adding, "I cannot see that it is always to the disadvantage of such a country as ours." Eisenhower concluded with the announcement that Dulles would shortly clarify the administration's position on nonalignment.[25]

The Dulles speech that followed barely two days later was anticlimactic. He reaffirmed Washington's hostility to nonalignment, and declared that United States mutual assistance treaties with forty-two countries in the Americas, Europe, and Asia "abolish, as between the parties, the principle of neutrality, which pretends that a nation can best gain safety for itself by being indifferent to the fate of others. This has increasingly become an obsolete conception and, except under very exceptional circumstances, it is an immoral and shortsighted conception."[26]

The State Department embraced Dulles' position. In a policy statement issued in June 1957, it held that "the major threat to world peace and security is international communism" because it "still has as its objective world domination." The United States, the department went on, "is reinforced in its belief that the most effective method of combating international communism, within the framework of the major objective—building enduring world peace with justice—is for the community of free nations to cooperate to safeguard their independence by creating a collective defense system." On this account, it was considered "unwise for any noncommunist nation to fail to avail itself of the benefits of free association with other independent nations for this purpose." For the department, the matter was further complicated because "[i]n some instances, 'positive neutrality' has expressed itself in propaganda attacks upon other independent states which have rejected the neutralist position for themselves, and which have joined in collective defense against communism. Such propaganda attacks have benefitted international communism and constitute unneutral conduct."[27]

Down to the end of its tenure, the Eisenhower administration hardly moderated its hostility towards nonalignment. At an NSC meeting in August 1960, the question was raised whether neutralism in Africa was "necessarily undesirable from the point of view of U.S. interests." What followed was an assertion that the only neutralism the United States could accommodate was a pro-Western alignment. Acting Secretary of State Douglas Dillon told the meeting that "neutralism was not undesirable if the countries were genuinely neutral—that is, friendly to the West and to free enterprise." Otherwise, "neutralism could be undesirable."[28]

Far more than the possibilities of Egyptian or Indian influence in Africa, the containment of "communism" as a policy objective loomed large in Washington's rhetoric. The standard position was the acknowledgment that "communism" had not made any real gains in Africa, but that was no reason for complacency; instead, the United States had to intervene, by maintaining an active presence in the region, in order to keep "communism" at bay. This vocabulary was well represented in the report turned in by Nixon after his tour of Africa in early 1957.[29] *Times* of London (8 April 1957) was quick to point out at the time that Nixon seemed "obsessed with the threat of communism in this area." While conceding that "[h]is fears are not wholly without basis," the newspaper suggested that "a very clear distinction needs to be made between communism as a domestic political movement and the Soviet Union as an international political force. Communism has never been a serious subversive threat in Africa."

Nixon was not alone in his assessment.[30] A State Department paper prepared in early 1956 held that United States interest in Africa had "assumed a new dimension," for two reasons. One was that Africa's large land mass "gives a present and potential importance in the conflict with the communist nations." The other was that Africa was "the last great area in which the issues of colonialism are being resolved." Both factors were said to be conditioned by the "world-wide sweep of events which has propelled the United States into a position of leadership in the struggle between the West and the Soviet Union."[31]

Given this kind of rhetoric, anti-Sovietism appears and is widely taken as *the policy,* rather than as *part of United States policy* in Africa.[32] In order to avoid being tautologous, I am reserving my response to this perspective for a later point in this chapter. For now, it is enough to emphasize that in assessing the impact of the Cold War on United States conduct in Africa, a distinction must be made between rhetoric and actual policy. Such a distinction is important and necessary because the archival records clearly show that actual policy did not reflect the urgency and concern evident in the official pronouncements.

Hegemonic Socialization

In seeking to shape the process of political change in Africa, Washington understood that it was not enough to focus on the negative strategy of restraining the penetration of "communism," nonalignment, or Egyptian/Arab nationalism. Like Antonio Gramsci,[33] Washington fully understood that influence can be wielded in the international system not only by manipulating material incentives but especially through normative controls that can alter the "'ways of seeing' and, implicitly, of organizing the world."[34]

In November 1950, the State Department emphasized that "[t]he position of the United States today makes it incumbent upon us to seek all practical means of integrating the peoples of the underdeveloped areas of the world into the free world." To achieve this end, the department envisioned "influencing non-official groups and individuals in underdeveloped areas" and therefore advocated that Washington's "contacts must not be confined to the transaction of day to day official business or to the simple exchange of information. They must be used to influence the thinking and actions of the people along the lines we consider most likely to produce the desired result."[35] Similarly, a 1955 NIE explained that containing Soviet expansion into the "Third World" entailed a " 'battle of ideas' for influencing the attitudes and allegiance of potential leadership groups."[36] To win this "battle," Washington put in place a number of mechanisms designed to ensure that the elites of the subordinate states in its world system internalized United States value orientations and claims about the nature of the international system. One such mechanism was the Foreign Leader Program, which was inaugurated by the State Department in 1947.[37]

The grantees—as participants in the Foreign Leader Program were known—were nominated by the United States diplomatic missions in their respective home countries.[38] Their first stop was Washington; after they had been attached to officials who helped to plan their individual study tours, the grantees moved to the American Council on Education, which had a contract with the State Department to offer a one-week program of lectures, discussions, films, and tours in Washington. This was intended to provide grantees with a general introduction to the United States, its history, economy, geography, government, institutions and customs. After their time with the American Council, the grantees were assigned to groups dealing with their more specialized interests. The Governmental Affairs Institute, a private organization in Washington affiliated with the American Political Science Association, catered to those who were interested in observing the United States political system, the civil service, local government and administration, the judiciary, and law enforcement as well to as university teachers of political science, public administration, and international relations. The National Social Welfare Assembly, a private New York-based organization, worked with grantees concerned with youth organizations, social group work, community recreation programs, and the operation of voluntary agencies in the social welfare field. The Office of International Labor Affairs of the Department of Labor saw to those interested in labor issues, while the Women's Bureau of the Department of Labor took care of women leaders. Leaders who wished to study matters relating to the educational system were assigned to the Office of Education of the Department of Health, Education, and Welfare. The Educational Exchange Service of the State Department took care of those who were interested in information dissemination (including media operations), cultural affairs, economic affairs (except agricultural and labor affairs), and foreign affairs (except the teaching of international relations in the universities).[39]

In the second phase of the program, the grantees individually toured a number of cities and one or two small towns. (Those not proficient in English were accompanied by "escort-interpreters.") In each city, the grantee met with professional colleagues, visited local tourist attractions, attended cultural and civic events, and spent some time with a local family. In addition, each grantee had to visit at least one small community with a population of 50,000 or less. After the "study tour," the grantees returned to Washington "for final interviews" with their program and area officers in the State Department. In addition, they participated in a three-day terminal seminar on "the American scene." Back in their home countries, United States diplomatic missions followed up, both formally and informally, "to maintain a relationship with the grantee and to evaluate the results of the visit."[40]

The Foreign Leader Program must not be confused with the Foreign Specialists Program, which was also administered by the State Department. As provided by Public Law 402 of the Eightieth Congress, both programs were intended to promote "better understanding of the United States in other countries and to increase mutual understanding between the people of the United States and the people in other countries" through the grantees' travels, observations, and consultations with their American colleagues. But while Specialists Program participants received specialized or technical exposure and training,[41] Foreign Leader Program participants did not.[42] And while participants in the former tended to be younger and stayed in the United States for longer periods, participants in the Leader Program were established individuals: journalists and publishers; members of national, state, and local legislatures; officials of government agencies at the national, state, or local levels; political party leaders; members of academia; high-ranking educational (including university) administrators; labor leaders; leaders of women's organizations; and youth leaders. In short, the grantees were, according to Robert Elder, "the sort of people anyone would select if he were looking about the United States for leaders and persons of genuine influence whose words will always not only be heard, but heeded."[43] It was required that each prospective Foreign Leader grantee should "be a person who now exercises, or may be expected to exercise in the relatively near future, unquestionable influence over a substantial segment of public opinion in his home country."[44] Students were therefore excluded from the program on the ground that they "are something of a gamble in that in most cases it is impossible to accurately ascertain their leadership potential."[45]

The thrust of Gramsci's proposition is that in order to neutralize popular challenges and thus bridge the historical antagonisms within civil society, the dominant class has to establish its leadership at the ideological and cultural levels. It is a basic requirement of this process that the dominant class must create its own intellectual cadre which would direct and organize its worldview. "The intellectuals," Gramsci insisted, "are the dominant group's 'deputies' exercising the subaltern function of social hegemony and political government."[46]

From the roll call of the Foreign Leader grantees, it is evident that Washington was clearly seeking to create "deputies" who would help ensure "the predominance of political society over civil society in such a way that the subaltern classes are held in a passive position because their potential leadership is co-opted."[47] From Nigeria came people who were in positions of power and influence such as Richard Doherty, speaker of the Western Region House of Assembly;[48] Ernest Nwanolue Egbuna, speaker of the Eastern Region House of Assembly;[49] Elizabeth Adekogbe, president, the Women Movement of Nigeria;[50] T. O. Ejiwuno, secretary of the Amateur Athletic Association of Western Nigeria;[51] B. R. Pam, development secretary, Jos Native Authority, and member of the Northern Nigeria House of Assembly; H. M. Katsina, education councillor, Katsina Native Authority; Ishaya Andrew, chief of Jaba; Muhammadu Aminu, district head, Sabon Gari, Zaria;[52] Ayo Bello, assistant publicity officer, Northern Nigeria Information Service; Talabi A. Braithwaite, manager of Law Union and Rock Insurance Company Limited; Jonathan Adeniyi, principal, Abeokuta Grammar School; E. N. Akpom, women's welfare officer, Nigerian Coal Corporation, Enugu; and Amos Okulaja, superintendent, Poultry Development Center, Fashola.[53] Some of the participants—for example, Festus Sam Okotie-Eboh,[54] Yusuf Maitama Sule,[55] Eyo Esua,[56] Godfrey Kio Jaja Amachree, Stephen Oluwole Awokoya,[57] and Theophilus Aribisala[58]—later occupied key public positions in Nigeria.

Participants from other parts of West Africa were no less impressive. For example, the grantees from French West Africa included Gabriel d'Arboussier, president of the Grand Council of French West Africa;[59] Ernest Boka, minister of public functions, Ivory Coast;[60] Seydou B. Kouyate, minister of rural economy and planning of the Republic of Soudan (later, Mali);[61] and Paul Amegee, Togo's minister of public works.[62]

There was certainly the hope that by socializing the grantees into the United States hegemonic vision of the world order, the Foreign Leader Program would ensure that the participants identified with and defended United States interests and aspirations. By definition, this role also entailed that, as opinion molders in their various countries, the grantees would transmit United States norms and thus influence the subaltern groups to achieve, as Gramsci put it, "not only a unison of economic and political aims, but also intellectual and moral unity."[63]

In the event, efforts such as the Foreign Leader Program achieved very little. European colonial rule and the entire process leading up to the transfer of power ensured an instinctive pro-Western orientation among West African political leaders. By contrast, the younger elements were more radical in their outlook, and even resentful of the West, including the United States. In September 1960 (a month before Nigeria's independence), John Emerson, the United States consul in Lagos, reported that Prime Minister Abubakar Tafawa Balewa "was unequivocal in his determination to stick to democratic institutions and firm relations with [the] west. He does not like the terms non alignment or neutrality as he considers himself committed to western ideals." In particular, Balewa cherished "close British ties" and wished to develop "close relations" with the United States.[64] Almost a year earlier (in August 1959), Emerson had given a talk on "American Foreign Policy toward Nigeria" to the Lagos Contemporary Society, which drew its membership from young professionals and civil servants. The questions that followed the talk were generally critical of United States foreign policy, ranging from its close relations with the apartheid regime in South Africa, to its hostility to nonalignment, to its support of dictatorships, as well as "feudal and fascist states," and even its policy in Latin America. Reporting to Washington, Emerson observed that while "not attaching too much significance to the trend of thought exemplified in this meeting, one must remind oneself that official declarations of solidarity with the West by government and political leaders may not always reflect accurately opinions held by many of the younger generation, not now in positions of influence but potential leaders of the future."[65]

Criticisms such as those voiced at the 1959 talk still resonated by the end of the period covered by this book. In early 1961, Paul Conklin of the *New Republic* interviewed some students of the University College, Ibadan

(Nigeria). They told him: "You Americans are the most obstinate people. You above all others should realize that Africa is not to be wooed like a child with no mind of its own. There is so much talk in the United States about winning Africa for the free world. Has it ever occurred to you that perhaps we don't want to be won, perhaps we don't regard your freedom as being particularly desirable."[66]

The sentiments expressed at Emerson's talk and by the students were more widely held. In March 1961, the same month when Conklin published his interview, the third All-African Peoples' Conference met in Cairo, attended by some seventy delegations—all representing, not the governments but the rising younger forces—from at least thirty-five African countries. In its communiqué, the conference labeled the United States as the leader of the international neocolonial conspiracy, which, while grudgingly acceding to the inevitability of independence, tries "to deprive this independence of its essence of real independence . . . through economic and political intervention, intimidation and blackmail." Independent African states were urged to be on their guard against this phenomenon. More particularly, the conference advised that the United States Peace Corps program should be "mercilessly opposed" since its aim was to "reconquer and economically dominate Africa."[67]

Of more significance than the anti-United States sentiments was that Washington had little leverage to affect political change in Africa. Indeed, it followed, rather than decided, the course and nature of change. In 1954, it was declared that a principal United States objective in Africa was "to try and influence their governments towards the building of sound democratic and integrated societies."[68] However, an NIE published in June 1959 showed that Western democracy had little prospects in West Africa. According to the report, an essential character of West African political parties was "personal loyalty to a leader; the trend is toward the domination of particular states by a single party." The result, it was noted, was "a highly personal and authoritarian style of government, which is regarded by the leaders as necessary to achieve unity and development in the face of ethnic diversity and economic backwardness." The estimate saw "little chance of a trend away from authoritarian methods"; on the contrary, it held that "in fact, as their problems become more complex many leaders will probably become more vigorous in their use of these methods."[69] By 1960, the Eisenhower administration had come to accept this reality and decided on building up the "strong men."[70] The objective, it seems, was no longer the institution of democratic client states, but client states that were pro-West, and especially pro-United States.

Economic "Assistance" and Related Issues

Gary Hess found that the "substantial growth of American influence" in South Asia "profoundly affected regional developments, and the United States has been the principal external political-economic-military force in South Asia."[71] By contrast, the "distinguishing characteristics" of United States aid operations in Africa, according to Rupert Emerson, were that they were "held down to modest proportions, that the military element has been slight, and that as a general rule they were deliberately made supplementary to those of the former colonial powers."[72]

The financial balance sheet, as shown in table 4.1, lends credence to the view that United States "aid" programs (under both the Truman and Eisenhower administrations) in Africa were perfunctory. In 1956, a State Department intelligence report recalled that the United States "has thus far devoted few of its resources to Africa." It calculated that "[d]irect official U.S. aid to Africa since World War II has amounted to about $650,000,000 or less than two percent of total U.S. economic abroad during this period."[73] In the same year, Senator Theodore Green did a study of United States economic aid and technical assistance in Africa and reported that "[i]n comparison with our Government's overall program of foreign economic aid, the amount budgeted for Africa has been very small." He found that of "a total sum of approximately $1,546.7 million appropriated for fiscal year 1957, it is estimated that somewhat less than $25 million will be allocated to Africa, or 1.6 percent of the total."[74]

A congressional report issued in 1957 also showed that "[s]ince the end of World War II the United States has given away without requirements of repayment, a total of $46,142,143,000. Of this total Africa received $71,595,000 or 0.15 percent."[75] Another study showed that in 1956–60, the total United States aid to the UDCs was $11.4 billion. Out of this figure, the Near East and South Asia received $4.6 billion, East Asia received $4.1 billion, $2.2 billion went to Latin America, but Africa received only $0.5 billion.[76] There was thus sufficient statistical justification for the NSC confession, in July 1960, that United States aid to Africa was "very modest compared with our assistance to other parts of the world and, of course, compared with the assistance of the European powers."[77]

The miserly reality of these figures is apparent when it is realized that United States aid to Africa essentially went to North Africa and to the racist enclaves in southern Africa. In 1959, Melville Herskovits and his colleagues at the African Studies Program of Northwestern University reported that Africa received only 0.15 percent of the global United States grants from

Table 4.1. United States Foreign Aid to West Africa during the Mutual Security Act Period, 1953–1960 (figures in U.S.$m)

	Economic Assistance		Military Assistance	Export-Import Bank Loans	Total
	Loans	Grants			
Chad	-	0.1	0.0	0.0	0.1
Dahomey	-	3.1	0.0	0.0	3.1
Gambia	-	0.3	0.0	0.0	0.3
Ghana	30.0	6.4	0.0	0.0	36.4
Guinea	-	4.0	0.0	0.0	4.0
Ivory Coast	-	2.1	0.0	0.0	2.1
Mali	-	2.5	1.2	0.0	3.7
Mauritania	1.4	0.2	0.0	0.0	1.6
Niger	-	2.0	0.0	0.0	2.0
Nigeria	4.0	14.9	0.0	1.3	20.2
Senegal	-	3.6	0.0	0.0	3.6
Sierra Leone	-	1.1	0.0	0.0	1.1
Upper Volta	-	2.0	0.0	0.0	2.0
Togo	-	1.9	0.0	0.0	1.9

Total U.S. Aid to West Africa, 1953–60 = $93.5million

Source: Agency for International Development, *U.S. Overseas Loans and Grants and Assistance from International Organizations: Obligations and Loan Authorizations July 1, 1945–September 30, 1960* (Washington, D.C., n.d.). Available at the U.S.A.I.D. Library, Washington, D.C.

1945 to 1956, and 2.12 percent of all its loans, of which "over two-thirds" went to South Africa and the Federation of Rhodesia and Nyasaland.[78] In 1958, $74 million out of a total package of $87 million was allocated to Libya, Morocco, and Tunisia; in 1959, $112 million out of a total package of $161 million went to the same three countries and Sudan; in 1960, the same four countries received $150 million out of a total of $178 million.[79]

According to Robert Pollard, "American leaders used foreign economic policy as the main instrument of U.S. security from 1945 to the eve of the Korean War"[80] in 1950. Even after 1950, Washington continued to rely on economic aid to safeguard its national security interests around the world. As Dean Rusk, secretary of state under presidents John F. Kennedy and Lyndon Johnson, told a congressional committee in 1965: "Foreign aid is basic to U.S. security. Without it, many countries undoubtedly would have been subverted or overrun in the past two decades. . . .In fact, foreign assistance has been our primary means of helping to guide the economic, social, and political evolution of most of the countries of the non-communist world."[81] Thus a discussion of United States foreign aid to a particular geographical region is at the same time a discussion of the nature and scope of its overall interests, policy, and involvement in that region. It is therefore imperative to investigate why Eisenhower presided over what the International Cooperation Administration (ICA)[82] mission in London, described as "a small aid program of marginal effect"[83] for Africa.

In the 1950s, Africa was still under European colonial rule. Ordinarily, investment, trade, and monetary ties all combine to orient colonial economies toward their respective metropoles. In the circumstance, colonies are, by definition, sheltered markets for the metropoles. It is thus understandable that there were occasional complaints in Washington that the European colonial presence constrained United States economic program in Africa. In March 1954, the Defense Department complained that the "orderly development" of Africa's agricultural and mineral resources for the "mutual benefit of non-African free world countries" and of the Africans themselves was being stifled because of the fragmentation of the region into "economic spheres of influence" controlled by the European colonial powers. The department also observed that while there were "development" programs in existence, such programs were aligned to the "narrow economic policy of the colonial powers involved, inhibit private investment from other nations, and are 'paternalistic' rather than designed to develop minor industry locally or in other ways to create slowly expanding markets."[84]

In the same vein, the 1959 study prepared by the Program of African Studies at Northwestern University attributed the limited scope of official United States economic involvement in Africa to the colonial powers, who "have showed preference for financing their African needs themselves, so that outside participation on the governmental level has not been sought."[85] In these two respects, the French were singled out as the most culpable. As late as August 1960, Secretary of State Herter complained that the "basic problems" of United States policy in the francophone countries stemmed from "the extreme reluctance of the French to let the United States or any other country operate aid programs."[86]

As demonstrated in chapter 3, the intricate web of the relationship between France and its African colonial economies was such that the latter were virtually isolated from the rest of the world. Nevertheless, Paris was not entirely unwilling to allow foreign capital into its colonies. In June 1954, the French government and the Foreign Operations Administration (FOA) concluded an agreement for a loan of 500 million francs. The loan was to enable the French to undertake a public works program in support of the mining activities of *La Société des Mines de Cuivre de Mauritanie*.[87] In

January 1958, the United States embassy in Paris observed that the French were becoming increasingly conscious of the need to develop their colonies and were therefore becoming more interested in attracting external capital into the territories.[88] However, as shown in chapter 3, even in the period 1950–52, the French had been adept at soliciting and simultaneously fending off American capital. Thus the signals coming from Paris in 1954 and 1958 need to be evaluated with care.

In April 1958, the United States embassy in Paris explored the prospects for United States capital in French Africa. The study revealed that the French government had come to the realization that the financial and technical investments required for the development of its African territories were beyond its financial capacity, as well as the capacity of French private enterprise. But it was also quickly acknowledged that this realization "in many liberal quarters . . . runs into severe nationalist opposition in Paris." The embassy observed that it was axiomatic for the French that their African territories should retain their purely French character, especially in the economic sphere. In this context, Paris regarded the entrance of a foreign country or multilateral agencies into the area as "tantamount to driving a wedge to separate these territories from France. As a consequence, France has taken almost no advantage of the United Nations Technical Assistance Program and relatively little advantage of bilateral U.S./French technical assistance save for a few exceptional cases where administrative control remained largely in French hands."[89]

The same underlying consideration, the embassy believed, informed the French insistence upon the overseas territories provisions included in the 1957 Rome Treaty that established the European Economic Community (EEC). As explained by the embassy, those provisions were designed to ensure the extension of French rights and privileges in French colonies to the other members of the EEC "as a concession to retain as much economic domination in the territories" as was possible. It therefore expected that France "will try to maintain a sort of economic Monroe Doctrine, particularly in the undeveloped Middle African territories, with the idea of retaining Africa as the natural economic hinterland of Western Europe. They will consequently probably try to discourage large-scale economic penetration of the area by other countries, particularly the United States."[90]

The British were, on the other hand, very receptive to United States economic participation in their colonies. This willingness was manifested in a 1955 ICA announcement that the fiscal year 1956 dependent overseas territories' (DOTs') program was to be focused on the British territories because "UK OT's wish an association of their territorial development and

U.S. technical assistance."[91] A year later, ICA/London reported that the British government was increasingly favoring greater United States official and private participation in the development of Africa.[92] There were, indeed, clear and persistent signals from British officials on the need for United States assistance in their colonies. In March 1957, Lord Perth, minister of state for the colonies, stated that London "warmly welcomed U.S. interest in assisting African territories via FY '58 programs." He pointed out that, having long recognized that the resources required for Africa's development were far beyond its resources, Britain would welcome any contributions that the United States could make. Lord Perth added that the Colonial Office was willing to make available its own experience and territorial development plans which might help the United States in preparing well-coordinated programs for the territories.[93] A month later, Secretary of State Alan Lennox-Boyd "expressed pleasure with [the] growing interest U.S. [was] taking in Tropical Africa."[94]

Perhaps because they expected so much from the United States, the British were very disappointed with the United States program in Africa on two grounds. One was the high cost of United States technical assistance. For example, the UN paid the full salaries of the technicians it provided, as well as their international transportation expenses and half of the local "sterling costs." By contrast, ICA technicians received allowances and other perquisites, paid for by the territorial governments, "at levels which exceeded the total salary and allowances of their British counterparts." This, the United States embassy in London pointed out, was harmful to the United States public image as "African politicians are already attacking the munificence of 'expatriate' emoluments and are demanding equal pay for African Government employees." The major British complaint, however, had to do with the limited scope of the United States program: London insisted that the exclusive focus on pilot and demonstration schemes precluded any meaningful financial participation by Washington in the economic development of Africa.[95]

Britain's disenchantment induced ICA/London, with the support of the United States embassy in London, to call for a substantial shift away from a program limited to technical assistance and at the "prevailing scale," "if appreciable progress in forwarding U.S. interests in the area [British African territories] is to be made." The mission emphasized that any accomplishment in this direction "would require an effort commensurate in terms of money and scope with U.S. efforts devoted to similar purposes in other areas of comparable size and stage of economic development. Continuation of a program of the restricted character of that now in effect cannot have the necessary impact." The technical assistance program, ICA/London recalled, had been characterized by: (1) narrow criteria in the choice of projects; (2) serious delays in the recruitment of technicians; (3) difficulties in negotiating the terms of contracts; and (4) a fairly evident lack of interest on the part of officials, both in London and in the colonies, "in a program of this sort, except when, as in the case of Kenya, technical assistance has been combined with substantial amounts of development capital."[96]

The mission urged that the United States should be prepared to supplement the efforts of Britain and its colonies in "basic fields" of long-term economic development such as highways, irrigation, agriculture, and public health. It also believed that assistance would be required in key situations where their resources were inadequate and other sources of financing, such as the World Bank, were unavailable. The mission suggested that $5 million be included in the fiscal 1958 budget submission to "provide for launching activity pending decision as to whether we are prepared to enter upon a more comprehensive economic program and the development of such a program with the British and territorial authorities if the decision is affirmative."[97]

The petitions by the ICA and the United States embassy in London clearly suggest that there was room for a substantial expansion of the United States program in British territories. They are also proof that the modest level of the official United States program in British African territories in particular cannot be explained in terms of any constraints imposed by colonial control. Even the French, Senator Green found, were unwilling to participate in a severely limited "technical cooperation program, divorced from a large development program [for Africa] financed by the United States."[98] It is significant that Washington never even bothered to engage the ICA and the embassy in a debate over aid for British African territories. Worse, all the signs pointed to a cutback in the scale of the United States program. Complaining of "limited technical cooperation funds available," ICA Washington notified USOM, London, that it should plan in terms of a $1.3–$1.5 million program for fiscal 1956,[99] and that was in spite of the warning given by USOM, London:

> Insofar as political stability in Africa is concerned, it would be extremely hard to prove that the very limited funds we provide to defray the salaries of American technicians have any appreciable effect on political stability in the African UK/DOT's. In view of our extremely limited financial contribution vis-à-vis Colonial Development & Welfare grants and other assistance in-

cluding that provided by the UN, we are not in a position to affect either the pace of development or political stability in the African territories concerned to any marked degree.[100]

The nature and outcome of United States program in Africa derived, in part, from the underlying philosophy of Eisenhower's foreign economic policy. He had come into office with a deep personal commitment to achieve an Open Door for American private capital. This predisposed him to a "trade not aid" policy,[101] and therefore an emphasis on the capacity of United States private enterprise to generate externalities strong enough to stimulate and sustain general development in other economies. This bent was legitimized by the Commission on Foreign Economic Policy. The commission's report, submitted in 1954, not only emphasized trade rather than aid, it proposed a drastic cutback in existing aid programs and the concentration of any future aid on Asia.[102]

In his foreign economic policy blueprint, sent to Congress on 30 March 1954, Eisenhower also embraced the commission's recommendation that United States assistance to the UDCs should continue to be essentially in the form of technical assistance. Such technical assistance programs were to provide only United States experts, not capital (money and equipment) for investment; they were to be fit into the existing development programs of the assisted countries; and they were to be related to anticipated private or public investments. Eisenhower added that these principles were to be embodied in the Mutual Security Program legislation that he would propose. In consonance with the spirit of this proposal, he stated that substantial reductions in external grant aid had already been made by his administration.[103]

Eisenhower's orientation meant that, as with his predecessor, United States "aid" program continued to be in the form of "technical assistance." In 1956, the State Department observed that "we are handicapped by certain regulations or provisions of the law which narrow the field of technical assistance and make our program less flexible. For example, we cannot go much beyond providing persons to give demonstrations in teaching, when facilities and supplies may be badly needed." Consequently, the department recommended, "If we are to make our program useful—and the African is avid for help of this nature—we have to restudy technical assistance as an instrument of foreign policy in order to make it fit in a more realistic fashion the situation in Africa."[104]

United States technical assistance in Africa was restricted to "demonstration projects." The stated objective was to develop, jointly with the participating country, "new or improved methods of tackling a given problem on the assumption that if the demonstrated method proved to be a solution, the country itself would continue to apply it to the same and similar problems." Such projects were, for the most part, in the general fields of agriculture, natural resources, vocational and technical training, public health, and transportation. United States participation in any given project involved the provision of equipment and American technicians (along with their dollar needs). The recipient country was obliged to put up (counterpart) funds (in its own currency) equal to, but usually greater than, those contributed by the United States.[105]

In terms of impulses, objectives, and practical application, Eisenhower's economic program in Africa replicated Truman's. As shown in chapter 3, the origins of United States "economic assistance" to Africa lie in the Marshall Plan, which was focused on the rehabilitation of Western Europe and the extraction of minerals for the United States strategic stockpiling program. This focus ensured that United States economic involvement during the Truman administration was rather modest in its scope and financial investment. In 1955, the State Department explained that the United States economic program in Africa was still placed "in the context of European recovery and the need for strategic materials"; it was therefore not, to quote the department again, a United States "policy towards Africa itself."[106] In his 1956 report mentioned above, Senator Green pointed out the implication of the United States program in Africa subserving the European, rather than the African, interest: "Little attention was given to the fundamental problems characteristic of underdeveloped colonial areas."[107]

Besides its institutional nature, practice, and objectives, there is another explanation for the limited nature and ineffectiveness of United States program in Africa. From its inception in 1948 and through the Eisenhower administration, Washington conceived the program as augmentative of the colonial governments' economic programs. In 1954, the FOA mission in London explained that United States economic assistance for Africa remained "very small in scale and designed to complement the primary" local and metropolitan programs "through emphasis on skills and resources in which the U.S. has a distinct lead."[108] In other words, in the realm of economic assistance, Africa was regarded as a European responsibility.

In June 1958, Clarence Randall, chairman of the (presidential) Council on Foreign Economic Policy, circulated to members of the council a paper contending that Britain and France were unlikely to be able or willing to maintain "a sufficient flow of public and private capital to their territories, particularly after these colonies achieve independence." Randall therefore advised that "it would be to our interest for the countries of the Free World (including the United States) to provide additional economic and technical assistance."[109] Rather than heed this advice, the administration reaffirmed the existing policy in May 1959, when Deputy Assistant Secretary James Penfield outlined the United States role in Africa's economic development. He readily conceded that in all respects—trade, administration, political and economic development, and education—the "European colonial or former colonial powers" had contributed "far more to Africa than we have" and were still "continuing their interest and contributions." Penfield then declared, "We regard this as natural, and we welcome it. We have no desire to interfere with the fruitful development of these new relationships."[110]

In March 1960, Joseph Satterthwaite, assistant secretary of state for African affairs, warned that "[c]omplete dependence on metropoles or former metropoles is dangerously unrealistic if we are determined to retain a Western-oriented African continent."[111] Undersecretary of State Douglas Dillon could only assure him that the United States would "fill the gap" if the "European countries did not supply [Africans'] needs or if the African territories were unwilling to accept aid from the former metropoles, and if additional aid were needed."[112]

Washington's option for what John Montgomery has called "a junior partner's role" in relation to the former metropolitan powers meant that in fiscal year 1960, Britain and France contributed "about $830 million" a year to Africa as against "some $209 million" contributed by the United States (with much of the latter going to North Africa).[113] This United States definition of its role vis-à-vis the Europeans in relation to economic assistance for Africa was common knowledge. In 1960, *New York Times* reported that the United States recognized the preponderant role of the European powers in providing foreign assistance to African territories, even after they had achieved independence.[114]

Apart from the Europeans, Eisenhower's other preferred source of aid to Africa was the UN and its agencies. This was a major theme of his address to the UN General Assembly on 22 September 1960. "An awakening humanity" in Africa, he said, "demands as never before that we make a renewed attack on poverty, illiteracy, and disease." This attack, Eisenhower asserted, could best be made in concert by all nations, through the UN. This led him to propose that the UN should help African countries to "shape their long-term modernization programs." To provide the financial base for this, he called for increased contributions to ensure that the UN Expanded Technical Assistance Program (EPTA) and the Special UN Fund for Economic Development (SUNFED) would jointly have $100 million at their disposal in 1961. Eisenhower also urged that the World Bank and the IMF should be encouraged to provide technical advice to African countries and hoped that "[w]e should also look forward to appropriate and timely financial assistance from the two multilateral financial sources as the emerging countries qualify for their aid." Finally, he called for an all-out UN effort to help African countries launch educational programs that would develop the skills required for their development programs. In this connection, Eisenhower announced that the United States was ready to contribute to an expanded program of educational assistance to Africa through the relevant UN agencies in accordance with the desires of the Africans themselves.[115]

On a number of occasions soon after his address, Eisenhower let it be known that he was strongly opposed to bilateral aid to Africa, "because, if it is carried too far, the relation between the giving and receiving countries tends to be one of domination." Meeting with Nigeria's Prime Minister Abubakar Tafawa Balewa, he modified this view, explaining that aid to Africa through the UN did not "necessarily preclude bilaterals" but that he preferred that aid be in the form of loans rather than grants. A loan, Eisenhower held, "requires the recipient to be responsible, independent, and self-respecting," and that while grants might occasionally be necessary, "they connote some feeling of obligation."[116]

According to Burton Kaufman, Eisenhower's readiness for cooperation (through the UN) with the Soviet bloc on aid for Africa and his preference for assistance in the form of loans instead of grants are best explained against the backdrop of the United States balance of payments problem. Treasury Secretary George Humphrey first alerted Eisenhower to the problem in 1955.[117] The situation worsened after 1955. In the period 1958 to 1960, the deficit involved an excess of payments over receipts of about $10.5 billion.[118] Put simply, during the period, the government and residents of the United States made payments abroad—for imports of goods and services, for net private foreign investment and economic assistance—which exceeded by an average of $3.5 billion a year the receipts from United States exports of goods and services.

In December 1960, Eisenhower reviewed the background of the balance of payments crisis. He recalled that the global responsibilities which the United States had assumed since after World War II—reconstructing the war-ravaged economies of Western Europe and Japan, bolstering their military strength, and providing economic assistance to the UDCs—had all combined to cause a substantial dollar outflow. This outflow had, in turn, created a balance of payment deficit that, according to him, had been noticeable "since about 1950." He confirmed that it was in an effort to contain the situation that the Development Loan Fund (DLF) adopted a new lending policy in December 1959, "so as to place primary emphasis on the financing of goods and services of United States origin."[119]

Eisenhower announced measures to reverse the deficit. These included an expansion of the new DLF policy: "we must," he stressed, "include in our efforts a reduction in certain governmental payments of dollars to foreign countries." To this end, the ICA director was instructed to "adopt a policy which will place primary emphasis on financing goods and services of United States origin in all its activities." At the same time, a ceiling was to be placed "on operations which do not finance direct procurement of United States goods and services, and efforts shall be made to minimize the balance of payments effect of those operations. The amount of commodities now being purchased abroad with ICA funds shall be reduced to the lowest figures." These measures essentially amounted to a retrenchment of United States aid to the UDCs. Of greater importance, however, the balance of payments problem generated some reexamination of whether the United States could afford to continue as the "free" world's dominant source for aid. This was indicated in Eisenhower's announcement that the United States was pushing for the formation of the International Development Association (which became a World Bank adjunct) "through which other countries will share with us the burden of assisting the newly developing countries."[120]

At any time, United States "economic assistance" was in the form of dollars and had to be ultimately used for buying American goods and services.[121] The new policy adopted by the DLF in 1959 and its expansion a year later meant that United States "aid" was directly "tied" to the purchase of United States goods and services on commercial terms by the receiving country. It can be said that such credits serve a useful purpose since the beneficiaries, being typically countries with serious capital shortages, may not qualify for the commercial loans they need to pay for their imports. But "aid" in this form is, as V. I. Lenin regarded it, "usury imperialism," which is "a means of encouraging the export of commodities."[122]

Africans had been irritated by the "Buy-American" policy as it had existed even before 1959. In March 1958, Clarence Randall had to urge that the policy be suspended because Africans were "offended by this policy, and regard it as a new form of colonialism, and exploitation by the United States. Their loans are hard loans, and they wish to buy in a free market. In many instances the equipment they need can be obtained at a lesser price in Europe, or it may be complementary to existing European equipment which they know how to operate."[123]

The balance of payments had a direct impact on Africa in other ways. It was, as Kaufman had contended, responsible for Eisenhower's preference for multilateralism in aid-giving, and it partly explains the shift from assistance in grants to assistance in loans. It also reinforced Washington's predilection that Western Europe had the preponderant role in economic assistance for Africa. For example, in December 1959, Henry Claude Blisson, the personal assistant to Prime Minister Mamadou Dia of Senegal, met with officials of the Brussels-based United States Mission to the European Community (USEC). At the time, the Mali Federation (which included Senegal) was sorting out its independence from France. Blisson's purpose was to do a "pre-reconnaissance" of aid possibilities from other Western sources for the federation after its independence. Deane Hinton of the USEC made it clear to Blisson that given its balance of payment deficit, Washington was more interested than ever in having its European allies carry more of the burden in the UDCs. Hinton added that the United States hoped that the French Community would endure and that France would continue to provide economic assistance to African members of the Community; that the United States saw no incompatibility between the independence of Mali, continued membership in the French Community, and continued association with the European Economic Community.[124]

No doubt, the balance of payments problem has its value in explaining much of Eisenhower's aid program in Africa. But the basic elements of the program (especially, its nature and scope) were so entrenched that even without the balance of payments deficit, the outcome would have been no different. In 1954, well before the deficit became an issue, the FOA mission in London explicitly stated that the "primary external responsibility for assisting development [of British African territories] lies with the British," and that "U.S. aid is essentially a specialized marginal adjunct to UK aid and is channeled via the UK."[125] In 1955, both the ICA and the United States embassy in London acknowledged that United States technical assistance to British colonies was "not only marginal but has been deliberately kept so," adding that the program was "in general not likely to be either very large or very effective in the immediate future, in view of the narrow limits established by our criteria." They explained the underlying reason for the United States "administering a small aid program of marginal effect" in Africa: Washington did not intend to increase its global political and financial commitments "by encouraging the peoples of British Africa to depend increasingly upon the U.S. Government for resources."[126]

Another reason why the United States consigned Africa to the Europeans was the perennial congressional hostility to aid-giving. This was manifested by the drastic cuts in foreign aid appropriations from 1952 onward. In that year, Congress slashed by 25 percent the amount that the White House had originally requested to aid "nations resisting communist aggression."[127] In vain, Eisenhower tried to restrain this tide. For example, sensitive to the congressional mood, the administration sought $3.5 billion for fiscal 1955, $1 billion less than had been appropriated for the preceding year. Yet Congress cut the total to $2.8 billion, largely at the expense of funds for NATO, but also through a 10 percent cut in funds for the UDCs. Above all, the Senate Foreign Relations Committee amended the legislation to put a specific termination date, 30 June 1955, on the aid agency. According to Andrew Westwood, "Many Congressmen voted for it as a way of expressing their desire that foreign aid be terminated."[128]

For fiscal year 1957, Eisenhower cited the Soviet economic "offensive" in requesting a mutual security appropriation of $4.67 billion. Congress was unmoved: it approved only $3.8 billion, erased the Asian Economic Development Fund that had been established in 1955, and refused to approve the request for a special $100 million fund for the Middle East and Africa. Furthermore, Congress ruled that 80 percent of the development assistance funds should be made available to recipients as loans not grants.[129] For the rest of his presidency, Eisenhower faced a Congress with an increasing distaste for aid-giving. In 1959, the Senate directed the White House to submit to Congress a procedure for phasing out all grant aid, excluding military and technical assistance programs. At the same time, many urged on the UDCs the introduction of disinflationary fiscal and monetary policies and better treatment of private foreign investors.[130]

The congressional disaffection with foreign aid was symptomatic of a deeper national mood, which desired Washington's retreat from some of the global responsibilities it had assumed after World War II. As early as 1950, this calculation was already shaping United States policy in Africa. In that year, the State Department enumerated "the basic attitudes" of Americans, attitudes that were influencing their government's policy toward Africa. One was "a strong desire to assume as few additional world responsibilities as possible."[131]

Congressional antagonism to aid-giving helped determine the essential elements of official United States economic involvement in Africa and, by extension, the overall nature of United States policy in Africa. In 1957, Assistant Secretary of State William Rountree argued for United States support of a "Colombo Plan" for Africa because he believed that such a plan would encourage the Western European powers to continue to assist both their colonial territories and former territories, encourage the African peoples to continue to collaborate with and look primarily to the European countries for assistance, and provide a continuation of the "mutual interdependence so vital" to both the Africans and the Europeans. Rountree believed that the achievement of these objectives would "[r]elieve the growing pressure on the United States to assume a major and expanding role in meeting Africa's need for external aid as our ability to do so is likely to be limited by the growing Congressional sentiment for reducing aid programs."[132]

Overall, there is every indication that Washington (in this case, both the Eisenhower administration and Congress) never considered itself a major player on African turf. At a meeting of the NSC on 18 August 1960, Acting Secretary of State Dillon insisted that the United States policy of relying on Western European nations to "influence and support their respective dependent and recently independent areas so long as such encouragement and reliance are consistent with U.S. national interest" was "adequate and realistic." He observed that France believed that it could take care of its ex-colonies and that the United States "was working with the French, trying to keep them in a position of supporting their ex-colonies." For Dillon, the "position with respect to the British areas" was "at present satisfactory," as Ghana and Nigeria had remained friendly with Britain.[133]

Contending that "there was a sense of urgency about the problem of eventual communist infiltration," Defense Secretary Thomas Gates, Jr., told the NSC meeting that he was disturbed by the policy of relying upon the Europeans to safeguard Western interests in Africa; first, because African states might not continue to welcome the Europeans; and second, because the Europeans might not be very willing to continue their assistance. Eisenhower's response was that the underlying principle of the French Community "was to keep the ex-colonies of France closely bound to France economically and culturally." In order not to disrupt the French scheme, he ruled that in the case of the French Community, "we should get the countries [to] go first to Paris." In the end, Dillon explained the basis of the policy of relying on the Western Europeans to bear Africa's foreign aid burden. "Our thinking," he told the meeting,

> was that, so far as any major effort was concerned, black Africa should have a relatively low priority. This did not mean that we should not make an effort but rather that our efforts should be limited to technical assistance and some individual projects like Volta Dam. Latin America, where U.S. responsibility is greater and the possibility of success is also greater, should have a higher priority. The same thing was true of India where the prospects

of success were also greater . . . We could not get ourselves into a position where we were committed to vast contributions to Africa.[134]

The Strategic Dimension of Minimalism

Dillon was essentially saying that geopolitical considerations, or the degree of United States "responsibility" in a particular region, were decisive in determining the extent of United States aid to (and general involvement in) such a region. Geopolitical considerations in this regard would have definitely included geographical proximity to the United States and the perceived danger of Soviet penetration: both would have applied to Latin America while the latter obviously worked in India's favor. On the other hand, the conscious effort to avoid "vast contributions" to Africa suggests the region's "relatively low priority" in this kind of strategic rating.

It has been demonstrated in this chapter that Eisenhower started off with a commitment to drastically curtail, if not eliminate, foreign economic assistance. Incidentally, this policy was being formulated at a time when Moscow was aggressively expanding its economic assistance to the UDCs. This Soviet initiative caused a great deal of nervousness in Washington in the period 1956–60[135] and therefore compelled a shift "within two years" from the original policy of "trade not aid." The new emphasis was to ensure "greater public assistance to less developed countries."[136] Even Congress, in spite of its growing aversion to foreign aid, still appreciated "the value of aid as a partial response to the problem of communist expansionism in Asia."[137] In 1958, the State Department rationalized United States aid to India solely in this context.

The department pointed out that "[i]n the apportionment of U.S. aid, one consideration must take priority over all others, and that is that U.S. aid must be directed toward those who need it most in order to remain free—this for the greater good of the Free World." The United States, it was further stressed, "is resolved to extend all possible, necessary support to the countries on the perimeter of the Soviet Union and Red China as well as to vulnerable areas further removed geographically from the communist bloc." This resolve was, however, constrained by two factors: the fact that United States resources were necessarily finite and the "conviction that the greatest aid must be extended at the points where the danger is greatest at any time." It was explained that the size of the aid to India, in particular, was informed by the country's population of nearly 400 million and its "enormous political and psychological importance in Asia." Other considerations included the fact that India, "the largest democracy in the

Free World," had to develop economically if political and social stability were to be maintained, "and it urgently needs economic assistance for such development." Besides, Washington held that the security and well-being of South Asia and the Middle East were all predicated on India's stability and independence (from "communist" control). Above all, it was believed that if India failed to obtain the external assistance it desperately needed from the countries of the "Free World, it may by force of circumstances make some arrangement for help from the Soviet Union which could eventually compromise its independence (and consequently that of the whole area)."[138]

The anti-Soviet focus on India raises a very important question: To what extent did strategic considerations and, especially, anti-Sovietism shape not only United States aid to Africa but overall United States policy in Africa during the Eisenhower era? In mid-August 1960, against the background of the Congo crisis, the Joint Chiefs of Staff emphasized that the "continued availability" of the Congo's Kitona airfield as well as the port of Banana, "to the Free World is strategically important as a base for maritime patrol aircraft in support" of operations in the South Atlantic as well as "for the control of ocean shipping, and as a major point of access to the Congo and Africa south of the Sahara." This view prompted Undersecretary of State Dillon to observe that the memorandum marked the first time, to his knowledge, that the Department of Defense had indicated that the United States had "any specific strategic interests in Africa south of the Sahara."[139]

Interestingly, in October 1960, the JCS drew attention to the strategic importance of another part of Africa: this time it was the "western bulge" and they warned that the air and maritime facilities there, "both actual and potential, would constitute a serious threat to U.S. interests in the South Atlantic and in South America, as well as in Africa itself, if they were to fall under the political influence of the Sino-Soviet Bloc."[140]

Until the Congo crisis, the long-standing calculation, expressed in various forms, was that there was no threat of Soviet expansion in Africa. A 1954 policy paper declared that the Western position in Africa was threatened, not by the possibility of Soviet penetration, but by "rising African dissatisfaction with the rate and manner in which their growing aspirations are being realized."[141] There were two main reasons for this reassurance: first, Africa was still very much under Western European political control; second was the region's geographic remove from the "danger areas" such as southeast Asia. These two factors meant that Africa was generally considered to be secure in Western hands and therefore free of Cold War complications. This consideration was frequently expressed along the lines of a 1951 State Department memorandum, which remarked that "Africa is fundamentally identified economically and politically with the Free World Democracies—countries aligned against communism."[142]

In May 1957, the State Department felt confident enough to reiterate that "the association of the northern and western half of Africa have been northward toward Europe and westward towards the United States."[143] This continuing assurance that Africa was in safe hands impinged heavily on the policy-making process. For example, a 1957 NSC paper conceded that Africa had enjoyed less priority than Western Europe, the Middle East, and the Far East, "where the weight of communist military and political strength was more powerfully and intensively applied."[144] Not only was Africa removed from the immediacy of the "communist" threat, it had no deep-seated or obvious bearing on United States national security. In 1959, a strategic contrast was drawn between North and sub-Saharan Africa, and the latter came out poorer. Given North Africa's geographical location (immediately south of Europe), it was obvious to the NSC that the "loss of North Africa to Soviet control would outflank Europe and it was doubtful whether the free world would survive such a disaster." In addition, both Britain and France had military bases in North Africa, while the United States had Strategic Air Force bases in Libya and Morocco. North Africa was therefore so strategically important that the United States was explicitly committed to maintain its base rights there "by all feasible means, being prepared, if necessary, to offer reasonable quid pro quos therefore."[145] On the other hand, Africa south of the Sahara was said to be "of less immediate strategic importance," except that "its vast [primary] resources could make a major contribution to the free world."[146]

NSC 5719 and a number of other high policy papers of the 1950s also reveal that, for Washington, Africa's real importance derived from its raw materials.[147] In 1959, a study for the Senate Committee on Foreign Relations reported that "U.S. strategic interest in sub-Saharan, as against North Africa, has been directed toward its value as a source of raw materials."[148] There was, at the same time, the conviction that in spite of any "prospective political changes," Western access to these raw materials "will generally be preserved."[149] This confidence was based on the assessment, even by mid-1959, that "[d]espite the socialistic and, in many respects, authoritarian outlook of many of the leaders in the area, communism has not become a strong force in West African internal politics."[150] This kind of assessment invalidated a real "anticommunist" response as far as Africa was concerned.

The truth, therefore, was that in a setting in which strategic considerations counted for so much, the strategic importance of black Africa to the

United States was minimal. Along with this was the persisting satisfaction that colonialism had so thoroughly acculturated the African political elite into the Western camp that there was hardly any prospect of a real shift on their part to the Soviet camp. It is therefore not surprising that Washington's anxiety over Soviet economic penetration of the UDCs did not rub off on Africa. The Mutual Security funds authorized for the entire continent (excluding South Africa and Egypt) actually dropped from $209 million in fiscal 1960 to "less than 'about $140' " million in fiscal year 1961.[151] The allocation pattern of the 1961 Mutual Security funds was a revelation in itself. Of the "less than 'about $140' " million that was allocated to Africa, $50 million went to Morocco, $20 million to Tunisia, $18 million to Libya, and $2 million went to Ethiopia. That left only $60 million for the rest of the continent. The allocations to the North African countries were justified as "special assistance . . . furnished to advance special U.S. military and political interests." The same preference was reflected by official United States lending institutions. The total DLF lending to Africa as at 1960 was $57 million. Out of this, Morocco, the Sudan, and Tunisia were allocated $23 million, $10 million, and $8.7 million respectively, "with smaller loans for Liberia, Somalia, Nigeria, Libya and Ethiopia."[152]

There is, of course, no denying that the United States sought to keep Soviet influence out of Africa in the 1950s. The first NSC position paper on Africa, NSC 5719, which was issued in July 1957, categorically declared that a major United States objective in Africa was "to deny the area to communist control." This was considered important, for according to the paper, "communist" control would ensure "both economic dislocations to Western Europe and communist access to strategic materials."[153] The point being stressed, however, is that containing "communism" was not the peg of United States policy in Africa, certainly not in the period 1950–60.

The discussion on aid to Mali is a clear pointer as to how policy making was influenced by the general feeling that West Africa in particular was not under any Soviet threat. On 1 November 1960, Undersecretary of State Dillon, Director of the Bureau of Budget Maurice Stans, and their assistants met with Eisenhower to discuss a $2.5 million mutual security program for Mali. Dillon introduced the subject, stating, "We are at the point where we should give consideration in policy terms to the question of aid for Mali." He estimated that France was still aiding Mali at the rate of $10 million annually but stressed "the importance of acting quickly if we are going to do this to avoid the possibility of close ties developing between Mali and Guinea."[154]

The aid was to be "in the form of commodities produced in the United States, including cement and POL [petroleum, oil, lubricants] with the counterpart funds thus generated being used to improve a transport route through the Ivory Coast and to Mali." Dillon opposed the idea that such aid should be channeled through the UN on the ground that the Soviets and Czechs "are pressing to give aid which would tie Mali to Guinea." At that point in the meeting, Eisenhower asked "whether our giving aid would result in an advantage to us in relation to the Russians and the Czechs. Mr. Dillon said that it would, adding that the Mali authorities look to us as the leader of the West. The hazard is that if we do not give aid, we will be closed out of the area, as they have attempted to do in Guinea. The great danger of a Mali-Guinea tie-up is that there would then be a route leading directly into Algeria." In spite of this response, Eisenhower still emphasized that he generally preferred "the UN approach" to aid for Africa. He reluctantly endorsed the aid for Mali, acknowledging that the surveys that precede UN and World Bank economic development programs usually take "a long time—a year or more—by which time the situation may have gone against us." Eisenhower did not retreat from his position that direct United States aid program for Africa should be regarded and planned as "essentially transitional in nature, over the next twelve to eighteen months, while a UN program [for Africa] is being organized."[155]

Conclusion

The factors discussed above: the fact that the United States program in Africa was based upon the paramountcy of Western European interests and its corollary (that is the subordination of Africa's interests to Europe's); the fact that the United States opted to have the Europeans take primary responsibility for foreign aid to Africa; and the absence of Cold War complications in Africa all combined to ensure that United States "aid" program in Africa was minimal and inconsequential. This, as has been argued here, mirrored the overall nature of United States policy in Africa.

More fundamentally, this chapter finds that United States involvement in Africa had a symbolic, as opposed to a substantive, content. For example, as far as Washington was concerned, aid-giving to Africa was the primary responsibility of the ex-colonial (European) powers—and secondarily, of multilateral agencies. This derived from the fact that in spite of United States standing after 1945 as the world's preeminent economic power, its leaders were anxious to avoid the burden of an "imperial overreach"— that is, their global responsibilities outstripping their resources. This ensured that there was a correlation between the level of Washington's involvement in a given geographical area and such an area's bearing on United States national security interests. Given Africa's low rating in this strategic accounting of costs and benefits, Washington was very disinclined to devote resources and attention to the region. In the event, the United States opted to rely on the Europeans to project and defend Western interests in Africa.

5

GHANA: HONEYMOON AND ESTRANGEMENT

Ghana's independence on 6 March 1957 was a momentous event in modern African political history. Dramatized by the vibrant presence of Kwame Nkrumah, Ghana at once appeared on the world stage as the one place where Africans were set to recapture their initiative in history. The significance of Ghana's independence and its long-term implication, in terms of relations with independent African states, was not lost on Washington. Secretary of State Dulles acknowledged Ghana's independence as one of the "most significant events of contemporary Africa," adding that the event would be watched with great interest by both colonial and anticolonial powers. He also recognized that "[t]he other emergent peoples of Africa will follow with particular attention the degree of interest and sympathy which the United States accords these developments."[1]

As explained by the United States embassy in Accra, Washington intended to encourage and help Ghana develop and maintain a stable political and economic setup so that it would neither seek nor accept assistance of "an obligating nature from any countries whose motives are inimicable [sic] to the national interests of the United States." Ghana was also considered "a good example for other areas in Africa which are approaching independent status."[2] Washington therefore saw the transfer of power in Ghana as the turning point that would decide whether Africa's rapport with the West, a rapport instituted by colonial rule, could be sustained in the postcolonial era. According to one official paper,

> The success of this newly independent African State in establishing an adequate framework of government dedicated to democratic principles and capable of maintaining political stability and progress in improving the productivity and living standards of the people should be a stabilizing influence throughout Africa and other underdeveloped areas. It will provide a concrete demonstration of the benefits of association with the West and an answer to the criticisms of western influence in Africa which are made for political reasons by the communists and others.

The paper believed that Ghana would need external assistance to help overcome the shortage of both skilled labor and capital, and other problems in relation to its effort to establish a stable political, social, and economic structure. There was an implicit promise that the United States would help tackle the problems as "Ghana will be a testing ground of the willingness and ability of the West to help underdeveloped peoples."[3]

In a broad sense, the United States objective was to ensure that Ghana remained closely aligned to the West. This goal involved warding off competing sources of influence, including, the Soviet presence. In a briefing for Vice President Nixon—leader of the United States delegation to Ghana's independence ceremonies—the State Department observed that aside from "various efforts at penetration and subversion in northern Africa, the Soviet Union and its allies have seized every opportunity to further their interests South of the Sahara." As an example of this effort, the department recalled that during the 1956 inauguration ceremony of Liberia's President William Tubman, the Soviets sent "a powerful delegation, sought to establish diplomatic relations, and made vague offers of economic assistance." Nixon was alerted that there would be an even more vigorous Soviet effort during Ghana's independence ceremonies.[4]

Nkrumah Cultivating Washington's Friendship

A key factor that worked in favor of United States policy in Ghana in the period 1957–60 was the ideological orientation of Nkrumah and his government. According to one biography, Nkrumah was preoccupied with "the total liberation of the African continent from colonialism, imperialism, neocolonialism and settler minority regimes," as well as the "political unification and the establishment of a socialist All-African Union Government."[5] This is an idealized image, which may have been true of the Nkrumah of the 1960s, but not the Nkrumah of the 1950s.[6] At the 1957

Commonwealth prime ministers' conference, for example, "he was unwilling to take a contentious stand on any issue," and more particularly, he quickly established a cordial relationship with racist South Africa. Nkrumah believed that the Commonwealth was "big enough for both Ghana and South Africa," and that the organization was not the forum in which to discuss apartheid. When they met at the 1959 UN General Assembly, Ajo Adjei, Ghana's foreign minister, invited Eric Louw, his South African counterpart, to visit Ghana.[7]

The Watson Commission, which investigated the 1948 riots in what was then the Gold Coast, believed that Nkrumah had strong "communist" leanings, and would, given an opportunity, translate this inclination into practice.[8] This forecast did not come true during the period under discussion here. Shortly after he came out of prison in February 1951,[9] Nkrumah declared: "I would like to make it absolutely clear that I am a friend of Britain . . . I want for the Gold Coast Dominion status within the British Commonwealth. I am no communist and never have been."[10] It was not long before he started living up to this profession. John Hargreaves says that by February 1954, Britain had secured Nkrumah's commitment to ban the entry of all "communist" literature into the Gold Coast; exclude any European with "communist" sympathies from the public service and Africans with similar inclinations from the administration, the ministry of education, and the police; and confiscate the passports of those who wished to travel to "communist" countries.[11]

Nkrumah's anticommunism did not begin in 1954. His government had first proposed restrictions on travel to the "communist" bloc in 1953. At the same time, Nkrumah threatened the editor of *Evening News,* the official organ of his party (the Convention Peoples Party, CPP) with dismissal if he continued to publish "pro-communist" materials.[12] Labor leaders and unions were the casualties of Nkrumah's anticommunist purge. On 22 October 1953, Albert Hammerton, representative of the International Confederation of Free Trade Unions (ICFTU)[13] in West Africa, met with William Cole, the United States consul in Accra, Vice Consul Robert Fleming, and Eugene Sawyer, USIS/consulate public affairs officer.

Hammerton, who was preparing for an international executive meeting of the ICFTU in Brussels, wanted a briefing on the Gold Coast. He was troubled that "the recent infiltration into the Gold Coast Trade Union Congress [TUC] of communist sympathizers such as [Anthony] Woode and Turkson Ocran" would be most unfavorably regarded in Brussels, especially given that the TUC had disaffiliated from the ICFTU at its annual conference in August 1953. To Hammerton, these were signals of something more fundamental, leading him to wonder about Nkrumah's ideological orientation and to stress the international public relations value of demonstrating at Brussels that "the CPP is not in fact conniving to support communist activities." Although Cole and Fleming assured him that it was their "understanding that Nkrumah held a sincerely neutralist position," they still felt the need for a clarification by Nkrumah himself. Fleming went to Nkrumah immediately after the meeting and impressed upon him the necessity of making a public statement on his position on "communist" activities in the Gold Coast. Another meeting followed, involving Nkrumah, Fleming, and Hammerton. In the course of the meeting, Nkrumah promised that the ICFTU would again be given a free hand in the Gold Coast, but he could not promise immediate reaffiliation of the TUC, to avoid the impression that he had been "bought over."[14]

On 23 October, Nkrumah convened the CPP central executive. Immediately after the meeting, it was announced that Woode and Ocran had been suspended from both the party's executive and the CPP itself. Two days later, Nkrumah used the platform of the national congress of the United Nations Students Association to publicly acknowledge that there was "confusion in the minds of some people . . . regarding where I and my Party stand in the present struggle between the Eastern and Western Democracies." To dispel any "future doubt," he declared that "we regard our country as being wedded to the democracies that are friendly to us."[15] Shortly after this, Ocran was relieved of his post as the TUC general secretary.[16] On 28 February 1954, the TUC reaffiliated with the ICFTU.[17]

Recalling its uneasiness with the "course of developments in the Gold Coast tending towards the complete domination of the local trade union movement by supporters of the World Federation of Trade Unions," the State Department commended its officers in Accra for sensitizing Nkrumah to the need for "drastic remedial measures."[18] It should be said that apart from helping America's cause, Nkrumah was also safeguarding his own political career. According to Jitendra Mohan, he feared that the labor leaders, "if allowed to prevail, could sabotage the neocolonial accommodation being essayed by CPP leaders and colonial interests. That was why those elements had to be subdued, and the trade union movement deprived of its autonomy and its political capacity."[19]

The purging of those with "communist" leanings from the public service, the censorship of *Evening News,* the suspension of Woode and Ocran from both the CPP and the TUC, and the TUC's reaffiliation with the ICFTU all point to Nkrumah's clear-cut pro-Western orientation. Writing in 1954, David Apter observed that although the CPP "lists as its primary aim the establishment of a socialist Ghana. . . . .the general conduct of the present Nkrumah government would make it difficult to see what efforts toward socialism are being made, other than broad state entrepreneurial functions similar to those of the colonial government before the present constitution."[20]

It is, of course, true that Nkrumah had a number of close associates with strong Marxist credentials. Notable in this category were Adviser on African Affairs George Padmore; Attorney General Geoffrey Bing, who had long been associated with the extreme British Left; and James Markham, secretary of the Pan-African Office, who had been with the Anti-Colonial Bureau of the Asian Socialist Conference in Rangoon. These were, however, more than matched by people of a different ideological persuasion: in 1956, St. Clair Drake observed, "All the members of the Cabinet are Western oriented."[21] In any case, even the Marxists were not averse to a visible Western (especially, United States) presence in Ghana. Padmore, for example, argued that if the United States was "really worried about communism taking root in Africa," it should undertake "a Marshall Aid program for Africa" and, more specifically, "construct the Volta River project in the Gold Coast."[22]

There was certainly a great deal of pragmatism in Nkrumah's foreign policy, a pragmatism dictated by the Volta River Project. His oft-repeated priority was to achieve a structural transformation of the colonial pattern of trade in which Ghana exported primary produce and imported manufactures. This entailed the diversification of the economy through the modernization of agriculture and the substitution of locally produced goods for imports. The key to this diversification, Nkrumah thought, was power generated from the Volta. In the early 1950s, he had banked on British funding for the Volta project. But by 1957, it was clear that funding from Britain would not be forthcoming. He then turned to the United States. In the circumstance, the need to attract Western and especially United States financial support for the Volta project shaped the orientation of Ghana's foreign policy in the period under study here.[23]

"Another cause for Ghanaian interest in the United States," explained Douglas Anglin in 1958, was that "the rising population of the States offers the brightest prospect for the export of cocoa on which Ghana's continued prosperity is so heavily dependent." In this regard, he noted that in 1958, about half of Ghana's cocoa exports went to the six countries that comprised the European Economic Community (EEC), especially West Germany and the Netherlands. Anglin pointed out that the overseas territories provisions of the 1957 Rome Treaty, which established the EEC, threatened this market in two ways: "by providing for the eventual importation of cocoa from the French and Belgian Congo duty free; and by clamping a 9 per cent tariff on Ghanaian cocoa, which now enters Italy and the Benelux countries free." Besides, the provisions "will encourage production of cocoa in French and Belgian overseas territories and thus contribute to a lowering of world prices." Against this background, the search for alternative markets became "a matter of increasing urgency to Ghana."[24]

"The nature of the situation, then, and the predisposition of the leaders," according to W. Scott Thompson, "made a 'pro-West' bias for Ghana inevitable at the beginning."[25] This bias was particularly noticeable in the case of the United States. So anxious was Nkrumah for a warm relationship with the United States that he went to great lengths to downplay the racial humiliation of Finance Minister Komla Gbedemah in the United States. The same consideration was at work in the establishment of Ghana/Soviet relations.

Gbedemah and the Orange Juice Palaver

On 7 October 1957, Gbedemah set out from New York by road for a speaking engagement at Maryland State College. He was accompanied by Bill Sutherland, his African-American personal assistant, and two African-Americans from the college. On entering Delaware State, one of the African-Americans[26] pointed to a Howard Johnson restaurant and told Gbedemah that by the state's practice, he would not be served there because of his skin pigmentation. Highly skeptical—especially because they had just been served in New Jersey at a restaurant belonging to the same chain—Gbedemah suggested that they stop at the next Howard Johnson. Just outside Dover, Delaware, they ran into one. Gbedemah and Sutherland went in, sat down, and ordered two glasses of orange juice. The drinks were packaged for them to take out. Their declared intention to have the drinks inside the restaurant was refused, even after Gbedemah had identified himself to the manager. The following day, Gbedemah issued a press statement in New York on the incident, which was widely attributed to racial discrimination. An embarrassed Eisenhower immediately invited Gbedemah to breakfast with him at the White House on 10 October.[27]

Meanwhile in Accra, Ghana's External Affairs Ministry had formally drawn the attention of the United States embassy to the incident and requested that "such action as appropriate" be taken as redress.[28] Before receiving the note, Wilson Flake, the United States ambassador to Ghana, had issued a statement expressing his personal regret, "assuming Gbedemah was quoted correctly."²⁹ The following day, Flake reported to Washington that Nkrumah had been annoyed with Gbedemah for creating a fuss over the incident. Nkrumah, who was personally acquainted with racial discrimination in the United States,³⁰ was reported to have said that he personally "understood these things" and emphasized that he would have kept quiet if he had been in Gbedemah's place. He believed that some day "everything will be all right" in the United States and counseled that in the interim, "Africans had to be understanding." In addition, Nkrumah was said to have made a "guarded but nevertheless uncomplimentary" reference to Sutherland. He held that Sutherland should have known better than to let Gbedemah stop at that particular restaurant.³¹ In Flake's presence, Nkrumah ordered the Information Ministry to "kill any further publicity" of the incident in government-owned media; he telephoned the same order to the editor of his party's newspaper, *Evening News,* and telephoned the *Daily Graphic* for "cooperation." Finally, he requested Flake to assure Washington that "this incident will not have the slightest effect on the happy relations between our two countries."³² The following day, Flake reported the silence of the Ghanaian media on the "Gbedemah story": the *Graphic,* he observed, "has not one word" on it.³³

Before Flake's despatch arrived in Washington, the State Department had sent a telegram narrating the incident and mentioning Eisenhower's breakfast with Gbedemah to the United States embassy in Accra. Flake was asked to personally communicate to Nkrumah the information and the regrets of the United States government.³⁴ The telegram reached Flake after his meeting with Nkrumah. He went back to Nkrumah, conveying its substance. Nkrumah opted not to release the telegram to the press. He told Flake that he had ordered Radio Ghana not to mention the incident in its local languages programs, and that he had sent telegrams to Gbedemah and Ghana's high commissioner in London advising them to let the matter rest.³⁵

Soviet Diplomatic Representation³⁶

While the establishment of diplomatic relations between Washington and Accra came on the eve of Ghana's independence and as a matter of routine,³⁷ the establishment of Accra/Moscow relations came almost a year later and was preceded by considerable foot-dragging and deference to United States opinion by Accra. It was as if Ghana was getting involved with the Soviets in spite of itself.

Shortly after Ghana's independence, A. L. Adu, permanent secretary, Ministry of External Affairs and Defense, informed the United States consulate general in Accra that the Soviets had requested the establishment of diplomatic relations and that Ghana would accede to the request.[38] But on 13 March 1957, the Ghanaian cabinet agreed that only those countries which already had consular representation in Accra would be allowed to establish embassies. This formula technically ruled out the Soviet Union and the Eastern European countries and was therefore considered a "victory" by the State Department.[39] Washington's opposition to diplomatic relations between Accra and Moscow weighed very heavily in the formulation of this policy.

The United States consulate general in Accra had, in its despatch of 23 January 1956, alerted the State Department that the Soviet Union was very likely to be invited to the Gold Coast independence celebrations.[40] The department responded that the "recent and current diplomatic efforts of the Soviet Union to interest itself much more directly" in Africa was a matter of serious concern in Washington. It believed that the establishment of diplomatic relations between African states and the Soviet Union was a Soviet device to pave the way for the "communist penetration" of Africa, because "[o]nce a Soviet mission is established in an African state it becomes only a matter of time before Russian blandishments and enticements of economic aid and technical assistance are likely to be accepted." Under these circumstances, the prospect of a Ghana/Soviet diplomatic relationship was viewed with grave "concern."[41]

In a separate note, the department notified the United States embassy in Monrovia that it remained "vitally interested in the problems" posed by the possible establishment of Ghana/Soviet diplomatic relations and would therefore appreciate the embassy's reports on the subject.[42] This prompted the embassy to contact Liberian officials, urging them to use their good offices to dissuade Ghana from entering into diplomatic relations with the Soviets.[43] President Tubman of Liberia was very willing to be of assistance. He sent a personal note to Nkrumah. In the note, which was shown in advance to the United States embassy in Monrovia, Tubman "earnestly" prayed Nkrumah to employ all means possible to forestall the "introduction in West Africa of any harmful ideology, i.e. communism."[44]

On 4 March 1957, William Tolbert, Liberia's vice president and head of the country's delegation to Ghana's independence celebrations, showed Nixon a copy of Tubman's letter to Nkrumah. Nixon told Tolbert that he had discussed Ghana's foreign policy with Nkrumah and was informed that it would be "nationalist rather than neutralist," that Ghana would pursue a policy of noninvolvement and nonalignment in the East/West confrontation, would protect its independence, and would resist domination from any quarter. Nixon also learned that Ghana might find it necessary to establish relations with the Soviet bloc, but that in the meantime firm decisions on diplomatic relations had only been made for Britain, France, Liberia, and the United States.[45] Nine days later, the United States embassy in London confirmed that during Ghana's independence celebrations, Nkrumah met with the Soviet representative and agreed to the establishment of a Soviet diplomatic mission in Accra. The British Foreign Office had shown the embassy a telegram to that effect from its high commission in Accra.[46] On 21 March, the embassy warned that "danger may already be upon us" as there were reports that the Soviets had already purchased 40,000 tons of Ghana's cocoa. "In this event British representatives would consider Nkrumah already following in Nasser's steps and danger exists Volta River could become another Aswan Dam."[47]

At the end of October 1957, the British Foreign Office informed the United States embassy in London that Ghana and the USSR were again in touch over the establishment of diplomatic relations "and decision possible in next few weeks."[48] At that point, Washington still believed that Ghana could be dissuaded from any Soviet "representation at all." The United States embassy in Accra was reminded that the State Department had long held that the establishment of a Soviet embassy in West Africa constituted a serious political threat to the stability of both the host country and its neighbors. In particular, it was felt that a Soviet diplomatic mission in Ghana harbored a "real danger [of] subversive activity which could be injurious [to the] internal security" of Nkrumah's government. Above all, the department did not wish to lose the gains the United States had achieved in "establishing friendly relationship with Nkrumah." It was considered "highly desirable" that Flake should explore the matter "along above lines at some length with [Nkrumah] now" through a "personal approach rather than give impression you are acting strictly on instructions."[49]

In return, Flake informed the department that the "basic question" had been settled during the independence celebrations, when Nkrumah "was pressured by USSR delegate and formally promised to exchange diplomatic mission with USSR. Timing was indefinite and now USSR wants action." He therefore held that it was futile trying to get Nkrumah to abort the deal. Flake preferred that the focus should instead be directed at delaying the exchange of diplomats between Accra and Moscow for as long as possible, using the interlude to give Ghana a "series of inoculations to make it resistant to activities of USSR mission when it eventually arrives." He agreed with the "wisdom of approach" suggested by the department and hinted that Nkrumah had invited him and the heads of five other diplomatic missions to meet him on November 6. Flake undertook to stay on after the meeting and "express as my own views the points covered" in the department's telegram.⁵⁰

The meeting mentioned by Flake was held between Nkrumah and the diplomatic representatives of Britain, Canada, India, France, Liberia, and the United States. The meeting revealed that Nkrumah was still trying very hard to walk the tightrope of accommodating the Soviets without offending the West. Before the meeting, Flake sent word to Nkrumah that he should not tell the group that the exchange of diplomatic representatives with the Soviet Union was imminent or even imply that he would turn to Moscow if the West failed to meet his expectations of economic assistance; that he should keep his options open until he heard from the group and "especially until I could talk to him privately."⁵¹

Nkrumah opened the meeting by emphasizing that although the Soviets were pressuring the Ghanaian high commissioner in London, he was yet to take a final decision on diplomatic relations with the USSR. Nonetheless, he made it clear that he could not keep the Soviets at bay much longer. He then inquired if the diplomats would accept a quantitative limitation on their personnel in Ghana so that he could have an excuse to set a ceiling on the numerical strength of the Soviet diplomatic staff. The diplomats asked for time to consult their governments before giving him an answer.⁵²

The establishment of Ghana/Soviet diplomatic relations was announced on 15 January 1958, with the exchange of representatives to follow in "due course."⁵³ Ghana remained anxious to ensure that this development did not damage its relations with the United States. In July 1958, Adu found it necessary to explain to the State Department that Ghana had been "bulldozed" into relations with the USSR at the time of independence; that Ghana had since then used every device to delay the actualization of such relations; but that in the end, the exchange of diplomatic missions with the Soviets had to be made; still, Ghana wanted the Soviet mission to be as small as possible and was therefore insisting that the embassy staff be limited in total numbers.⁵⁴ It is of significance that Ghana did not accede to a Soviet ambassador until 10 April 1959. The first Soviet ambassador, Mikhail Sytenko, arrived in August 1959; and it was only in early 1960 that Ghana sent "an advance party" to open an embassy in Moscow.⁵⁵

The United States Cultivating Ghana's Friendship

As already indicated, the basic objective of United States involvement in Ghana was to use it as springboard for securing Western hegemony in postcolonial Africa. To achieve this objective, Washington strove to create goodwill for itself in Accra.

In the week of 15 April 1957, officials of the United States embassy, the International Cooperation Administration (ICA), and Ford Milam (the United States regional agricultural attaché in Accra) held discussions with Ghanaian officials on "the subject of possible American aid to Ghana." In his meeting with Minister of Trade and Labor Kojo Botsio and Finance Minister Gbedemah, Milam outlined the general provisions of Public Law 480 and listed the various commodities declared as surplus by the United States Department of Agriculture. The United States embassy later reported that following the discussions, both ministers "gave the impression that their government is interested in receiving commodity aid assistance."[56] On 28 June 1957, Flake called on Gbedemah and conveyed to him "the sense of the [State] Department's [Instruction] A-87 of June 14, 1957, which had to do with possible United States assistance to Ghana on the latter's five-year industrial development program." Gbedemah was told that he "could take it for granted that the United States would consider carefully and sympathetically any specific request which Ghana might make for assistance under the Development Loan Fund if and when the Development Loan Fund should become a reality in the Fiscal Year 1958."[57]

In September 1957, Gbedemah was in Washington for a World Bank meeting. The occasion enabled ICA officials to arrange a series of meetings with him, all on possible United States aid to Ghana. From Stuart Van Dyke, director of the ICA Office of African and European Operations, Gbedemah received assurances that the United States was interested in assisting Ghana and was therefore prepared to receive requests for specific forms of aid, and that Ghanaian officials had been encouraged to talk to "our representatives." In turn, Gbedemah explained that his government was taking its time in studying its needs for assistance and would communicate them to the appropriate United States agencies "as soon as they were crystallized."[58] Earlier, when he paid a courtesy call on Henry Kearns, assistant secretary of commerce, Gbedemah was briefed on Public Law 480 and expressed interest in Ghana's participation in the program. He was equally enthusiastic about Kearns' proposals for a United States trade mission to Ghana and about an investment study of Ghana by the department, on behalf of United States business interests.[59]

During Nkrumah's visit to the United States in 1958, the issue of United States assistance to Ghana featured prominently in meetings between officials of the two countries. Undersecretary of State Dillon opened one of the meetings, stating that the United States was deeply interested in the improvement of the welfare of the peoples of the UDCs and was "always desirous of lending assistance." He pointed out that Ghana's requirements for technical assistance in education, agriculture, and related fields could be examined by the ICA, and he added: "We are, moreover, willing in principle to help in Ghana's industrialization if we receive specific requests." Gbedemah focused the discussion on Ghana's Second Development Plan and the Volta River Project. Dillon returned with the suggestion that the United States could assist in the plan by adopting the procedure it employed in the case of India: once the plan was ready, United States officials, including DLF staff, would study it and indicate the general fields where the DLF could entertain applications; Ghana could then make an application for assistance for specific projects in those fields. This suggestion was acceptable to the Ghanaians.[60]

In spite of these efforts, the level of United States assistance to Ghana remained rather modest. It was not so much that Ghana did not desire such assistance as that the United States packages were not attractive enough. In practice, United States "economic assistance" essentially meant technical assistance. Ghana certainly had some need for technical assistance: its request for an ICA survey team in October 1957[61] led to the conclusion of an agreement for the staffing of an ICA mission as well as technical assistance in geophysical surveying and agricultural development in Ghana.[62] However, Ghanaian officials never hesitated to emphasize that they desired external assistance not for "frivolous" projects but for those that were clearly beyond their country's own financial resources. In this regard, the Volta River Project came up for specific mention at every turn in their discussions with Washington.[63] As the next chapter reveals, for quite some time, the United States tried very hard to avoid getting seriously involved in the project.

The point being emphasized at this stage is that while Nkrumah was trying hard to achieve the best possible relationship with Washington, the Eisenhower administration was similarly cultivating Accra's friendship. Besides the approaches on aid, the administration employed more subtle means for this purpose. On the first anniversary of Ghana's independence, Eisenhower sent a congratulatory message to Nkrumah. "It is gratifying to note," the message said, "the developing ties between Ghana and the United States, many of which reach back into the history of our two countries." On a personal level that must have touched a sensitive chord with Nkrumah, Eisenhower noted with pride that "hundreds of your young people, including yourself, have chosen to come to America to study in our schools, to establish friendships." He used the opportunity to invite Nkrumah to pay an official visit to the United States in July of that year.[64] In his reply,

Nkrumah talked of the "deep impression" that Eisenhower's letter had made on him and his colleagues in government, adding that the message would be accepted by all Ghanaians as "an expression of the very great interest which Your Excellency, your Government and the people of the United States of America have always taken in the affairs and aspirations of the people of Ghana." He accepted Eisenhower's invitation to visit the United States.[65] It is also worthy of note that Acting Secretary of State Christian Herter sent Nkrumah a congratulatory message on his forty-ninth birthday, 9 September 1958,[66] and another on the second anniversary of Ghana's independence.[67]

Just as Nkrumah overlooked the treatment meted out to Gbedemah in the Dover restaurant, Washington was equally willing to accommodate and rationalize complaints against Nkrumah's internal politics. In March 1958, Tom Mboya, African elected member of the Kenya Legislative Council, was in Ghana for the celebrations marking the first anniversary of its independence. Coming from a white settler colony, Mboya had positive impressions of Ghana, which he published in the *East African Standard*. He regarded Ghana "as yet another success in the struggle of the colonial peoples against imperialist colonial regimes." Mboya held that Ghana "stood out as the first and real challenge to those who believe in the myth of the White man's supremacy, or superiority, over the Black." He noted that the Africanization of the public services had not led to an exodus of expatriate civil servants or businessmen; on the contrary, many were renewing their contracts, business was expanding, and economic prospects were very bright. He also noted the absence of racial discrimination, that primary schools were being opened at the rate of one every other day with attendance up from 25 to 85 percent in five years, that the cabinet enjoyed the full confidence of the country and the civil service, and that Finance Minister Gbedemah was highly regarded in Western capital markets. Mboya dismissed foreign media reports of Ghana's slide into dictatorship and economic chaos. "Ghana," he concluded, "was a land of hope. In this experiment, Africa's White settlers have the challenge of their times. This is not Black racialism but democracy."[68]

The United States consulate general in Nairobi passed Mboya's article on to the State Department and requested that the United States embassy in Accra be invited to comment on it. The consulate general was skeptical of Mboya's observations, stressing that they were made against the "background of local criticism of conditions in independent Ghana, suggesting economic chaos, tribal [sic] fragmentation, and dictatorial administration—conditions bordering on civil war." In essence, the consulate general wanted to test the validity of Mboya's account, but even more importantly, to assess "his sincerity and the trend of his political and economic philosophies."[69]

At a time when Nkrumah's regime was under a barrage of criticism for deporting two Muslim leaders (Larden Lalemie and Ahmadu Babu) from Kumasi to Nigeria (in July 1957) and there was serious talk in Accra of a "preventive detention" law under which political opponents were to be incarcerated without trial, the State Department showed a surprising degree of appreciation of Nkrumah's perspective on the situation in Ghana. It pointed out that in general, the reports on internal conditions in Ghana, "particularly those reports of late 1957, were, and to a lesser extent still are, unduly pessimistic and biased. Those comments have placed undue emphasis upon the problems of Ghana rather than pointing up the very real accomplishments in that country." The department (and the embassy in Accra) dismissed the "impressions of near-chaos and dictatorial excesses" as incorrect, adding, "There appears to be little danger of serious deterioration of the Ghanaian economy or of any successful challenge to Prime Minister Nkrumah's strong support by the majority of the people of Ghana. In almost every recent test the Convention People's Party has severely beaten the Opposition in polling for governmental representation in generally free and fair elections."[70]

The department was also impressed by the fact that Nkrumah's government was consciously and gradually undermining ethnicity as a factor in Ghana's internal politics. While stating that Washington would have preferred that the government of Ghana be more tolerant of political opposition, it observed that "those in conflict with the CPP and the Government have not hesitated to use strong-arm or other violent tactics against the Administration." Taking another line in its defense of Nkrumah, the department held that "[i]n a country where passion, superstition, and rumor play such a large part in political activities, it is most difficult for a new Government faced with the problem of modernization of a backward state to allow complete freedom of action to dissident elements. The Department does not foresee a critical danger in these Government activities, and, though they are certainly not to be condoned, the overall tenor of Nkrumah's regime thus far definitely appears to be moderate."[71]

High Noon of the Honeymoon

The United States/Ghana relationship was deepened by Nkrumah's official visit to the United States in July 1958. In a very elaborate manner, Washington rolled out the red carpet for Nkrumah. As *Time* observed, "seldom was a guest from a small country more welcome. The State Department saw the nationalism of his year-old country and the promise of his African leadership as a possible future counter-balance to rampant nationalism spreading from the Mideast."[72] In a briefing for Eisenhower on the visit, the State Department observed that Ghana had "received flattering attention from many nations, particularly the Soviet Union" and Egypt and that Nkrumah was "the inspiration" of all nationalists. United States relations with Ghana were assessed as "good" in spite of the latter's policy of "non-involvement in the East-West struggle." According to the department, the "primary objective" of the United States was to use the visit as a demonstration of its "recognition of the importance of Ghana's independence and acceptance of that nation as a full-fledged member of the community of nations."[73]

Nkrumah's party arrived in Washington on 23 July. The official visit lasted three days, after which the party left Washington for Pennsylvania, New York, and Chicago. Nkrumah and his entourage headed home on 1 August. For Nkrumah, the visit to New York was a personal triumphal return: in his early student days in the United States, cash-strapped Nkrumah peddled fish on a Harlem street corner and occasionally slept in the city's subway during one summer vacation. His reception in the city was tumultuous: more than 10,000 people filled Harlem's National Guard Armory to hear Nkrumah, and they rose and cheered as he spoke. To them, he explained that "Ghana's freedom is meaningless without the total freedom of the African continent." He invited them to Africa as doctors, technicians, and teachers. In Chicago, where he was accorded a city hall reception with full military honors, similarly enthusiastic crowds greeted his motorcade. The welcome was no less boisterous in Philadelphia where confetti was strewn over the motorcade.[74]

Nkrumah was very moderate in his public utterances, saying only things that were pleasing to his hosts. At a press conference, he assured his hosts that "communism" had made no mark and indeed posed no danger in Ghana because "our better institutions and the like . . . do not allow the ideology to have any fruitful set-up in our country." He asserted that the issue of racial discrimination against blacks in the United States "has often been exaggerated deliberately by those who hoped to bring the country into disrepute." On the Middle East, where the United States had a special interest and had just landed its marines (in Lebanon), Nkrumah proposed a "quarantine" for the whole region, with the sovereignty of every state there "guaranteed by the Great Powers" and the oil resources "brought under international control, and used for the benefit of the local people."[75] In the joint communiqué with Eisenhower, he agreed that a solution to the problems of the Middle East should be found within the UN framework, and he expressed his concurrence with the United States plan to withdraw its troops "as soon as the UN can act effectively" to assure Lebanon's independence and integrity.[76]

Speaking to the Council on Foreign Relations in Washington, Nkrumah envisaged a dominant place for the West in postcolonial Africa. He observed that colonialism had ensured that most of Africa's ties were with Europe. Africans, he asserted, welcomed such links, stressing, "You cannot cancel 100 years of history, and history has brought Africa and Europe into close community." For Nkrumah, the Western impact on Africa was very deep-rooted: he equated "modern life" with "Western life," a culture that had been adopted by Africans. In his words: "The hopes and ambitions of [Africans] have been planted and brought to maturity by the impact of Western civilization. The West has set the pattern of our hopes, and by entering Africa in strength it has forced the pattern upon us." In large part, the speech was a call for more Western involvement in Africa's economic development: "the Western Powers," Nkrumah emphasized, "have the opportunity to play a new and vital role in Africa. The colonial phase is dead or dying. But a new phase is opening in which the whole of this continent will struggle to achieve the institutions and opportunities of modern life."[77]

On 28 July 1958, at a luncheon meeting with the National Foreign Trade Council, Nkrumah announced Ghana's willingness to enter into an investment guarantee agreement to insure United States private investments in Ghana.[78] Two days before this announcement, Ghana's External Affairs Ministry had submitted an *aide-mémoire* to the United States embassy in Accra, expressing Ghana's willingness to enter into an agreement with the United States that "would bring investment in Ghana by United States Government citizens or corporations under the protection of the United States Investment Guaranty Program." The note explained that Ghana was willing to enter into an agreement on guaranties "against expropriation and refusal of permission to permit conversion of capital and profits into United States currency."[79] On 30 September 1958, Ghana adhered to the United States Investment Guaranty Agreement.[80]

Nkrumah's visit was more about appearance: the most he got from Eisenhower was a "mutual interest" (as opposed to a commitment) in developing the Volta River Project,[81] the issue of the moment to the Ghanaian government. Yet, beyond diplomatic niceties, Nkrumah and his associates did not disguise the fact that they were highly pleased with their United States trip.[82] Nkrumah himself personally believed that the visit strengthened "Ghana-America friendship."[83] That Washington must have shared this feeling was evidenced by its response to a food crisis that plagued northern Ghana (in the areas of south Mamprusi, Nanumba, Dagomba, and Gonja) in the third quarter of 1958. In July 1958, the ICA mission in Accra alerted its Washington headquarters to the food crisis, that stemmed from extremely dry weather conditions in the areas. By the beginning of August, the Ghanaian government had started to confront the crisis: it appointed a food commissioner, embargoed the export of foodstuffs from Ghana, and set up a committee to monitor the situation.[84] The Ministry of Agriculture later calculated the total crop loss in the affected areas as 50 percent.[85]

On 4 September, the ICA mission in Accra reported to Washington that the Ghanaian Ministry of External Affairs had requested United States assistance in the form of 10,000 tons of maize under Title II of Public Law 480 for famine relief in northern Ghana, and that Ghana was prepared to pay for the ocean freight charges. It stressed the political capital to be reaped from Ghana receiving the maize at the "earliest practicable date." The mission was also quick to draw attention to the standard ICA practice: that Title II assistance could only be provided in cases where the recipient lacked the resources to grapple with a disaster. The exception to this rule, it recalled, was when, for political reasons, the State Department made a request on behalf of the recipient country. Based on this rule, the mission held that Ghana's food crisis did not constitute a famine as defined by law. It further noted that food could not be given to a country under Title II for the purpose of stabilizing prices during a food shortage since such assistance was intended to be distributed free to disaster victims. The mission did, however, concede that Ghana would be eligible to benefit from Title II if weather and crop reports indicated the failure of "current maize crops" in northern Ghana.[86]

The United States embassy in Accra disagreed with the ICA, emphasizing that there were "reasonably good economic" as well as psychological and political justifications for Title II assistance to Ghana. It argued that by its own understanding, the principal criteria for Title II assistance were crop failure "or similar problem and inability of final consumers [to] pay for food both of which apply here." While maintaining that the situation had not yet attained the proportions of a famine, the embassy referred to the measures already put in place by the government to cope with the crisis and insisted that the matter "is certainly urgent." It also noted that Ghana was prepared to pay for the maize and "excluding other considerations government would have started procurement through Crown Agents three weeks ago." The embassy cautioned that notwithstanding the technicalities, a negative response would immediately result in an unfavorable official and public reaction in Ghana and such a reaction would impair the diplomatic position of the United States in the country. In "this underdeveloped country," it continued, "tangible and easily identifiable aid like food" was bound to have a "maximum impact on government and public" particularly in the northern part of the country where Egypt was eager to play on Muslim ties. The embassy recalled that Nkrumah and his cabinet were delighted with their visit to the United States and were "now looking for concrete aid." It believed that no such aid was coming to Ghana in any meaningful sense: there were "no assurances of significant U.S. contribution" to the Volta project, and DLF assistance for Ghana was "most unlikely even if excellent projects [were] available"; in the "foreseeable future," Ghana "will receive only technical assistance which for all its virtue is viewed by government as marginal contribution." It therefore argued that generous and prompt Title II aid "could do much to remove impression of U.S. stinginess or indifference" to Ghana.[87]

The embassy also emphasized that Nkrumah had been cooperative and understanding of the United States position on diplomatic issues involving the Middle East and Chinese representation in the UN. It was emphasized that he had been equally "sensible on racial issue and more cautious on Pan-Africanism than many of his colleagues would like him to be. He has thus far remained aloof from formal relations with communists." As a consequence, they embassy argued that Nkrumah needed to be compensated for his "positive neutralism," which "has on the whole been helpful to U.S." The embassy believed that given the time constraint, Ghana would not turn "elsewhere" for food supplies, but a negative response "would offer incentive and of course opportunity for communists far more attractive than Volta," and would signal to Ghana that its pro-United States orientation was not paying off.[88] Swayed by the political arguments, Washington brushed the technicalities aside and offered 5,000 tons of yellow dent corn valued at $650,000 under Title II. The agreement was signed in Washington on 8 October.[89]

Some Trying Moments

The United States/Ghana relationship was not altogether a fairy one. The year 1958 saw Nkrumah's foreign policy begin to take a new, bold turn, with an emphasis on "positive neutralism," the termination of colonialism and neocolonialism in Africa, African unity, and the projection of the "African Personality" in international diplomacy. These were the benchmarks of the speech on foreign policy that Nkrumah gave to the National Assembly on 15 July 1958.

Hitherto, there had been no clear-cut statement of Ghana's adherence to nonalignment. On the eve of independence, Nkrumah pledged that his government would neither be "aligned with any particular group of powers or political bloc" nor did it "intend to follow a neutralist policy in its foreign policy." Ghana, he declared, only desired "to preserve its independence to act as it sees best at any particular time."[90] Until 1958, this was the only statement on Ghana's nonalignment policy. A foreign policy that is at one and the same time nonaligned and nonneutral is quite likely to pose conceptual complications, both in articulation and execution. The July 1958 speech cleared away the ambiguity. Nkrumah now stressed Ghana's adherence to "an independent foreign policy," a policy of "positive neutralism and nonalignment" with ideological or political blocs. This policy, he explained, implied that Ghana would act "as it sees best at any particular time in the light of the country's obligations under the United Nations Charter, our position in relation to the African continent, our adherence to the principles enunciated at the Accra and the Bandung Conferences, and our desire to safeguard our independence, sovereignty and territorial integrity."[91]

The speech was significant in another respect. Not only did it highlight the increasing emphasis that Nkrumah placed on Ghana's policy in Africa, it also served notice that he was retreating from his embrace of apartheid South Africa. Ghana, he said, accepted the principle of equality of all races in Africa and condemned "unreservedly racialism in all its forms and shapes anywhere it occurs in Africa." There was also an unequivocal commitment to the liberation of colonial Africa. Nkrumah promised that it was the intention of his government "to do everything within its power" to encourage all nationalist movements "in any part of Africa that are dedicated to the emancipation of colonial peoples and to the welfare and prosperity of their peoples." To this end, he announced that Ghana would host a conference of the nationalist movements in all the dependent territories of Africa. It was hoped that "a blue-print for the total liberation of other dependent territories in Africa" would emerge from the conference. He assured the colonial powers that if they were prepared to cooperate with the "newly invigorated spirit of nationalism" sweeping through Africa, "the result might well be beneficial to them as it will be to us in Africa." This was followed by the warning that the struggle for freedom and independence in Africa "cannot be stayed."[92]

The speech also gave clear indication that Nkrumah envisaged Ghana playing a leadership role in and for Africa. He talked of the "fundamental unity of outlook on foreign policy" that was emerging among independent African states and pledged that Ghana would promote this "distinctive African personality" in international affairs and also work for African cooperation in the economic, social, and cultural fields.[93] The increasingly African focus of Ghana's foreign policy and Nkrumah's bid for the leadership of Africa were already in evidence before the July 1958 speech. Accra had hosted the meeting of independent African states in April 1958.[94] Nkrumah followed that up with a tour of the participating states. And in December of the same year, he hosted the All-Africa Peoples Conference.[95]

Washington was uncomfortable with the increasing assertiveness of Nkrumah's foreign policy rhetoric. A memorandum circulated in the State Department in June 1958 observed that at a state banquet during his visit to Cairo, Nkrumah had stressed the importance of liberating Africans still under colonial rule, and the need for independent African states to unite in order to consolidate their independence. Concern was particularly expressed over his statement that the acquisition of independence undermines "forces of reaction, forces of imperialism, and forces of intrigue." The memorandum also recalled that in October 1958, the organizing secretariat of the All-African Peoples' Conference issued an advance leaflet that adopted the "following communist-type cliches": "Peoples of Africa, Unite! You have nothing to lose but your chains. You have a continent to regain! You have Freedom and Human Dignity to attain! And to our oppressors we say: 'Hands off Africa! Africa must be free!'" It was pointed out that the leaflet listed colonialism, imperialism, and racialism as the chief items on the agenda. The department worried that the conference would

> evolve into an emotionally-charged, intemperate and leftist-dominated circus along the lines of the Cairo Afro-Asian Solidarity Conference of last December. The net result would be to further encourage neutralist and anti-Western tendencies in Africa and increase tensions in dependent areas and particularly pressures for premature independence while at the same time hardening the attitudes of the metropoles. Outbreaks of violence could result.[96]

It was no coincidence that when they met on 30 June 1958 (a few days after Nkrumah's visit to Egypt), President Tubman of Liberia told Nkrumah that he did not like his (Nkrumah's) foreign policy rhetoric because it was "too provocative, warlike, and antagonistic." Quoting the biblical exhortation that a mellow voice extinguishes anger while a grievous word stirs up anger, Tubman advised him to tone down his public statements and moderate his attitude towards the British.[97] The voice was certainly Tubman's, but the message sounded like Washington's.

The point is that by 1958, Washington did not wish for any strain in the relationship, which was why it hid its exasperation with Accra's rhetoric from the public. Washington must have believed that through its embassy in Accra and through third parties (notably, Liberia), it could privately express its worries and even exercise some restraining influence on Nkrumah. Above all, it must have been satisfying to the United States that the strident rhetoric was not translating into a shift away from the West. After his 1958 tour of independent African states, Nkrumah confided in Flake that he was impressed by the level of economic development that Nasser of Egypt had achieved with Soviet assistance; but that he had also noticed that Nasser was not happy with Egypt's dependence on Moscow for assistance because none was forthcoming from the West. Nkrumah also mentioned that he had advised Nasser to visit Yugoslavia's President Josip Broz Tito, who was in the vanguard of the nonalignment movement, to demonstrate his independence of Moscow. More significantly, he believed that the countries he visited saw Ghana as the vanguard of progress in Africa, and that if he could industrialize Ghana with United States assistance, other African countries would be encouraged to hitch their stars to the United States and the West instead of the USSR.[98]

Washington must have also taken note of the fact that in his July 1958 speech, Nkrumah reiterated the importance Ghana placed not only on the UN and its specialized agencies but also on its Commonwealth relations, noting that for small countries such as his, international organizations were the only hope for a peaceful world. In addition, he reiterated his desire to improve Ghana's economy as a means of improving the people's quality of life. To achieve this goal, he said that his government had sought to create "stable internal conditions" in which foreign (read Western) capital could flourish, and had entered into technical aid arrangements with the UN and some of its specialized agencies as well as with the United States, Britain, Israel, and Canada.[99]

"Close and Trusting Friends"?

In 1958, Douglas Anglin observed that Ghana's neutralism was different from India's because the former "is more clearly oriented to the West and more dependent on it economically and militarily than is India." This meant that "[d]espite Ghana's declared intention of seeking friendship with all nations . . . her relations with the Soviet bloc have not been on the same footing as her relations with the West."[100] While acknowledging that Nkrumah was personally attracted to Marxism, Anglin emphasized that this personal preference had still not "translated into a policy of conciliation to communism either at home or abroad."[101] A year later, it seemed that the "communists" were enjoying some visibility in Ghana.

In January 1959, Ghana hosted an East German trade mission led by that country's deputy minister of trade. A member of the mission stayed behind as acting commercial counselor. A similar Polish mission, led by that country's deputy minister of foreign trade, followed just a few days later. Shortly afterward came the announcement that Poland would assign a trade commissioner to Ghana and that both countries would later establish diplomatic relations. In the following month, East Germany announced that it was about to establish a diplomatic mission in Ghana.[102]

In the second half of 1959, a total of eighteen Polish engineers were in Ghana, all involved in the preliminary phases of an iron mining and foundry project; by October, all but three had returned to Poland. By the end of the year, the Polish shipping line was calling at Takoradi twice a month. A party of three Czech businessmen was in Ghana in September, doing feasibility surveys on small industries.[103] In the following month, it was announced that discussions were being held on the possibility of the Soviets establishing a steel industry in Ghana.[104] In the same month, Ghana congratulated the People's Republic of China on its tenth anniversary. The message expressed the "earnest hope that succeeding anniversaries will bring continued prosperity" to China and "a strengthening of the ties of friendship" between Ghana and China.[105]

In spite of this widening "communist" presence, the truth was that the Western position in Ghana was not being eclipsed. Accra was, at the most, giving a symbolic expression to its nonaligned posture—which was why it still used a long spoon in its dealings with the "communists." For example, in September 1959, Ghana granted "limited consular rights" to the East German trade representative, bestowing certain privileges such as the free entry of specified personal effects. The representative was not allowed to perform any consular functions. It was understood that Ghana was highly sensitive to its cocoa trade with West Germany and therefore had no plans to establish even a trade mission in East Germany.[106] And as earlier noted, Ghana was yet to open an embassy even in the Soviet Union.

Above all, Washington must have found comfort in the fact that Israel was actually Ghana's best friend. By 1959, Israel was assisting Ghana in several key spheres: in establishing and running a flying training school to train officer pilots for the Ghana Air Force; in operating a nautical training college; and in providing both capital and management for the Black Star Line (Ghana's official shipping line) and the Ghana National Construction Company. According to the United States embassy in Accra, Israel was also having "a profound influence" on the Ghana labor movement, the United Ghana Farmers Council, and on the development and expansion of cooperatives in Ghana. Besides, Israeli technicians were reported to have "given advice on such matters as rural water development and the establishment of a textile industry."[107] The prominent, and definitely influential, Israeli presence in Ghana certainly worked to the advantage of the United States. In November 1957, the United States embassy in Accra proposed that Washington should exploit the "present high favor of Israel" with Accra "to neutralize [the] influence of Egyptian Embassy when established" in Accra.[108]

It took a potential threat to reveal the strength of United States/Ghana relations by 1959. The background was Foreign Minister Ajo Adjei's meeting of 2 October 1959 with Fred Hadsel of the United States mission at the UN. It was later reported that in the course of their conversations, Adjei sharply criticized the United States position on African questions in the UN, asserting that the United States was in the habit of supporting the colonial powers. This caused Washington to explain the motivating principle of its UN votes on African issues, noting that the metropolitan powers had also frequently protested that the United States was siding with the Africans against them in the UN.[109]

In a memorandum intended for Accra, the State Department stressed that rather than taking positions on African questions "on purely political grounds," the United States had usually sought to deal "honestly with each problem on its merits." The objective, it was stated, had been to fashion out "constructive compromises between the two [African and European] positions" within the confines of the UN Charter. While regretting that achieving such compromises had not been easy and had in fact "often led to criticism from both sides," the department insisted that the efforts were in accordance with the United States view of the UN as a forum for solving international problems and the "role of the United States as a leading member of the United Nations." Ghana was reminded that "cooperation in the United Nations is a two-way street," and that the United States itself had not been receiving such cooperation from the authorities in Accra. As the department put it, "On some of the major political issues before the General Assembly, many of the African delegations, especially Ghana, have voted with the Soviet Bloc and against the United States and other Members of the Free World." Washington's checklist of seventy-nine votes in the General Assembly in 1958 showed that Ghana voted eight times with the United States, forty-eight with the Soviets, and abstained or was absent twenty-three times.[110]

The protest note was not passed on to Accra as the State Department had originally framed it. The United States delegation at the UN had reservations about the tone of the memorandum. It emphasized that in spite of its "exaggerated nature," Adjei's criticism was in fact made in a "most friendly manner . . . which should not be destroyed by unnecessarily contentious reply." The delegation believed that while cooperation is usually a two-way street, the United States should not give the impression that it would abandon either its principles or its friends simply to obtain votes. The department's attention was also drawn to the "real danger in citing exact statistics of voting record, since without careful analysis such statistics may be unintentionally misleading." It was explained that some of the votes were "procedural" while others were on issues that Ghana considered "as dividing along East-West lines." While conceding that Ghana was very emotional on African issues (especially on Algeria and on France's atomic tests in the Sahara), the delegation emphasized the cordial relations that existed between the United States and Ghanaian missions at the UN, particularly in the Fourth Committee where, according to the delegation, "African matters are holding center of stage" and the two delegations were engaged in "constructive give-and-take discussions and real cooperation." On these grounds, the department was advised that the memorandum should not be passed on to Ghana and that a "carefully planned oral presentation [of the] essential points" would be more appropriate.[111]

The delegation had a restraining impact on the State Department. A fresh directive went to the United States embassy in Accra: the cordial relations between the United States and Ghana at the UN were noted, and the embassy was advised that in discussing the earlier memorandum with the appropriate officials in Accra, it should stress United States "appreciation" and desire to continue "frank discussions [on] all UN problems" with Ghana.[112]

On 3 December, William Flake, the United States ambassador to Ghana, who had been away on leave since the beginning of November, called on Adjei. Flake later reported to Washington that "[e]ven by digging almost to the point of gouging, I was unable to bring forth any remarks as strong as those he had expressed to Mr. Hadsel in New York." Flake observed that although Adjei regretted that the United States could not more openly and more forcefully support Africa on certain issues, he was equally understanding of the fact that the United States was torn because of the loyalty to its NATO allies and assured Flake that such loyalty would not strain Ghana's relations with the United States. On independence for Algeria, Adjei was reported to have urged the United States to continue to exert such pressure as was possible on de Gaulle, "short of wrecking the NATO" alliance.[113]

Adjei defended Ghana's voting record at the UN, emphasizing that there was no commitment to side with the Soviets as Accra treated each case on its own intrinsic merits. According to Flake, "The Foreign Minister seemed relieved to have me imply that a Ghana vote with the Soviet Union on some specific issue had no wider meaning than a United States vote on some specific issue that did not agree with Ghana's vote on the same issue." Adjei was said to have concluded by noting that Ghana and the United States "are and must remain close and trusting friends," even though they might occasionally differ or be disappointed with each other's response on a given matter. While recognizing that Adjei could have been more cautious with him than with Hadsel, Flake took pains to assure Washington that he had no reason to doubt that Adjei had been quite sincere in their conversation, "and his actions generally have supported what he has said to me in the past." The State Department was therefore advised that the matter should no longer be pursued.[114]

Flake's assessment was confirmed a week a later. During the National Assembly debate on Nkrumah's annual foreign policy statement on 16 December, there were suggestions that Ghana should strongly protest the United States/British abstentions from the UN vote on French atomic tests in the Sahara.[115] Adjei rejected any such protest, explaining that Ghana too had on several occasions voted against the United States and Britain, "So that if on this particular occasion they did not see eye to eye with us we should not quarrel with them; we have exercised our sovereign rights and they too have exercised their sovereign rights."[116]

On the whole, there is no doubt that the declared United States objective of getting Ghana "associated with the West"[117] was clearly on track at various levels by the end of 1959. In October 1959, the United States embassy in Accra was able to conclude: "Our trade relations with Ghana, including access to raw materials produced in Ghana, are good. Our political relations with Ghana are friendly and fruitful."[118]

Things Fall Apart

At the beginning of 1960, there was still no obvious strain on United States/Ghana relations, and the "communists" still seemed hard put to gain a firm footing in Ghana. An early draft of NSC 6005, dated 29 February 1960, contended that in spite of the overtures of the Soviet bloc, "Ghana remains basically Western in orientation."[119] But as the year wore on, Washington's assessment changed dramatically. The United States Senate study mission that toured some African countries in November/December 1960 found that "[s]omething has gone sour in our relationship" with Ghana. "The extreme symptom of this condition," the mission observed, "is Ghana's angry opposition to U.S. policies, primarily toward the Congo, and secondarily toward Algeria and colonial issues raised at the UN. On our side, conjectures in the press about Ghana slipping into the communist bloc have materially affected our official relations."[120]

The breach in United States/Ghana relations was first brought into the open by Secretary of State Christian Herter. On 23 September 1960, he charged that Nkrumah, by his speech before the UN General Assembly earlier that day, "has marked himself as very definitely leaning toward the Soviet bloc."[121] Before then, the State Department had already privately expressed concern that the "communists" were gaining ground in Ghana. In its telegram of 12 August 1960 to the United States embassy in Accra, the department cited China's opening of an embassy in Accra, the alleged Soviet interest in the Volta project and steel industry, the alleged purchase of Soviet aircraft by Ghana, and the use of Soviet aircraft by Nkrumah as evidence of an "apparent increase [of] Bloc influence [in] Ghana." It asked the embassy for an "appraisal of [the] seriousness [of] this apparent drift toward Soviets."[122]

Flake assured Washington that what seemed to be an apparent drift towards the Soviets was only a reflection of Ghana's "determination to pursue more actively its policy of positive neutralism (like India, it now seeks political support and material benefits from any source as long as it feels this can be done without dangerous involvement). It is not a turning away from the West. . . .It is what Ghana regards as the final breaking of chains that before independence kept Ghana confined entirely to the West." He explained that the United States could not stem this development and advised that "we must expect some more manifestations of closer relations with Soviets."[123]

On the specifics, Flake recalled that Ghana had always recognized China but had never taken the initiative to exchange diplomatic missions. He believed that Ghana must have accepted the opening of an embassy by the Chinese as "a routine process." The alleged Soviet interest in the Volta project, he said, "does not attract Nkrumah so long as he has faith in effective support from U.S. as he now has." But at the same time, Nkrumah "sees no reason to turn down USSR offer to build steel mill if it proves feasible," especially since United States public and private agencies were not interested in the project. Ghana's purchase of four Soviet aircraft was explained as part of an expansion scheme that also involved the simultaneous purchase of five new British aircraft and three used aircraft from the United States. Flake pointed out that the Soviet terms were more favorable than the others, and that the Soviet aircraft had already been delivered and were therefore being used "pending the delivery of the new aircraft."[124]

Flake was emphatic that "Ghana is not communist and I detect no desire here that it become so." While he would not minimize the dangers inherent in the increasing contact with the "Soviet Bloc," he urged that "we must be careful not to attribute motives to G[overnment] O[f] Ghana that do not exist." Flake assured the department that "[t]he West has always had a dominant position in Ghana and in my opinion this will continue." He advised that to match the Soviets fully in cultivating Ghana's friendship, the United States needed to be "more positive in supporting Africa against European NATO powers. We would also have to oppose 'neo-Colonialism' in Africa and encourage Ghana's desire to create (in the words of Nkrumah) 'a socialist New Jerusalem' in Ghana."[125]

The compelling and unambiguous tone of Flake's response must have reassured the department that Ghana was not yet lost. There is no evidence of a sudden accretion in the "communist" strength in Ghana in the month that followed. Indeed, until the end of 1960 at the least, Ghana still put its faith in the West and especially the United States.[126] A clear pointer to this was Accra's handling of an unsolicited, generous aid package from Moscow. In August 1960, trade union leader, John Tettegah, and Tawia Adamafia, both board members of Ghana's Bureau of African Affairs, went to Moscow and met with Soviet Premier Nikita Khrushchev. The Kremlin and its guests concluded agreements on trade, and on economic and technical cooperation. The agreements provided for Soviet aid in prospecting for Ghana's mineral resources, in building industrial plants and power dams, in the organization of model state farms, and in cooperation in training Ghanaian workers. In addition, the two sides agreed to give each other most-favored-nation treatment in all trade and shipping matters. The Soviets undertook to send to Ghana machinery and equipment, rolled steel, petroleum products, and building materials. In return, Ghana was to send to the Soviet Union cocoa beans, coffee, copra, and rubber. To underwrite its commitment to these projects, Moscow instantly extended a long-term credit of 160 million rubles (£G14.7 million) to Accra.[127]

"In its three years of independence," W. Scott Thompson writes, "Ghana had sought aid for only one major project, the Volta scheme, and had spent two full years in negotiations with the Americans for it. Suddenly, £14,700,000 [Ghanaian] was offered to develop Ghana, almost without asking for it and apparently with no strings attached." The Soviet gesture was definitely tempting. But according to Thompson, "Caution could still be detected in Accra. There was a significant period of delay before the government made public the communiqué of 4 August 1960" containing the agreements with the Soviets; and it was not until the end of April 1961 that Accra approved the Soviet credit.[128] It is thus safe to conclude that by September 1960, Nkrumah was not "leaning toward the Soviet bloc" and that the state of "communism" in Ghana at the time was not strong enough to strain United States/Ghana relations.

The circumstances leading up to the rupture of United States/Ghana relations in 1960 were more complex than Herter implied. It is, for example, certain that Washington was irritated by Nkrumah's move (in 1958) towards an activist, African-centered foreign policy and more so by its accompanying rhetoric.[129] While United States/Ghana relationship may have been sufficiently resilient to withstand this development in 1958, it appears that the more Accra asserted itself in Africa, the more Washington worried about the general direction of Ghana's foreign policy. By February 1960, Washington had resolved to "[d]iscourage, whenever possible, Ghana's current tendency to support extremist elements in neighboring African countries."[130] It is, however, worthy of note that until September 1960, Washington kept its exasperation with Accra away from the public domain. The clear departure in this sequence was the Congo, which imploded in July 1960.[131]

The Congo—The Last Straw

As Thomas Hodgkin aptly observed, the Belgians who colonized the Congo formulated for themselves a role similar to that of the philosopher-king in Plato's *Republic*: their task, as members of "a benevolent, wise and highly trained elite," was to manipulate the "plastic minds" of their African subjects, to instill in them certain "unquestioned and unquestionable moral values," to provide them with certain amenities, but to prevent them from ever coming into contact with such "contaminating" concepts as liberty and self-determination.[132] In terms of its remote cause, the Congo crisis was a result of this paternalism. By the end of 1958, Belgium still envisaged that independence for the Congo belonged to an infinite future. This meant that there was as yet no shift in the essence of its colonial policy, which was to ensure that Africans remained hewers of wood and drawers of water. It was only in 1954 that a Congolese, Thomas Kanza, was first admitted into an undergraduate university program.[133] By 1960, only thirty Congolese had university degrees. African political parties were not allowed until December 1957. As with the civil service, the upper cadres of the military were blocked to the Congolese.[134] At independence, the army consisted of "some 24,000 soldiers and non-commissioned officers, all of them Congolese, and about 1,000 officers, all of them Belgian."[135]

The riots of 4–7 January 1959 in Léopoldville forced Belgium to hastily open negotiations on independence with Congolese political leaders. Thereafter, events moved so fast that the Congo was hurried into independence on 30 June 1960 with Joseph Kasavubu as president, and Patrice Lumumba as prime minister. Six days later, Congolese troops mutinied because General Emile Janssens, their Belgian commander, had told his Congolese noncommissioned officers that independence had no bearing on the military and their service conditions. Almost immediately, the mutiny spread to the civilian population and escalated into large-scale anti-European unrest. On July 11, Moïse Tshombe complicated the crisis by announcing the secession of Katanga, the Congo's richest province. That same day, and without consulting the Congolese government, Belgium injected its metropolitan troops into the crisis, ostensibly to secure European lives and property. The arrival of more Belgian troops and the fact that they were actively supporting the Katanga rebels led to widespread suspicion among the Congolese that Belgium was embarking on a reconquest of its former colony.[136] In this way, the Belgian military intervention "contributed to a spiraling deterioration in relations between the local Belgians and the Congolese, and so to further disorder."[137]

On 14 July, after they had been denied landing rights at Elisabethville, which was under the control of Belgian troops, Kasavubu and Lumumba broke off relations with Belgium. At the same time, they appealed to Soviet Premier Nikita Khrushchev to "watch hourly over the development of the situation" as "we may have to ask for the Soviet Union's intervention should the Western camp not stop its aggression." Moscow pledged "resolute measures" if the West did not stop its "criminal actions."[138]

Lumumba, according to Carole Collins, was driven by the desire for "true independence": above all else, he was anxious not to compromise his country's newly won independence and this predisposed him to strong and total opposition against any Belgian influence in the Congo. His other preoccupation was national unity, "the preservation of the Congo's territorial integrity at any cost." Thus Lumumba could not countenance accommodating the secessionists in any way.[139]

By mid-July, the objectives of the Congolese government were to expel the Belgian troops and end Katanga's rebellion. To achieve these objectives, Lumumba first appealed to the United States, without success, for assistance.[140] He had no better luck with the UN: the Congolese government had, on July 13, requested UN intervention to end both the Belgian aggression and the Katanga rebellion. The following day, the UN Security Council approved a peacekeeping operation in the Congo. The resolution establishing the operation merely "call[ed] upon" Belgium to withdraw its forces from the Congo, and was silent on Katanga. On 9 August 1960, the council adopted another resolution, which, with specific reference to Katanga, again "call[ed] upon" Belgium to "withdraw its troops immediately." Belgium heeded neither of these resolutions.[141] In desperation, and especially as Belgium was arming the Katanga rebels (even supplying them with planes), the Congolese government turned to the Soviets. The arrival of ten Soviet planes, sixty trucks, weapons, and military advisers to help Lumumba "confirmed the worst fears of the Eisenhower Administration. The President and his advisers realized that the Soviet leader was taking an unprecedented step, one which threatened to alter the balance between the two superpowers. It was the first time the Russians had ever intervened militarily in a conflict thousands of miles from their borders."[142]

In this setting, Lumumba immediately fell out of Washington's favor.[143] CIA Director Allen Dulles informed the NSC on 21 July 1960 that Lumumba was "a Castro or worse,"[144] an agent for the Soviet penetration of Africa. Eisenhower himself hardly disguised his antipathy for Lumumba. On one occasion, he wished that "Lumumba would fall into a river full of crocodiles."[145] In addition, there was general agreement in Washington that Lumumba was the obstacle to national reconciliation and stability in the Congo.[146]

On 5 September 1960, Kasavubu, who had been converted to the United States cause, announced Lumumba's dismissal. Lumumba was in a strong position to turn the tables: he had majority support in Parliament as well as in the army, and he was noted for his fiery oratorical skills and charming, persuasive personality.[147] Besides, as Andrew Cordier, the UN special representative in the Congo, observed, Lumumba "worked around the clock without regard for sleep or meals . . . rounding up support and generally beating down efforts made by the President [Kasavubu] and his few active supporters."[148] Lumumba was hobbled by the UN or rather, by Cordier, an American. Like Washington, Cordier paired Lumumba with Cuba's Fidel Castro: "persons," he wrote, "who are themselves destroyers and who therefore not only become the symbols of Russian influence abroad but the outposts of their effort." To him, Lumumba was "completely irresponsible—if not a mad man," and the "only real solution" was "to remove Lumumba from his position" as prime minister.[149]

Cordier, according to Carole Collins who has studied his private correspondence, not only "had advance notice of Kasavubu's intention to dismiss Lumumba," but he "welcomed the move." Collins has also established that Cordier sent UN troops to close the airport and seize the radio station at Kasavubu's behest. Unlike Lumumba, Kasavubu was not handicapped by these moves: Kasavubu still had access to the government radio station in nearby Congo-Brazzaville, Lumumba had no such means to counter Kasavubu's anti-Lumumba speeches; more telling, the airport was closed only to the Lumumba camp since Kasavubu's supporters were still allowed to use it. Lumumba was thus blocked from shifting his troops from their operations in Katanga to Léopoldville. In the circumstances, Cordier's actions served only to consolidate Kasavubu's "control of the capital and [the] silencing [of] his charismatic rival."[150]

On 12 September, Joseph Mobutu, a Congolese army colonel who had also been won over by the CIA,[151] announced that he was "neutralizing" the civilian government and that the Congo was to be governed until the end of the year by a "collectivity of students and technicians"; in addition, he asked the Soviet and Czech technicians to leave within 48 hours and placed the embassies of the "communist" countries under guard.[152] In the ensuing power struggle, the United States sided with the Kasavubu/Mobutu camp.[153] On 26 September 1960, Clare Timberlake, the United States ambassador in the Congo—who was very influential in shaping Washington's hard-line policy against Lumumba—informed Kasavubu that the United States diplomatic personnel in the Congo were at his (Kasavubu's) absolute disposal. Timberlake added that he had avoided frequent meetings with Kasavubu and his entourage in order not to give the "impression to their opponents" that Washington and the president "were working too closely" together.[154]

Like the United States, the UN was anything but a disinterested arbiter in the Congo. In addition to the anti-Lumumba bias of Cordier and his close collaboration with Washington, it is now clear that, between Kasavubu and Lumumba, UN Secretary-General Dag Hammarskjold favored the former.[155] In August 1960, he asserted that the Congo situation "must come to crisis shortly and that Lumumba must be broken."[156] A few days later, he confided in the United States mission at the UN that all "he was trying to do was to get rid of Lumumba without compromising UN position and himself through extra-constitutional actions."[157] Briefing Harold Beeley, the British deputy permanent representative at the UN, Hammarskjold conceded that "in practice the action of the United Nations favored and was designed to favor Kasavubu."[158]

In large part, the bias of these high UN officials derived from the fact that they saw no contradiction between their positions in an international, neutral, mediatory organization and their pro-Western, as opposed to pro-Soviet, bent. Hammarskjold, for example, believed that Lumumba "has decided to play with [the] East against. . . .the UN," and that "the communization of the Congo" would be inevitable if Lumumba won. Besides, Cordier's contempt for Lumumba was shared by his colleagues. Early in the crisis, Ralph Bunche, the special representative of the UN secretary-general in the Congo (July–August 1960), reported that Lumumba was an "utterly maniacal child." In Hammarskjold's perception, he was "an ignorant pawn, in his utter lack of experience of the big political currents, balances and pressures."[159] No less significant was the considerable influence that the United States wielded over the UN operations in the Congo, especially by largely underwriting the operations to the tune of $100 million a year.[160]

The standard explanation is that the United States objective in the Congo was to hold the line against Soviet incursion[161] and that the UN shared this objective and was thus the "transmission belt for American policy."[162] "Both the UN intervention and United States policy," according to Michael Schatzberg, "were more a consequence of the fear of Soviet expansion" than a response to the Congo's territorial integrity and security needs.[163] There is, however, more plausibility in arguing that there was a fusion of strategic interests (especially anti-Sovietism, access to Congo's uranium deposits,[164] the geographical size of the country and its location at the heart of Africa), as well as what Stephen Weissman has identified as a deeply ingrained "NATO reflex in [United States] African policy."[165] The weighting of each of these factors is an entirely different matter.

Whatever the motives for Washington's conduct, it seems that with Eisenhower's personal knowledge and approval, United States agencies and agents masterminded not only Mobutu's coup but the deposition, arrest, and possibly the murder of Lumumba. A United States Senate report issued in 1975 found that the "chain of events and testimony is strong enough to permit a reasonable inference that the plot to assassinate Lumumba was authorized by President Eisenhower."[166]

Like the United States, Ghana was deeply involved in the Congo crisis, and almost from the beginning, the two had fundamental differences on the issue. To begin with, Nkrumah felt a marked mutual affinity with Lumumba. The latter had attended the December 1958 All-Africa Peoples conference held in Accra. The conference was a watershed in Lumumba's career; it marked "the beginning of Lumumba's Pan-Africanist affirmations. . . .It also marked his transformation from a liberal to a radical nationalist."[167] From then on, the two men took to each other. In addition, from then on, Lumumba consciously imitated Nkrumah's pattern of politics. For obvious strategic reasons—notably, the size, resources, and geographical location of the Congo—Nkrumah welcomed the opportunity of acting as a role model for Lumumba.[168] This camaraderie allowed Ghana some place in Congo's public life. Before the crisis, Ghana sent doctors, engineers, and civil servants and provided Lumumba with a flying secretariat during his tour of Africa and North America in July/August 1960.[169]

It was therefore quite natural that once the crisis erupted, Ghana was the first country to pledge (on 13 July) "all possible aid including, if it is desired by the Government of Congo, military assistance," either directly and alone or through and in concert with the UN.[170] The Congolese responded to the offer and requested Ghanaian troops, the first such request they made. The first set of Ghanaian troops landed on 15 July. By 25 July, Ghanaian troops (numbering 2,340), were the largest single national contingent in the UN force, which then totaled 8,396. At the same time, there were about 370 Ghanaian police officers in the Congo. Besides, "Ghanaian ministers and officials visited and revisited the Congo in quick succession during the coming months."[171]

The United States was well aware of Nkrumah's influence over the Congolese government. This led to the belief, at least, until August 1960, that Nkrumah could be enlisted to serve United States ends in the Congo. As early as April 1960, Washington was already disturbed by what it regarded as the "extent of communist penetration [of the] Congo in the period prior to independence." It considered that Nkrumah's influence could be quite helpful in countering the anticipated "communist" threat "as seen by his urging [the] Congolese [to] keep Belgian Civil Servants and avoid outside influence." Against this background, the State Department chose to encourage Nkrumah to increase his influence over the Congolese, although it was recognized that "this may mean expansion Nkrumah-type extreme anti-colonialism and Pan Africanism should his influence increase in the Congo."[172] Following this policy option, Flake met with Nkrumah on 30 April 1960 and inquired whether he shared Washington's concern that the Congo might become susceptible to Soviet designs. Nkrumah assured him that he was doing all he could to prevent such an outcome.[173]

Early in August 1960, after the Congo had exploded, Eisenhower sent a "personal and confidential" message to Nkrumah, emphasizing that the crisis presented "grave dangers to world peace." According to the message, the United States "agreed that the immediate problem is the speedy resolution of the Belgian troop and Katanga questions." Eisenhower believed that Hammarskjold was "doing his best to carry out his S[ecurity] C[ouncil] mandate" and stressed that the United States was "backing and supporting him to the hilt" because of its conviction that the council's resolution "is the right one" and that "if the UN were unsuccessful or discredited in the Congo, the results for world peace and cooperation would be disastrously tragic." The essence of the message was to invite Nkrumah to look beyond "these immediate problems" to the state of a postcrisis Congo. Eisenhower contended that since it would have "almost no trained experienced personnel to administer the country and operate the economy," the Congo would "be forced for a period of a few years at least, to entrust the country's essential services to outsiders." Anxious that, in this context, the Congo "be effectively protected against conflicting power politics," Eisenhower sought Nkrumah's support for his proposal that "this protection might be provided by means of a contract between the UN and the Congolese Government under which the former would be the exclusive agent for the supply of administrative, technical and financial assistance to the latter."[174]

Nkrumah agreed with Eisenhower's view that the crisis constituted a serious danger to world peace and stressed that the "immediate problem" was the speedy withdrawal of Belgian troops from all of the Congo, including Katanga. He regarded Katanga's secession as the "product of Belgian maneuvers" and held that it would have "the most disastrous consequences not only upon African opinion, but upon the whole balance of political forces in the world." Nkrumah acknowledged that although it was important to shield the Congo from "conflicting power politics and other pressures," the "first task before any other issue can be considered is the withdrawal of Belgian troops." Set in this context, his major disappointment was "the failure to act quickly in the implementation of the United Nations resolution." He therefore urged that the first step towards a resolution of the crisis was to "establish the authority of the United Nations." Nkrumah hinted at his distrust of Western intentions, mentioning the widespread African suspicion that the United States, France, and Britain were "not giving their full support to the United Nations decision that all Belgian troops should be withdrawn from the whole of the Congo. The view which is being taken by some African states is that these powers are deliberately delaying on this issue in the hope that a Katanga state can be created and that the Belgian military occupation can continue and be ultimately justified on a de facto basis."[175]

Nkrumah had cause to feel disappointed with the West. At the onset of the crisis, he was "determined to have the first troops in Leopoldville, but was totally dependent on the great powers to get them there." While the United States and Britain, whom he had approached for help, dithered, the Soviets promptly volunteered two Ilysuhin 18's. The tardiness of the West was not helped when Hammarskjold chided Nkrumah for his haste in demonstrating Ghana's nonalignment by accepting the Soviet offer.[176] The lines were thus drawn early in the crisis. But the tension smoldered until 23 September 1960, when Nkrumah addressed the UN General Assembly. Hardly had he stepped off the podium than the United States took the speech as a signal that he had crossed over to the Soviet side. Secretary of State Herter had called a hasty press conference to denounce Khrushchev's address before the General Assembly. He did so in the strongest possible language. When asked to comment on Nkrumah's speech, he responded:

> There again, very strongly. I would want to read the speech over, as I didn't hear all of it. As much as I heard of it, it sounded to me as though he were very definitely making a bid for the leadership of what you would call a Left-wing group of African states. He, I think, went out of his way from the point of view of showing a very close relationship to what Mr. Khrushchev said. . . .I think he has marked himself as very definitely leaning toward the Soviet bloc.[177]

Nkrumah promptly issued a statement professing surprise since, as he put it, Herter "was, in fact, the last person from whom I would expect such a remark."[178]

Herter's umbrage was indeed ironic. Like the United States, Ghana was also suspicious of Soviet intentions in the Congo. Thus Accra's preoccupation was to insulate the crisis from the dynamics of the Cold War and this meant minimizing, if not excluding, any superpower involvement. This explains Nkrumah's efforts to discourage Lumumba from seeking any Soviet assistance, except under the auspices of the UN. For the same reason, Ghana sought to Africanize the crisis by forestalling all non-African intervention. Nkrumah hoped to achieve this objective "not only by claiming for the U.N. a virtual monopoly of all outside intervention in the Congo" but even more forcefully by his demand that the UN force in the Congo "should predominantly be an African affair composed mainly of African troops."[179]

Much later, Eisenhower, reechoing Herter, wrote in his memoirs of how "Mr. Nkrumah went directly from my room to the United Nations

General Assembly and within forty-five minutes cut loose with a speech following the Khrushchev line in strong criticism of Secretary-General Hammarskjold."[180] Eisenhower could not have meant this as a fair assessment. Using the Congo as an illustration, Khrushchev had spoken very harshly of Hammarskjold for manipulating the UN machinery to further Western interests. In order to achieve an impartial UN, the Soviet premier demanded the substitution of a three-person committee (representing the West, the Eastern bloc, and the nonaligned nations) for the office of secretary-general.[181] Nkrumah did not subscribe to the Soviet proposal to eliminate the office of secretary-general, even after he met with Khrushchev at the Soviet villa at Glen Cove, Long Island, on 25 September.[182] Indeed, Nkrumah went out of his way to canvass support for Hammarskjold among other leaders.[183]

In his speech, which immediately preceded Khrushchev's, Nkrumah expressed his "personal appreciation" of the way Hammarskjold had "handled a most difficult task" in the Congo. His complaint against the UN in the Congo was that it had attempted to restore order without distinguishing between legal and illegal authorities. Nkrumah was, however, willing to accept such a lapse as "in essence growing pains of the United Nations"; he even added that "it would be entirely wrong to blame either the Security Council or any senior officials of the United Nations for what has taken place."[184]

Nkrumah's support of Hammarskjold reflected a remarkable consistency (and independence from the Soviets) in Ghana's policy. At the General Assembly on 17 September, the United States castigated the Soviet Union for unilaterally sending "hundreds of so-called technicians" as well as planes and trucks to the Congo. The Soviets defended their action, insisting that they had acted not only in full compliance with Security Council resolutions but also at the request of the Congolese government. In addition, the Soviets charged that the United States had used the UN secretary-general to oust Lumumba because he represented a threat to Western interests. Following this, Hammarskjold protested his impartiality and asked for a vote of confidence.[185] The next day, Alex Quaisson-Sackey, Ghana's UN representative, on behalf of seventeen African and Asian countries, introduced a draft resolution that endorsed Hammarskjold's Congo policy, asked him to continue to take "vigorous action" toward the restoration of peace and order in the Congo, and urged all UN member states to "refrain from any action which might tend to impede" the restoration of peace and security and to work only through the UN in attending to the crisis. The resolution was adopted by seventy votes to none, with eleven abstentions (including the Soviet bloc).[186] The resolution "was seen as a huge defeat for the Soviet Union."[187] There was thus hardly anything to suggest Ghana's acquiescence in the Soviet criticism of Hammarskjold's performance in the Congo nor was there any basis for the more general charge that Ghana fell behind the Soviet position on the Congo.

Nonetheless, one can easily explain Washington's anger. Nkrumah's speech ranged widely over the world's problems and offered solutions for each. He demanded that permanent UN Security Council seats should be created for Africa, Asia, and the Middle East; that China should be admitted into the UN to make it "more realistic and more effective and useful"; that South Africa should surrender its mandate over South-West Africa; that the NATO countries should pressure Portugal to grant independence to its African colonies; and that France should enter into negotiations with the Algerian Nationalist Government.[188] In case after case, these demands approximated Moscow's and conflicted with Washington's.

On the Congo, which was the primary focus of his speech, Nkrumah amplified positions that had typified Ghana's perspective on the crisis. Incidentally, this perspective immeasurably offended Washington as it was antithetical to the Western interpretation, objective, and approach on the Congo. In detail, he reviewed the origins of the crisis, criticizing Belgium at every step for employing "a system of calculated political castration in the hope that it would be completely impossible for African nationalists to fight for emancipation." He accused Belgium of inciting the riots in the Congo to create a pretext to recolonize the country. He emphasized that the Congo crisis "has more than justified my continuous outcry against the threat of balkanization in Africa and my daily condemnation of neocolonialism, the process of handing independence over to the African people with one hand only to take it away with the other." He upheld the Kasavubu/Lumumba coalition as the legitimate government of the Congo and therefore insisted on Lumumba's reinstatement as prime minister, denounced Katanga's secession, dismissed Mobutu as a "fake," and blamed "imperialist intrigue" as the reason why a document of reconciliation "drafted in the presence of my Ambassador in Leopoldville" had not been signed by Lumumba and Kasavubu. He declared the Congo "an acute African problem which can be solved by Africans only" and therefore proposed that the UN should "delegate its functions in the Congo to independent African states," especially those who had contributed most to the UN Congo operations; such forces, he said, should be under a unified African command with responsibility to the Security Council.[189] On account of its apparently anti-United States tone, Nkrumah's hour-long speech drew a very enthusiastic response from the Soviet bloc. To cap it, Khrushchev stood up and shook Nkrumah's hand as the latter returned to his seat.[190] This spectacle could not have pleased Washington.

On 24 September, Joseph Satterthwaite, the assistant secretary of state for African Affairs, attempted (on Herter's instruction) to meet Nkrumah and formally protest against the latter's General Assembly speech. Nkrumah refused to see him.[191] Satterthwaite could only secure a telephone conversation with Quaison-Sackey. He used the opportunity to indicate that the United States was offended less by Nkrumah's speech per se than by the apparent communality with the "communists." Satterthwaite noted that although Nkrumah was in New York, he was absent when Eisenhower delivered his speech; on the other hand, Nkrumah "with great display, took his seat at the head of his delegation to listen to the 2 hour and 20 minute speech of Premier Khrushchev." On the contents of Nkrumah's speech, Satterthwaite observed that "except for Nkrumah's personal praise of Secretary Hammarskjold, it was difficult to find a word in the speech showing any understanding of the position of the West in the East-West conflict." Besides, Nkrumah made no allusion to the unilateral intervention of the Soviets (in responding to Lumumba's request for assistance) outside UN channels, an intervention the United States held as the cause of the Congo crisis. "Certainly, therefore," Satterthwaite concluded, "the content of the Nkrumah and Khrushchev speeches and the display attached to the reception by the eastern bloc delegates of the Nkrumah speech gave us every reason to believe there had been collusion between the two."[192]

Despite the plausibility of Satterthwaite's explanation, Nkrumah's speech—along with all its supporting scenes—was only a subtext in the United States/Ghana divide. An underlying anti-Ghana resentment seems to have been building up in Washington since mid-August 1960. This had to do with Ghana's role in the Congo crisis. Well before 23 September, Washington knew that Lumumba was receiving very strong backing from Nkrumah. On 17 August 1960, Timberlake, the United States ambassador to the Congo, cabled Washington that "Ghana is at least giving aid and comfort to Lumumba and the communists." He added that Washington should "count on the strong possibility" that Ghana, along with Guinea, "would oppose any change in the Government of the Congo and any action of the UN which would reduce Lumumba's power or change his political course."[193] A month later, he reported that Lumumba was "reportedly hiding out somewhere under Ghanaian protection."[194] At the same time, the United States mission at the UN reported that Nkrumah was the "man who is steering Lumumba."[195] Reports such as these and their broader implications could not have endeared Nkrumah to Washington. In the circumstances, the events of 23 September 1960 merely provided Washington with an excuse to vent its resentment of Ghana's position and role in the crisis. It is, for example, significant that Herter passed judgement on the speech without even hearing or reading all of it.

Nkrumah had decided to attend the fifteenth session of the UN General Assembly because he expected that "the Congo crisis would loom large in the discussions."[196] And with heads of state and government such as Eisenhower, Khrushchev, Prime Minister Harold Macmillan of Britain, Tito of Yugoslavia, Nehru of India, Nasser of Egypt, and Fidel Castro of Cuba attending, he must also have felt that the session afforded a good opportunity to resolve the crisis. In this respect, Nkrumah hoped that he could, with Eisenhower, forge a strategy to be put before the UN for the resolution of the crisis. This hope stemmed from Nkrumah's belief that United States/Ghana relations still had its old flame.

Nkrumah and Eisenhower met on 22 September 1960. For the latter, the meeting went very well. "Mr. Nkrumah," Eisenhower later wrote, "professed, to my surprise, considerable optimism regarding the situation in the Congo. He said the situation was not insoluble, and said that the solution had to be worked out through the United Nations. Indicating his respect for the United States, he said he had taken special steps to arrange a visit to me before going to see Mr. Khrushchev, upon whom he had been invited to call."[197] On the other hand, W. M. Q. Halm (Ghana's ambassador to the United States), who was at the meeting, noted that Nkrumah left the meeting "heartily dissatisfied"[198] because Washington did not share his sense of urgency and concern about the Congo.

At their meeting, Eisenhower and Nkrumah agreed that the UN provided the best forum for a solution of the crisis; both also spoke highly of Hammarskjold's handling of the crisis. From there, Eisenhower launched into a reminiscence of his military exploits during World War II. Nkrumah raised the issue of the Congo again. Herter, who was in attendance, could only say that the United States was opposed to a Soviet effort to place the crisis before the General Assembly.[199] Of course, Eisenhower and his secretary of state had no need to be concerned. They were satisfied with the turn of events in the Congo at the time: that is, the ascendancy of the Mobutu/Kasavubu faction. Washington's celebration was, however, Accra's agony. In essence, Eisenhower and Nkrumah were separated by their allegiance to different causes and personalities in the Congo.

Washington's overriding objective was to ensure that, at the minimum, Lumumba was permanently excluded from political office in the

Congo. A telegram of 24 September 1960 from CIA Director Dulles to the CIA representative in Leopoldville was explicit: "We wish to give every possible support in eliminating Lumumba from any possibility [of] resuming governmental position or if he fails in Leopoldville, setting himself up in Stanleyville or elsewhere."[200] By contrast, Ghana, Guinea, and Egypt were working tirelessly to rehabilitate Lumumba's political fortunes and thus negate the accomplishment of Washington's goal. Their effort involved reconciling him with Kasavubu and restoring the legitimate balance of power in the country. At one point, Timberlake informed Washington that

> Evidence has steadily accumulated that Ghana, Guinea and the UAR have been putting continuous and mounting pressures on Kasavubu and [Joseph] Ileo to reach a compromise with Lumumba. Their maximum goal is reestablishment of status quo ante dismissal Lumumba; failing that, at least his inclusion as one of ministers. I believe this move is sparkplugged by Nkrumah who clings to dream of Ghana-Guinea-Congo union as stepping stone to Nkrumization of Africa. If Lumumba is out of Congo, so is that part of dream. . . .I can think of no greater disservice to the realization of the aspirations of the Congolese people and to our own for them than to stand aside and let these three countries have the field to themselves in such pressure play.[201]

Washington shared Timberlake's apprehension with regard to the efforts to restore Lumumba to power and must have been thoroughly displeased with Ghana for spearheading those efforts.

On 23 September 1960, the day Nkrumah addressed the UN General Assembly, the State Department claimed that "[i]t has unfortunately become clear" that Guinea, Ghana, and Egypt were "deliberately intervening in internal affairs of Congo in violation [of] repeated S[ecurity] C[ouncil] and G[eneral] A[ssembly] resolutions." The interference, according to the department, was in the form "of refusal [to] permit arrest of Lumumba" and attempts to persuade Kasavubu and his camp to embrace a power-sharing formula that accommodated Lumumba.[202] Washington was, in the meantime, very hard at work to frustrate any attempt to reconcile the Congolese factions. On 24 September 1960, the State Department instructed the United States mission at the UN to approach the Ghanaian, Guinean, and Egyptian delegations to make a case against their support of Lumumba.[203]

In Léopoldville, Timberlake notified Kasavubu that Washington was fully aware of the efforts of Guinea, Ghana, Egypt, Morocco, and Tunisia to "effect a reconciliation between Kasavubu and Lumumba" and emphasized that "it would not be profitable to come to an understanding with Lumumba." To drive his point home, Timberlake claimed that "[d]uring the two months he [Lumumba] was in power, he created anarchy throughout country, he fought with his collaborators, the UN and the UN Secretary General, helped bring [the] cold war to Congo by accepting direct assistance [of a] military nature from Soviets, he fanned fires of civil war in [the] country and in summary constituted a centrifugal rather than centripetal force." Timberlake strongly impressed on Kasavubu that for these reasons, the United States was "squarely against" Lumumba, "an evil influence who would be bad for the Congo." Besides, he pointed out the absurdity of Lumumba's continued use of the prime minister's official residence; this, Timberlake cautioned, "constituted psychological advantage for Lumumba."[204]

In dealing with the Congo crisis, both the United States and Ghana started from the assumption that they could mutually develop a common ground robust enough to accommodate their differences and end the crisis.[205] By the end of August 1960, this expectation and all the efforts built on it had foundered because the two governments had opposing perspectives, preferences, and objectives. To Eisenhower and his men, Lumumba was a "communist stooge" and the author of the Congo's crisis, and their ultimate objective was to physically eliminate him.

By contrast, Nkrumah saw Lumumba as a nationalist striving to safeguard his country's sovereignty and territorial integrity. It is true that as the crisis deepened, Nkrumah became Lumumba's chief patron and adopted Lumumba's cause as his own. But he allowed for a middle ground that could accommodate all, provided the nationalist goals were upheld. On this account, Nkrumah held to the legitimacy of the Kasavubu/Lumumba government and hoped for the restoration of the status quo: the expulsion of Belgian troops, the reintegration of Katanga into the Congo, and the reinstatement of the central government with Kasavubu and Lumumba as president and prime minister respectively.[206] Thus at every turn, he readily endorsed the legitimacy of Lumumba's claims to power. When he arrived in New York on 21 September 1960 for the UN General Assembly meeting, Nkrumah did not hesitate to declare that Lumumba was the head of the "legitimate government" of the Congo.[207] By insisting on Lumumba's restoration, Nkrumah put himself sharply at odds with the United States. And by the logic of guilt by association, Washington labeled him a "communist," the label assigned to Lumumba.

Back in Accra, Nkrumah tried to mend the relationship. A few hours after his return, he invited Flake to his office. Their discussion covered a number of issues related to United States/Ghana relations. Inevitably, Nkrumah referred to Herter's comments on his speech and regretted that he was misunderstood.[208] The State Department's response to the Nkrumah/Flake discussion suggested that Washington wished for some distance with Accra. The department noted that Nkrumah's performance at the UN "made [a] most unfortunate impression in this country because it reflected a complete lack of appreciation of Western position on almost every issue and, while consistently critical of the West, failed to find fault with flagrant unilateral Soviet intervention in Congo." It believed that by his actions and deeds, Nkrumah seemed determined to abet the Soviet cause.[209]

In addition, the department found that many other African states did not endorse Nkrumah's performance at the UN. "Under these circumstances," it continued, the United States was disinclined to take any action that would "encourage Nkrumah's role in Africa unless and until he shows greater signs of stability and that his actions are not furthering Soviet objectives in such matters as Congo and UN machinery." "Nkrumah," it was stressed, "has grandiose view [of the] part he is to play in future Africa," a view the department abhored. To its relief, Washington noted that resistance to and resentment of Nkrumah's leadership were being expressed in Africa and especially hoped that a "counter force such as Nigeria will now begin to assert strong [a] moderating influence" on the continent.[210]

Reflecting Washington's changed perception, *New York Times* of 17 October 1960 ran a front-page news analysis, entitled "Nkrumah brands all of Ghana with the Stamp of his authority." Essentially, the piece detailed how Nkrumah had transformed Ghana into his "personal political kingdom": "The state of Ghana is authoritarian and the authority is Mr. Nkrumah. He has followed the classic modern pattern—the creation of a personally controlled party that reaches into every village and directs every aspect of social and political life."

Conclusion

Ghana has traditionally derived its real significance on the world stage from being a leading cocoa supplier. Incidentally, this makes it extremely dependent on the goodwill of cocoa consumers. In the 1950s, the United States was very important in this regard: according to David Apter, a " large part" of Ghana's income at the time came from "American bulk purchases of cocoa."[211] Like other commodity exporters, Ghana is a price-taker for cocoa in the sense that it cannot not fix or even influence the price of the produce. And since Ghana is heavily dependent on cocoa exports for its public revenue, it can ill afford to cut supplies: a serious falling-off in the value of exports would have deep repercussions throughout the economy, with the general level of incomes, the expenditure on imports, and the yield of taxes (especially import duties) falling in a cumulative process.

The United States did, however, have an international public relations need for Ghana in the late 1950s. At the time, Washington needed to demonstrate that it had an enlightened African policy, and Ghana was the most attractive platform for this purpose. From 1958, the resulting romance started losing its warmth: Ghana was becoming increasingly assertive on the African diplomatic and political scene. To the United States, the anticolonial dimension of this assertiveness was akin to an anti-Western (though not pro-Soviet) posture. From then on, the United States regarded Ghana warily. By early 1960, the United States could finally afford, and had indeed planned, a redefinition of its relationship with Ghana.[212] A major incentive for this redefinition was that Ghana was no longer alone on the African stage. By the end of 1959, it was all but certain that independence was also coming to the francophone African territories, and this actually took place between June and August 1960. Thus in September 1960, eleven francophone African states were admitted into the UN. Of even more significance (because of its size, its population of 30 million at the time, and its resources) was Nigeria's independence, which was to come on 1 October 1960. The emergence of these states meant that Ghana was immediately crowded out in the international arena.

In other words, by the beginning of 1960, Ghana had lost its diplomatic significance as the lone African bride. More complicating yet for Ghana was the fact that the francophone states and Nigeria not only eschewed Nkrumah's strictures on Western neocolonialism in Africa, but they were distinctively pro-Western without veering off to "positive neutralism"; and they were also inclined to be conservative on issues such as African unity, the projection of an "African 'Personality,'" and the "liberation of Africa"—issues that Nkrumah held close to his heart.[213] Against this background, the United States had sufficient incentive to redefine, though not necessarily to chill, its relationship with Ghana by 1960. The Congo crisis provided a convenient excuse to do so, although in an acrimonious manner.

Without question, Eisenhower's handling of the Congo crisis generated intense frustration, even resentment, in Accra. It is, however, very unlikely that Nkrumah was prepared to confront Eisenhower to the point of impairing the relationship between their two governments. The restraining factor must have been that by 1960, Ghana was at last beginning to see the possibility of the Volta project materializing, with United States financial and political support. The turning point was 23 September 1960: on that fateful Friday, Nkrumah lost all hope that Washington could be counted upon as a partner in the resolution of the Congo crisis. After Herter's outburst, he spent an hour with Khrushchev at the residence of the Soviet mission at the UN.[214] Ghanaian sources contrast the "frosty" forty-five-minute Eisenhower/Nkrumah meeting of the previous day with the geniality of the Khrushchev/Nkrumah meeting.[215] It is therefore not surprising that Nkrumah accepted Khrushchev's invitation to spend part of the weekend at the Soviet estate on Long Island.[216]

In retrospect, it seems that with these gestures, Ghana was finally appraising the possibilities of closer ties with the Soviet camp. The real first step in this direction was occasioned by Lumumba's murder on 17 January 1961. (His death was announced on 13 February.) According to Richard Mahoney, this had "a shattering effect on Nkrumah. His belief in the UN and in the process of multilateral compromise was deeply undermined. His doubts about Western intentions drifted toward paranoia."[217] It is in this context that one must understand the Accra visit of President Leonid Brezhnev in February 1961. The Soviet leader had not originally intended to visit Ghana; but while in Guinea, Ghana "hurriedly extended an invitation to him which he accepted the same day that Lumumba's death was announced."[218] In July–August 1961, Nkrumah reciprocated the Brezhnev visit with a tour of the Soviet Union, Eastern Europe, and the People's Republic of China. There is thus a causal link between Nkrumah's sense of Western (and particularly, United States) deception in relation to the Congo and his shift to the Soviet camp.

6

THE POLITICAL ECONOMY OF THE VOLTA PROJECT

"The first essential thing," Nkrumah told a press conference in Accra after his visit to the United States in July 1958, "is to build a dam and get the hydroelectric power. Exploitation of the bauxite deposits and production of aluminum would follow." He emphasized that "Ghana needs new industries, and new industries need power. Aluminum production could be dealt with as an industry after the power supply was established."[1] Nkrumah was talking about the Volta River Project (VRP), intended to establish large-scale aluminum production in Ghana by harnessing its bauxite deposits and the Volta's potential for producing sufficient hydropower to make possible the conversion of bauxite into aluminum.

As far as Nkrumah was concerned, the VRP had easily demonstrable justifications. To begin with, colonial rule ensured Africa's entrenchment in an international division of labor that consigned it to the production of primary materials. Ghana's particular inheritance was an economy precariously balanced on cocoa exports.[2] Thus by March 1957, when it achieved independence, the price of cocoa was under £180 per ton, having fallen sharply from a peak of £560 in July 1954.[3] Prices did move upward thereafter, settling at £260 per ton in 1958/59.[4]

"Fragility" is the term suggested by Tony Killick to describe the inherent tendency of the Ghanaian economy towards instability on account of its excessive dependence on cocoa. "First and foremost," he says, "there is the large fluctuation in the earnings that Ghana derives from her cocoa exports. . . .Partly as a result of the unreliability of cocoa tax revenues, the general government budgetary balance is unpredictable."[5] In the circumstance, the Nkrumah government was confronted with the task of devising a fiscal strategy for capital mobilization in an economy constrained by the combination of a weak productive base and very limited private capital formation.[6] Phrased differently, Ghana had to boost its income, either by expanding existing sources of revenue or by establishing new ones. The former option, which implied a vigorous expansion of cocoa exports, had little appeal. The basic market problem with commodities such as cocoa is that they have a very low income-elasticity of demand. Thus with a generally inelastic demand, an aggressive supply behavior only depresses prices further.

Speaking in Accra on 14 January 1957, at the inauguration ceremony of the All African Regional Conference of the International Confederation of Free Trade Unions, Nkrumah regretted that African countries were excessively dependent on commodity exports. "This situation," he observed, "has rendered us extremely vulnerable to fluctuations in world prices for our dominant crops. These fluctuations have had unsettling effects on long term plans and crippled attempts to raise the standard of living." As a consequence, Ghana considered that "it is necessary to develop heavy industries," and the VRP was "designed for such a purpose."[7] Eight months later, Finance Minister Gbedemah told Deputy Assistant Secretary Joseph Palmer 2nd that the Ghanaian government considered that having to rely on cocoa for 60 to 70 percent of its national revenue was unhealthy and that was why Ghana put a very high premium on the VRP. He believed that the project would have a trigger effect by providing power for new industries and for irrigation, which would allow for agricultural diversification.[8]

More fundamentally, Nkrumah regarded poverty as a self-perpetuating vicious circle that could only be broken by a "big push" for industrial development.[9] "One thing," he insisted, "is certain, unless we plan to lift Africa up out of her poverty, she will remain poor. For there is a vicious circle which keeps the poor in their rut of impoverishment, unless an energetic effort is made to interrupt the circular causation of poverty. Once this has been done, and the essential industrial machine has been set in motion, there is a snowballing effect which increases the momentum of change."[10] This deep-seated belief that industrialization held the key for African economies led him to the observation that "[t]here are, however, imperial specialists and apologists who urge the less developed countries to concentrate on agriculture and leave industrialization for some later time when their populations shall be well fed. The world's economic development, however, shows that it is only with advanced industrialization that it has been possible to raise the nutritional level of the people by raising their levels of income."[11] The ordinary Ghanaian agreed with this proposition. In 1948, the Watson Commission reported that "[a]t every turn we were pressed with the cry of industrialization." The commission thought that this demand could be assuaged by the establishment of small-scale industries in such areas as fish canning, furniture, and textiles.[12]

Nkrumah and his fellow Ghanaians were not alone in their faith in the efficacy of industrialization to remedy underdevelopment; it was the orthodoxy of the 1950s and 1960s, whether one talks of Rosenstein-Rodan's model of "balanced growth" through a "big push" for industrialization, Albert Hirshman's "unbalanced growth" through growth poles, Arthur Lewis' two-sector growth model or Walt Rostow's "stages of economic development."[13] These development theorists had their ideas of how the UDCs could achieve what Rostow had called the " 'take-off' to mass production and mass consumption."[14] But for Nkrumah, and he said so repeatedly, electricity was the key. In February 1961, he told the Ghana National Assembly that "[a]ll industries of any major significance require, as a basic facility, a large and reliable source of power." Contending that the industrialization of Europe, North America, Russia, and everywhere else was the result "of the invention of sources of power of hitherto undreamt of size," Nkrumah emphasized that "[n]ewer nations such as ours, which are determined by every possible means to catch up in industrial strength, must have electricity in abundance before they can expect any large-scale industrial advance. Electricity is the basis for industrialization. That, basically, is the justification for the Volta River Project."[15]

There was, of course, a political justification for the Volta project. In 1958, Nkrumah wrote of the "rising expectations" created by independence. African leaders, he said, "are now expected, simply as a result of having acquired independence, to work miracles. The people look for new schools, new towns, new factories. . . .In this situation, however poor the country, the new government cannot sit and do nothing. . . .There must be something to show for independence."[16] Given this mind-set, the VRP must have been perceived as a dramatic dividend of independence.

In March 1957, Nkrumah described the VRP as "my baby and my ambition."[17] He certainly made the project his rendezvous with history, but he had adopted it. As long ago as 1924, the bauxite deposits in the Gold Coast and the Volta's hydroelectric possibilities had induced the colonial administration to draw up plans for an integrated aluminum industry. From then on, thoughts and plans on the project advanced through various stages. By 1957, much time and money had already been invested in planning and discussing the VRP that many believed it was a worthwhile scheme.[18]

Nkrumah, as should be obvious at this point, had an absolute belief that electricity had enormous external economies for the entire economy, and for industrialization in particular. Consequently, his focus was almost entirely on the hydroelectric component of the VRP. The hitch was that Ghana did not have the wherewithal to build the dam. This put the project (and Nkrumah) at the mercy of external parties. In the event, the British and then the United States governments insisted that the existing and estimated future demands for electric power in Ghana were insufficient to justify the hydroelectric project, and therefore that it would make economic sense only if an adequate demand could be guaranteed in advance. Incidentally, Ghana also had considerable deposits of bauxite, and a lot of power is required for the conversion of bauxite into alumina and then into aluminum. This was how and why aluminum production became the economic justification for the dam project.

The British White Paper

Aluminum established itself as a nonferrous metal of major importance in the aftermath of World War II. Beginning with the aircraft industry, it was soon in heavy demand for shipbuilding, residential construction and home improvement, for the production of cans, cylinder blocks for cars, railway and bridge carriages, and in the electrical industries (as both a conductor and in associated metallic compounds).[19] Increased and increasing demand created worries about supply possibilities as every industrialized country wanted an assured source of aluminum.

By the late 1940s, Britain, which had to pay scarce dollars to obtain 80 percent of its aluminum supplies from Canada, was anxiously seeking new sources in the sterling area. Aluminum of Canada Limited (ALCAN) and the British Aluminum Company (BAC) were willing to help by establishing a smelter in the sterling area. A study by both companies considered the Gold Coast a promising site. Meanwhile, the Gold Coast government had in 1949 appointed William Halcrow and Partners to investigate the potential value of the Volta River to the economy of the Gold Coast. In August 1951, the firm submitted a favorable report on the prospects of developing hydroelectric power for aluminum production.[20] Following these reports, discussions were held in October/November 1951 and in May 1952 in London and in June 1952 in Accra between the British and the Gold Coast governments as well as the aluminum companies. Based on this groundwork, the British government was

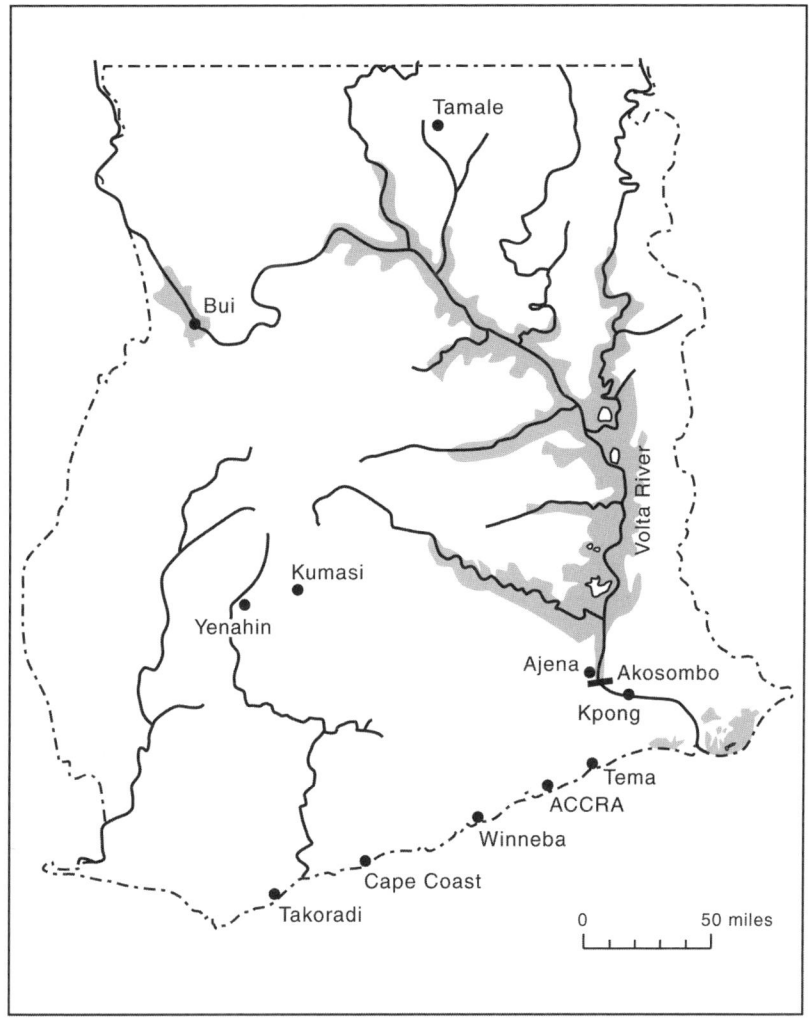

Ghana: The Volta River Project

able to issue a white paper in November 1952 declaring that, in principle, it favored a hydroelectric-bauxite-aluminum project in the Gold Coast.[21]

The white paper envisaged the construction of a dam, 2000 square miles, across the Volta River, as well as a power station capable of generating about 600,000 kilowatts. Both were to be located at Ajena, seventy miles from the mouth of the river. There was also to be an aluminum smelter at Kpong, twelve miles from Ajena, which would use all but about 50,000 kilowatts of the Volta-generated power to manufacture aluminum from the Gold Coast's bauxite deposits. The smelter was to have an initial installed annual capacity of 80,000 tons and an eventual annual capacity of 210,000 tons. Along with the construction of the power station, the dam and the smelter, there was provision for an extensive investment in public works, ranging from the provision of new port facilities to the building of new railways, roads, and houses.[22]

The financial estimates projected an ultimate capital outlay of some £144 million, of which £100.5 million was earmarked for the initial stage. Of the overall figure, the Gold Coast government was to provide the £26 million for the public works. The cost of the power project was estimated at £54 million, toward which the British government would provide £46 million as loan financing and the Gold Coast at least £8 million. The cost of the smelter was estimated at £64 million, to be shared in the ratio of 1:1:4 between the British and Gold Coast governments and the aluminum companies. The maximum expenditure of the British government on the entire project was to be £57 million. In return, up to 75 percent of the aluminum produced was to be assured to the British domestic market for thirty years.[23]

The white paper showed that Britain was interested only in securing an assured supply of aluminum from the sterling area. In 1951, British consumption of aluminum was 316,000 tons, and it was calculated that this would rise at an average annual rate of 5 percent over the period 1950–60. It was estimated that the Gold Coast project would supply close to fifty percent of total British requirements by the early 1970s.[24] For Ghana, the project was a completely integrated aluminum—producing operation that promised a broad multiplier effect on the economy and society: the provision of an assured source of electricity that would support industrialization; aluminum-related secondary industries; the realization of the fishery and irrigation possibilities of the lake to be created by the dam; the development of technical skills and the generation of employment opportunities; a broadening of the narrow base on which the economy rested, through a valuable export material; infrastructural expansion, with the construction of new transportation and communications facilities and other public utilities; and an increase in public revenue through taxes from all these activities.

The Preparatory Commission's Report

After the white paper was issued, the two governments and the two aluminum companies still considered it necessary to have a preparatory commission further examine the project. The commission, established in 1953 and headed by Robert Jackson,[25] became so bogged down with details that it took until December 1955 to complete its work. Its report noted that the primary object of the project was to produce 210,000 tons of aluminum per annum. This was predicated on the accomplishment of five conditions: the development of the bauxite mines (especially those in Aya and Yenahin); the construction of an aluminum smelter and township around Kpong; the completion of the port at Tema; the building of new railroads to link the mines with the smelter and the port; and the construction of a dam across the Volta River. The commission hoped that the dam, to be located at Ajena, would hold back the river for about two hundred miles and thus create a 3,500–square-mile lake, the largest body of dammed water in the world. It envisaged that the water would be capable of generating 600,000 kilowatts of continuous power supply. Most of the power would go to aluminum production, but there would remain "ample reserves of power available to the Gold Coast Government for many years to come." The commission estimated that the construction of the dam and power installations would take seven years; the rail lines, approximately six years; the smelter, four years; and that the Tema port would be ready in "good time."[26]

The commission pronounced the Volta project economically, technically, and commercially sound. More specifically, it held that the project would bring large-scale industry to the Gold Coast and provide the country with a new export along with a reliable market for it; that in this way, the project would relieve the Gold Coast of its excessive dependence on cocoa and make it less vulnerable to fluctuations in cocoa yields and prices; that since aluminum would earn twice as much per worker as cocoa, the VRP would double the earning capacity of the Gold Coast; that the loans for the dam and power installations would be repaid from the sale of power, with the implication that the Gold Coast would eventually own the dam and power installations free from debt. The commission also demonstrated that the VRP would benefit Britain: by developing a large-scale source of aluminum within the Commonwealth, the project would save Britain £35 million a year (which was the amount the sterling area would otherwise expend for the purchase of the commodity from dollar sources). The commission was satisfied that the problems of health and sanitation, including river blindness, which would arise with the new lake, could be effectively controlled.

The commission's financial estimates were substantially higher than those put forward in the 1952 white paper. The figure for the initial phase was now £162 million instead of the £100.5 million quoted in 1952, and the cost of the smelter had shot up by 42 percent to £91.2 million. The overall cost of the project jumped from the £144 million proposed in 1952 to £231.3 million (or £309 million if allowance was made for the commission's anticipated 40 to 50 percent increase in costs before the work was completed).[27] In part, these increases had to do with the fact that the commission was far more ambitious than the white paper. For example, its public works were estimated at £72.5 million instead of the original £26 million. Similarly, cost of the dam and power project increased by 12.5 percent to £67.6 million because the commission envisaged a 10 percent increase in generating capacity.

The British and Gold Coast governments as well as the participating aluminum companies knew of the commission's report some months before it was made public. This enabled them to discuss the report among themselves ahead of its publication. On the side of the British government, Peter Thorneycroft, the president of the Board of Trade, circulated a memorandum among his cabinet colleagues at the end of February 1956. After noting that from the commission's findings, the VRP "can be judged to be economically and technically sound," he was quick to add: "however desirable the Volta scheme may be, I am greatly troubled at the prospective financial burden." Thorneycroft pointed out that the British government would be required to make a direct investment of £72 million (and possibly £107 million if account was taken of the 40 to 50 percent allowance for inflation suggested by the commission) instead of £52 million as originally estimated. In addition, the Gold Coast would be able to draw on its sterling balances for the investment of £75 millions, and the aluminum companies had the option of raising half of their investment on the London market. Based on these figures, the memorandum estimated that the cost of the project on Britain's balance of payments could add up to more than £150 million.[28] Given this picture, Thorneycroft expressed "the deepest misgivings about our embarking on capital commitments of this order."[29]

By 1956, the cost-benefit analysis of the VRP had gone beyond economic considerations. This was not lost on Thorneycroft. On purely economic grounds, he would "regard the sums involved as a quite disproportionate insurance against a possible shortage of aluminum in the United Kingdom." Nonetheless, he felt that "there is no doubt that an abrupt withdrawal by the United Kingdom at this stage would cause a major breach of relations between this country and future Gold Coast Governments, which would probably turn elsewhere for assistance to bring about the Volta scheme." Indeed, as he put it, withdrawal would incur a heavy political cost: "It is not too much to say that a decision to withdraw Her Majesty's

Government would adversely affect our influence on, and relations with, West Africa for years to come." Caught in this dilemma, Thorneycroft recommended that the Gold Coast and the aluminum companies should be assured that the British government remained "ready to participate in the scheme"; that the pattern of investment contemplated in 1952 would be reconsidered "in view not only of the substantial increases in costs disclosed in the Preparatory Commission's reports, but also in view of the United Kingdom's many other commitments and serious economic situation"; and therefore that the British government could only participate in the scheme "if there is an assurance of substantial financial support from outside the sterling area," and that in this regard, the World Bank should be approached as a possible source of funds.[30]

Alan Lennox-Boyd, the secretary of state for the colonies, endorsed the views of Thorneycroft: "I agree that in our present financial circumstances we cannot shoulder the same proportion of the increased cost of the scheme as we envisaged in 1952 and that we should therefore seek to enlist the support of the International Bank." Lennox-Boyd was equally concerned that "our withdrawal from the scheme would adversely affect our influence on and relations with West Africa for years to come." More than Thorneycroft, he drew attention to the wider implications: "the example of the Aswan dam and the Indian steel works has not been overlooked in Africa and there would be no surer way of driving the present anti-communist Gold Coast Government to seek economic ties with the Soviet bloc than to fail in our endeavors to bring the Volta scheme to fruition."[31] At their meeting of 8 March 1956, the cabinet approved Thorneycroft's proposals "for handling the next stage of the negotiations," including inviting World Bank participation in the project.[32]

As a result of the cabinet decision, talks were held from 4 to 10 April 1956 between officials of the British and Gold Coast governments as well as the participating aluminum companies. On purely commercial grounds, and this was what mattered for the companies, the commission's estimates made the Gold Coast a high-cost producer (and this meant poor returns on investment). For one thing, the estimates were so high that any resulting power rates would have made aluminum smelting uneconomical. As a consequence, the only way the companies could possibly have been induced to invest in the VRP would be for the Gold Coast to subsidize the cost of power used by the smelter. The companies, according to the official British account of the meeting, were also concerned "at the uncertainties attendant upon a project of this magnitude in an underdeveloped country. And they are troubled about the risks of a political and administrative deterioration in the Gold Coast following independence." Their overall strategy was thus "to keep the scheme alive, presumably with a view to keeping others from taking their place in it, but not to commit themselves to embarking upon it (even to the limited extent of their present proposals) until they have seen how the Gold Coast conducts its affairs as an independent country."[33]

The companies were, in effect, no longer prepared to have the smelter company buy power on a cost-plus basis; instead, they proposed that the smelter company should buy power under a long-term contract "at a price fixed before the power plant was constructed." In addition, the companies "thought that a price tolerable to them in conditions of today would only enable the power plant to operate profitably if the interest on the capital investment" did not exceed 3.75 percent; they also proposed that for the "first few years of the project they would not use local bauxite but rely on imported alumina"; and that their contribution to the cost of the smelter at the first stage (120,000 tons) would be limited to about £24 millions, "all in equity capital."[34]

On its part, the British government stressed that its contribution "would be for a finite sum at fixed rate of interest." This meant that it would not share in the equity risks; that it could not "contemplate advancing money at less than the full cost to itself of borrowing for a comparable period; in the present circumstances this would be between 5 percent and 5½"; that it could not provide capital for the scheme to the extent contemplated in 1952; and therefore that steps should be taken to seek substantial assistance for the scheme from sources outside the sterling area, "notably the International Bank."[35]

As would be expected, the combined effect of these proposals confronted the Gold Coast delegation with a great difficulty. Above all else, it was certain that even with the involvement of the World Bank, the Gold Coast would have to shoulder a far greater financial burden in seeing the project through than it had ever contemplated. The only decision taken at the meeting was the agreement that officials of the British and Gold Coast delegations should recommend to their respective governments that the World Bank should be invited to consider "at an early date the whole project in the light of the report of the Preparatory Commission and of the April discussions."[36] The parties ruled out soliciting official United States participation on the grounds that Washington was unlikely to contribute directly to financing an aluminum project sited in the sterling area.[37]

The report of the preparatory commission was released on 27 July 1956. In its public reaction, the Gold Coast government pointed out that an agreement would be negotiated "satisfactorily" between it, the British government, and the two aluminum companies. The statement added that "[i]t has for a considerable time been contemplated" that the World Bank "might be associated with the project and both Governments and the aluminum companies have agreed that the bank should now be invited to make a general assessment of the scheme. The bank will send a mission to the Gold Coast later in the year to make a general survey of the country's economy, and this survey will naturally give particular attention to the possibilities of the project."[38]

Speaking for the British government, Lennon-Boyd declared that "because of the substantial increase in the estimated capital cost of the project, it will be necessary to review both the framework and the method of finance." He added that "as the next step," the World Bank "is being invited to make a general assessment of the project and to indicate the extent to which it would be willing, in principle, to participate in it if agreement on the framework could be reached between the two governments and the aluminum companies."[39]

It should be said that as far as the British government, ALCAN, and BAC were concerned, the VRP had run into serious difficulties well before the commission's report was released. By July 1956, the aluminum companies had committed large financial and technical resources to projects in many other parts of the world. In Africa alone, the VRP had its rivals in terms of projects combining hydroelectric power with aluminum production: Konkoure in Guinea, Kouilou in French Congo, Inga in the Belgian Congo, and Edea in the Cameroons.[40] These commitments lessened the interest of the companies in the VRP. Besides, the expansion schemes ensured that aluminum supply was likely to meet demand for as far ahead as the experts cared to forecast. In point of fact, supply matched demand in Britain and the United States at the end of 1956.[41] These factors combined to ensure that, as with ALCAN and BAC, Britain's enthusiasm for the VRP and its readiness to back it financially waned.

Enter Washington, Enter Kaiser

As early as 1950, the VRP was attracting sufficient interest from American firms for the State Department to request its consulate in Accra to submit a detailed report on developments "to date."[42] This level of private interest was not evident within official circles. The ECA, the only official United States agency that gave it a thought, cited the time span (seven years) required to construct the project to explain its unwillingness to participate in it.⁴³ By 1952, however, Washington was beginning to give consideration to some financial participation in the VRP: Secretary of State Acheson informed the United States consulate in Accra and the embassy in London that no loan or grant for the project was under consideration by the United States government either directly or through its agencies because no request for any such loan or grant had been received. He explained that if it so desired, two avenues for United States funds were open to the Gold Coast: the Export-Import Bank (which could consider a loan request within its statutory limits) and the Mutual Security Assistance program. The latter, Acheson explained, could finance some aspects of the project under the Basic Materials Program and would consider a request submitted through the British Colonial Office.⁴⁴

Of greater significance was that Nkrumah himself was opening the VRP door to private American interests. In June 1951, he was at Lincoln University, his alma mater, to receive an honorary doctorate degree and deliver the commencement address.⁴⁵ It seems that Nkrumah used the opportunity to ask Horace Mann Bond, Lincoln University president, to assist him in developing a plan whereby American companies and the United States government could be interested in making available capital (finance and machinery) and expertise (in management, engineering, and construction) to help develop the economic and mineral resources of the Gold Coast. Bond called this matter to the attention of Louis Detwiler, a financial and management consultant. With the help of a very enthusiastic Detwiler, Bond was able to arrange elaborate discussions on the subject with the heads of a number of engineering, construction, mining, and industrial organizations. Leading companies such as the Anaconda Corporation and Reynolds Metals were involved. The discussions yielded a plan for the development of the Volta River Project and the Gold Coast's natural resources, for which purpose the United American Management Corporation was formed. The corporation had Detwiler as president, and its offices in New York.⁴⁶

The plan called for a self-liquidating loan of $600 million from the United States government to the Gold Coast government, with American private interests undertaking the engineering, construction, and operation of the VRP in cooperation with the Gold Coast government. The loan was contingent upon the United States government being privileged either to purchase up to two-thirds of the total aluminum production or to delegate others to purchase various amounts of this share. Primary rights to purchase the remaining one-third or to designate others to purchase various amounts of it were reserved for Britain on the same terms and conditions on which the Gold Coast government agreed to sell to the United States and its designees. While the British white paper proposed an initial total annual aluminum production of 80,000 tons, with an eventual production increase up to 210,000 tons per year, the Bond/Detwiler plan contemplated a total annual aluminum production of 600,000 tons.[47]

Some time between December 1952 and early January 1953, Bond and Detwiler traveled to Accra and presented their plan to Nkrumah. Detwiler reported that Nkrumah authorized them to pursue the matter further and to arrange such meetings between officials of both governments as might be necessary. As a follow-up, Detwiler wrote to Secretary of State Dulles in January 1953. The letter, written on behalf of the United American Management Corporation, stressed the urgent need for the United States to step into the VRP in order to secure important natural resources for rearmament and the maintenance of its national economy as the keystone of prosperity in the "free world." "The current annual United States demand," Detwiler recalled, "is now over 1,500,000 tons of aluminum, and it has been forecast that within twenty years the United States will need three times as much, but the free world's needs will, by then, have soared to more than four times its current requirements. Yet the Gold Coast, as stated above, has a high-grade bauxite ore deposit estimated in excess of 225,000,000 tons which is lying idle." The VRP, Detwiler further argued, "offers the additional advantage of being in position to develop a substantial capacity of low cost hydroelectric power for the manufacture of aluminum from its bauxite deposits."[48]

It does not apear that Dulles even acknowledged Detwiler's letter. And that letter was the most the United American Management Corporation achieved. Its world collapsed quickly. On 21 March 1953, Bond and Detwiler returned to Accra. A little later, Nkrumah mentioned that he was embarrassed by Detwiler's presence as it created the impression that he was being duplicitous with the British on the VRP.[49] It is worthy of note that Bond and Detwiler were met at the airport by Archie Casely-Hayford, the minister of agriculture and natural resources.[50] It was highly unlikely that the minister would have done so without Nkrumah's knowledge and consent. It seems that Detwiler created the difficulties for himself: he was too much in the open at a time when Nkrumah desired that his dealings with the Americans be kept discreet so that he could still keep the door open for the British government, ALCAN, and BAC.

There was another, perhaps, more important, reason why Nkrumah had to cut Detwiler off: there were signals that the United States government itself would be willing to help. Earlier in March 1953, the State Department informed its consulate in Accra that United States interests held "over 50 percent shares" in ALCAN's parent company, Aluminum Limited.[51] On 24 March 1953, the day before Nkrumah disowned Detwiler, William Cole, Jr., the United States consul in Accra, met with Nkrumah and explained to him the American interest in Aluminum Limited and thus in ALCAN. The consul also showed him a memorandum from the State Department on the possibility of obtaining a grant or loan from official United States sources for the VRP. With reference to Detwiler's efforts, Cole explained that official bilateral loans were pursued through government channels. Nkrumah was said to have expressed a keen interest in United States involvement in the aluminum companies, emphasizing that he would like to see American capital in the VRP as that "should help put an end to silly stories to the effect that I'm a communist!" He emphasized that the scale of the project was such that there was room for investment from other sources besides those mentioned in the British white paper and hinted that he intended to explore the possibilities at the official United States end, even though he knew that the British would not take kindly to such an exploration. Nkrumah derided Detwiler and the Bond/Detwiler plan, saying that the VRP was "much too large for a small man like Detwiler."[52]

Neither the United States nor Ghana pursued the opening created by the Nkrumah/Cole meeting. Indeed, it was more than three years before officials from both countries discussed the VRP together again, and that was in December 1956, when Robert Jackson met in Washington with State Department officials. For Ghana, the restraining factor all along may have been that Britain was still very much in the picture. But by December 1956, there was every indication that Britain would rather have the United States take the lead in generating external assistance for the VRP. It seems that the objective of Jackson's trip to Washington was to build confidence for the project in Washington, especially against the background of the preparatory commission's report. He readily admitted that the VRP had two unsettling features: its staggering cost and the seven years it would take to build the dam. He, however, placed more emphasis on the project's redeeming features. One, according to Jackson, was that the project had wide political support in the Gold Coast. There was thus the assurance that it would continue irrespective of which political party was in power. Second, Nkrumah was personally very keen on attracting Western capital investments, which should gave confidence in the security of foreign investments in the Gold Coast. Jackson finally emphasized that the Gold Coast government would "continue to look primarily to the Atlantic Community," that

Nkrumah wanted no help from the Soviets for the VRP and that if the project did come to fruition, it would "represent a sound political and economic investment in Africa."[53]

Ghana's independence celebrations in March 1957 afforded the next opportunity for an exchange of Ghana/United States views on the matter. Meeting with Vice President Nixon, Nkrumah spoke at length and with intense passion on the VRP. "History," he asserted, "has shown that political and economic independence must proceed *pari passu* and that the former cannot be effective without the latter." He returned to his oft-repeated theme: that Ghana's economy was predominantly agricultural and heavily dependent on cocoa exports. "This means," Nixon heard, "that the health of its economy is directly related to the price of cocoa which has fluctuated widely. Only a year ago cocoa brought £500 per ton. Currently the price has dropped to £180." With these figures, Nkrumah dramatized the unhealthy situation created by such heavy reliance on cocoa and reiterated his deep commitment to diversify the economy through agricultural development and by exploiting the country's mineral resources, particularly bauxite. However, he left little doubt that his main focus was on the latter, and that its execution was hampered only by the lack of funds. Besides considering the VRP as a matter for exploration with the interested British, Canadian, and World Bank parties, Nixon could only assure his host that the United States would "continue to watch the situation carefully."[54]

Some United States private interests were not content with simply watching the situation. In April 1957, a group of American businessmen representing Utah Construction Company of San Francisco, Foreign Construction Associates of Houston, and Winslow Cohn and Stetson of New York presented Ghana with a proposal for an American syndicate to finance the VRP. They planned to complete the project in four years and thereafter exercise complete control over it, although the returns were to be split equally with Ghana. G. van B. Slagle and Fraser Leith, who led the group, assured the United States embassy in Accra that twenty large United States corporations and investment houses such as Halsey Stuart, Kuhn Leob, Chase, and Boston First Bank could be counted upon to follow on the plan.[55] On the basis of the proposal, Nkrumah gave the Slagle/Leith group a written three-month "first refusal," effective 18 April 1957, to negotiate for the financing, construction, and operation of the project.[56]

In addition to the VRP, the Slagle/Leith group had undertaken to help Ghana raise money for a housing scheme in Tema. The arrangement was that Ghana would contribute half of the £11 million needed for the housing scheme while the syndicate would raise the balance from United States and UN agencies.⁵⁷ The real interest of the Slagle/Leith group was in the VRP. As Slagle was later to explain, they threw in the housing scheme to convince Ghana of their good faith and ability to raise money (even from official United States sources).⁵⁸ It would also seem that they intended it as a *quid pro quo* for the possible extension of their ninety-day option on the Volta project.

With Nkrumah's guarantee in hand, Slagle and Leith made frantic efforts to raise the money they needed to retain the project. Although their efforts came to naught, they did signal to other United States interests that the VRP was well within their reach. On 1 May, Leith approached Kaiser Industries Corporation with his proposal. The Kaiser people, who were hearing of the VRP for the first time, were certainly not attracted to the idea of working under Leith's direction. But they smelled gold in his proposal and immediately arranged for a meeting with the State Department to discuss the matter. The meeting was held the following day, between William Duggan, the international relations officer of Southern African Affairs, and Chad Calhoun, vice president of Kaiser Industries. Essentially, Calhoun (Kaiser's point man in Washington) stated that his company "might be interested" in the project if ALCAN and other non-American groups "do not now enjoy a legally-based favorable position." He wanted the department to help him ascertain from Accra how things stood in this regard.⁵⁹ The day after the meeting, the department asked the United States embassy in Accra about the "existing legal commitments if any," and whether the Ghanaian legislature had taken specific steps to terminate such commitments.⁶⁰ The reply was that ALCAN had a ninety-nine-year concession for the bauxite deposits and that there was as yet no legislative action to cancel the commitment. The overall thrust of the message, however, was that the way was open for any party interested in the project.⁶¹

Meanwhile in Washington, Slagle was making frantic attempts to meet Nixon. The latter's office helped him secure an appointment with the State Department instead. At the department on 10 May, he showed Deputy Assistant Secretary Joseph Palmer 2nd the agreement he and Leith had secured from Nkrumah, in which they had been given three months to obtain financial backing to execute the VRP. Slagle said that he urgently needed financial support from the United States government in order to cement the deal. He asked for an Export-Import Bank loan of $100–200 million, confident of raising the rest in the form of equity investments from private interests such as automobile companies, the Sun Life Insurance Company of Canada, aluminum companies, and Petrofina (a Belgian oil company). Slagle was less confident of raising any loans from private sources for the Tema housing scheme; he therefore requested that the United

States government should open a credit line of $30 million for this project. He worried that he was running out of time to raise funds for the housing scheme, which was why he wanted Nixon's intervention to help secure a government loan without much red tape. Palmer recalled that Leith had earlier agreed, but failed, to submit evidence of his group's financial standing. He advised Slagle to forward his problem to the department in writing. Palmer also advised that the ICA was the only official source for the kind of loan they needed, but that ICA funds for the year were virtually exhausted. All the same, he indicated that he would be willing to arrange for Slagle to meet with the ICA.[62]

The department's record of the meeting noted that "Mr. Slagle did not give the appearance of being either a financier or a wealthy man. He seemed tense and wrapped up in this project to the exclusion of all else."[63] This psychoanalysis may partly explain why the Slagle/Leith group was unable to secure official backing in Washington. A more decisive factor may have been that the department had instantly taken to Kaiser the moment Calhoun first showed up a few days earlier. On 15 May, Slagle and Leith were told that the ICA had no funds "either for the present or the coming fiscal year" for the Tema housing program and that in any case, "this type of project was not usually undertaken."[64]

Without the necessary funds, the Slagle/Leith group fell out of contention for the VRP. This left the Kaiser group as the most visible American presence on the Volta. When he met State Department officials again on 23 May 1957, Calhoun reiterated that Kaiser "might be interested" in the project, especially as part of a syndicate of aluminum and financial companies. Such a syndicate, he stressed, had to be exclusive of Slagle and Leith.[65]

In July 1957, London served notice that it was shifting the primary responsibility for assisting Ghana to realize the VRP to Washington. Meeting with State Department representatives, officials of the British embassy in Washington explained that not only was Britain intimidated by the cost of the project, but that "the pressure on the British for greater supplies of sterling aluminum has been steadily relieved by developing production elsewhere in the Commonwealth." Apparently, London had formally conveyed its withdrawal to Nkrumah. The embassy explained that "[a]gainst this background of reduced British interest, Prime Minister Nkrumah plans during his visit to the United States in September to investigate the possibilities of assistance from the World Bank, the American banking community, the American aluminum industry, and the U.S. Government." In this context, the British intended the meeting with the State Department as a reconnaissance of Nkrumah's chances.[66]

The prospects seemed hopeless on all fronts. The embassy was informed that the MSA legislation for the 1958 fiscal year and provision for a development loan fund were still under congressional consideration; but even if the fund was approved and appropriated in the amount requested by the White House, the money would be inadequate for mutual security requirements and would be carefully allocated on the basis of existing priorities, and the VRP was definitely not on the list. With respect to the World Bank, the embassy was reminded that the bank's preliminary survey of the project doubted its economic feasibility and desirability, and that the bank had therefore concluded that its financial involvement would require a fresh, extensive survey not only of the project but the entire economy of Ghana. Several United States aluminum companies, the department also noted, had expressed interest in the aluminum component of the project; but the companies, it was added, usually planned their expansion programs years ahead and were already heavily committed. For private enterprises generally, the outlook was further compounded by the steady rise in interest rates and the accompanying increase in the cost of loan funds and capital goods.[67]

Another official United States/Ghana discussion on the VRP occurred in Washington on 25 September 1957, at a meeting between Gbedemah and Palmer. Gbedemah had come for a World Bank meeting and found time to call on the State Department. The VRP featured prominently in the discussions, but only within the wider context of Ghana's economic development and possible areas of United States assistance. Gbedemah explained the importance of the VRP in the structural transformation of the Ghanaian economy, indicating that until its financing had been settled, the government saw no point in devoting any attention to technical assistance issues. Like Jackson before him, Gbedemah made no requests for official United States assistance, either for the VRP or for any other project.[68]

Enter Eisenhower

A little less than a fortnight later, the VRP was fortuitously thrust at the White House. As discussed in the preceding chapter, a Howard Johnson restaurant just outside Dover, Delaware, had refused to allow Gbedemah and his entourage to have their drinks inside the restaurant; as a consequence, Eisenhower invited Gbedemah to breakfast at the White House. In the course of the meal, Eisenhower heard of the VRP, possibly for the first time, and promised to see how the United States could help.[69] It is possible that Eisenhower did not take that pledge as committing him to anything; it might well have been intended to make Gbedemah feel good after his encounter at the restaurant. But that breakfast can be seen, in retrospect, as the first serious step in Washington's involvement with the VRP.

The breakfast pledge encouraged Nkrumah to write to Eisenhower. In a letter dated 17 October 1957, Nkrumah set out the basic conception of the VRP. The project was described as involving an overall capital expenditure of some $865 million, "though of this a considerable proportion can be found by Ghana and in fact is now being provided in the shape of a new port at Tema and of railway and other related facilities." Nkrumah referred to the work of the preparatory commission and noted that it had pronounced the project technically sound, that it could be carried out successfully, and that it should be competitive in relation to similar projects elsewhere. He was therefore able to emphasize that all aspects of the VRP had been examined with unusual thoroughness and that it been "advanced to such a state of preparedness that should adequate financial resources be available work could commence immediately." Nkrumah explained that his government regarded the VRP "as being of supreme importance to the future of Ghana and we are determined to do all in our power to implement it." He mentioned that the British government, ALCAN, and BAC had been actively involved in the project and expressed the hope that they would continue their participation, but added that his government "is at present completely free to negotiate with other Governments and/or other prospective commercial partners. Indeed, it is more than probable that a much wider consortium will be needed to finance a project of this size." The letter was accompanied by a copy of the report of the commission, to give Eisenhower "full information."[70]

Eisenhower replied on 8 November, thanking Nkrumah for his letter and the enclosed report. Nkrumah had not made any requests and Eisenhower could only assure him that "your country has our best wishes for success in its efforts to solve its problems and to realize its aspirations for a peaceful, stable and prosperous future."[71] Four days later, Nkrumah wrote Eisenhower again, this time specifically requesting United States financial support through a DLF loan for the VRP. Eisenhower replied that there were a number of factors that "we must take into account before making a full reply of your letter." However, Nkrumah was assured that "we shall give your proposal prompt and careful consideration and will communicate with you further as soon as possible."[72]

Washington was indeed treading cautiously, weighing various factors and options. The day before Eisenhower replied to Nkrumah's first letter, the State Department had advised the United States ambassador in Accra to avoid giving Ghanaian officials any hint that the United States would be forthcoming on the VRP "(even in a reduced form) at least at this stage."[73] There is every possibility that the World Bank's conclusions on the VRP considerably influenced the department. The bank had in 1956 sent a small group, not to do a detailed investigation of the VRP per se but to conduct an economic survey of Ghana. As it tried to fit the preparatory commission's findings into its report, the World Bank team concluded that the VRP was too expensive and its size, too gigantic, for Ghana's economy to sustain. In March 1957, World Bank President Eugene Black sent copies of the report to Nkrumah and the State Department.[74]

Even without the World Bank report, the department too was scared by the price of the project, especially since there was as yet no financial commitment from any quarter. In December 1957, an internal memorandum noted that the British and Canadian aluminum interests that held rights to Ghana's bauxite deposits had yet to give firm financial guarantees of their willingness to participate in the VRP, nor were there any such guarantees from the American aluminum companies that had expressed interest in the project. Besides, it was calculated that at most, Ghana itself could put up only $150 million out of the total cost of the project. In the circumstances, the department laid down what was to be the United States position throughout: there had to be concrete assurances of "alternative financing for the major portion of the cost" of the VRP before the United States "can give specific consideration to possible governmental financial assistance."[75]

The department's apprehensions shaped Eisenhower's lengthy letter of 3 January 1958, which was a detailed response to Nkrumah's second letter. He assured Nkrumah that he personally appreciated the importance that Ghana attached to the diversification of its economy, adding, "we are not only interested in this vital task of Ghana's economic development and diversification, but desire to help in such ways as are within the limitations of our resources and other heavy commitments throughout the world." He went on to predicate United States participation in "a project of the magnitude of the Volta" not only on the confirmation of its economic and commercial viability but also on the acquisition of "the total financing which would be required to bring it to fruition." To meet the viability test, Eisenhower asked Ghana to secure firm assurances of participation from the aluminum industry, multilateral agencies, and other governments. He promised that once Ghana had obtained such assurances, the United States would be willing to explore the possibility of financing a part of the project, "such as a portion of the hydroelectric installation."[76]

Nkrumah, it should be said, had turned to Eisenhower as something of a last resort, precisely because he was meeting with no success from other quarters. The British had by 1957 become singularly quiet about the project and there was no indication that they were prepared to stand by their original undertaking to contribute to the cost of the dam. And for all practical purposes, ALCAN and BAC had also dropped out of the project by then. In February 1958, Nkrumah explained to Ghana's Parliament that the government had run into a "vicious cycle" in its discussions on the VRP. Interested governments required that Ghana should first make a satisfactory arrangement with the aluminum companies; the companies wanted to be assured in advance of certain things, for example, the cost of power, which in turn depended on the conditions under which governments might raise loans for the project. He stated that Britain's 7 percent bank rate made it impossible for the project to be financed entirely from sterling sources. So in an attempt to break the deadlock, he had written to Eisenhower, who had offered his good offices in examining possible ways of starting the project.[77]

Nkrumah was being generous in his public interpretation of Eisenhower's letter. In reality, the letter was only reinforcing the "vicious cycle." Like everyone else, Eisenhower was saying that Ghana should come to agreement with other sources, but especially the aluminum companies, as a precondition for any official United States assistance. Having known only frustration over the VRP, Nkrumah was grasping at straws from somewhere, anywhere. Therefore he easily saw hope, not despair, in Eisenhower's letter. In his reply, he expressed appreciation for the interest Eisenhower had shown in the project and mentioned that it "has encouraged us in trying to get this great scheme started."[78]

A more reassuring development for Nkrumah came from other quarters in Washington. On the same day that Eisenhower's letter was prepared, ICA Director James Smith, Jr., wrote to Undersecretary of State Herter that Eisenhower's letter had placed on Ghana the burden of inducing the aluminum industry to "active participation" in the VRP. Smith felt that the ICA, rather than Ghana, was better placed "to serve as the catalyst . . . in this situation." He made it very clear that in assuming this responsibility, the ICA was not committing itself to finance the project, but only "to use our best efforts toward bringing together the necessary elements of the total project." Although skeptical of the outcome of such an effort, Herter gave his blessings: "the ICA," he approved, "should do what it can with regard to the Volta River Project so that in Ghana itself it will be felt that we have given every possible assistance, even though in the end the results prove to be negative."[79]

As things stood by early 1958, the United States was willing to "explore the possibility" of providing a loan to help finance the power plant "if and when private enterprises wanted to finance and operate the smelter." In addition, the ICA was to act as a "catalyst" to determine the interest of United States companies and the possibility of securing financing from any source if Ghana so desired and provided it first cleared up the question of the bauxite concessions held by ALCAN.[80] However, the feedback from the United States aluminum industry was anything but encouraging. Meeting with State Department officials on 24 February 1958, Thomas Covel, vice president of Aluminum Limited Sales Company, New York and Washington, DC, considered the VRP very costly. He stressed that the size of the loans required for the scheme would involve a high interest burden, and that there were therefore serious doubts in the industry as to the feasibility of the project.[81]

According to Covel, the VRP was doomed on another score. Market conditions for aluminum, he contended, were no longer falling, but were "now on a relatively stable plateau," rendering any new investment, and especially one of the size of the VRP, quite unattractive. To drive his point home, he emphasized that plans for the development of the bauxite rights his subsidiary company (ALCAN) held in Ghana had been shelved.[82] Some three weeks later, ALCAN followed up on Covel's intimations: it conceded that "in the present circumstances," it was not in "a position to proceed with the scheme immediately, but that [it] did not wish to stand in the way of other interested parties."[83]

The exit of ALCAN satisfied the basic condition Kaiser needed to play its cards with more vigor. Early in May 1958, Kaiser came into the picture again. Richard Ward, assistant to the vice president of Kaiser Aluminum Company, called at the State Department to confirm his company's interest in the VRP. Ward related that following an inquiry by Carroll Flesher of the ICA, he had—with the authorization of Edgar Kaiser, president of Kaiser Industries (the holding company of the Kaiser conglomerate)—reaffirmed the company's interest in establishing an aluminum smelter in Ghana if and when bauxite and low cost power were available. But Kaiser, he said, would neither participate in financing the construction of the dam nor conduct, at its own expense, the survey to determine the cost of the smelter.[84]

Kaiser's renewed interest was the bait that began to hook the department to the VRP. On 6 May 1958, the department met with the ICA to appraise the latter's efforts to get American private capital interested in the VRP. The ICA reported that ALCAN was not interested in the project "at this time" and was willing to make appropriate arrangements concerning its bauxite concessions in Ghana with any other company or companies interested in the VRP. Reynolds Metal and Kaiser Aluminum were said to be "definitely interested" if assured of cheap power; but only the former was willing to invest a "substantial amount" in the project. Kaiser's interest was in mining the bauxite and in erecting a smelter; it was not interested in financing the costs of the dam and power and actually preferred to purchase its power requirements. In addition, Kaiser Engineering was reported to be interested in obtaining the entire engineering and construction contract for the VRP.[85]

The ICA wanted an American firm to undertake the engineering and construction of the entire project and was therefore enthused by the interest shown by Kaiser Engineering.[86] Subsequently updating the United States embassies on the ICA's efforts, the department reported that two American aluminum companies appeared to be independently interested in the VRP, and that the companies might finance the mining and smelting components, perhaps with Export-Import Bank support, if they were assured of adequate power at cheap rates. Such an arrangement would leave the financing of the dam and the other facilities to Ghana; and at the same time it raised the question of additional financial commitments.[87]

Nkrumah's Visit: Kaiser Wins Round One

More than anything else, Nkrumah's impending July visit put the United States on the spot: it was anticipated that the VRP would be the major concern of the Ghanaian visitors and this put considerable pressure on Washington to decide its position on the matter. On 27 May 1958, the State Department, the Department of Commerce, and the ICA met to develop the position to be taken on the VRP in discussions with Nkrumah and his aides. The meeting reaffirmed previous positions. For example, it was agreed that Nkrumah should be informed that appropriate official United States agencies would be prepared to consider granting loans to help finance the cost of the dam and the power installation when Ghana was able to show the United States that it had "most of the funds in hand necessary for financing the dam and power component of the project and definite commitments from one or more qualified aluminum companies covering the private sector investments."[88]

The major new ground was the ICA view that the only way to get the VRP off the ground was to start with the construction of the dam and power facilities, with Ghana putting up at least $75 million. The ICA believed that such a commitment would induce Kaiser or any other company to seriously consider investing in the VRP. The meeting recommended that if Ghana accepted this proposal, it would then be essential to update the preparatory commission's data to determine whether the production of aluminum in Ghana was still economically feasible. Financing of such a study was considered to be Ghana's responsibility; but as an expression of its "continuing interest in Ghana and the Volta River Project," it was suggested that the United States should offer, through the ICA, to cover half the cost of the study.[89]

Five days before Nkrumah's arrival, the ICA asked Kaiser for an estimate of the cost of such a study. Anxious to gain a firm hold on the project, Kaiser was willing to make a quotation, even without a profit margin: they offhandedly quoted "around $120,000."[90] Assured that Kaiser was interested in doing the updating study on contract with the United States government and/or the government of Ghana, the State Department endorsed the State/Commerce/ICA recommendations. The department stressed that it should be made clear to Nkrumah that no business enterprise worth its salt would be willing to invest in a project of the magnitude of the VRP on the basis of a report as old as the 1955 study. The department agreed that the United States should assist in financing the updating study, and should even be prepared to bear the entire cost if Ghana was not enthusiastic about it.[91]

As envisaged by Kaiser, the study was to cover all phases of the scheme except the analysis of the bauxite deposits, which it intended to do for its own information and at its own expense. Kaiser was also reported to have indicated its desire to explore the possibilities of forming a consortium or a joint venture with other United States firms to build what it called the "production plant" of the VRP.[92] On 23 July, the day Nkrumah arrived in Washington, Kaiser was assured that the State Department would suggest the study to Nkrumah, would offer to split the cost with Ghana, and would recommend Kaiser to do the study.[93]

As was expected, the VRP was for Nkrumah the essence of his presence in Washington. Well before his arrival, the White House, the State Department, and the ICA were fully aware of the VRP story. Thus to them, there was nothing new in Nkrumah's presentation. For Eisenhower on 24 July, Nkrumah painted a graphic picture of his government's struggle to raise the quality of life in Ghana. These efforts, he added, were institutionally constrained by Ghana's dependence on cocoa. Nkrumah's conviction, Eisenhower was informed, was that this limitation could only be overcome by diversifying the productive base of the economy, through agricultural modernization and industrialization. Nkrumah returned to his belief that such a structural transformation required power, the possibilities of which had been investigated in connection with the VRP.[94]

Eisenhower identified the United States with Ghana's objectives of expanding its economy and raising the peoples' living standards. On the VRP in particular, he assured Nkrumah that the United States "always tries to be helpful with respect to projects of this kind." The rider was that private capital provided the best medium for such undertakings. Eisenhower then recycled orthodoxies that were well known in Accra: "If it is possible to get private aluminum companies interested in this project," he stated, "then the remaining financing could be explored" with the World Bank, the Export-Import Bank, the DLF, and other similar sources. He pledged that official United States agencies would be delighted to continue their exploration of those possibilities and that the State Department in particular would continue its efforts to bring the project to fruition.[95]

Nkrumah was grateful for the assurances and pledges of support he received from Eisenhower. His government, he said, would appreciate any assistance that could be given in exploring the matter with private aluminum interests. He, however, hoped that even if such companies were not interested, it would still be possible to press on with the power aspect of the scheme, which would have a lift-pump effect on Ghana's other development requirements and ultimately attract the aluminum industry.[96]

The Eisenhower/Nkrumah meeting was followed the next day by a high-powered meeting exclusively devoted to the VRP.[97] Early in the meeting, Gbedemah emphasized that the VRP was "the most important item for discussion" with the United States. Introducing the Ghanaian viewpoint, Nkrumah emphasized the need for additional electric power to create the springboard for Ghana's economic and industrial development. Observing that "recent" considerations of the project had consistently tied aluminum to the power project, he urged that the two should be de-linked.[98] Ghana's position, as Nkrumah put it, was that the power component of the VRP was necessary for uses other than aluminum production. He mentioned £65 million as adequate for the construction of the power plant. It was Gbedemah who hit the nail on the head. He explained that with Britain and Canada having pulled out, United States public and private capital remained the only hope for the project. Herter spoke in general terms of United States willingness to be helpful, after which he and Nkrumah left the meeting.[99]

Dillon continued the meeting, stating that the United States was "most anxious to see increased interest" by the aluminum companies in the VRP, but that as Nkrumah and his colleagues had observed, the companies wanted assurances of cheap electricity before making any investment. In outlining the ICA efforts to attract United States aluminum companies to the project, he emphasized the proposal to update the preparatory commission's study of the dam and the hydroelectric facilities and to translate it into American terms. The United States, Dillon explained, was willing to bear half the cost of the study, which he proposed should be done by Kaiser. He added that Kaiser had indicated a willingness to take the lead in exploring the possibilities for the formation of a joint company in connection with the aluminum production segment of the VRP.[100]

Worried that the VRP seemed forever jinxed, Gbedemah was not satisfied by Dillon's offer and asked for a more explicit statement of what exactly the United States would do to help bring the VRP to fruition. In response, Dillon said that the United States could not promise anything without the new data the proposed study would provide. Whether or not Kaiser would be selected for it, he said, was still a matter to be worked out with Ghana. But he left no doubt that, in his view, Kaiser was the best candidate for the job. Citing the quality of the jobs Kaiser had done in Australia, Jackson gave his consent to Kaiser doing the study. Trade and Industries Minister Kojo Botsio strongly felt that the next step ought to go beyond the study because aluminum production was not Ghana's priority. He returned to the point earlier made by Nkrumah, that the dam and the hydroelectric facilities should not be tied exclusively to aluminum operations. Like Nkrumah, Botsio stressed that Ghana's primary concern was power that would stimulate new industries with or without aluminum production. Dillon admitted that Washington had been led to believe that 95 percent of the power was meant for aluminum production and that no other substantial consumption would be possible. He held that other potential uses for power might change the picture and that the United States would be glad to consider them. The conferees agreed that a statement would be issued indicating United States willingness to help Ghana with the VRP.[101]

Later that same day, the ICA arranged for Nkrumah and his aides to meet with Calhoun, the vice president of Kaiser Industries. It was at that meeting that Nkrumah accepted the proposal for an updating study of the VRP and agreed to meet half the cost. In addition, he wanted Calhoun to explore the possibility of Edgar Kaiser paying a visit to Accra.[102] Kaiser immediately jumped at the invitation and asked to meet Nkrumah before he left the United States. The two met in New York on 28 July 1958.[103]

From all the discussions, it was clear that United States interest lay primarily in the aluminum aspect of the VRP. It was equally obvious that the United States would not contribute to the project unless United States aluminum companies were keen on it. There was no indication that Washington would contribute to the dam, the power station, and the ancillary works or even "explore the possibilities" of helping Ghana in these respects. According to the Eisenhower/Nkrumah joint communiqué that followed, the United States committed itself only to explore "the aluminum manufacturing phase of the project" with private American interests. It further agreed "to consider how it might assist with loans if the required private financing were assured." The communiqué spoke of Washington's willingness to examine proposals that Ghana "might advance for the use of power from the Volta River for purposes other than the manufacture of aluminum." The two governments agreed on the desirability of the updating study and to share its cost.[104] In concrete terms, Nkrumah may have received far less than he expected. But overall, the trip had the net effect of drawing the United States still further into the execution of the VRP.

A month after Nkrumah's visit, Ghana signed an agreement (in Washington) with the Henry J. Kaiser Company of Oakland, California, to update the engineering reports on the VRP.[105] Two weeks later, seven Kaiser engineers arrived in Ghana to undertake the study. On 22–26 September 1958, Edgar Kaiser and Calhoun visited Ghana. They resumed with Ghana the discussions that had been initiated during Nkrumah's visit to the United States in July.[106]

The Kaiser Report

The Kaiser *Reassessment Report,* published in February 1959, chose Akosombo as the dam site, over Ajena, which had earlier been proposed. The report held that Akosombo would permit a higher dam, would mean less cost, and would permit a larger electricity potential (768,000 kilowatts, 25 percent higher than the preparatory commission's figure). It was estimated that five years (against the previously envisioned seven) would be enough to build the dam at Akosombo; but a year could be saved if the contract was negotiated directly (with Kaiser) rather than by calling for tenders on an international basis. Further, Kaiser believed that it could establish an aluminum plant producing 200,000 tons of aluminum a year with 70 to 75 percent of the Volta dam power potential. On funding, the report hoped that the hydroelectric project including the transmission lines and any civil works would be largely, if not entirely, financed by Ghana. On the other hand, the burden of the aluminum smelter was to be borne by the aluminum industry.[107]

The major problem raised by the report was the question of demand for the power generated over and above the needs of the aluminum industry. The report allocated 330,000 kilowatts for use by the aluminum smelter and allowed another 175,000 kilowatts for the transmission network, to supply various cities and new industries. At the same time, it calculated that the total installed capacity in Ghana was 84,000 kilowatts, of which 53,000 kilowatts were in the mining sector and the rest was available for general utility services and industry. These figures meant that even if the new hydroelectric project displaced the entire installed capacity, there would still remain a huge amount of power to be absorbed by new general and industrial users. This led Kaiser to strongly recommend the development of an industrial market in addition to the aluminum smelter if Ghana was not to subsidize the cost of selling power to the aluminum companies.[108]

The *Reassessment Report* lowered the cost of the project from the previous estimate of $900 million: the dam, power station, and smelter could all be built, Kaiser said, for $339.1 million. Included in this was a five-hundred-mile transmission network, to be built at an estimated cost of $33 million. With the network, it would be possible to deliver part of the Volta power to customers other than the smelter. In the preparatory commission's report, only $450 million was estimated as essential for the basic production of aluminum; most of the balance was for other investments regarded as essential for the general benefit of the country regardless of the decision on the VRP. Kaiser achieved its scale-down by eliminating the expenditure on such ancillary investments: the cost of resettling the lake area population; the cost of health and sanitation works; and the construction of new town sites, port facilities, roads, and railways. Taking these approaches, the difference between the two estimates was not as wide as it would seem.

Over and above anything else, the Kaiser report was in favor of the VRP. This was particularly invigorating for Nkrumah. He promptly invited Edgar Kaiser to Accra for a meeting, held on 14 March 1959. Nkrumah reiterated his determination to have cheap power from the Volta "as soon as possible" and declared that he would therefore like to see the first stage of the Akosombo project "carried out as quickly and as cheaply as possible." As a demonstration of his commitment, Nkrumah asked Kaiser to immediately begin some preliminary work at Ghana's expense; this involved further drilling at the dam site, engineering and design, and the construction of access roads and some housing project.[109]

Nkrumah Rouses Washington

Rising from the meeting with Kaiser, Nkrumah forwarded a summary of the discussions to Flake, the United States ambassador to Ghana. In an accompanying letter, he reminded Flake that the Kaiser report was in favor of the VRP. The implication was obvious: during their visit to the United States, Nkrumah and his ministers were left with the impression that Washington would be more forthcoming if the VRP was certified to be a sound business venture by the updating study. With the ground thus cleared, Ghana expected Washington to stand by this commitment. In the course of the meeting with Edgar Kaiser, Ghana undertook to approach the United States government to "immediately" assist it, as Eisenhower had promised Nkrumah, both in generating interest among industries that would be major consumers of Volta-generated power and also in working out a plan for the public sector financing of the dam construction and power installation.[110] The hope that the United States would assist along these lines was embodied in Nkrumah's letter to Flake. In conclusion, Nkrumah recalled that "President Eisenhower has assured me of his interest in this project which can mean so much to Ghana, and my Government would be most grateful for any action which he and the Government of the United States could now take to bring the project into operation."[111]

Commenting on the Nkrumah/Kaiser meeting and Nkrumah's letter, Flake observed that the Kaiser report had breathed new life into Nkrumah's determination to go ahead with the VRP, with a serious expectation of United States assistance. Washington's response, Flake emphasized, would have a "profound effect on U.S.-Ghana relations and indirectly on U.S. relations with Africa." He therefore urged that the United States "should press forward earnestly to assist Kaiser's effort" to bring the project to fruition.[112]

In the wake of the Kaiser report, Accra was bursting with energy and expectation over the VRP. To Flake's chagrin, Washington did not share this sense of urgency. On 1 April 1959, two weeks after he had transmitted Nkrumah's letter, Flake had to remind Washington that a feedback for Nkrumah was overdue.[113] The State Department could only assure him that a reply was "presently under consideration" and would "be submitted soonest."[114] On 10 April, Daniel Chapman, Ghana's ambassador to the United States, called on the department to get some sense of how the United States was responding to the letter. He gathered that Calhoun was then in Ghana and that the department would be better placed, upon his return, to determine how Nkrumah's request could be met.[115] Calhoun had gone to Ghana to submit his company's proposal for the initial design and construction of the power project. He reported back to the department on 20 April.[116] Still there was no action by the State Department. On 29 April 1959, Flake sent an angry telegram to Washington, pressing that "some message" should be given to Nkrumah "immediately."[117] It was only then that the department drafted a letter which the ambassador was asked to sign and deliver to Nkrumah.

On Ghana's request that the United States assist it in attracting major industrial consumers of power, the draft recalled the efforts to interest United States aluminum companies to establish an operation in Ghana. It was reported that as a result of those efforts, the companies had started to discuss the possibility of forming a combine that could meet Ghana's needs. The draft promised that United States officials would continue discussions with other American industries that were large consumers of power, to see if they could locate some plants in Ghana. On Nkrumah's major concern about United States assistance in financing the dam construction and power installation, the department reiterated Washington's "sincere desire to help Ghana in such ways as are within the limitations of its resources and other heavy commitments throughout the world."[118]

The department also drew Nkrumah's attention to the point made in Eisenhower's letter of 3 January 1958, "that the active participation of the aluminum industry and its ability to undertake the mining and manufacturing part of the project were essential to the success of the entire project, particularly in view of its great magnitude." He was reminded that given this context, Eisenhower had insisted that the United States would be willing to "explore with you what possible assistance it might be able to provide toward financing a portion of the hydroelectric project," but only when "you have firm indications of intention from the aluminum industry to participate and necessary assurances of financial support from either private or public sources for a major part of the required financing." An accompanying note to Flake conceded that the letter was "not completely responsive to Nkrumah's second request" but explained that it was inappropriate for the United States to assume the primary role of arranging the financing of the VRP.[119]

The department's draft was disappointing to both Flake and Abbot Moffat, the director of the United States Operations Mission in Ghana. Arguing that the draft seemed to be an attempt to "disengage from our prior constructive attitude," Flake urged that "we should face squarely the explicit and implicit promises" made to Nkrumah when he visited Washington in July 1958. He observed that the records of the meetings held during that visit justified Nkrumah's expectation that with a favorable report by Kaiser, the United States would not only "take reinvigorated initiative" to interest private enterprise in establishing a smelter but also to consider how it could assist with loans for the dam. Flake informed Washington that in the light of his strong reservations he was withholding the delivery of the letter until it was modified to reflect a "more active participation" by the United States in attracting aluminum companies to the VRP. He suggested that the question of financing the dam could even be deferred on the grounds that it was contingent on the decisions on power construction and consumption.[120]

The pressure from Flake persuaded the department that he was better placed to set the tone of the letter to Nkrumah. He was therefore asked to draft the letter, but within parameters set by the department. It was clearly spelt out that the United States had no intention of assuming the initiative in working out the financing of the VRP, and that the United States position had not departed from the thrust of Eisenhower's letter of 3 January 1958. Besides, it was pointed out that the *Reassessment Report* had pronounced the VRP to be economically feasible, but with a serious qualification: that the aluminum industry must be prepared to make the necessary investment in the smelter, which was to be the major power consumer. Flake was told that in the light of this condition, the United States regarded the participation of the industry as essential before the project could move ahead. Finally, Flake was advised to omit any reference to either the DLF or the World Bank in his draft.[121] Limiting himself within these guidelines, Flake drafted the letter, which was approved by the department and then delivered to Nkrumah.[122]

The department's draft and the guidelines given to Flake suggest that Washington was yet to reconcile itself to any real responsibility for the VRP and that it agreed with Nkrumah's suggestion that probably only a consortium of governments, firms, banks, and international agencies could finance it. In that case, Washington's most important contribution was perceived as convening such a consortium. This role excused the United States from reacting quickly and in more concrete terms to the logic of the Kaiser report. However, the dynamics of the situation—the assurances Eisenhower gave Nkrumah in Washington and the fact that Ghana had no one else to lean on—swept the United States, in spite of itself, deeper into the Volta currents.

On 11 May 1959, Chapman hand-delivered to Acting Secretary Dillon a memorandum on the financing of the dam and power installation components of the VRP. A number of aluminum companies, the memorandum said, had indicated that they would like to have a firm statement from Ghana as to the rate at which power would be sold to potential industrial consumers before making any commitments on the VRP. But without any idea of the approximate interest rates and loan amortization costs of the project, Ghana was in no position to give even a rough estimate of such a rate. The memorandum recalled the sentiments expressed on the VRP in the joint communiqué following Nkrumah's visit to the United States and stated that Ghana "would now wish to know the general basis upon which it may expect to be able to secure" United States financial aid for the VRP. Ghana was, more specifically, anxious to know how financing could be arranged so that it could establish a price for the power to be provided to the aluminum companies. Ghana's calculation at this point was that the construction of the dam and the generation of power would cost $180 million. Out of this figure, only $53 million was expected to be raised internally.[123]

Chapman had no answer to Dillon's query on the status of Ghana's talks with the World Bank. Citing the case of India, Dillon explained that in similar situations where projects had been too large for any one country to finance, talks with the bank had been most helpful and had served as a "focal point." Nonetheless, he found the memorandum illuminating, noting that until then, no one in Washington had understood why Ghana had been pressing for some idea of the extent of United States financing of the VRP. He reaffirmed the United States position that the aluminum industry should be tied in with the project. On possible United States financing, Dillon promised that a DLF loan would be available. The fund's usual interest rate, he explained, was 3.5 percent and repayment on dam projects ran for twenty to twenty-five years. However, he cautioned that the DLF was in no position to fund the entire project, or even a substantial portion of it—which meant that Ghana had to explore other sources for funding. In any case, the United States could not make any commitments until Congress voted on the 1960 fiscal year appropriations (by August 1959). Given these obscure baselines, no specific figure was quoted to Chapman as what Ghana could expect from the United States. But in order to get the VRP off the ground and especially to help Ghana determine an approximate power rate, Dillon promised that the United States would be willing to explore with the World Bank the possibilities of their financing a portion of the hydroelectric project and also discuss with Kaiser "where they were going."[124]

Nkrumah was pleased with both Flake's letter and the Dillon/Chapman conversation. Although he welcomed the idea of bringing in the World Bank to serve as a "focal point," Nkrumah preferred to have Washington on the frontline. To him, the United States was a "powerful friend," and he wanted to have it acting "from the side" to urge the aluminum industry on, "stimulate World Bank's interest in close and helpful examination of financing the project," and possibly help at a later date with some DLF financing.[125]

By 1959, the World Bank's only contact with the VRP had been tangential, through the bank's 1956 economic survey of Ghana. As already noted, the survey had reported unfavorably on the VRP. Shortly after his meeting with Dillon, Chapman visited the bank and explained Ghana's need for the determination of adequate rates for power, which would help the aluminum companies decide whether or not to invest in the smelter. Chapman requested the bank's assistance in this regard as well as in putting together a financial package. The bank's response was that it would need time to study the Kaiser report, look at the new scheme as developed by the report within the overall context of Ghana's economy, and consult with the United States government.[126]

Doubts Linger, but Washington is Converted

On 28 May, World Bank Vice President J. Burke Knapp called on the State Department and reported on his meeting with Chapman. It was then that the department stated that loans from the DLF and the Export-Import Bank were the only sources of official United States financing for the VRP. There was thus no prospect for grant assistance, nor was there any possibility that the two agencies could together lend Ghana anything near $100 million. Knapp dwelt on the difficulties that confronted the VRP. He noted that aluminum companies were scouring the world for power sites, sources of bauxite, and sites for smelters. Compared with these other projects, he said, the VRP was not competitive. He mentioned all the other hydroelectric-aluminum projects in Africa as being more attractive than the VRP. Knapp also observed that a number of companies had already established smelters in Latin America and made tremendous bauxite discoveries in Australia and Borneo. These facts, he stressed, meant that very generous incentives had to be offered to attract aluminum companies to Ghana. In addition, Knapp believed that there would be difficulties finding a market for Ghana's aluminum. He insisted that in the face of these conditions, the bank needed to take a close look at Ghana's economy "in order to determine investment priorities."[127]

Ironically, the gloomy World Bank picture challenged the department to face the issue head on. Apparently, it had come to accept the point that Flake had emphasized all along: that the VRP was important for United States foreign policy in Africa and that this political factor should be given more weight than economics.[128] On the day following the meeting, Dillon wrote to the Export-Import Bank inquiring whether it could help Ghana to prepare estimates of adequate rates for the cost of power from the Volta.[129] Equally indicative of the department's newfound enthusiasm was a meeting Dillon had with Calhoun on 8 June 1959. At the meeting, Dillon professed Washington's continuing interest in the economic development of Ghana and reported that he had discussed the VRP with the World Bank.[130]

Calhoun's assessment of the VRP was far more optimistic than that presented by Knapp only ten days earlier. According to Calhoun, Kaiser's estimate showed a 13 percent shortfall in the supply of aluminum in the United States and therefore predicted a long-term increase in the demand for the metal. On the VRP, Kaiser remained convinced that it was economically feasible, that low-cost power would be available for the production of aluminum, and that there would be no problem finding a market for the product at competitive prices. Calhoun also assured Dillon that, in terms of execution, the VRP was ahead of similar projects in Guinea and the Belgian Congo. Regarding discussions on the formation of a joint company or consortium for the construction and operation of an aluminum smelter in Ghana, Calhoun reported that Kaiser had been conferring with a number of aluminum companies, especially ALCAN and BAC, both of which controlled the bauxite deposits in Ghana. ALCAN, which also had bauxite concessions in Guinea and had plans to construct an alumina plant there, was said to have invited Kaiser to join in the Guinea project and then process the alumina in Ghana.[131]

On the financing of the VRP, Dillon gave an undertaking that the DLF and the Export-Import Bank would be able to help with the hydroelectric project. But he quickly added that it had also become clear that the aluminum smelter was so essential to the overall project that the dam could not proceed without it. This centrality of the smelter, Dillon emphasized, made it imperative that there had to be a firm commitment from the aluminum industry before the United States government and the World Bank could begin discussions on any loan. "Somebody," he said, "had to start putting all of the parts together." Calhoun cut in to say that Kaiser was set to do just that, a response that delighted Dillon.[132]

Washington was being helpful in other ways. Ghana had on 18 June 1959 informed the State Department of its acceptance of the World Bank's offer to appraise its economy; the department was urged to communicate this acceptance to the bank with an indication that Ghana would want the exercise completed by September 1959.[133] Conveying this development to World Bank President Eugene Black, Dillon stated that "[f]rom the point of view of the U.S. Government, it would be useful if the proposed survey be undertaken and completed as soon as possible." Black was also notified that the United States government had agreed to assist Ghana "in exploring with the Bank and the aluminum companies the possibilities for financing, and [had] suggested that the Bank might be helpful in determining an appropriate power rate." More significantly, Dillon tried to narrow the options open to the bank or, at least, make it difficult for the bank to come up with an unfavorable report on the VRP. Concluding, he emphasized that "[t]he Volta project is obviously of considerable economic and political significance. I therefore hope the necessary further studies as to its economic and financial feasibility can be completed as soon as possible."[134]

Although the State Department was throwing more weight behind the VRP, there was still strong opposition to United States involvement in the project. On 10 August 1959, Export-Import Bank President Samuel Waugh wrote Dillon claiming that the bank had received numerous calls from the United States aluminum industry opposing the investment of huge public funds in Ghana for the reduction of bauxite to aluminum, especially as "there are sufficient facilities for this in the United States for the foreseeable future." He therefore advised that a study should be conducted to determine United States requirements for new sources of aluminum "over the years to come."[135]

Waugh went on to stress that according to his bank's analysis of the Kaiser *Reassessment Report,* the feasibility of the VRP "has not been clearly established." He endorsed the view that the hydroelectric project should not be considered unless there were firm commitments from the aluminum industry or some other large industrial user that would consume a very substantial portion of the power. He mentioned the power supply, which would be in excess of the demand of the aluminum industry (or any other large industrial user), and agreed with the Kaiser report that the viability of the VRP also depended on the possibility of additional industrial power consumers, besides the aluminum project. Waugh insisted that without effective demand for the extra power, "estimated rates will be incorrect and rates to the aluminum company will have to be revised upwards unless the government is willing and able to sell power to the aluminum company at a loss." The Kaiser estimate for the VRP was dismissed as unrealistic since it discounted the cost of the ancillary projects related to the project. It was contended that a more realistic estimate must include the cost of the infrastructure to attract new industries, the availability of skilled and unskilled labor, and the cost of various social and welfare provisions in the affected area, including resettlement, housing, hospitals, and schools. "In short, a careful study," Waugh insisted, "should be made to ascertain the ability of the economy of Ghana to absorb a project of this magnitude."[136]

Waugh's letter did not dampen the State Department's enthusiasm, which certainly says something of the extent to which it had embraced the VRP. On the bank's point that the VRP should not be given too much encouragement unless it was thoroughly planned in all its aspects, Dillon replied that Ghana had, on its own initiative, requested the World Bank to send a team to undertake an economic survey that would evaluate the VRP within a wider context, adding that he expected that the World Bank would be quite realistic in its report.[137]

Kaiser was partly responsible for the confidence the department exuded. The company had become so upbeat on the prospects of the VRP that it was not in the least bothered by the worries or by calls such as that of the Export-Import Bank for a reassessment of construction costs. From the preliminary quotations it had received on hydroelectric equipment, Kaiser had found that the costs were much less than previously thought. Nor was the company bothered about the surplus power to be generated from the VRP. Instead, it noted that Ghana's power demand had not been static and that the demand could even outstrip supply within five years after building the power installation. In this calculation, Kaiser drew on examples such as India, where there was also a very low demand for power when a hydroelectric project was planned.[138] So optimistic was Kaiser about the VRP that in September 1959 it expanded its interest in the VRP from the contract for the construction of the hydroelectric power dam to include aluminum production. As explained by Edgar Kaiser, the reason for this new dimension was that all the other major aluminum companies had some strong footing in West Africa: ALCAN, BAC, and Olin Mathieson were all involved in the Guinea project.[139]

VALCO Is Born

Kaiser's optimism lifted the VRP into the realm of possibility. Nkrumah had in January 1959 asked ALCAN to assume primary responsibility for organizing a private consortium to construct and operate the aluminum smelter. After several months, ALCAN had made no headway. In mid-August 1959, Edgar Kaiser met with ALCAN President Nathaniel Davis, and as a result, ALCAN surrendered responsibility for organizing the consortium to Kaiser. On 10 September 1959, Edgar Kaiser convened a meeting of potentially interested aluminum companies: ALCAN, the Aluminum Company of America (ALCOA), Kaiser Aluminum and Chemical Corporation, Olin Mathieson, and Reynolds Metals. The firms asked Edgar Kaiser to prepare a detailed financial and organizational proposal for the formation of the consortium. Four days later, Edgar Kaiser and Calhoun were in Accra. Following their briefing, Nkrumah welcomed the consortium arrangement. The Ghanaian government subsequently announced that it had asked Edgar Kaiser, and that he had accepted, to take the lead in forming the consortium.[140]

At his meeting with Ghanaian officials, Kaiser explained that under the consortium arrangement, the smelter company was to be a nonprofit operation and would therefore have to sell pig aluminum to the participating companies in proportion to their investment and at cost. Each company was thus required to market its share of the aluminum and reap the profit or loss. Nkrumah picked this arrangement apart. First, he pointed out, and Edgar Kaiser agreed, that it was unworkable if government or private individual stockholders were brought in, since these would not have made any initial investment. In particular, he indicated that although his government was primarily interested in producing power as cheaply as possibly, it was equally interested in having "a reasonable" share of the profits and/or risks in the smelter and that this implicitly undercut the proposition of a nonprofit-making smelter. With these preliminary observations, Nkrumah asked Kaiser to come up with "a sound proposal" for the development of a consortium that would establish a smelter company in Ghana and purchase sufficient power to justify the construction of the dam and power project.[141]

While conceding that the smelter should initially be financed entirely by the consortium, Ghana demanded that it should be given the option to purchase 50 percent of the stock at "a reasonable" price within about twenty years from the start of the operation. Nkrumah pledged that once the consortium was established, his government would "be prepared to take responsibility for financing" the construction of the dam and the hydroelectric installation. He added that Ghana intended to sell power to the smelter company at cost plus minimal profit. It was agreed that in drawing up its final plans, Kaiser would have to take the issues raised by the Ghanaian government into full account.[142]

On 4 November 1959, ALCAN, ALCOA, Kaiser, Olin Mathieson, and Reynolds Metals met in New York to consider Kaiser's proposal for the consortium. Agreement was reached to form a company called the Volta Aluminum Company (VALCO) under Ghanaian law with a capitalization made up of a $75,000 contribution from each firm. Kaiser indicated that it would take a one-third interest in the smelter project, while ALCAN and Olin Mathieson wanted 10 percent each. ALCOA and Reynolds Metals reserved their positions, with the latter expressing strong misgivings about Ghana's desire for equity participation in the project. In spite of this, Ghana was informed that there was a genuine interest among the firms for the formation of the consortium. The meeting agreed that VALCO would expect some tax concessions to be provided by specific legislation. Ghana was also expected to give definite assurances of "a reasonable power rate" to the consortium.[143]

As might have been expected, the formation of VALCO was very welcome news in Accra. At long last, the VRP seemed on the verge of achievement. Nkrumah assured Kaiser that Ghana was prepared to finance the dam construction alone if that was the only way to secure power from the Volta for the smelter. To give force to this commitment, Ghana immediately signed two new contracts with Kaiser. One, at a cost of $1,600,000, covered a new engineering design for the dam. The other, which amounted to $5,500,000, was for additional construction at the dam site and the provision of some equipment such as dredgers. When added to the earlier contract for preliminary works, these brought the total amount of the contracts with Kaiser to $9,600,000, all of which was being financed by Ghana.[144] Kaiser was also required to complete by, 1 September 1960, the design and drawings of the dam and power installation together with the tender documents that would enable Ghana to call for bids on an international basis.[145]

The formation of VALCO also induced Ghana to finally invite the World Bank, just before Christmas 1959, to send a team to study the VRP. Reporting this development to the State Department, Flake observed that Nkrumah had been very reluctant to invite the bank because he felt the economic feasibility of the project had already been amply demonstrated and that a new survey was only a delaying tactic. He emphasized that Nkrumah was in no mood to have anybody query the wisdom of the VRP any longer and would be quite prepared to look beyond the World Bank for financial assistance. Flake therefore advised that the department should urge "speed and utmost tact by World Bank team even if World Bank eventually has to refuse loan." A minute on Flake's telegram shows that the department telephoned the bank, urging that it should waste no time in sending a team to Ghana.[146]

In January 1960, World Bank officials arrived in Ghana to determine the economic feasibility of the VRP and its probable effect on the national economy. The bank's report, submitted to Ghana in July 1960, was not encouraging. "Even taking all the intangible benefits into account," it concluded, "the over-all balance of costs and benefits is on the positive side to only a modest extent at best." The report put the cost of the first stage of the project higher than the $300 million calculated by Kaiser.[147]

The Final Negotiations

By the time the report was issued, the VRP had gathered so much momentum that it could not even be delayed. Two weeks after the World Bank report was submitted, Kaiser officials arrived in Accra on behalf of VALCO to discuss the power cost with Ghana. This turned out to be a very thorny issue. The expectation of cheap power had attracted the aluminum companies to consider setting up a smelter in Ghana. Kaiser engineers figured that the power rate should be in the neighborhood of 2.5 mills per kilowatt.[148] On the other hand, the World Bank insisted that in order for the hydroelectric project to be self-sustaining, power had to be sold at a profit. Basing themselves on the bank's argument, the Ghanaians asked for 4.5 mills. A stalemate ensued.[149]

In August 1960, Gbedemah had a series of meetings in Washington with the World Bank, the State Department, the Treasury Department, the Export-Import Bank, and the DLF. Ghana received "tentative assurances" that the United States, the World Bank, and Britain would assist in financing the hydroelectric project. Of the total cost, finally put at $168 million, Ghana was to provide 50 percent; the World Bank, a loan of $40 million; and the Export-Import Bank and the DLF combined, a loan of $30 million. At the same time, the United States persuaded Britain to provide an additional loan of $14 million for the project.[150] The foreign components of the financing were to be provided only when Ghana "reaches a satisfactory arrangement with the owners of the proposed aluminum smelter."[151] This meant that if Ghana failed to reach an agreement with VALCO, there was hardly any chance that the smelter would be built and—as Washington had emphasized on countless occasions—without the smelter, Ghana might as well as forget the VRP or at least any United States assistance for it.

The fate of the VRP thus hinged on negotiations between Ghana and VALCO over the cost of power for the smelter. By this point, the consortium was the only member of the aluminum industry ready to work with Ghana. In the circumstances, Ghana had little option but to reach an agreement, any agreement, with VALCO if the project was to move ahead. This put VALCO in a very strong bargaining position.

The World Bank had confided in the State Department that the VALCO offer (of 2.5 mills per kilowatt) was "disappointingly low"[152] and would never be enough to cover the debt service of the power installation.[153] The bank was finally persuaded, not by the force of Kaiser's argument, but by another consideration: the Soviets had, in May 1960, mentioned to a Ghanaian parliamentary delegation in Moscow the possibility of a substantial loan, at low interest, for the VRP.[154] Faced with this Soviet interest in the project, the bank relented.[155]

In the final negotiations, VALCO played its strength to the fullest and extracted onerous terms from Ghana. In the agreement reached in November 1960, Ghana lost out on its original proposal for equity participation in the smelter. Imports by VALCO for the construction of the smelter and its operations were to be duty-free for the first thirty years; imported alumina was to be duty free for thirty years; there were to be no restrictions on, control over, or taxation of aluminum exports; VALCO was to be granted pioneer company relief, which exempted it from all taxation on its income for at least five years, extending beyond that period to a maximum of ten years if profits had not totaled £20 million (Ghanaian); and from the years when income tax became payable until 1997, the tax rate would be that which was applicable to companies on 2 January 1961, that is, 40 percent of retained profits plus a further 2.5 percent of profits transferred out of Ghana. Two other major concessions involved the agreement to sell power to the smelter at 2.625 mills per kilowatt, which was a little more than the cost price and was the lowest rate in the world, and to retain this price for thirty years. Besides, in order to keep the cost of the project down and thus ensure a low price for power, VALCO stripped the VRP of its ancillary public works.[156]

VALCO was even able to evade any firm commitment to install a plant to convert locally mined bauxite into alumina. Instead, it was allowed the anomaly of importing alumina processed by Kaiser plants in the United States from bauxite mined in the Jamaican concessions of Kaiser and Reynolds Metals. This was a major departure from the original conception of the VRP, which included a bauxite mine and an alumina plant. Even the Kaiser *Reassessment Report* found that there were "ample reserves of acceptable quality bauxite to support a substantial aluminum industry in Ghana" and recommended an alumina plant and smelter, to be built at Tema.[157]

The net result of VALCO's arm-twisting was that although Ghana's bauxite deposits could sustain a fully integrated industry, from mining the ore to processing it and manufacturing finished products, Kaiser was able to get Nkrumah to agree that the Ghanaian plant should process Kaiser's bauxite. In addition, Kaiser was able to secure electricity at the lowest rate paid in the industry. This ridiculously cheap rate meant that Ghana subsidized Kaiser to process its own bauxite to provide aluminum ingots for the United States economy.[158] The VRP was thus to be an integrated scheme, but integrated within the vertical confines of the United States aluminum industry. It is for this reason that the VRP remains a very emotive issue in the history of United States relations with Africa; the project comes in handy as a classic case study of the development of underdevelopment and neocolonialism in Africa by the West.[159]

Conclusion

On 21 September 1960, Ghana invited tenders for the construction of a rock-filled dam, 370 feet high, over the Volta River at Akosombo, with a volume of 10.9 million cubic yards and a saddle dam 120 feet high. The specification called for the dam to be ready for water storage by July 1964 and for the first generating unit to be producing commercially by September 1965.[160]

No doubt, strategic considerations—notably, forestalling Soviet involvement in the VRP[161] and flashbacks of the United States offhanded treatment of Egypt's Aswan Dam project—counted for much in Washington's commitment to the VRP. Nonetheless, the United States loan for the VRP was, by any measurement, a sound economic investment. In the first place, it reflected Washington's continuing interest in guaranteed access to Africa's valuable raw materials, achieved in this case through Kaiser. This was of particular significance because by 1960, the aluminum industry had recovered from the trade setbacks which plagued it in 1957–58 and was expanding dramatically. In the United States itself, Aluminum Limited had plans to increase its smelter capacity from 750,000 tons to a million tons. In France, Péchiney was constructing a plant near Pau with a production capacity of 56,000 tons per annum, representing an increase of one-third in France's aluminum output. At the same time, Greece signed a contract with French companies for a $75 million aluminum industry; and a $7 million aluminum plant in Buenos Aires, the largest in Latin America, was under construction. There were, at the same time, reports of plans for some of the world's largest plants in Australia and Poland. Everywhere, there was confidence not only that demand would keep pace with supply but also that aluminum would continue to be in greater demand than all other metals: in 1960, the use of aluminum in industrial construction and equipment in the United States was expected to reach 650,000 tons, an increase of 100,000 tons over the previous year.[162] This confidence certainly rubbed off on the VRP. Given the expanding global demand for the metal, Washington was well aware of the benefits to be derived from the control of the VRP by the United States aluminum industry.

It will be observed that the bickering over the Congo did not affect United States commitment to the VRP. The basis for this paradox can be found in NSC 6005, which was adopted as a policy statement in April 1960. A February 1960 draft of the paper simultaneously committed Washington to contain Nkrumah's activism in Africa and encourage Ghana "in its political development and economic growth and to support the preservation of its basically Western orientation." It was well known that for Nkrumah and his government, economic development was virtually synonymous with the VRP. Washington feared that Ghana would turn to the Soviets if "Western sources fail to assist in the Volta River Project." Along with this fear was the belief that "[t]he success of this major project (with Western assistance) will reinforce Western and U.S. interests in Ghana."[163] In other words, months before the Congo exploded, Washington had fashioned a carrot and stick policy for Ghana: oppose its activism in Africa but support the Volta project.

7

GUINEA: THE WEIGHT OF RESIDUAL INTERESTS

In chapter 2, it was demonstrated that Washington did not consider the transfer of power to Africans a topical issue in European colonial administration. The 1959 study prepared for the United States Senate Committee on Foreign Relations by the Program of African Studies at Northwestern University regretted that the United States had "been reluctant to acknowledge the principle of self-government as fully applicable" to Africans, with the result that

> We [the United States] write many prescriptions for self-government. African leaders must be able to withstand "extremist" pressures, and forsake "short-term" domestic political rewards; they must show moderation; they must be able to "rise above mere chauvinism" in border disputes; they must show preference for democracy as a political form; they must expand the area of their competence as legislators; they must be friendly to the metropolitan powers, recognizing the colonial contributions and showing a willingness to continue or expand existing ties with the metropole; they should demonstrate a preference for free enterprise, at least to the extent of choosing a "mixed" economy; they should be receptive to Western economic cooperation.[1]

Eisenhower himself acknowledged that "In spite of the relatively high regard in which the United States was held in most of the newly emerging nations because of our anti-colonial tradition, our close alliances with some of the former colonial powers caused vexing complications in Africa."[2]

Guinea is a splendid example of the complications that resulted from Washington's "close alliances" with the colonial (and ex-colonial) powers. In his memoir, John Morrow, the first United States ambassador to Guinea, blamed those he called "Washington officials" who "wanted everyone to exercise great care that nothing was done in Guinea to offend General de Gaulle" even when

> [i]t was perfectly clear that De Gaulle hoped that the Guinean experiment would fail and that its failure would serve to deter other French African territories from taking a similar leap toward independence. . . .American officials were unwilling to heed my fervent pleas concerning the necessity of treating Guinea as an independent nation and making good on our oft-repeated assertions of interest in the self-determination of emerging nations. Instead of seizing the initiative . . . the State Department saw fit to stick to its 'notion of residual interest' in its dealings with Guinea.[3]

The Background

On 13 May 1958, the French army in Algiers seized power, created "a civil and military Committee of Public Safety," and demanded the formation in Paris of a government capable of keeping Algeria as an integral part of metropolitan France. This government, they insisted, had to be headed by Charles de Gaulle, the man who had symbolized French opposition to Germany during World War II. The authorities in Paris proved totally incapable of containing the coup. On 1 June 1958, de Gaulle was called out of retirement to restore governmental authority in Paris. This marked the end of the Fourth French Republic.

More than any other French political leader in the 1940s and 1950s, de Gaulle was aware that his country's claim to world power status derived from its empire.[4] Consequently, he saw every need to continue with the old French strategy of reshaping, not unscrambling, the empire. On 13 July 1958, he outlined the thrust of his program: "We are going toward a vast and free community. In 1958 we must construct new institutions, establish according to federal principles the links of our union, organize a great political, economic, and cultural ensemble that fits modern conditions of life and progress." Sixteen days later, he convened a constitutional consultative committee, which was to create the institutional framework of the "free community."[5]

There was no consensus among the Africans on the committee: those led by Felix Houphouet-Boigny (of the Ivory Coast) wanted a tight federation between France and its African territories; those led by Léopold Senghor (of Senegal) preferred a confederal set-up, which would secure African territories a place within the French system and at the same time provide for their independence.[6] The latter group won an early victory: Article 66 of the committee's proposal provided that autonomous member states of the proposed French Community could, in the fifth year after the promulgation of the constitution, choose to become independent with the approval of France and of the Community's legislature. This victory was illusory and short-lived.

On 8 August, de Gaulle went before the committee and noted that, under the proposed constitution, the overseas territories "shall govern and administer themselves, which constitutes, to be sure, a very important step towards self-determination." But this was to be within a tightly knit federation. He declared: "The overseas territories are not States. We must therefore have a federation. It might even be called a confederation in view of certain special agreements that may have to be made. . . .But these are just words; and I prefer to stick to 'Federation.' " This preference implicitly ruled out the principle of independence but conceded that of "secession." De Gaulle explained that the proposed constitution would be subject to a referendum, to "verify, in particular in Africa, whether the idea of secession carries the day or not. In case the proposed *Communauté* is refused, it is evident that this shall signify independence, but independence with all that it includes in burden, in responsibility and in danger." For him, a "No" vote meant not just a rejection of the constitution but also "secession" from the proposed French Community. Anxious to avert this outcome, which he deemed repugnant, de Gaulle dangled the carrot and the stick at the same time: "what is inconceivable," he said, "is an independent state which France continues to help."[7] The same day, de Gaulle made a radio broadcast, warning: "Of course one might want secession, but it held duties. It carries with it dangers. Independence has its cost."[8]

In the constitutional proposal published by the de Gaulle government on 21 August 1958, Article 86 allowed for independence but also made it incompatible with membership of the French Community; and Article 66 of the committee's draft was expunged. Overall, the constitution, like that of 1946, proposed a federal relationship uniting France with its empire. However, this federation was, by its practical implications, a unitary system, for it was intended to be overwhelmingly dominated by France. Just before the proposal was published, de Gaulle set out on a tour of Africa.⁹ The purpose of this tour was to win Africans over to his vision of Greater France.

De Gaulle encountered his most rancorous reception in Conakry, on 25 August 1958. Prime Minister Sekou Toure, who was also the leader of the Parti Démocratique de Guinée (PDG), began his speech with a diatribe against French colonialism, blaming it for his territory's material destitution. Above all, he rejected de Gaulle's conception of a Franco-African community. "We have to tell you bluntly, Mr. President," Toure told de Gaulle, "what the demands of the people are. . . . We have one prime and essential need: dignity," which had been compromised by colonialism; to Toure, independence was the precondition for the rehabilitation of his people's dignity. Quite unambiguously, he told de Gaulle: "We shall never renounce our legitimate right to independence. There is no dignity without freedom. We intend to exercise our sovereign right to independence, but we also intend to remain linked with France. In an association with France, we will become a free, proud and sovereign people. These new relations must be free of all paternalism." Toure felt that de Gaulle had been vague in defining the conditions under which overseas territories might leave the French Community. He said that Guinea would vote "Yes" only if the constitution embraced the Africans' "right to independence" and acknowledged the "right to divorce" in the Franco-African "marriage" as well as the "active solidarity existing between the Associated States and the populations."¹⁰

De Gaulle responded that France was proud of its record in Africa and had no cause to be apologetic. After inviting Guinea to join the Community, he declared

> France proposes this Community and no one is compelled to belong to it. Independence has been mentioned. I say more loudly here than elsewhere that independence is at Guinea's disposal. She can take it by voting 'No' on September 28 to the proposal which is under consideration. In such an event, I pledge that the Metropole will place no obstacle in the way. Naturally she will draw the conclusion, but will place no obstacles on the way. Your territory can, if it so desires and under the circumstances it prefers, follow the path of its choice.¹¹

In addition to Toure's impassioned rhetoric, de Gaulle could scarcely have viewed with equanimity the crowds that lined the street from the airport and interrupted his speech. Much later, he wrote that a watershed was reached during his trip to Guinea, where he found himself "enveloped by the organization of a totalitarian republic. There was nothing that was hostile or offensive towards myself. But from the aerodrome to the center of the town, the crowd lined up on both sides of the road in well distributed battalions, and cried Independence with a single voice."[12]

By the time the reception in Conakry was over, de Gaulle had come to the conclusion that Guinea was already lost. "Come now, the thing is clear," he told his entourage, "we shall leave on 29th September, in the morning." The "consequences" he had so often talked about started unfolding immediately: an invitation for Toure to fly with de Gaulle to Dakar was withdrawn; Toure was informed that de Gaulle would not meet him at the party to be given that evening by the governor; and Cornut-Gentille, the minister of the Overseas Territories, was no longer to stay the night with Toure.[13]

The preamble of the final text of the new French constitution recognized the right of "free determination" by overseas territories to accept or reject the new constitution. The constitution provided for a federal Community with a president, an executive council, a senate, and a court of appeal. The French president, elected by an electoral college in which overseas members were in a small minority, was the president of the Community. The executive council consisted of the president, the prime ministers of the French Republic and the overseas territories, and the ministers responsible for those subjects that fell within the jurisdiction of the Community's government. The senate consisted of delegates chosen by the parliaments of member states in proportion to their populations and the responsibility each assumed in the Community. The Community's government was responsible for foreign policy, defense, currency, overall economic policy, strategic raw materials, and, if the member states agreed, justice, higher education, and communications. Member states had full autonomy over all other matters.

The constitution permitted agreements to be made between the Community and states that "wish to associate with it in order to develop their civilizations." It also allowed overseas territories to group themselves into primary federations. Territories that accepted the constitution and opted to become members of the proposed Community were to become "self-governing" and retain the right to leave the Community and "become independent." In the referendum of 28 September on the constitution, any territory that registered a majority of "No" votes would have rejected the constitution and thus "seceded" from the Community. More plainly, such a territory would have chosen immediate independence.

On 14 September 1958, Toure signaled Guinea's rejection of the constitution. He told a PDG conference, "It will fall to us to preserve, for Guinea and for Africa, the honor of African Man. . . . We shall vote 'No' to a Community which is merely the French Union rechristened—the old goods with a new label. We shall vote 'No' to inequality. We shall vote 'No' to irresponsibility. From the 29th September we shall be an independent country." The conference decided on voting "No."[14]

Overnight, by simply voting massively against the constitution of the Fifth French Republic on 28 September 1958, Guinea, alone of all the French territories in Africa, automatically opted out of the French Empire and immediately became independent. In the eyes of the French, however, Guinea had sinned. A day later, all French economic and financial aid to Guinea ceased; and Paris told Conakry that French officials, some 3,000, would be withdrawn over the next two months. The seriousness of this withdrawal and the degree of disruption it must have caused can only be appreciated if it is realized that at independence, Guinea, with an estimated population of 2.6 million and a geographical spread of 160,000 square miles, had only fifteen secondary schools, no tertiary institution, and an illiteracy rate of 95 percent.[15] This meant that its public services, as in other French African territories, were run by French officials.

As a colonial economy, Guinea had no banking institution and no currency of its own. Its economy was so overwhelmingly dominated by the French that domestic capital accumulation was virtually nonexistent. The "modern" sector was defined by a mercantile capitalism so rudimentary that its vital foreign component was no more than the exchange of primary goods for manufactured ones. Again, much of this exchange was with France, the destination of about 80 percent of Guinea's total exports. There was an excess of imports over exports; France covered the deficit through direct budgetary support and by cushioning commodity exports with price supports. Thus, agricultural exports from Guinea to France sold at protected prices about 20 percent higher than the prevailing world market rates. (In return, French goods enjoyed preferential treatment in Guinea even though they were dearer than similar goods from elsewhere.) In the period 1945–57, France provided roughly $150 million or 80 percent of all public sector capital and recurrent expenses in Guinea. In 1957 alone, France paid $6.5 million to cover administrative expenses in areas such as the judiciary, customs, and telecommunications; provided $10 million for military costs; and financed Guinea's budget deficit with a $1 million loan.[16]

In the event, the French "withdrawal" was more of a scorched-earth retreat: immediately, it ceased to buy Guinea's bananas, which it had done at subsidized prices; equipment—including files, maps, telephone sets and lines, medical supplies, and even plates and cutlery in the Government Palace—were either "withdrawn" or destroyed. The police and army left only after destroying their barracks. Guinean students in Paris and Dakar suddenly lost their French scholarships. French officials who remained in Guinea lost their seniority in the French public service.[17] By October 1958, Guinea was operating on an overdraft of 1.2 billion CFA francs ($6 million) with the French treasury. This meant that if France canceled the overdraft, as it did, Guinea would be without public funds, except those from customs duties (and possibly income taxes).[18] In the short run, Guinea's lifeline was a loan of £10 million from Ghana.[19]

The Weight of Residual Interests

Guinea formally proclaimed its independence on 2 October 1958. From then until the end of the Eisenhower administration, it was treated like a pariah by Washington. And that was in spite of Guinea's overtures. Joseph Satterthwaite, assistant secretary of state for African Affairs, was in Conakry in June 1959 and reported that he found on his arrival "an exceptionally cordial atmosphere toward [the] U.S."[20] Senator Stuart Symington, a Democratic presidential aspirant, visited Guinea in December 1959. Morrow recalled that the senator was "very much impressed by the fact that wherever we went . . . Guineans, old and young, stopped to wave, call out friendly greetings, and applaud. The senator told me that this was the first time he had ever seen this happen. I do believe that he must have concluded after three days of this kind of treatment that the showing of friendship was genuine and not something arranged for his visit."[21]

The explanation as to why Guinea made no headway in its efforts to cultivate cordial relations with the United States was provided in a State Department memorandum of 21 August 1959, which observed that "[s]ince September 1958 when French Guinea voted to secede from the French Union as it was transformed into the new French Community, United States policy has been hesitant. In the earlier period of Guinean independence the State Department deferred to French sensibilities."[22] Similarly, the NSC noted that "[i]n an effort to support France's special relationship, the U.S. after close consultations with France, recognized Guinea about three weeks after receiving Guinea's request for recognition although strongly urged to grant immediate recognition by Liberia and other African states."[23] Deference to French sensitivities delayed the recognition of Guinea and also affected its admission into the UN, the assignment of an ambassador to Conakry, and the provision of economic assistance.

At least three days before the referendum of 28 September 1958, Washington was certain that Guinea would vote "No." This created a dilemma for the United States. In the first place, the State Department believed that it made better sense for France to take the lead in according any *de jure* recognition following the referendum. Nonetheless, there was also a strong feeling that the United States should not wait for a French decision, if countries such as Egypt and the Soviet Union offered recognition. On 25 September, the department instructed the United States embassy in Paris to inform the French that barring the Egypt-Soviet dimension, the United States would have preferred to "proceed cautiously in recognizing Guinea since recognition would create serious complications in other African areas, could be interpreted as endorsement [of the] fragmentation of Africa and of [a] regime of questionable ability and political orientation."[24]

A day before the referendum, Amory Houghton, the United States ambassador in Paris, reported on a meeting he had with Louis Joxe, the secretary-general of the French foreign ministry. Joxe told Houghton that negotiations would be necessary to establish Guinea's status, that immediate United States recognition would cause a "catastrophic moral reaction" in France, and that the United States "should therefore wait and see what relations Guinea wished to have with France before taking any action."[25]

Without a nod from Paris, Washington decided to hold back on the recognition of Guinea. Meanwhile, on 2 October 1958, Toure circulated a message to various governments, requesting them to recognize Guinea and enter into diplomatic relations with it. When this message reached the White House two days later, Deputy Undersecretary Robert Murphy turned to Hervé Alphand, the French ambassador in Washington, on how the United States should respond. Alphand confirmed Houghton's report: that an agreement would have to be concluded between France and Guinea before the latter could be considered independent, and that this would not take long. Murphy emphasized the delicate nature of the matter, "particularly in view of the possibility of recognition of Guinea in the near future by the Soviets and other governments." On this account, he hoped that France would "regularize the situation promptly" and requested that the State Department be kept abreast of the discussions with Guinea.[26]

The Soviet Union recognized Guinea on 5 October and the Eastern Europeans quickly followed. This development made the pressure on the United States more immediate. But there was also Toure's own pressure. In response to his message of 2 October, the United States consulate general in Dakar could only promise Toure a reply "when all aspects of the juridical position of Guinea are clarified."[27] For Toure, this must have seemed quite incomprehensible as he could not think of anything about Guinea's status that still required clarification. Against this background, he wrote to Eisenhower on 13 October, emphasizing the importance he attached to recognition by the United States, requested diplomatic relations with the United States, and stated that he realized that it was in Guinea's interest to remain aligned to the West. This letter induced the State Department to assure Toure that the United States was "giving due consideration to the question of the recognition" of Guinea as an independent state.[28]

On 14 October, the department instructed the embassy in Paris to take up the question with French Foreign Minister Couvre de Murville. The embassy was to stress the "increasingly difficult posture of the United States" as more countries recognized Guinea and to inquire at "what point France's friends can extend recognition with French acquiescence."[29] The embassy gathered the reason why France was in no hurry to clear the way for Guinea: it was loath to "reward" Guinea for its choice so that the other African territories would not feel that they too would have been better off with a "No" vote. In the end, the embassy could only extract a pledge that France would consult with its allies, especially the United States and Britain; this was coupled with a renewed French request that they postpone recognizing Guinea "for some weeks."[30]

By 21 October, Washington had information from London that France had withdrawn its objections to the recognition of Guinea.[31] Details of the revised French position were conveyed to Washington three days later. France held that Guinea had "juridically speaking become a separate entity" by its "No" vote, and that France would not object to the recognition of Guinea's "new status" by the United States. However, Paris hoped that it would be "a qualified rather than formal recognition of a full sovereign state." It would "be very premature," France further contended, to consider the establishment of diplomatic relations or admission to the UN. The department found the French position too garbled to be helpful.[32]

A meeting Dulles had on 25 October with Alphand did not clarify matters either. There was "no question," the ambassador said, "that Guinea would be independent and a member of the UN, but we did not wish to go too fast. Guinea will be separated from the French Community and will be recognized." This confusing explanation was silent on when France would relent on Guinea, as Paris claimed to be still preoccupied with matters concerning the territories that had voted in favor of the Community. "If the others believed [Guinea] was favored," Alphand pointed out, "they would be encouraged to follow the same course with the resulting Balkanization of Black Africa, a development which would be against the interests of the West as a whole." France was also pressing its allies not to "rush diplomatic representation or UN membership" for Guinea. Dulles drew Alphand's attention to the discomfort the nonrecognition of Guinea was causing Britain, especially "because of the effect in Ghana and elsewhere." On UN membership, Dulles pointed out that while his "basic sympathy" lay with the French, it was tempered by the fact that "precedents for delaying UN membership were not good."[33]

On 31 October, Britain informed the United States that it was set to recognize Guinea the following day.[34] There was a ready consensus in the State Department that the United States should not delay recognition beyond a day or two after the British.[35] Dulles immediately informed Eisenhower that France had "reluctantly given qualified concurrence to the recognition of Guinea" and that Britain was to announce its recognition the following day. On these grounds, he recommended that the United States should follow suit.[36] This enabled Eisenhower to write to Toure on 1 November 1958, informing him of United States recognition of Guinea.[37]

In advising Eisenhower on the question of recognition, Dulles had informed him that France disapproved of the establishment of diplomatic relations with Guinea "at present" and had "also requested assistance in delaying Guinea's entry" into the UN. On both scores, Dulles went along with the French: he recommended that "the question of establishment of diplomatic relations with Guinea be held in abeyance for the time being," adding that the State Department would consult with Britain and France "to determine what practical steps might be taken to dissuade Guinea from requesting admission to the United Nations during the current session."[38] Not only would the United States dissuade Guinea from seeking UN membership, it also discouraged other countries from taking the alternative action. In October 1958, Nkrumah had revealed to Wilson Flake, the United States ambassador in Accra, his intention to sponsor Guinea for UN membership "this session." Flake tried to talk him out of it, suggesting that his efforts would be in vain since "it would be a while before Guinea met the criteria for UN membership." This had its effect: Nkrumah now felt the need to test the waters first and assured Flake that he "would sponsor only when [he was] sure of [a] favorable outcome."[39]

Meanwhile, Guinea continued to work towards cultivating United States diplomatic support and relationship. In November 1958, Toure despatched Telli Diallo as his personal emissary to Washington. Part of Diallo's brief was to express Guinea's appreciation of the recognition accorded it by the United States and to request the establishment of diplomatic relations, as well as Washington's support for Guinea's admission to the UN.[40] Diallo's reception was cold as Washington was still very much attached to the French position. On 26 November 1958, the State Department assured Charles Lucet, the minister of the embassy of France, that it intended to consult with Diallo "concerning the possibility that Guinea might delay its application for membership of the United Nations."[41] In spite of this maneuvering, Guinea was admitted as a member of the UN in December 1958 following a motion sponsored by Iraq and Japan. There was no opposition to the motion, but France abstained as it did when the issue was put to vote in the Security Council.[42]

As with the recognition of Guinea, Washington awaited the endorsement of Paris before establishing its diplomatic mission in Conakry. In February 1959, Robert Rinden assumed duties as the United States chargé d'affaires at Conakry. Although he welcomed this development, Toure again urged action on the exchange of diplomatic missions.[43] But in Washington, French opinion carried greater weight, and until the end of April 1959, Paris not only insisted that it did not "wish to honor the Guineans by sending an ambassador" to Conakry but asked that the "U.S. also not send one."[44] Washington was released from this dilemma on 11 May, when information came from Rinden that Paris no longer objected to the "immediate naming of an American Ambassador to Guinea." The French were now convinced that Western interests would be better served by a United States embassy in Conakry.[45] This was why the nomination of John Morrow as the first United States ambassador to Guinea was not announced until 28 May 1959.[46]

As in the diplomatic sphere, the United States allowed France to influence—better, inhibit—its policy towards Guinea in terms of economic (and other forms of) assistance. In spite of the obviously inauspicious circumstances, the United States initially predicated its policy on the assumption that France would continue as Guinea's primary source of external assistance.[47] A shift from this policy was only contemplated because of the increasing "communist" presence in Guinea. In April 1959, Satterthwaite expressed concern that Guinea had closer economic ties with "communist" countries than with the West and recalled that the United States had "left to France the leading political and economic role in Guinea since independence." He urged that in the light of "the growing influence in Guinea of the Soviet bloc," it was time "to determine that it is in the interest of the United States to provide assistance to the Republic of Guinea." To prepare the ground for such a determination, Satterthwaite proposed that an ICA team should be sent to Guinea to discuss its economic and technical needs and to ascertain the areas where the United States could offer assistance.[48] Following this proposal, Washington instructed its embassy in Paris that it had decided that it was in the United States national interest to consider an aid program for Guinea and that an ICA team was therefore being sent there for an assessment of the country's needs.[49]

Before the ICA team left Washington, there were already a number of unaddressed Guinean requests for United States assistance: the Ministry of Education had asked for English language textbooks and teaching materials; the commander of the army had asked for uniforms and other noncombatant materials; and the Ministry of Public Works wanted to buy a DC-3 aircraft for Sekou Toure's use.[50] In the light of these requests and the "communist" interest in Guinea (which had prompted Satterthwaite's memorandum in the first place) the ICA mission was an empty ritual. The team recommended several technical assistance projects in agriculture and education, sending four or five teachers of English, and assisting Guinea to establish a development bank that would finance cooperatives and small-scale industries.[51] None of these recommendations was acted upon.

Guinea ended up with one teacher, and that was only after Toure himself had personally taken up the matter with the United States embassy. As recalled by Morrow, after "[s]everal weeks and many messages," from the embassy, Washington sent only one teacher as its "answer to the hurry-up request" for English language teachers. Morrow found himself in the difficult situation of explaining why the United States was so short of English language teachers that it could spare only one.[52]

On one occasion, Satterthwaite reminded Deputy Assistant Secretary James Penfield that the determining factor in United States dealings with Guinea was "the importance to the United States of cordial relations with France and of the NATO alliance."[53] The Konkoure dam project shows that this consideration cast its spell not only in the diplomatic sphere but also over United States economic assistance to Guinea. The dam, an ancillary part of the Fria aluminum project, was a major issue Guinea had to confront following its rupture with France. The aluminum plant was being built by an international consortium, but it was coupled to a scheme to harness the Konkoure River for hydroelectric power. By the original arrangement, the French government had a minority equity interest in the dam company. In addition, the company was to secure loans from the Bank of France and the World Bank, both guaranteed by the French government.[54] The dam project ran into a problem as France withdrew economic support after Guinea's independence.

In May 1960, in the course of a meeting with Undersecretary of State Douglas Dillon, Diallo inquired as to the possibility of the United States assisting in building the dam.[55] Washington was prepared to make some gesture in this regard, but not without approval from Paris. On 9 June

1960, the State Department informed France of the possibility of a United States-sponsored updating survey of the dam project. France asked for time to consider how the proposal would be received by the Conseil de l'Entente states;[56] meanwhile, it disapproved of Guinea being informed of the United States proposal on the grounds that it would "have adverse effect elsewhere in Africa, especially in [the] evolving [French] Community." But if Conakry had to be informed, Paris suggested that the Konkoure project be placed in the wider context of all the hydroelectric developments in West Africa. Following this prompting, the United States agreed to delay informing Guinea of its intention and also accepted that any announcement on the Konkoure project should be linked to all similar projects in West Africa.[57] In addition, France received assurances that the "commitment to make [the] study is not tantamount to commitment [to] construct [the] project," and that the study only afforded a period of grace "to think [the] subject through more thoroughly."[58]

On 8 July, Dillon gave Alphand a draft press release and told him that the United States intended to inform Guinea of its proposal on the dam the following week. Alphand again told him that Paris would prefer a postponement. Four days later, inquiries by the State Department showed that while Paris had not changed its position, it "fully understood what the United States intended to do."[59] On 21 July, the United States finally informed Guinea that it was prepared to undertake, at its own expense, an update study of the Konkoure hydroelectric project. Guinea was promised that if the project proved to be economically feasible and private financing for the related aluminum smelter facilities was assured, the United States would "consider how it might assist financially, in addition to financial participation of other private and public sources, in the construction of this project." To mollify the French, the aide-mémoire added: "It is observed that the proposed Konkoure Dam and related aluminum operations in the Republic of Guinea form one of a number of power-aluminum complexes, such as the Volta, Kouilou and Inga projects, which are at some stage of consideration in several states of Africa by various governments, enterprises or international institutions."[60]

Guinea declined the United States offer. In the first place, it was, according to Diallo, qualified by "so many conditions," that "Guinea was unable to conclude whether the U.S. was genuinely prepared to go ahead with this project or not. For this reason the American offer was considered as possibly constituting a delaying action."[61] More decisive, however, was the fact that Guinea already had a more attractive offer from the Soviet Union: a long-term loan to finance the entire construction of the dam and an undertaking to send all the technicians and equipment necessary to ensure that work on the project started by New Year's Day 1961. Conakry was perplexed to no end by the United States proposal. As Toure put it, "If the USSR, which is not acquainted with this project, had replied that it would have to undertake a new survey, the Guineans would have some understanding of the necessity for such a delay; they find it more difficult to understand why the United States, which already has the French plans for this dam, should propose another survey." Nevertheless, he did challenge Satterthwaite in October 1960: "If the U.S. should make an offer equivalent to that of the Soviets', there would be no question that Guinea would accept the U.S. offer instead."[62] This challenge was never taken up.

In a large measure, Washington's offer on the Konkoure dam was symptomatic of its general attitude towards Guinea. By routinely deferring to France and offering too little too late, it missed out in Guinea and thus created openings for the "communists." This pattern was evident in the case of the delivery of Czech arms to Conakry in March 1959. Satterthwaite told the House of Representatives Foreign Affairs Committee that the arms delivery was a signal that the "communist offensive" had emerged in Africa with "startling rapidity."[63] Amidst the furor in Washington, Toure revealed his efforts in November 1958 to get arms from the United States through the intermediation of Liberia's President William Tubman and that it was only after a long wait for a United States response that he accepted the Czech offer.[64] In spite of this disappointment, Toure still believed in the possibility of a warm United States/Guinea relationship. In a telegram sent to Eisenhower, he hoped that the United States would "analyze the necessity of pursuing a genuine policy of friendship devoid of any ulterior motives or disloyal intentions, and establish direct contacts with the Guinean Government in order to evaluate correctly the facts exploited by French diplomacy."[65]

The delivery of Czech arms did indeed induce some effort, in Washington, to establish "direct contacts" with Conakry. When Diallo visited the State Department on 24 April 1959, the officials he met focused much of the discussion on the delivery of Czech arms to Guinea and worried "at the circumstances which had caused such a large quantity of arms to arrive in Guinea at the same time as communist bloc specialists and a Soviet diplomatic mission."[66] Later that same day, the department advised Eisenhower to invite Toure for an official visit to Washington.[67]

The State Department's memorandum to the White House stressed that "[r]ecent developments in the relations of Guinea and the Soviet bloc countries are causing serious concern." The department observed that since

Guinea's independence, "the Soviet Union and bloc countries have been actively wooing her by the signing of trade, cultural and educational agreements. This has culminated in a Czech arms gift and the assignment of Soviet, Bulgarian and Czech representatives in Guinea." Eisenhower was advised that an invitation to Toure "would be most effective in counteracting the rapidly developing communist influence in Guinea."[68] "Our principal objective in Guinea," the department explained, "is to maintain the presence of the United States and the West in the country and to establish a position for future United States action to stem the flood of expanding Soviet influence and reinforce our influence when this flood recedes."[69] The expectation that the so-called flood would recede was informed by the assessment that "[d]espite this definite tendency towards the East, President Toure is committed to a policy of non-alignment."[70]

The invitation for Toure's visit was delivered on 4 June 1959 by the United States embassy in Conakry, and Toure accepted it immediately. Guinea, an official announcement stated, was "sincerely gratified by this initiative which, in the wake of other concrete, positive attitudes on the part of the United States, inaugurates in such felicitous fashion an era of understanding, the basis of amicable and fruitful cooperation between the Government of the Republic of Guinea and the Government of the United States of America."[71] The visit, which took place in late October 1959, did little to improve relations between the two countries, or for that matter, between Guinea and the West.

In 1960, the always tense United States/Guinea relationship finally dissolved. On 2 March 1960, the same day Guinea pulled out of the franc zone, it was announced that the Soviet Union and Guinea had concluded a three-year technical agreement, which involved the establishment of a number of factories and a polytechnic for 1,500 students.[72] Increasing trade with countries outside the franc zone had made possible the withdrawal from the zone, but French shortsightedness had made it essential. After Guinea's independence, France had sought a veto right over Guinea's choice of trading partners. In return, Paris offered to continue financial and economic assistance on a "provisional basis" but on condition that Guinea remained in the franc zone.[73] Membership of the zone entailed requirements that were unacceptable to Guinea in the light of its near frozen relations with France. For example, trade and payments agreements between franc and non-franc countries had to receive the concurrence of other franc zone members. In addition, if Guinea had not broken with the franc zone, all of its foreign currency would have gone into its account in Paris, giving France a great deal of control over Guinea's external commercial dealings.

Withdrawal from the franc zone enhanced Guinea's control over its economy. But Washington could not help relating this development to the increasing presence in Guinea of diplomats, engineers, farmers, and businessmen from the Soviet bloc. Nor could it fail to notice that Guinea's new trading links were essentially with the Soviets, the Chinese, and the Eastern Europeans.[74] On 10 March 1960, CIA Director Allen Dulles reported to the NSC on "the recent actions of Guinea," highlighting its "definite drift toward closer relations with the Sino-Soviet Bloc": the recognition of East Germany, "the probability of a similar action for North Vietnam," the withdrawal from the franc zone, and the printing of its new currency in Czechoslovakia. Other indicators were Guinea's Three-Year Economic Plan, which, according to Dulles, had "a strong socialist flavor"; further, "six Soviet Bloc nations were, or were about to be, represented in Guinea; Bloc economic and technical assistance in Guinea surpasses that for any other African state; and Guinea has a great deal of barter trade with the Bloc. The Czechs, East Germans, and Poles have about 100 advisors in Guinea and there are about 100 Guinean students behind the Iron Curtain."[75] For the rest of 1960, Washington continued to monitor the expanding "communist" presence in Guinea.

An April 1960 State Department intelligence report asserted that the "Soviet bloc has established a position of considerable influence in Guinea," and that "[b]loc aid is massive, relative to the scale of things in Guinea." The report found that Eastern European countries had donated a fleet of buses for use in the city of Conakry, powerful radio transmission equipment, a sophisticated printing plant, and arms to replace those removed by the French; and that there were plans for the People's Republic of China to undertake a large technical assistance program in rice cultivation and livestock development. It was also reported that educational "and other exchanges of persons with the Bloc go on constantly, and several Bloc nationals hold positions in Guinean ministries and state services," and that between 50 and 60 percent of Guinea's trade were directed to the "communist" states under several bilateral trade agreements. For the department, the expansive "bloc" involvement in Guinea was dramatized, above all else, by a line of credit opened for Conakry by Moscow in August 1959: $35 million (140 million rubles, which converted to about 8.6 billion CFA francs), repayable over twelve years, at 2.5 percent interest.[76] *West Africa* (5 September 1959) pointed out that this interest rate was "much lower than any obtainable from Western lending institutions or the International [World] Bank."[77]

In October 1960, Washington formally complained to Conakry of "recent indications that Guinea is deviating from a neutral foreign policy in favor of close alignment with Soviet positions."⁷⁸ By then, Conakry and Washington had all but gone their separate ways.

The United States senators who undertook a study mission of Africa in November/December 1960 concluded that Guinea had "become very deeply involved with the East." They had, according to their report, noticed "over 450 bloc technicians" in advisory positions in nearly every ministry and department of the government; that following Guinea's adoption of a new currency, "the great bulk of its trade has abruptly shifted away from the franc to the bloc," and that it had accepted "total bloc credits of over $100 million, as well as barter deals which have mortgaged at least one major export crop to the bloc for a minimum of 2 years." Even Guinea's political system, the senators noted, was "indistinguishable from a communist one." Writing Guinea off as a lost cause, they recommended that "[p]ending clearer evidence that Guinea indeed wants our friendship and wishes to—and can—preserve its independence from the bloc, we believe that the United States should maintain no more than a token aid program just to keep the door open."⁷⁹

As early as 1951, the United States consulate general in Dakar had notified the State Department that Toure was an "African communist leader."⁸⁰ Washington scarcely ever saw him in any other light. Among French African politicians, Sekou Toure was certainly atypical. Born in 1922, he was younger than all the other leading politicians of French West Africa. The others were born into a rarefied world of old money, privilege, and power; alumni of classical education in Dakar and Paris, and thoroughly bred Frenchmen. By contrast, Toure came up the hard way and almost despite himself: his schooling came in fits and starts; by eighteen, he was eking out a living as a post office clerk, without passing his *licence*. In 1945, however, he formed the first trade union in Guinea and found himself at last. In retrospect, it seems that trade unionism was far better suited to Toure's temperament than politics in the French West Africa of the 1940s. His work as a labor leader brought him into contact with the French communist officials of the Confédération Générale du Travail (CGT). In 1953, Toure—as the secretary of the Guinea chapter of the CGT—organized a two-month-long strike in Conakry; the strike resulted in a 20 percent wage increase for the lowest-paid public sector workers. This outcome turned him into a folk hero in Guinea and, indeed, in all of French West Africa.⁸¹ It was from this background that Toure worked himself into politics. Trade unionism provided him with an education in Marxist ideology as well as superb organizational skills; and through those employed in the expanding wage economy, it also provided him with a loyal political constituency.

No doubt, Toure—a self-educated man, a former trade union leader—drank deep of Marxist lore. It is equally beyond dispute that, in terms of doctrine, structure, and method, the PDG which he led seemed a close replication of the European communist parties. Toure brought to his politics the oratory and organizational skills of his trade union days. As a Muslim, he was able to secure the support of his country's influential religious leaders. At the same time, he gained mass popularity by drastically curtailing the power and privileges of the traditional chiefs.[82]

In all, Toure, his party, and his country all stood at the far left of the West African political spectrum. Nonetheless, as late as July 1960, *Economist* posed the question to Toure: "It is often said that Guinea is 'disappearing behind the iron curtain.' Is this opinion justified?" He replied, "We are not concerned with whether we are on one side of the iron curtain or the other. Our interest is whether our actions further the evolution and emancipation of our people. Before all ideological considerations, we have to face up to the essential realities which everyone knows about: such things as human misery, total lack of education, bad health conditions, and lack of economic development."[83]

When he visited Washington in October 1959, Toure recounted for Eisenhower the difficulties created by the French "withdrawal" and explained that so hard pressed was Guinea that his government "would have accepted help from the devil." The relief, he recalled, came from the Soviet bloc countries: barter arrangements, 2,500 guns, three tanks, a number of field kitchens, and several thousand plows, "all of which were given to Guinea without their having made a request for them of any kind either orally or in writing."[84]

By sharp contrast, Washington did not make even a symbolic gesture to Guinea. There was no lack of imagination or effort on the part of the African Bureau of the State Department and the embassy in Conakry. For example, the bureau pressed the need to "make favorable impression" on Toure during his October 1959 visit to Washington. Taking into account the fact that Guinea had inquired about acquiring a DC-3 through commercial channels, both the bureau and the embassy recommended that an aircraft (valued at $250,000) be presented to Toure. Sattterthwaite recalled the precedents for such a gesture: "the Coast Guard patrol vessel given Liberia after the Nixon visit and the Constellation given the Emperor of Ethiopia." In addition, he recommended the supply of pharmaceuticals, a refrigeration plant, earth-moving equipment, jeeps, tires, and spare parts.[85] Morrow says that these recommendations were not acted upon as "it was next to impossible to deal with Guinean matters in the State Department without consulting with the division that handled French affairs—namely, the Bureau of European Affairs."[86]

From October 1958 to 1960, Toure never missed an opportunity to deny that he was in the warm embrace of the "communists," to stress Guinea's neutralism in international affairs, and to demonstrate that he was simply being pragmatic in the face of his country's dire straits. In April 1959, Stanley de Osborne, the president of Olin Mathieson Company, visited Guinea and later reported to the State Department that Toure was "basically friendly to the West but ready to accept aid from any place it was given."[87] More fundamentally, Morrow found that "although Sekou Toure was a Marxist in orientation, he was not a communist and he had no desire to see his country taken over by the Russians or the Chinese. For that matter, he didn't want to see Guinea taken over by the Americans, French, British, or Germans." Morrow emphasized that "[i]n spite of the discrepancies which marked the carrying out of Guinea foreign policy—and there were many—I remained convinced that the cornerstone of this policy was positive neutralism."[88]

The Last Straw

Morrow described the reception Toure accorded the senators who visited in late 1960 as "notably cooler" than that received by United States public figures who had previously been in Conakry. Placing the matter on a broad canvas, he cabled Washington that Toure left a distinct "impression that he has all but written off [the] possibility of any significant cooperation with United States."[89] In his memoir, Morrow ascribes Toure's attitude on this occasion not to any "communist" hold but to his disaffection with United States policy over the Congo crisis. Toure, like Nkrumah, was a strong partisan of Lumumba. According to Morrow, Toure was therefore "very much irked" by the leading role played by the United States in seating the Joseph Kasavubu delegation at the UN General Assembly in September 1960.[90]

Toure initiated his communication with Washington over the Congo in August 1960, when he sent a message to Eisenhower urging that the United States should "take vigorous action" to effect the implementation of the UN Security Council resolution calling for the evacuation of all Belgian troops from the Congo and for respect for its territorial integrity. "We are certain," he added, "that if you will contribute your support, only a few hours will be needed to save the peace, which will benefit the African peoples and the entire world."⁹¹ Eisenhower saw the note as an opportunity to educate Toure on the need to support the UN in the Congo. He affirmed that the United States was not inclined to act unilaterally in the Congo because of its belief that the crisis there could be surmounted "only through the united efforts of all countries . . . coordinated through the United Nations under the effective leadership of Secretary-General Dag Hammarskjold." He contended that it would be a great contribution to peace if Toure himself were to use his influence in Africa to "encourage the fullest possible support for the United Nations effort in the Congo."⁹²

Incidentally, two days after Eisenhower's reply to Toure, the State Department agreed with a request by Baron Scheyven, the Belgian ambassador to the United States, that Washington should use its influence to forestall any changes in the Security Council resolutions under which Hammarskjold had been operating in the Congo.⁹³ Like Scheyven, Toure must have been motivated by the fact that international organizations such as the UN are only as effective as their most powerful members want them to be. He was therefore definitely not asking the United States to sidestep the UN but only to help see that UN resolutions were implemented, and so ensure that the organization was more effective.

It was not that Toure was out of order as that his request, the evacuation of Belgian troops, did not serve United States interests. On 16 August 1960, five days before a UN Security Council session on the Congo, the State Department instructed the United States mission at the UN to ensure that the withdrawal of Belgian troops received "minimum attention and [to ensure] that discussion will focus on crux of issue," which it defined as the dispute between Lumumba and the UN secretary-general on the future role of the UN in the Congo.⁹⁴ The fact was that Toure was never in good standing in Washington; the Congo merely complicated matters in this regard. In August 1960, the United States mission at the UN suggested that the Soviet Union could only disrupt UN operations in the Congo "through 'flag of convenience.' This would only be Guinea or Ghana."⁹⁵

A meeting between Toure and Satterthwaite in New York on 6 October 1960 failed to bridge the differences over the Congo. Satterthwaite reiterated the United States position that the problem revolved around Lumumba, who "seemed determined to curtail the United Nations role in the Congo and facilitate that of the Soviet Union." To Toure, this was reductionist: the issue, he insisted, was the independence and territorial integrity of the Congo. He wanted the legality of the Congolese government, as established through free elections, to be respected and reproached the UN for ignoring the needs of the government that had invited it into the country.⁹⁶

In November 1960, Toure cabled Eisenhower again, complaining of "our concern at the development of a partisan position by the United States in the situation in the Congo." He "earnestly" requested Eisenhower to "cease supporting the position of the enemies of African emancipation, who are employing every possible means against the legitimate Government of the Congo to attack the unity and territorial integrity of the Congolese nation." Toure warned that if the United States maintained its "present position," Guinea would decline participation in any conciliation effort and would "take any position in African affairs consistent with Congolese interests."[97]

Eisenhower regretted that Toure's cable reflected "a serious misunderstanding" of the United States policy "in support of African freedom." Toure was reminded that the United States had been "in the forefront of those nations who have favored emancipation of all peoples, including Africans, in accordance with the purposes and principles of the Charter of the United Nations." On the Congo, Eisenhower recalled that the United States had welcomed its independence, had "recognized and upheld its unity and territorial integrity through United Nations actions," and had refrained from unilateral intervention in its internal affairs. He held that "[a]lthough considerable partisanship has been demonstrated by some states, our support for the recognition of M. Kasavubu as Chief of State, a constitutional position which is universally accepted and recognized in the recent report of the UN, is not a question of partisanship but an attempt to strengthen one of the essential foundations of stable and effective government in that unhappy country." Eisenhower insisted that such a position was "in strict conformity with the interests of the Congolese Government and people" and that, in any case, "a large number of African states have taken a similar stand." Concluding, he invited Toure to fully support the UN effort in the Congo, given "the fact that the United Nations success is vital for the welfare of the Congolese."[98]

Morrow recalls that Toure was "very unhappy" with the way the second message he had sent to Eisenhower was handled. He was not only surprised at the tone of the response, but he was particularly displeased with the fact that Eisenhower released the reply to the press. Thereafter, Toure sent a message to President-elect John F. Kennedy but also "received a rebuff on this score when Kennedy let him know that he too was supporting the stand" taken by Eisenhower. According to Morrow, Kennedy's reply "surprised and nettled Toure, who expected a difference of opinion" between him and Eisenhower. Toure reacted by recalling Guinean troops from the Congo. It was against this tense background that the senators met with Touré,[99] who, at that point, had finally given up any hope of a relationship with the United States.

Conclusion

The most charitable comment is that both Guinea and the United States regarded each other warily and tried as far as they could to put the best possible face on their relationship. More seriously, the United States/Guinea relationship was essentially non-existent even before the Congo crisis: in deference to France (and to de Gaulle in particular), Washington had kept its distance from Conakry. Consequently, the relationship was, at best, very superficial, which explains its inability to withstand the strain of the Congo crisis.

The treatment meted out to Guinea did not endear Washington to West Africans. Even thoroughly pro-Western elements such as Prime Minister Tafawa Balewa of Nigeria were in sympathy with Touré "since [the] French, Britain and [the] U.S. had turned [their] backs on him."[100] In October 1958, the United States embassy in Monrovia had advised that even while respecting French opposition to any United States/Guinea relationship, Washington should issue a public statement of "sympathy and interest in Guinea's development and many current problems as well as a declaration of intention to extend formal recognition." It warned that "a definite and positive U.S. response on Guinea could not be long deferred without considerable damage [to] U.S. prestige [in] West Africa."[101]

Explaining his frigid relationship with the Eisenhower administration, Touré pointed out that "there is incontestably a sort of hiatus in these relations, conditioned, I think, on the side of the United States by French-American relations. If you prefer, we have a feeling the evolution of our relations with the United States is closely dependent on the evolution of relations between France and Guinea. There is a sort of subordination of our interests which has been particularly marked recently."[102] This was a remarkably perspicacious observation. Yet, any explanation of Guinea's difficulties with the United States must take into account the fact that Touré violated Eisenhower's model of the transfer of power from the European colonial powers to Africans: Guinea's transition to independence was anything but gradual or "evolutionary"; indeed, Touré had been "radical" enough to rupture relations with his former colonial overlord. In addition, it is almost certain that Eisenhower took Guinea's "secession" from the French Community as a personal rebuff and an affront to de Gaulle.

The sharp contrast afforded by Ghana adds more explanatory power to Washington's behavior towards Guinea. In all respects, Ghana's transition to independence accorded with Eisenhower's model of "evolutionary independence." Unlike Guinea's abrupt break with France, Ghana's transition was well calibrated, the result of mutual agreements between Nkrumah and his colleagues on the one hand and the British on the other—and so, in the end, independence came without the bitterness and rancor which marked Guinea's. Thus while Guinea "seceded" from the French Community and the franc zone, Ghana remained in the sterling area and joined the British Commonwealth (as it was then known); and while Franco-Guinean relations were practically frozen, Anglo-Ghanaian relations were very warm. This undoubtedly paved the way for an equally warm relationship between Ghana and the United States.

Implicit in this causal analysis is a more fundamental observation: Eisenhower's response to Guinea's independence suggests that in dealing with Africa, Washington was unable to divest itself of the a priori thought that it needed to give first consideration to Western European sensitivities, even after colonial rule had ended.

8

SUMMING UP

The previous chapters have explored the subtleties that shaped United States policy in Africa. There is much evidence that ideology, as conceptualized by Michael Hunt, underpinned much of United States conduct in Africa. One constituent of this ideology was a racial construction that privileged those of European descent and ghettoized those of African descent. In this way, racial postures derived from domestic race relations shaped the United States perspective and, by extension, policy towards Africa. The other element of the ideology was the legitimation of the international status quo—which in the 1950s, included the European colonial empires. Other findings in this book substantiate and elaborate upon the works of other scholars, particularly in stressing that Africa was a terribly neglected region (given the extremely limited attention and resources accorded to it relative to other "Third World" regions) as well as the overly European orientation of United States policy.

There are, of course, major points of departure from earlier works. One is the primacy of material considerations, especially the importance of Africa for European recovery and prosperity as well as a source of raw materials, in the determination of policy. Much of the existing literature pushes every United States policy decision in Africa during the period under study here into a rigid anti-Soviet framework. Anti-Sovietism was certainly an important consideration in policy making, but my evidence leads to the conclusion that it was not as consequential as is popularly believed.

A major United States objective identified in the earlier chapters was to ensure the pro-Western orientation of African states. The means to this end was influencing the process and content of (political) change. In general, this book shows that, in terms of both the means and the end, Washington fared badly. In the first place, the effort at "hegemonic socialization," although very limited in scope, hardly yielded any dividend. The major obstacle in this regard was the United States record in Africa. Africans, as John Morrow (the first United States ambassador to Guinea) observed in 1958, "had followed with great interest" United States "policies in Europe and Asia after the Second World War and had come to believe that the United States would not only have a sympathetic understanding" of African "aspirations but also would stand ready to help realize them."[1]

No doubt, Africans and especially, their political leaders, had high expectations that the emergence of the United States as a superpower and its presence in Africa would provide them with a negotiating space, distinct from the Western European sphere, in the world system. Sekou Toure, for example, was optimistic that the United States was "better situated than most Western powers to adopt correct policies towards Africa because it has no colonies and it has a colonial past."[2] More specifically, some thought that relations with the United States would help them reduce their economic dependence on Western Europe, which they considered pernicious. Niger's Prime Minister Hamani Diori was thus anxious for United States private investment "in order to break up the monopoly of French trading companies."[3] There was also a widespread expectation that the United States would lend its weight to the cause of self-determination in Africa. On each of these counts, Africans were greatly disappointed, as indicated by their criticism of United States policies, which is very much in evidence in the preceding chapters.

Eurocentricism and its Critics

The basic and recurring complaint by Africans was that the United States marched in lock step with the colonial powers, that Washington was too given to waiting for the green light from Western European capitals. In August 1959, John Emerson, the United States consul general to Nigeria, visited Claudius Akran, the Western Nigerian deputy premier and minister of economic planning. While anticipating an increase in United States assistance to the region, Akran talked of a widespread impression that the United States "has a tendency to hold back in matters of economic aid out of deference to the position and interest of the UK in this area."[4] In July 1960, Kenyan nationalist, Tom Mboya, publicly urged that United States assistance for Africa should be sent directly to African governments and not channeled through London, Paris, and Brussels.[5]

By 1960, this complaint was coming from American public officials as well. A 1959 study prepared for the United States Senate Committee on Foreign Relations was particularly critical of the "tendency to allow U.S. policy towards Africa to be formulated in the capitals of Europe."[6] Senators Frank Church, Gale McGhee, and Frank Moss, who toured Africa at the end of 1960, observed that the United States had been agonizing about one particular dilemma "ever since new emphasis has been given to our relations with Africa": trying to steer a careful course "between harmless expressions of idle sympathy for African nationalism, and active support of independence which we fear might unduly antagonize certain of our NATO allies." In this context, they found that "[w]ithout any adequate evidence of the truth of the equation—one established under different world conditions—we apparently cannot escape the habit of weighing our policies towards Africa against the chances that they would shatter our alliance system in Europe."[7]

While there may be some truth in the view that the European colonial presence narrowed Washington's latitude for independent action and thus stymied its policies in Africa, this book shows that there is greater merit in arguing that those policies were, by definition, self-negating. The preceding chapters have identified and dwelt at length on the self-negating policies that the United States adopted in its dealings with Africa. These included the instinctive European bias of the policymakers; the overriding concern with European economic recovery and well-being; the perception of Africa as a European sphere of influence; the policy of minimalism which flowed directly from the foregoing factors, and the format of decolonization-as-neocolonialism in Africa. For example, the notion that Africa was a European sphere of influence, and therefore the primary responsibility of the Europeans, made it very convenient for the United States to opt for a rather symbolic role in Africa. The point has been made, especially in chapter 4, that the fundamental factor in the determination of these policies was Africa's low rating in the strategic calculus of the United States.

On the Absence of Domestic Influence and Lobby

In the introduction, I asserted that policy formulation was "entirely a bureaucratic affair," without even congressional input. This assertion, clearly borne out by the preceding chapters, generates questions such as: Were Democratic politicians such as Chester Bowles, Hubert Humphrey, and Adlai Stevenson not persistent in their criticism of Eisenhower's inattention to Africa? Did John Kennedy not make the administration's lack of attention to Africa a major issue in his 1960 campaign for the presidency? Did these criticisms not provide any causal context for some of the decisions discussed in this book? It is equally legitimate to wonder whether the State Department was, as this book suggests, working in a vacuum, totally removed from other issues and individuals in the United States of the 1950s. The African-American bus boycott in Montgomery, Alabama, which started on 5 December 1955, marked the emergence of Martin Luther King, Jr., and the beginning of America's civil rights movement. The success of that boycott and the end of segregation on buses in Montgomery was the movement's first fruit. And this raises the question: How did this emergence of race as an issue—and more specifically, the mobilization of African-American political power—in the United States affect Washington's response to decolonization in Africa?

The Washington Dimension

I am well aware of the criticisms leveled by Democrats against the nonvisibility of Africa on Eisenhower's agenda. Kennedy, for one, made headlines with his sharp criticism, in 1956, of Eisenhower's "indecision, confusion, haste, timidity, and . . . excessive fear of giving offense" on the colonial question, and with his 1957 speech on Algeria.[8] There is no discussion of these speeches in this book because they did not bear directly on sub-Saharan Africa—and in any case, they had no bearing whatsoever on policy. It is instructive, in this regard, that (as shown in chapter 2) Eisenhower merely reiterated his lack of confidence in the ability of Algerians to "run their own government in the most efficient way," when informed of Kennedy's proposed resolution in favor of Algerian independence.

Kennedy is said to have made 479 references to Africa during his fall 1960 presidential campaign, emphasizing that "we have lost ground in Africa because we neglected and ignored the needs and aspirations of the African people."[9] Richard Mahoney has pointed out that much of this was sheer political opportunism. Kennedy's "Senate record on liberal issues," he says, "was weak and, in the case of civil rights, particularly so." Set in this context, "Kennedy's handling of the African issue in the 1960 campaign—his pitch to the liberal and black vote—was a minor classic in political exploitation in foreign policy." Mahoney therefore dismisses the references to Africa as a strategy to woo "American blacks without alienating Southern whites."[10] The more relevant issue here is that administrations are hardly ever influenced by the campaign rhetoric of the opposing party—and in this particular instance, the Eisenhower administration did not change its policy towards Africa on account of Kennedy's campaign rhetoric, a rhetoric, that in any case came very late in the day for the administration and the period covered by this book.

The preceding chapters do, indeed, point to some domestic political pressures in favor of a more meaningful African policy. At the same time, they show that the policymakers were indifferent to such pressures. This is well illustrated, in chapter 3, by the response of Secretary of State Dean Acheson to Senator Theodore Francis Green's urging that "the sympathy of the American people for those who were trying to get self-government should be broadcast even if all we can do is to put this sympathy in words." Chapter 4 shows that the United States embassy and the ICA mission, both in London, Clarence Randall (chairman, Eisenhower's presidential Council on Foreign Economic Policy), and Assistant Secretary Joseph Satterthwaite all pressed for an expansion of United States economic programs in Africa during the Eisenhower presidency. Typically, these efforts were of no causal consequence in terms of policy formulation.

Following his 1957 tour of some African countries, Vice President Richard Nixon prepared a report for Eisenhower. Among other things, the report urged that the United States should support African leaders such as Ghana's Nkrumah, become better acquainted with African peoples, staff its diplomatic missions in Africa with people capable of explaining Washington's policies in a clear manner, encourage private investment in Africa, and give more economic and technical assistance to African states.[11] A 1959 study prepared for the Senate Committee on Foreign Relations recommended that the United States "must treat Africa as a majority policy area, to be approached on a level of equality with other policy areas." As a prerequisite, the report urged that the United States "must relinquish the negative, ad hoc," and Eurocentric approach that had characterized its African policy. Neither of these reports was taken into account by the policymakers, which explains why the senators who toured Africa at the end of 1960 found that "the impression given by our activities in Africa as a whole is one of improvisation. . . .We have been reacting rather than initiating."[12]

Certainly, there were occasional domestic demands for a "dynamic" approach to Africa. It is worth emphasizing again that they bore no fruit: Africa was just not important enough. And this was true not only for the Truman and Eisenhower administrations, but also for Congress as well. Africa was the one corner of the world where Congress had no policy initiative and therefore routinely followed the executive branch. For example, in May 1959, the Senate Foreign Relations Committee established a subcommittee on Africa. This was a "consultative" subcommittee, which meant that it could not hold formal meetings unless the White House needed legislation on Africa—and there was none, since the executive did not submit any legislative recommendations on Africa.[13]

The African-American Dimension

There is now an impressive body of scholarship showing the concern and impact of African-Americans on United States diplomacy in Africa during the period under study here.[14] There are, however, other studies in the mold of Milton Morris' 1972 finding that "there is very little evidence that the black population has indeed affected substantially U.S. policies towards Africa."[15] African-American leadership has, recalled James Roark, "traditionally concerned itself almost exclusively with the issue of race advancement." Consequently, "American black leaders from 1943 to 1947 raised a vigorous protest against European colonialism and against the American foreign policy which they found in support of that colonialism." Yet after this burst of activity, "[m]ost black leaders again narrowed their horizons and once more defined their problems largely within the domestic context."[16] Writing in 1965, Elliot Skinner pointed out that until 1957–60, when they were "drafted by the State Department" to attend independence celebrations in Africa, the African-American intellectual community had "often looked askance at Africa." Ghana's independence in 1957, he observed, passed "relatively unnoticed" by them: "the event was celebrated only by a handful of [African-American] intellectuals and veterans of the Garvey Movement."[17]

A major survey found that in 1957, only 1 percent of African-Americans, contrasted with 6 percent of whites, could name as many as five countries, colonies, or other territories in Africa; 70 percent of African-Americans compared with 55 percent of whites could not name any at all.[18] A more recent study, by James Meriwether, confirms this disinterest in Africa, in the period 1935 to 1963. Meriwether identified several factors that inhibited African-American relations with Africa: "negative, racist imagery of Africa; an ambivalence about the continent and its peoples; a tendency to concentrate exclusively upon the domestic struggle rather than view it as part of a worldwide struggle for freedom and equality; a frustrating inability to influence U.S. foreign policy towards Africa."[19] It is therefore the case that there are conflicting perspectives on the African-American influence on United States policy towards Africa in the 1950s.

Given the mass of official reports, despatches, and position papers that form the resource base for this book, it is only to be expected that my interpretations and conclusions will reflect the "official mind." Nonetheless, it is also to be expected that in one way or the other, the officials would have in—their "internal memoranda," "memoranda of conversations," despatches, or reports—given some indication of a letter or letters, a petition or petitions, a rally or rallies, a public lecture or lectures, a meeting or meetings with one African-American group or the other, which had do to with Africa. In the event, my archival research—which was clearly extensive and thorough—turned up nothing along these lines. Phrased differently, I saw no hint of any African-American input, lobby, or pressure in connection with Washington's policies and behavior in Africa in the 1950s. It is important to bear in mind that this was a period when the American civil rights movement was still very much in its infancy, a period when there was no Congressional Black Caucus or TransAfrica and similar organizations that today lobby and influence United States conduct in Africa.[20]

Africa and the Issue of Race in America

While my research revealed no African-American influence on United States policy towards Africa, there are strong indications that the independence of African states, beginning with that of Ghana in 1957, contributed, in some way, to reshape the dynamics of race in the United States. Reporting after his 1957 visit to Africa, Nixon insisted that advocacy for Africa's independence could not be divorced from the domestic racial crisis: "We cannot talk equality to the peoples of Africa and Asia," he asserted, "and practice inequality in the United States."[21]

Rupert Emerson and Martin Kilson have since pointed out that there was an official acknowledgment of the interplay between domestic race relations and United States foreign policy at the end of World War II.[22] This, they say, induced both "the Truman and Eisenhower administrations . . . however, fitfully, to give executive leadership to the protection of a wide range of civil rights long guaranteed" to African-Americans "by the Constitution but subverted by the states." They argue that this process was helped by Africa's independence and the resulting increased contact which followed between Africans and the American public.[23]

In part, chapter 5 discussed how Ghana's Finance Minister Gbedemah and his entourage were prevented from eating inside a Delaware restaurant simply because of their skin color. This was not an isolated experience. In

November 1960, immediately after presenting his credentials to Eisenhower, Gallin Douathe, the ambassador of the Central African Republic to the United States, left Washington for New York City. On the way, he, his wife, and his secretary stopped at a restaurant at Pulaski Highway, near Baltimore, Maryland. The three sat at a table but were told that dinner was no longer being served, which was not true as they saw nonblacks being served at the same time. When Douathe pressed the matter, and even revealed his identity, the proprietor still insisted that they could not be served and advised that they could buy sandwiches to eat on the road. At that point, Douathe ordered four bottles of orange juice. Not only were these served without glasses, but the waitress would not allow them to drink inside the restaurant. Like Gbedemah, the Douthe group paid for the drinks, which they did not touch, and left. A few days later, Ferdinand Oyono, the Cameroonian representative at the UN, had a similar experience in New York City.[24]

As the Gbedemah case showed, racial discrimination against African dignitaries was a serious embarrassment for Washington. Consequently, such incidents received urgent attention at the highest levels. On 28 September 1960, British Foreign Secretary Lord Home informed Eisenhower that the first secretary of the Nigerian delegation to the UN was "finding it difficult to get a place to live in New York [City] because of his color." Secretary of State Christian Herter described the situation as "a terribly difficult one," and Eisenhower ordered that the New York [City] mayor and police commissioner should take up the matter "at once."[25]

It is clear, from the foregoing, that the emergence of Africa on the international arena was in conflict with white America's established patterns of segregation and discrimination against peoples of African descent. "American whites," according to Skinner, "had become somewhat accustomed to the Asian diplomats at the United Nations, but Africans presented a new and different challenge. For the first time in its history, America found itself compelled by world events to deal with black men on the basis of full equality."[26] Furthermore, African-Americans "witnessed the unusual spectacle of White House and other American officials apologizing to such Africans as Mr. Gbedemah of Ghana and Mr. Karifa-Smart of Sierra Leone who had been mistaken for Afro-Americans and been refused glasses of orange juice in restaurants. . . . For generations, Afro-Americans had been routinely subjected to worse indignities. Now, for the first time in the history of the Republic, American Negroes found themselves welcomed in the White House and the official receptions at which African Heads of State were entertained."[27]

True, "Africans did find that their presence was not appreciated by many white Americans," who "refused to rent apartments to Africans or to serve them meals in restaurants."[28] Nonetheless, even outside official circles, the increasing presence of Africans—diplomats, students, and visiting public officials—was redefining white-black relations in the United States. According to Skinner, Africans who came to the United States from the late 1950s onward found "themselves being received in homes, associations, and neighborhoods which had been closed to Afro-Americans. Many schools and colleges in the north, and even in the south, opened their doors to Africans while they still barred Afro-Americans." At the same time, "[m]any a policeman found out too late that the black man he had beaten up and taken to the police station for being 'cheeky' actually was carrying a diplomatic passport." Skinner added that, often, "embarrassed 'City Fathers' tried to make amends."[29]

The emergence of independent African states had another result. According to Alfred Hero, it "stimulated increased interest in that aspect of world affairs and, perhaps indirectly, in foreign policy" generally among African-Americans in the American South. Hero says that black integrationist leaders used the changing relations between the races in Africa and the end of colonial control by whites to arouse Southern blacks against local white supremacy: essentially, they argued that "progressive relations between the races in the South would improve" America's "public image" and the effectiveness of its policies towards Africa and other colored areas; that Africans had terminated white supremacy very quickly whereas Southern blacks had been unable to achieve their constitutional rights even a century after the abolition of slavery; and that "more equalitarian race relations is part of a worldwide movement against colonialism."[30] In Skinner's words, "The new interest in Africa was intimately related to the stepped-up drive for full integration in America. The new Africa was being employed by Afro-Americans as a weapon in their fight for 'Freedom Now!'"[31]

A more specific evidence that the United States civil rights movement drew some inspiration from Africa's political transition is furnished by Martin Luther King, Jr., himself. King was one of the African-Americans who attended Ghana's independence celebrations in 1957. There, he met Vice President Nixon. King used the opportunity to invite Nixon to visit Alabama, where "we are seeking the kind of freedom Ghana is celebrating."[32]

Against this background, it is quite plausible to argue that the independence of African states, Washington's attempt to address the racial discrimination directed at Africans, and the entire psychological adjustment in dealing with top-ranking African—and therefore, black—public officials had some redemptive impact on the United States domestic racial problematic. There are also grounds to argue that Africa's political transition energized the civil rights movement in the United States.

The Soviet/Cold War Factor

Another subject which calls for clarification at this point is the importance of the Soviet (or the Cold War) factor or the lack of it as a policy determinant. As chapter 6 shows, the fear of Soviet influence contributed in finally deciding Washington's participation in the Volta project. Nonetheless, the evidence is overwhelmingly in support of my contention that the Soviet factor was not a major determinant of United States diplomacy in West Africa.

On account of the manner in which it became independent, the petulant French reaction to it, and the depth of its structural economic weakness, Guinea was the country most vulnerable to "communist" penetration. Thus, Guinea, far more than any other West African country, provides a litmus test of Washington's anti-Soviet concerns and strategies in Africa in the 1950s. As shown in chapter 7, the "communist" countries were among the first to recognize Guinea, establish diplomatic missions in Conakry, and offer economic and military aid. Even with this apparent "communist" threat, the United States, in deference to France, kept its distance from Guinea and, indeed, shunned its overtures for a cordial bilateral relationship.

No doubt, Washington was from time to time worried by the Soviet presence in Guinea. For one thing, this concern—as chapter 7 shows—informed the decision to invite Sekou Toure for an official visit to Washington in October 1959. Paradoxically, and in spite of the efforts of the African Bureau of the State Department and the embassy in Conakry, and although Toure gave Eisenhower himself graphic details of Guinea's dire straits, Washington did not as much as make a symbolic gesture, in the form of material assistance, to Guinea.

In October 1960, the Joint Chiefs of Staff worried that Guinea was "increasingly following the path leading to domination by international communism."[33] In spite of this apprehension, Washington spent more than a year negotiating with Conakry for agreements on technical assistance, investment guarantees, commerce, and navigation. That was in spite of the well-known fact that the "communists" had moved in without such agreements, established a radio station that carried Guinea's voice all over Africa, and built a four-lane highway linking the capital city with its airport.[34]

A State Department intelligence report acknowledged that "[t]he Soviet Bloc has established a position of considerable influence in Guinea, and this former French West African territory may now have veered somewhat from its neutral course in foreign affairs." Yet, the department believed that "Guinea is drawn towards the communist states mainly by substantial Bloc economic aid." Above all, the report did not sense any indication that the "communists" aimed at seizing power in Guinea: "Rather, Soviet activities in Guinea are part of a many-sided effort to erode Western positions and brighten the public image of the communist system in Africa and the underdeveloped world generally." This did not perturb Washington, which played down the "communist" presence in Guinea: "Guinea," it was noted, still "lies within a Western politico-military sphere of influence."[35]

There is, in this entire sequence, not the slightest indication that the evident Soviet presence and influence in Guinea translated into a containment strategy of any form by the United States. On the contrary, and this is amply demonstrated in chapter 7, each "communist" gain can be matched against a prior "tactical withdrawal" by the United States. In Guinea, the underlying explanation for United States behavior was not the Soviet factor, but the accommodation of French sensitivities.

The United States response to "communism" in Guinea was, if anything, rather complacent. And as the evidence showed in chapter 4, this was emblematic of the general United States approach in West Africa during the period under study here. For a variety of reasons that were explored in that chapter, Washington did not consider West Africa, indeed all of sub-Saharan Africa, to be a real or potential theater for any threatening Soviet expansion. This explains why, by 1960, Washington was willing to accommodate—rather than oppose or "contain"—some degree of "communist" presence in Africa. While it believed that the end of European rule "opens the door to Sino-Soviet Bloc penetration," the NSC itself felt that it was futile, even unnecessary, to attempt to stem such penetration. It conceded that "African countries cannot be prevented from accepting some economic aid, technical assistance, and cultural exchanges from the Bloc." In the circumstances, the United States objective "should be to meet (together with the Metropoles and the multilateral agencies) the legitimate needs of the African countries wherever possible, to encourage them to accept only a minimum of Bloc aid, to limit Bloc activities to less sensitive fields, and to place those activities under strict controls."[36]

Decolonization as Neocolonialism

This book started with an articulation of decolonization as the co-optation of the "independent" African states and their political elite into a European-constructed neocolonial network. The attractiveness of this definition, as pointed out in the introduction, stems from the fact that as the end of European rule became a reality, the translation of decolonization into neocolonialism in Africa became a pressing matter in Washington. Although this subject has received occasional mention in some of the earlier chapters, its centrality as a policy objective was such that it merits a more systematic exploration at this point.

One reason for adopting 1950 as the opening date for this book was that the year saw the first attempt to formulate a United States policy for Africa: in 1950, the State Department became convinced, Assistant Secretary George McGhee recalled, of "the importance of developing an overall African policy in view of the 'malleability of the African people' and our influence with the colonial powers."[37] In spite of this conviction, no policy actually emerged in 1950 or in the years immediately following it. In 1955, the State Department realized that the United States still did not have an "African policy," that is, a policy independent of the European colonial powers in Africa. The stated objective of the resulting position paper was to "seek to create a greater sphere of activity which is identifiably American." This, it said, "would be a matter of creating policy where none has ever existed." The paper, intended to outline United States policy in Africa up to 1965, divined that until then, the colonial powers "will continue to dominate the African scene," albeit "under conditions of declining influence," which would "pose a number of difficulties for American policy, since the Metropolitan Powers may tend to become more suspicious of outside influences, less confident that they can manage the situation, and hence less inflexible in their policy towards the dependent territory." There was a simultaneous recognition that with the increasing political strength of African nationalism, the United States "may be constantly pressed to endorse either the European or African point of view."[38]

The paper suggested that the way out of the dilemma lay in "the development of a more independent policy in Africa." This policy was to be of "a triangular nature," taking into account United States needs and interests, the policies of the Western European powers, and the aspirations and attitudes of Africans themselves.[39] It is difficult to see how such a triangular balance could have been practicable, which may explain why Richard Jones, then United States ambassador in Monrovia, criticized the paper as "a holding-position aimed at preserving the status quo."[40] In any case, the preceding chapters amply show that the United States made no effort towards maintaining any such equilibrium.[41]

It was not until the end of July 1957 that the first NSC policy statement on Africa, NSC 5719, entitled "U.S. Policy toward Africa South of the Sahara Prior to Calendar Year 1960," was issued. Remarkably, even with the issuance of papers such as NSC 5719, there was really no United States policy for Africa all through the 1950s, that is, if by "policy," one is thinking of *a coherent plan for action*. It is instructive that in 1957, the year when NSC 5719 was issued, the NSC embarked on a proposal for "A Study of Africa in Transition," which derived from the recognition that "since the end of World War II, Africa was the only major geopolitical area where the U.S. had not systematically defined its national interests and formulated a coherent policy."[42]

By 1959, the "coherent national policy" had still not materialized. Thus in February 1959, *New York Times* carried a news analysis that showed how Africa's "political awakening" had caught Washington off guard and compelled the State Department to search for "meaningful African policies." One anonymous official was quoted as saying: "The African demand for political independence and improved living standards has begun to erupt much sooner than the experts anticipated. We are still laying the foundation for policy and action."[43] It was therefore appropriate that a 1959 study prepared for the United States Senate Committee on Foreign Relations opened with the observation that "[t]he United States has never had a positive, dynamic policy for Africa." The report observed that the United States had "looked to the continuing control by friendly European powers as a guarantee of stability and dependable cooperation"; otherwise, "a negative, ad hoc approach" had characterized Washington's attitude towards Africa.[44]

John Morrow, who was appointed as United States ambassador to Guinea in May 1959, reported that "[d]espite the briefings, and the conscientious reading of available documents," in late June 1959, "I was finding it difficult to ascertain the current United States policy in Africa." He recalled that

> As I continued my talks with State Department officials and those in other governmental agencies, I began to sense that there was an unwritten policy on Africa which would make it extremely doubtful that the State Department would produce in the foreseeable future a blueprint for coping with the profound political, economic, and cultural changes taking place throughout Africa.

According to Morrow, what passed for policy was the hope that "the ties, economic and otherwise, which formerly had bound African nations to the British or French, would be sustained in some fashion."[45] Again, it is worth emphasizing that this was, indeed, the fundamental objective—or better, desire—of the Eisenhower administration. The expectation that decolonization would translate into neocolonialism defined much of United States policy in Africa from the mid-1950s onward. Even the general European-orientation of policy stemmed, in part, from the desire for strong neocolonial relations between Europe and postcolonial Africa.

Underlying the desire for European neocolonialism was the fact that the United States never intended to assume any responsibility in Africa. In July 1959, Washington instructed its consul in Freetown that he should be "guided by the following policy considerations: (1) It is the general policy of the United States that the metropoles be encouraged to continue their close relationships, with, and support of, their former territories; (2) Although the United States does not wish to assume any part of what it conceives to be the role and responsibilities of the metropoles, it does desire to show its interests in the emerging territories by appropriately assisting them in a manner that will tend to supplement rather than to replace continuing activities of the metropoles."[46] This instruction was not an isolated case; its essence, as chapter 4 shows, recurred quite often in NSC and State Department working papers.

Neocolonial relations, it was calculated, would enable the Western European powers (especially Britain and France), which still had considerable political, economic, and cultural leverage in Africa, to safeguard Western interests there. This strategy and its broader implications were expressed in April 1956, when Assistant Secretary George Allen reminded the American Academy of Political and Social Sciences that the relationship between Africa and Western Europe was established when the concepts of international relations "were different." Continuing, he emphasized that "in the course of this relationship between the metropolitan powers and the African territories, there grew up interlocking economic relations, the violent disruption of which would seriously weaken" both Africa and Europe. Given this assumed mutual relationship between Africa and Europe, he proposed that what was required was "transforming existing relationships into a cooperative endeavor" in which African states "can achieve and maintain their national self-respect. . . . We need friendly and cooperative relations with Europe and Africa, just as their own interests require the maintenance of intimate ties with each other."[47]

Allen was in effect saying that the taproot of the colonial relationship should still subsist, even if "independence" inevitably occurred in Africa. A year later, Deputy Assistant Secretary Joseph Palmer 2nd expressed the same hope, using words essentially identical with Allen's. After noting that Africa and Europe were "fundamentally complementary areas," Palmer held that the "essential problem" confronting the West was "that of bringing about a new relationship" between the two "in a manner which will assure the most beneficial results for both parties." It was therefore Washington's hope, he said, that "the transition of Africa from a colonial to a national status will take place in a manner which will preserve the fruitful ties which bind the two continents together."[48]

More than colonialism, neocolonialism is a collaborative arrangement between the former European colonial rulers and the indigenous political elite. Thus to function at all, neocolonialism requires pliant local mediators.[49] In turn, this requires that no rupture occurs in the transition to independence between the indigenous elite and the "departing" colonial power, as was the case in Guinea. It was for this reason that the United States cautioned the anticolonial forces that their zeal should be balanced by patience, preferred that independence should be evolutionary, and frowned at "premature independence." This context also provides the explanation for Washington's declared commitment to encourage "insofar as we are able, moderate African leaders." In May 1958, Julius Holmes, special assistant to Secretary of State Dulles, defined "moderate leaders" as those "who recognize the benefit to their own people of following the evolutionary, rather than the revolutionary, approach to social, political and economic progress." The African political elite was therefore urged "to consider seriously the numerous pitfalls that confront a newly independent state today and to realize that premature independence can carry with it more dangers than a temporary prolongation of a dependent status."[50]

The decolonization-as-neocolonialism format and its enabling conditions received their most eloquent elaboration in NSC 5719, which was issued in July 1957. Its running theme was that the United States was "concerned that Africa South of the Sahara develop in an orderly manner towards self-government and independence in cooperation" with its European colonial powers. "We hope," the paper continued, "that this transition will take place in a manner which will preserve the essential ties which bind Europe and Africa—which are fundamentally complementary areas....The United States, therefore, believes it to be generally desirable that close ties and mutually advantageous economic relationships between the European powers and Africa should continue after the colonial period has passed."[51]

In a sense, the desire that European colonial networks in Africa should not be disrupted after independence was informed by the need for the Europeans to continue as the primary source of external capital assistance for Africa. Washington calculated that by virtue of their suzerainty over Africa, the Western European countries were necessarily bearing a large part of the burden for Africa's economic development. But the extent to which they would continue doing so after independence was not clear. The authors of NSC 5719 reasoned that factors other than the European countries' financial capabilities would influence any decision taken in this regard by the Europeans. "One very important factor," they believed, "will necessarily be a metropolitan power's appraisal of the likelihood that it will be able to maintain close political and economic ties with a particular colonial territory, either through an extension of the colonial relationship itself or through the development of a mutually-satisfactory new relationship." Where the prospects for such a relationship did not exist, "the incentives of the metropolitan powers to provide financial or economic support, either through public or private investment, are likely to suffer rapid deterioration." And in such a circumstance, the United States saw itself having to carry the "white man's burden" in Africa. The only way to avoid such a burden was to encourage an "orderly," and therefore harmonious, transition that would ensure continued heavy European responsibility in Africa. In the words of NSC 5719: "Thus our success in attaining the previously-stated U.S. objective of preserving the essential ties between Europe and Africa will probably have an important impact upon the rate of Africa's reliance on U.S. assistance."[52]

The singular significance of NSC 5719 is that it tied together what ordinarily appear as disparate elements of United States policy in Africa during Eisenhower's presidency: its heavy Eurocentric bias; its option for "a junior partner's role" to the Western Europeans, not just in terms of foreign aid but in a more general sense; its opposition to "radical" nationalism that could rupture the relations between Western Europe and Africa; and its endorsement of European neocolonialism.

It was not simply that the Eisenhower administration wished to avoid responsibility for aid to Africa; its broader strategy was to retain European influence as the "stabilizing" element in Africa. At the April 1959 tripartite (Britain, France, United States) talks on Africa, the United States delegation surveyed the political developments in Africa at the time and assured the Europeans that Washington considered it "essential" that the changes should take place "in an orderly manner and in the closest cooperation with the Western European powers. Europe and Africa are complementary, and the closest ties must be preserved after the colonial period has passed." The Europeans were further assured that the United States regarded them as "best equipped" for defending and projecting Western influence in Africa, and therefore that Washington was "most anxious to work in the closest cooperation with the former administering powers of the newly independent areas."[53]

Washington's strategy of relying on European influence as a stabilizing force for Western interests and settling for a supporting role was not exclusive to Africa: it was a strategy applied whenever and wherever United States national security interests were not in any immediate danger. A 1949 CIA report confessed that "[e]verywhere in the world outside the Western Hemisphere and Northeast Asia, British power is an essential component in the present structure of U.S. security. . . .In consequence the United States has counted on the British, sometimes pursuant to formal agreement but more generally by implication, to assume primary affairs in the Middle East, South and Southeast Asia, and most of Africa."[54] There was thus what H. W. Brands has called America's "Commonwealth strategy," that is, relying on the Commonwealth framework as the mechanism to safeguard South Asia in the period from 1947 to 1950. This strategy sprang from the realization that "a direct assumption of responsibility for the securing of India and Pakistan was entirely out of the question" at a time when the American public was just getting accustomed to the idea of its commitment to Europe. Consequently,

> American officials sought to pursue a policy of indirect influence. The United States would work through collaborators, through agents who would extend the American reach in South Asia beyond the limits set by American resources and American domestic politics. This was where the Commonwealth—Britain especially, but also Canada, Australia and others—could be persuaded to accept continued responsibility for the security of the subcontinent.

Brands shows that Washington held on to this strategy, even with Mao Tse-tung's accession to power in China in late 1949. It was the outbreak of the Korean War in June 1950 that finally forced the United States to assume direct responsibility for securing its national security in the region.[55] In the case of Africa, there was no equivalent of the Korean War to induce a change of policy.

One does not need to strain too hard to understand the rationale for this reliance on the Europeans as a stabilizing influence in their colonial and former colonial areas. Even as American leaders aspired to the universalization of their power and interests, they were acutely aware that while their country was the world's preeminent power, it was far from being omnipotent. This meant that although Washington considered that its domestic stability and prosperity was intertwined with the stability of every other unit of the international system, there was at the same time the realization that it lacked the wherewithal to singlehandedly police all the world. There was thus an early recognition of the need to assign supervisory roles to the other major powers as well. It was no wonder, then, that when in April 1943, Roosevelt was asked what would replace Article 10 of the League of Nations Covenant—to maintain world peace—he replied that the United States and China "would police Asia, Africa would be stabilized by Britain and Brazil, and Europe by Britain and Russia."[56]

By the same token, the CIA and JCS rankings mentioned in chapter 2, like those of George Kennan,[57] differentiating between areas of vital and peripheral importance to United States national security, were informed by this awareness of Washington's limits to project its preeminent power worldwide. This limitation was made quite real by the perennial unwillingness of Congress, as shown in chapter 4, to provide the financial support for an expansive, activist, internationalist foreign policy.

In the circumstances, resigning supervisory responsibility to the Europeans over some "Third World" regions made perfect sense: Washington entrusted to its chief partners in the world system the responsibility of producing the public good of international stability in the areas where they were best equipped to do so. That was a highly cost-saving division of labor based on comparative advantage. It remains to be said that under this arrangement, Africa was in a class of its own by 1960: in August of that year, Acting Secretary of State Douglas Dillon reminded the NSC that "[t]he U.S. position in Africa . . . was different from that in other underdeveloped areas in that we were supporting other industrial countries rather than assuming the main role."[58]

NOTES

Notes to the Introduction

1. Thomas J. Noer, "'Non-Benign Neglect': The United States and Black Africa in the Twentieth Century," in *American Foreign Relations: A Historiographical Review*, eds. Gerald K. Haines and J. Samuel Walker (Westport, CT: Greenwood Press, 1981), 271–92.

2. Obafemi Awolowo, *Path to Nigerian Freedom* (London: Faber & Faber, 1947), 23.

3. Olajide Aluko, "Politics of Decolonization in British West Africa, 1945–1960," in *History of West Africa, vol. 2*, eds. J. F. Ade Ajayi and Michael Crowder (Essex, England: Longman Group UK, 1987), 694–95. For a similar view, see H. S. Wilson, *African Decolonization* (London: Edward Arnold, 1994), 54–56.

4. Wm. Roger Louis and Ronald Robinson, "The United States and the Liquidation of British Empire in Tropical Africa, 1941–1951," in *The Transfer of Power in Africa: Decolonization 1940–1960*, eds. Prosser Gifford and Wm. Roger Louis (New Haven, CT: Yale University Press, 1982), 48–49.

5. Jeffrey A. Frieden, "The Economics of Intervention: American Overseas Investments and Relations with Underdeveloped Areas, 1890–1950," *Comparative Studies in Society and History*, 31, 1 (January 1989). D. Cameron Watt, *Succeeding John Bull: America in Britain's Place, 1900–1975* (Cambridge: Cambridge University Press, 1984), 250–52, also argues that the United States was hostile to European colonial rule after World War II.

6. Louis and Robinson, "The United States and the Liquidation of British Empire in Tropical Africa, 1941–1951," 31.

7. NIE-83, "Conditions and Trends in Tropical Africa," 22 December 1953, *FRUS, 1952–1954, vol. 11* (1983), 71–89. National intelligence estimates (NIEs) were "high-level interdepartmental reports presenting authoritative appraisals of vital foreign policy problems. NIEs were drafted by officers from those agencies represented on the Intelligence Advisory Board Committee (IAC), discussed and revised by interdepartmental working groups coordinated by the Office of National Intelligence Estimates of the Central Intelligence Agency (CIA), approved by the IAC, and circulated under the aegis of the CIA to the President, appropriate officers of the cabinet level, and the National Security Council." See *ibid.*, n. 1, 71–72.

8. That was NSC 5719/1, "U.S. Policy toward Africa South of the Sahara Prior to Calendar Year 1960," 23 August 1957, *FRUS, 1955–1957, vol. 18* (1989), 75–87. (The first draft, NSC 5719, dated 31 July 1957, can be found under RG 273, at NA).

9. Dwight Eisenhower (president, 1953–61) recalled that "[i]n early 1960, when the independence movement really began to snowball, it became obvious that our traditional

policy of refraining from involvement in areas considered to be under the hegemony of other nations had to be re-examined." The result, according to him, was that "in early April," he approved that "the United States would be prepared on the basis of a case-by-case appraisal of a country or project to extend economic development assistance where needed to the nations of Africa." See his *The White House Years: Waging Peace* (Garden City, NY: Doubleday, 1965), 572–73, n. 13.

10. Gabriel Kolko, *Confronting the Third World: United States Foreign Policy, 1945–1980* (New York: Pantheon Books, 1988), 115.

11. The countries were Chad, Cameroon, Central African Republic, Congo-Brazzaville, Congo (Zaire), Dahomey (Benin), Ivory Coast, Gabon, Madagascar (Malagasy), Mali, Mauritania, Niger, Nigeria, Senegal, Somalia, Togo, and Upper Volta (Burkina Faso).

Notes to Chapter 1

1. Aguibo Y. Yansane, *Decolonization in West African States with French Colonial Legacy—Comparison and Contrast: Development in Guinea, the Ivory Coast and Senegal (1945–1980)* (Cambridge, MA: Schenkman Publishing, 1984), xv.

2. Martin Kilson, "African Political Change and the Modernization Process," *Journal of Modern African Studies*, 1, 4 (December 1963), 427, 431–32. Also see Martin Kilson, "Nationalism and Social Classes in British West Africa," *Journal of Politics*, 20, 2 (May 1958); Immanuel Wallerstein, "Elites in French-speaking West Africa: The Social Basis of Ideas," *Journal of Modern African Studies*, 3, 1 (May 1965). For a broad discussion, see David E. Apter, *The Politics of Modernization* (Chicago and London: University of Chicago Press, 1965); Rupert Emerson, *From Empire to Nation: The Rise to Self-Assertion of Asian and African Peoples* (Cambridge, MA: Harvard University Press, 1960); Edward Shils, "Political Development in the New States (I)," *Comparative Studies in Society and History*, 2, 3 (April 1960); Shils, "Political Development in the New States (II)," ibid., 2, 4 (July 1960).

3. See David E. Apter, *Ghana in Transition* 2nd rev. edn. (Princeton, NJ: Princeton University Press, 1972); Dennis Austin, *Politics in Ghana, 1946–1960* (London: Oxford University Press, 1964); James S. Coleman, *Nigeria: Background to Nationalism* second printing (Berkeley and Los Angeles: University of California Press, 1960); Kalu Ezera, *Constitutional Developments in Nigeria* (Cambridge: Cambridge University Press, 1960); Thomas Hodgkin, *Nationalism in Colonial Africa* (New York: New York University Press, 1957); David Kimble, *A Political History of Ghana: The Rise of Gold Coast Nationalism* (Oxford: Clarendon Press, 1963); Martin Kilson, *Political Change in West Africa: A Study of the Modernization Process in Sierra Leone* (New York: Atheneum, 1969); Ruth Schachter Morgenthau, *Political Parties in French-Speaking West Africa* (London: Oxford University Press, 1964); Gabriel O. Olusanya, *The Second World War and Politics in Nigeria, 1939–1953* (Lagos, Nigeria: University of Lagos and Evans, 1973).

4. A. G. Hopkins, *An Economic History of West Africa* (London: Longman, 1973), 260, 271.

5. The metropolitan side of the narrative of the transfer of power in Ghana can be followed in Richard Rathbone, ed. *British Documents on the End of Empire: Ghana*, 2 vols. (London: HMSO, 1992).

6. Cohen was assistant undersecretary in charge of the African Division in the Colonial Office, 1947–52; in 1952, he became the governor of Uganda.

7. Andrew Cohen, *British Policy in Changing Africa* (London: Routledge & Kegan Paul, 1959), 20–26. Indirect rule refers to the British model of colonial local government. It consisted of a resident at the head of a political territorial unit (a province), assistant residents, district officers, and assistant district officers, all Europeans. Under these came the native authority consisting of a paramount chief who, in turn, had his own hierarchy of lesser officials (district heads, village heads, etc.).

8. Ebere Nwaubani, "Getting behind a Myth: The British Labour Party and Decolonization in Africa, 1945–1951," *Australian Journal of Politics and History,* 39, 2 (1993).

9. Kofi Frimpong, "The Joint Provincial Council of Paramount Chiefs and the Politics of Independence, 1946–58," *Transactions of the Historical Society of Ghana,* 1, 14 (June 1973).

10. For an elaboration, see Nwaubani, "Getting behind a Myth: The British Labour Party and Decolonization in Africa, 1945–1951."

11. Under the 1946 Gold Coast constitution, only five of the eighteen unofficial seats in the LegCo were to be elected directly. Since the opportunities were thus very narrow for non-chiefs, many Western-educated elites had to lobby the chiefs to enter the LegCo on the ticket of the Joint Provincial Council. In 1946, only J. B. Danquah and C. Baeta were successful in winning that ticket. See Frimpong, "The Joint Provincial Council of Paramount Chiefs and the Politics of Independence, 1946–58."

12. Austin, *Politics in Ghana,* 58–73.

13. *Report of the Commission of Enquiry into the Disturbances in the Gold Coast, 1948,* Colonial No. 231, s. 263. (London: HMSO, dated 9 June 1948, the report was published on 4 August 1948.) Also, David Rooney, *Kwame Nkrumah: The Political Kingdom in the Third World* (London: I. B. Tauris, 1988), 34–35.

14. Rhoda Howard, *Colonialism and Underdevelopment in Ghana* (New York: Africana Publishing Company, 1978), 75.

15. Quoted in Polly Hill, *The Gold Coast Cocoa Farmer: A Preliminary Survey* (London: Oxford University Press, 1956), 67, n. 1.

16. *Report of the Commission of Enquiry into the Disturbances in the Gold Coast,* s. 192.

17. Dennis Austin, *Ghana Observed: Essays on the Politics of a West African Republic* (Manchester: Manchester University Press, 1976), 15; W. B. Birmingham, "An Index of Real Wages of the Unskilled Labourer in Accra," *Economic Bulletin of Ghana,* 4, 3 (1960), 2–6.

18. Austin, *Ghana Observed,* 15; Rooney, *Kwame Nkrumah,* 35.

19. Much of the hardship arising from the scarcity of imported goods and the resulting inflation was widely attributed to AWAM. Just before World War II, the United Africa Company, in concert with a number of other leading European trading firms, formed a merchandise agreement group—that is, a group of firms that agreed on prices and shares of the market for a number of imports into the Gold Coast. This cartel, which later transformed itself into AWAM, survived until April 1948. See Howard, *Colonialism and Underdevelopment in Ghana,* 106.

20. Austin, *Ghana Observed,* 18; Rooney, *Kwame Nkrumah,* 35.

21. Kwame Nkrumah, *Autobiography* (London: Thomas Nelson, 1957), 76.

22. Austin, *Ghana Observed,* 18.

23. Rooney, *Kwame Nkrumah,* 38.

24. The other members were Keith Murray of Lincoln College, Oxford University; Andrew Dalgleish, a trade unionist; and E. G. Hanrott of the Colonial Office, who acted as secretary. They arrived in the Gold Coast in April 1948.

25. *Report of the Commission of Enquiry into the Disturbances in the Gold Coast.*

26. Ibid.

27. *Statement by His Majesty's Government on the Report of the Commission of Enquiry into the Disturbances in the Gold Coast 1948,* Colonial No. 232 (London: HMSO, 1948).

28. *Gold Coast: Report to His Excellency The Governor by the Committee on Constitutional Reform 1949,* Colonial No. 248 (Accra, 1949).

29. *Statement by His Majesty's Government on the Report of the Committee on Constitutional Reform 1949,* Colonial No. 250 (14 October 1949).

30. Ibid.

31. J. H. Price, *Political Institutions of West Africa* (London: Hutchinson, 1966), 53.

32. J. M. Lee, *Colonial Government and Good Government: A Study of the Ideas Expressed by the British Official Classes in Planning Decolonization 1939–1964* (Oxford: Clarendon Press, 1967), 1.

33. "Self-government," in British political practice, had long meant the steady devolution of political authority through legislative institutions until parliamentary sovereignty—that is, the executive becoming collectively responsible to the legislature—was attained. This approach derives from the notion that within Parliament resides the sovereignty of the citizenry and thus that representation and legislative decision making are the means by which legitimacy is incorporated into the political process. The first stage is a LegCo consisting entirely of officials and nominated members; in the second stage, a few elected members are brought into the council, to complement the official and nominated members; the third is a council consisting of official, nominated, and elected members, with the elected members in the majority; but certain subjects are still reserved. The fourth and final stage is a council consisting of elected members to whom ministers forming a cabinet or executive are responsible for the entire administration without reservation, the governor being reduced to a position analogous to that of the monarch in the British metropolitan system. See A. B. Keith, *Responsible Government in the Dominions, vol. 1* (London: Oxford University Press, 1928); Martin Wight, *The Development of the Legislative Council, 1606–1945* (London: Faber & Faber, 1946).

34. Like that of the British, French political policy in Africa, even by 1950, was conservative. The 1946 French constitution, which was still in effect, was intended to achieve the integration of the overseas territories into the French Union. The political change in the Gold Coast immediately put some pressure on the French. By the mid-1950s, the need for reforms had become more pressing: Britain clearly wanted British Togo's future settled along with Ghana's independence; this made France concede the principle of autonomy in French Togo. The same concession could not be denied to other African territories, especially because the French became "increasingly concerned about the possible 'separatist' influence on French tropical Africa" of the independence of Ghana which would soon follow the June 1954 elections there. The outcome of this concern was the *Loi Cadre.* See Morgenthau, *Political Parties in French-Speaking West Africa,* 61–62; John D. Hargreaves, *Decolonization in Africa* (London and New York: Longman, 1988), 154.

35. Michael Blundell, *So Rough a Wind* (London: Weidenfeld and Nicolson, 1964), 83.

36. CO 583/287/30, A. B. Cohen to Sir J. Macpherson, 12 June 1948 (PRO, Lon-

don). Zik was the nickname of Nnamdi Azikiwe who, through his Lagos-based *West African Pilot* had, since 1938, advocated far-reaching political reforms in Nigeria—and indeed, in all of British West Africa—along Westminster lines. In 1946, Arthur Richards, Macpherson's predecessor, introduced the constitution, discussed earlier in this chapter, which was based on indirect rule and the chiefs. Azikiwe led the National Council of Nigeria and the Cameroons to campaign against the constitution. See Coleman, *Nigeria*; Ezera, *Constitutional Developments in Nigeria*; Olusanya, *The Second World War and Politics in Nigeria*.

37. CO 583/287/5/30453/4, Sir J. Macpherson to A. B. Cohen, 28 June 1948 (PRO, London). (Emphasis in original).

38. F. M. Bourret, *Ghana: The Road to Independence, 1919–1957* (Stanford, CA: Stanford University Press, 1960), 164. Kwame Nkrumah noted that J. B. Danquah, who later became a leading UGCC member, "supported the Burns Constitution so strongly that he allowed himself to be nominated by the Joint Provincial Council of Chiefs as their representative in the Burns Legislative Council." See Nkrumah, *Autobiography*, 69.

39. In 1947, the UGCC invited Nkrumah to become its secretary. He accepted the invitation and left England on 14 November 1947. See ibid., 61–63.

40. Ibid., 74–75.

41. Ibid., 76.

42. Hargreaves, *Decolonization in Africa*, 115.

43. Nkrumah, *Autobiography*, 79–80.

44. See *Report of the Commission of Enquiry into the Disturbances in the Gold Coast*; Nkrumah, *Autobiography*, 85–87.

45. Austin, *Politics in Ghana*, 19; Nkrumah, *Autobiography*, 77; Rooney, *Kwame Nkrumah*, 39.

46. Austin, *Politics in Ghana*, 81–85; Austin, *Ghana Observed*, 20–26; Nkrumah, *Autobiography*, chaps. 8–9; Rooney, *Kwame Nkrumah*, 42–45.

47. Nkrumah, *Autobiography*, 103.

48. Ibid.

49. *Gold Coast: Report to His Excellency The Governor by the Committee on Constitutional Reform*, sections 443–64.

50. Austin, *Ghana Observed*, 23.

51. Nkrumah, *Autobiography*, 113–14. "Positive Action," according to Nkrumah, was the "adoption of all legitimate and constitutional means by which we could attack the forces of imperialism in the country. The weapons were legitimate political agitation, newspaper and educational campaigns and, as a last resort, the constitutional application of strikes, boycotts and non-cooperation based on the principle of absolute non-violence as used by Gandhi." See ibid., 111–12. But Fitch and Oppenheimer have pointed out that "Nkrumah's is a conservative interpretation of Gandhi, who never stipulated that non-violence must be 'constitutional.'" See Bob Fitch and Mary Oppenheimer, *Ghana: The End of an Illusion* (New York and London: Monthly Review Press, 1966), 28 n. 23.

52. Nkrumah, *Autobiography*, 116; Rooney, *Kwame Nkrumah*, 53–54.

53. Reginald Saloway, "The New Gold Coast," *International Affairs*, 31, 4 (October 1955), 470–71.

54. Fitch and Oppenheimer, *Ghana*, 29.

55. Nkrumah, *Autobiography*, 115.

56. Richard Jeffries, *Class, Power and Ideology in Ghana: The Railwaymen of Sekondi* (Cambridge: Cambridge University Press, 1978), 54–55.

57. Ibid., 48.
58. Saloway, "The New Gold Coast," 470–71.
59. Fitch and Oppenheimer, *Ghana,* 31.
60. Austin, *Politics in Ghana,* 88–90, 114; Rooney, *Kwame Nkrumah,* 54–55.
61. Austin, *Politics in Ghana,* 138–51.
62. Nkrumah, *Autobiography,* 103.
63. Jeffries, *Class, Power and Ideology in Ghana,* 58–59.
64. Basil Davidson, *Black Star: A View of the Life and Times of Kwame Nkrumah* (London: Allen Lane, 1973), 128.
65. Nkrumah, *Autobiography,* 171–77; D. J. Morgan, *The Official History of Colonial Development, vol. 5: Guidance towards Self-Government in British Colonies, 1941–1971* (London: Macmillan, 1980), 83–84.
66. In British colonial practice, "internal self-government" or "responsible government" meant a government with full responsibility for local affairs but none in the "imperial sphere" (that is, foreign affairs, defense, trade, and constitutional matters), which remained in the hands of the "mother country." See Keith, *Responsible Government in the Dominions, vol. 1.*
67. For details, see Nkrumah's "motion of destiny" in Nkrumah, *Autobiography,* chap. 17.
68. This found expression through the National Liberation Movement, formed in September 1954. See Jean Marie Allman, "The Youngmen and the Porcupine: Class, Nationalism and Asante's Struggle for Self-Determination, 1954–57," *Journal of African History,* 31, 2 (1990); Allman, *The Quills of the Porcupine: Asante Nationalism in an Emergent Ghana* (Madison: University of Wisconsin Press, 1993).
69. Austin, *Politics in Ghana,* chap. 6.
70. *Report of the Advisory (Monckton) Commission on the Review of the Constitution of Rhodesia and Nyasaland,* Cmd. 1148 (October 1960), *Parliamentary Papers* (London, 1959–60), xi, 21, para. 31.
71. Davidson, *Black Star,* 126.
72. Rooney, *Kwame Nkrumah,* 123.
73. Ibid., 123–24.
74. Nkrumah, *Autobiography,* 282. (Emphasis in original).
75. Austin, *Ghana Observed,* 28.
76. Michael Crowder and Donal Cruise O'Brien, "Politics of Decolonization in French West Africa, 1945–1960," in *History of West Africa, vol. 2,* eds. J. F. Ade Ajayi and Michael Crowder (Essex, England: Longman Group, 1987), 736. Also see Michael Crowder, "Independence as a Goal in French West African Politics: 1944–60," in *French-Speaking Africa: The Search for Identity,* ed. William H. Lewis (New York: Walker, 1965).
77. Guy Martin, "The Historical, Economic, and Political Bases of France's African Policy," *Journal of Modern African Studies,* 23, 2 (June 1985), 191.
78. Hargreaves, *Decolonization in Africa,* 162.
79. Coleman, *Nigeria,* 312.
80. Dennis Osadebay, *Building a Nation* (Ibadan, Nigeria: Macmillan, 1978), 76.
81. The definitive work on this subject is Ehiedu E. G. Iweriebor, *Radical Politics in Nigeria, 1945–1950* (Zaria, Nigeria: Ahmadu Bello University Press, 1996). But also see Gabriel O. Olusanya, "The Zikist Movement: A Study in Political Radicalism, 1946–50," *Journal of Modern African Studies,* 4, 3 (November 1966); Olusanya, *The Second World War and Politics in Nigeria,* 113–17; Coleman, *Nigeria,* 296–302; Richard L. Sklar, *Nigerian*

Political Parties: Power in an Emergent African Nation (Princeton, NJ: Princeton University Press, 1970), 72–83.

82. Gary Wasserman, *Politics of Decolonization: Kenya Europeans and the Land Issue, 1960–1965* (Cambridge: Cambridge University Press, 1976), 5.

83. Obafemi Awolowo, *AWO: The Autobiography of Chief Obafemi Awolowo* (Cambridge: Cambridge University Press, 1960), 299.

84. Austin, *Ghana Observed*, 2.

85. Judith Marshall, "The State of Ambivalence: Right and Left Options in Ghana," *Review of African Political Economy*, 5 (1976), 50–51. This theme is pursued at length in Fitch and Oppenheimer, *Ghana*.

86. Wm. Roger Louis, *The British Empire in the Middle East 1945–1951: Arab Nationalism, the United States, and Postwar Imperialism* (New York: Oxford University Press, 1984), viii.

87. Rudolf von Albertini, *Decolonization: The Administration and Future of the Colonies, 1919–1960*, trans. Francisca Garvie (New York: Doubleday, 1971), 284, 266; John Chipman, *French Power in Africa* (Oxford: Basil Blackwell, 1989).

88. Michael Crowder writes that French colonial policy for Africa, from the 1944 Brazzaville Conference to the creation of the French Community in 1958, was intended "to assimilate Africa into Greater France, which was why France at no point envisaged independence for its African colonies." See Crowder, "Independence as a Goal in French West African Politics: 1944–60."

89. See Edouard Bustin, "The Limits of French Intervention in Africa: A Study in Applied Neo-Colonialism," Working Paper No. 54, African Studies Center, Boston University (1982); Chipman, *French Power in Africa*; Richard Joseph, "The Gaullist Legacy: Patterns of French Neo-Colonialism," *Review of African Political Economy*, 6 (May–August 1976).

90. Martin, "The Historical, Economic, and Political Bases of France's African Policy," 191.

91. William J. Foltz, *From French West Africa to the Mali Federation* (New Haven, CT, and London: Yale University Press, 1965), 83–84, 89.

92. *West Africa*, 28 June 1958.

93. Sekou Toure, *Expérience guinée et unité africaine* (Paris: Présence africaine, 1959), 71.

94. Quoted in Teresa Hayter, "French Aid to Africa: Its Scope and Achievements," *International Affairs*, 41, 2 (April 1965), 240–41.

95. For the results, see *West Africa*, 11 October 1958.

96. Elliot J. Berg, "The Economic Basis of Political Choice in French West Africa," *American Political Science Review*, 54, 2 (June 1960); Boubacar Barry, "Neocolonialism and Dependence in Senegal, 1960–1980," in *Decolonization and African Independence: The Transfer of Power, 1960–1980*, eds. Prosser Gifford and Wm. Roger Louis (New Haven, CT, and London: Yale University Press, 1988), 277. The close integration of the West African economy with the French is treated in detail and contrasted with the British approach in David K. Fieldhouse, "The Economic Exploitation of Africa: Some British and French Comparisons," in *France and Britain in Africa: Imperial Rivalry and Colonial Rule*, eds. Prosser Gifford and Wm. Roger Louis (New Haven, CT, and London: Yale University Press, 1971).

97. *West Africa*, 12 October 1957. Also see Felix Houphouet-Boigny, "Black Africa and the French Union," *Foreign Affairs*, 35, 34 (July 1957).

98. Quoted in Kenneth Robinson, "West Africa: A French View," *West Africa*, 7 September 1957.

99. Crowder, "Independence as a Goal in French West African Politics," 40.

100. Coordinator of Information, British Empire Section, Special Memorandum No. 27, "Native Manpower and Morale," 10 January 1942, in *OSS/State Department Intelligence and Research Reports Part 13: Africa, 1941–61* (Washington, DC: Union of America Publications Inc., 1980), microfilm Reel I. (This is available at the Robarts Library, University of Toronto)

101. *West Africa*, 13 February 1960.

102. Quoted in Colin Legum, *Pan-Africanism: A Short Political Guide* (London: Pall Mall, 1962), 254.

103. *West Africa*, 8 April 1961.

104. Panaf Great Lives, *Kwame Nkrumah* (London: Panaf, 1974), 72.

105. Wasserman, *Politics of Decolonization*, 6, 14–15.

106. Colin Leys, *Underdevelopment in Kenya: The Political Economy of Neo-Colonialism 1964–1971* (Berkeley and Los Angeles: University of California Press, 1974), 9.

107. In March 1952, Nkrumah assumed the title of prime minister. But this was simply a change in nomenclature; it did not enhance his position in the allocation of power. In his discussion of the transition process in Ghana, Arden-Clarke pointed out: "We learnt a good many lessons during that period. We learnt, for example, how effective the device of changing names could be. It is, I suppose, true that 'a rose by any other name would smell as sweet,' but we learnt that if we changed the name of Leader of Government Business to Prime Minister and Executive Council to Cabinet, without in any way altering their functions and powers, or the name of Chief Commissioner to Regional Officer, or District Commissioner to Government Agent, they all seemed to smell much sweeter in the public nose. That device certainly helped to get us over some difficult periods." See Charles Arden-Clarke, "Eight Years of Transition in Ghana," *African Affairs*, 56, 226 (January 1958), 35.

108. John Gallagher and Ronald Robinson, "The Imperialism of Free Trade," *Economic History Review*, 6, 1 (1953).

109. Frantz Fanon, *The Wretched of the Earth* (New York: Grove Press, 1963), 77.

110. Bade Onimode, *Imperialism and Underdevelopment in Nigeria: Dialectics of Mass Poverty* (London: Macmillan and Zed, 1983), 130.

111. Wasserman, *Politics of Decolonization*, 4.

112. John Darwin, *Britain and Decolonization: The Retreat from Empire in the Postwar World* (London: Macmillan, 1988), 7; J. G. Darwin, "In Search of Decolonization," *History*, 73, 237 (February 1988), 55–56.

113. Wasserman, *Politics of Decolonization*, 174, 13.

114. Henry Luce, "The American Century," *Life*, 17 February 1941.

Notes to Chapter 2

1. The quotations are, respectively, from Peter J. Schraeder, *United States Foreign Policy Toward Africa: Incrementalism, Crisis and Change* (New York: Cambridge University Press, 1994), 2; and Jean Herskovits, "Subsaharan Africa: The Lowest Priority," in *The

Dynamics of World Power: A Documentary History of United States Foreign Policy 1945–173, vol. 5, ed. Albert M. Schlesinger, Jr. (New York: Chelsea House, 1973), 539.

2. Telegram from the United States embassy in France to the State Department, 31 August 1963, *FRUS,1961–1963, vol. 13* (1994), 971.

3. Deborah Wing Ray, "The Takoradi Route: Roosevelt's Prewar Venture beyond the Western Hemisphere," *Journal of American History,* 62, 2 (September 1975), 355–56.

4. *West Africa,* 3 March 1945.

5. See Thomas C. Wasson, "The Mystery of Dakar: An Enigma Resolved," *American Foreign Service Journal,* 20, 4 (April 1943), 169; William L. Langer, *Our Vichy Gamble* (New York: Alfred A. Knopf, 1947), 187; William L. Langer and S. Everett Gleason, *The Challenge of Isolation, 1937–1940* (New York: Harper & Bros., 1952), 736.

6. "Tripartite Dinner Meeting, November 28, 1943, 8.30 p.m., Roosevelt's Quarters, Soviet Embassy," *FRUS: The Conferences at Cairo and Teheran, 1943* (1961), 509.

7. William L. Langer and S. Everett Gleason, *The Undeclared War, 1940–1941* (New York: Harper Publishers, 1953), 369.

8. *Life,* 9 June 1941, 32.

9. "Africa and the U.S.A.," enclosure in Memorandum by Sherman Kent, chief, Mediterranean Section, 11 December 1941, *OSS/State Department Intelligence and Research Reports: Part 13: Africa, 1941–61* (Washington, DC: University of America Publications Inc., 1980, microfilm). (Available at the Robarts Library, University of Toronto.) I found nothing on how the OSS proposal was received by the State Department or the White House or any follow-up on it.

10. Samuel I. Rosenman, compiled, *The Public Papers and Addresses of Franklin D. Roosevelt, vol. 12, 1943* (New York: Russell and Russell, 1969), 87.

11. Arthur L. Funk, *Charles de Gaulle: The Crucial Years, 1943–1944* (Norman: University of Oklahoma Press, 1959), 280.

12. ECA Document Brief, "ECA Objectives and Program in French Overseas Territories," 6 September 1951, RG 469, Overseas Development Subject Files, 1949–53, Box 15 (Suitland).

13. CIA, "Review of the World Situation as it Relates to the Security of the United States," 12 September 1947, PSF, Intelligence File, Box 257 (HSTL).

14. Memorandum by the JCS to the State-War-Navy Coordinating Committee, "Policies, Procedures and Costs of Assistance by the United States to Foreign Countries," 12 May 1947, *FRUS, 1947, vol. 1* (1973), 737.

15. Report by the Policy Planning Staff, "Review of Current Trends: U.S. Foreign Policy," 24 February 1948, *FRUS, 1948, vol. 1* (1976), 510–511.

16. CIA, "The Break-up of the Colonial Empires and its Implications for U.S. Security," 3 September 1948, PSF, Intelligence File, Box 225 (HSTL).

17. See Study Mission to Africa, November–December 1960, *Report of Senators Frank Church, Gale W. McGhee, and Frank E. Moss to the Committee on Foreign Relations, Committee on Appropriations, and Committee on Interior and Insular Affairs, United States Senate, February 12, 1961, 87th Congress, 1st Session* (Washington, DC: United States Government Printing Office, 1961), 2–4.

18. Foster Rhea Dulles and Gerald E. Ridinger, "The Anticolonial Policies of Franklin D. Roosevelt," *Political Science Quarterly,* 70, 1 (March 1955), 1–8; Elliot Roosevelt, *As He Saw It* (New York: Duell, Sloan and Pearce, 1946); Willard Range, *Franklin D. Roosevelt's World Order* (Athens: University of Georgia Press, 1959), 102–19.

19. See Walter LaFeber, "Roosevelt, Churchill, and Indochina: 1942–45," *American Historical Review*, 80, 5 (December 1975); John J. Sbrega, "The Anticolonial Policies of Franklin D. Roosevelt: A Reappraisal," *Political Science Quarterly*, 101, 1 (1986); Christopher Thorne, "Indonesia and Anglo-American Relations, 1942–1945," *Pacific Historical Review*, 45, 1 (February 1976); M. S. Venkataramani, "The United States, the Colonial Issue, and the Atlantic Charter Hoax," *International Studies* (Delhi), 13, 1 (January–March 1974), 25; Scott L. Bills, *Empire and Cold War: The Roots of U.S.-Third World Antagonism, 1945–47* (New York: St. Martin's Press, 1990), 5–22; Wm. Roger Louis, *Imperialism at Bay, 1941–1945: The United States and the Decolonization of the British Empire* (New York: Oxford University Press, 1977).

20. "The War and Human Freedom" (a radio broadcast by Cordell Hull on 23 July 1942) *Department of State Bulletin*, 25 July 1942, 642. Also see Cordell Hull, *The Memoirs of Cordell Hull, vol. 2* (New York: The Macmillan Press, 1948), 1599.

21. See Samuel I. Rosenman, complied, *The Public Papers and Addresses of Franklin D. Roosevelt, vol. 11, 1942* (New York: Russell and Russell, 1969), 474–475.

22. Louis, *Imperialism at Bay*, 567–68.

23. Hull, *The Memoirs of Cordell Hull, vol. 2*, 1599.

24. OSS, "Problems and Objectives of United States Policy," 2 April 1945, Rose Conway File, Box 15 (HSTL).

25. Ibid.

26. Bills, *Empire and Cold War*, 21.

27. Harry S. Truman, *Memoirs, vol. 1: Year of Decisions* (Garden City, NY: Doubleday, 1955), 275, 237–38.

28. Paper prepared by the Colonial Policy Review Sub-Committee of the Committee on Problems of Dependent Areas, "United States Policy Toward Dependent Territories," 26 April 1950, *FRUS 1952–1954, vol. 3* (1979), 1077–1102.

29. The difference between the two is not merely semantic. A major policy paper explained that "[w]hile self-government should be a goal for all dependent peoples, independence can be the goal only for those territories where conditions are suitable. There are, of course, widely varying degrees of self-government up to full independence. " See ibid., 1082.

30. Minutes of the 45th meeting of the United States delegation held at San Francisco, Friday, 18 May 1945, 9 a.m., *FRUS, 1945, vol. 1: General—The United Nations* (1967), esp. 792–93, 795.

31. CIA, "The Break-up of the Colonial Empires and Its Implications for U.S. Security," 3 September 1948, PSF, Intelligence File, Box 255 (HSTL).

32. Ridgway B. Knight, "Preliminary Thoughts on the Subject of a U.S. Policy towards Colonial Areas and Colonial Powers," 21 April 1952, *FRUS 1952–1954, vol. 3* (1979), 1106–07.

33. CAB 129\24, CP (48)36, Memorandum by colonial secretary, "United Nations General Assembly, 1947: The Colonial Question," 30 June 1948 (PRO, London).

34. CO 537/7136, Confidential Desp. from the British ambassador in Washington (Oliver Franks) to the secretary of state for foreign affairs, 14 January 1950 (PRO, London).

35. Policy paper prepared by the Bureau of Near Eastern, South Asian, and African Affairs, "Future of Africa," 18 April 1950, *FRUS, 1950, vol. 5* (1978), 1528. As far as the colonies were concerned, the 1946 constitution (which created the Fourth French Republic) was anything but liberal. No local autonomy was intended by the creation of territorial

assemblies in the colonies—as the assemblies had no legislative powers and no control over local administration. The fundamental aim of the constitution was integrationist. The preamble pronounced the French Republic "one and indivisible" and promised "to bring France and its overseas colonies into a single political, economic and social unit for cooperation in an association which represents the distinctive personality of each of its members." See Georges Catroux, "The French Union: Concept, Reality and Prospects," *International Conciliation,* 494 (November 1953); Ruth Schachter Morgenthau, *Political Parties in French-Speaking West Africa* (London: Oxford University Press, 1964).

36. Summary Record of Colonial Policy Talks with the UK, 5 July 1950, File 350, Accra Consulate, Classified General Records, 1950–52, Box 5 (Suitland).

37. Summary Records of Colonial Policy Talks with the French, 11 July 1950, Lot 53 D246, Records of the French Desk, 1941–51, Box 1; also 350/8–1450, enclosure in Memorandum, State Department to AmCongen, Dakar, 11 August 1950 (all at NA).

38. George C. McGhee, "Africa's Role in the Free World Today," *Department of State Bulletin,* 16 July 1951, 97–101.

39. Ibid.

40. Desp. No. 15 from AmCongen, Dakar, to the State Department, 15 July 1952, File 350, Dakar Consulate General, General Records, 1951–55, Box 6 (Suitland).

41. Gaddis Smith, *Dean Acheson* (New York: Cooper Square Publishers, 1972), 16.

42. Letter from Lucius Battle to Helen Kitchen, 19 January 1988, quoted in Helen Kitchen, "Still on Safari in Africa," in *Centerstage: American Diplomacy Since World War II,* ed. L. Carl Brown (New York and London: Holmes & Meier, 1990), 177.

43. Douglas Brinkley, *Dean Acheson: The Cold War Years, 1953–71* (New Haven, CT, and London: Yale University Press, 1992), 303; also 45–46.

44. Ibid., 303.

45. Memorandum of Telephone Conversation, 25 March 1952, Papers of Dean Acheson, Box 67 (HSTL).

46. Brinkley, *Dean Acheson,* 46.

47. Ibid., 303.

48. Dean G. Acheson, "The Foreign Policy of the United States," *Arkansas Law Review and Bar Association Journal,* 18, 3 (Fall 1964), 232.

49. Ibid.

50. See his criticism of United States opposition to the Anglo-French Suez operation of 1956 and of John F. Kennedy's speech on Algeria, in Dean Acheson, *Power and Diplomacy* (Cambridge: Harvard University Press, 1959), 110–26. In 1969, he appeared before the House Committee on Foreign Affairs to oppose economic sanctions against Rhodesia and support Portuguese colonial and South African racist policies. See Dean Acheson, *Grapes from Thorns* (New York: W. W. Norton, 1972), 177–82. Also see Dean Acheson, "U.S. Involvement in South West Africa," *Washington Post,* 2 January 1971; Acheson, "Fifty Years After," *Yale Review,* 51, 1 (October 1961); Douglas Brinkley and G. E. Thomas, "Dean Acheson's Opposition to African Liberation," *TransAfrican Forum,* 5, 4 (Summer 1988); Brinkley, *Dean Acheson,* chap. 10.

51. Brinkley, *Dean Acheson,* 304.

52. Henry A. Byroade, assistant secretary of state for Near Eastern, South Asian, and African Affairs, "The World's Colonies and Ex-Colonies: A Challenge to America," speech delivered to the World Affairs Council of Northern California on 31 October 1953, *Department of State Bulletin,* 16 November 1953, 655.

53. Personal letter to Churchill, 22 July 1954, AWF, DDE Diary Series, Box 7 (DDEL).

54. Ibid. In his reply, dated 8 August 1954, Churchill stated that the "sentiments and ideas" expressed by Eisenhower were "in full accord with the policy now being pursued in all the Colonies of the British Empire. In this I must admit that I am a laggard. I am a bit skeptical about universal suffrage for the Hottentots even if refined by proportional representation. The British and American Democracies were slowly and painfully forged and even they are not perfect yet." Personal letter to the President, 8 August 1954, AWF, DDE Diary Series, Box 8 (DDEL). ("Hottentots" is a derogatory Afrikaner name for the Khoikhoi of South Africa.)

55. Letter to General Alfred M. Grunther, marked "Personal and Confidential," 30 November 1954, AWF, DDE Diary Series, Box 8 (DDEL).

56. Ibid. (Emphasis added.)

57. On 6 January 1953, two weeks before his first inauguration as president, Eisenhower's diary entry was: "Nationalism is on the march and world communism is taking advantage of the spirit of nationalism to cause dissension in the free world. Moscow leads many misguided people to believe that they can count on communist help to achieve and sustain nationalist ambitions. . . .The free world's hope of defeating the communist aims does not include objecting to national aspirations. We must show the wickedness of purpose in the communist promises and convince dependent peoples that their only hope of maintaining independence, once attained, is through cooperation with the free world." See *The Eisenhower Diaries,* ed. Robert H. Ferrell (New York: W. W. Norton, 1981), 223.

58. 611.71/4–951, Desp. No. 480 from Amlegation, Tangier, to State Department, 9 April 1951 (NA).

59. Stephen E. Ambrose, *Eisenhower, vol. 2: The President* (New York: Simon & Schuster, 1984), 378.

60. Memorandum of Conversation with Prime Minister Harold Macmillan and others, 27 September 1960, AWF, DDE Diary Series, Box 53 (DDEL).

61. Dwight D. Eisenhower, *The White House Years: Waging Peace* (Garden City, NY: Doubleday, 1965), 429.

62. Minutes of the 45th Meeting of the United States delegation, held at San Francisco, Friday, 18 May 1945, 9 a.m., *FRUS 1945, vol. 1: General—The United Nations* (1967), 795.

63. Minutes of the 78th Meeting of the United States delegation, held at San Francisco, Saturday, 23 June, 1945, 10.30 a.m., ibid., 1417.

64. See Ronald W. Pruessen, *John Foster Dulles: The Road to Power* (New York: The Free Press; London: Collier Macmillan, 1982), esp. 408–505.

65. Letter by John F. Dulles to General Dwight D. Eisenhower, 14 November 1952, AWF, Dulles-Herter Series, Box 1 (DDEL).

66. Telegram No. 1772 from Karachi to the secretary of state, 22 May 1953, Dulles Papers, Box 6 (DDEL).

67. Conference with the president, secretary of state, counselor McArthur, etc., 5 May 1954, AWF, Miscellaneous Series, Box 2 (DDEL).

68. The speech was frequently described as such. For example, see letter from the secretary of state to the United States representative at the UN (Lodge), 9 February 1955, *FRUS, 1955–1957, vol. 18,* (1989), 3; Memorandum from the assistant secretary of state for International Organization Affairs (Key) to the deputy undersecretary of state (Murphy), 20 April 1955, ibid., 6.

69. John F. Dulles, "The Moral Initiative," a speech before the Congress of Industrial Organizations at Cleveland, Ohio, on 18 November 1953, *Department of State Bulletin,* 30 November 1953, 741–44.

70. Byroade, "The World's Colonies and Ex-Colonies: A Challenge to America."

71. Paper prepared by the NSC Staff for the NSC Planning Board, "Africa: Major U.S. Interests," n.d., *FRUS, 1952–1954, vol. 11* (1983), 102. (This paper was sent to the NSC Planning Board by NSC Executive Secretary Lay on 17 March 1954. See ibid., n. 1, p. 101.)

72. CO 936/317, no. 13, "Notes on Colonialism for Washington Talks": Note prepared in the Colonial Office for use by Sir W. Churchill and Mr. Eden, June 1954 (PRO, London).

73. State Department Memorandum, "United States Foreign Policy," 16 May 1954, AWF, Dulles Papers, Box 8 (DDEL).

74. Lodge's letter, entitled "New Anticolonial Statement by You," was dated 26 June 1956. Dulles' reply was dated 29 June 1956. Both are in Dulles-Herter Series, Box 7 (DDEL).

75. Telegram No. 4325, from AmEmbassy, Paris, to the secretary of state, 20 March 1956, AWF, Dulles-Herter Series, Box 6 (DDEL).

76. *New York Herald Tribune,* 30 June 1959.

77. Ibid.

78. Thomas J. Hamilton, "Colonialism at UN: United States is Again Accused of Lining up with 'Imperialists,'" *New York Times,* 18 December 1960.

79. *New York Times,* 16 December 1960.

80. See *General Assembly Records* (15th session), 947th Plenary Meeting, 14 December 1960, 1273–74.

81. Ibid., 1283; *Department of State Bulletin,* 2 January 1961, 26–27.

82. Wayne Morse, "The United States in the United Nations, 1960: A Turning Point," *Supplementary Report to the Committee on Foreign Relations, United States Senate, 87th Congress, 1st Session* (Washington, DC: United States Government Printing Office, 1961), 8–10, 12–13, 16–24.

83. Arthur M. Schlesinger, Jr., *A Thousand Days: John F. Kennedy in the White House* (Boston: Houghton Mifflin, 1965), 510–11; *New York Times,* 16 December 1960.

84. *Africa Special Report,* April 1959, 2.

85. 611.70/6–859, Memorandum of Conversation, "Liberian Concern about the United States, France, and British Positions on Africa," 8 June 1959 (NA).

86. *New York Times,* 9 July 1959.

87. Memorandum of Conversation, "Africa and Aid," 27 October 1959, *FRUS, 1958–1960, vol. 14* (1992), 702–06.

88. 611.70B/6–3059, Incoming Airgram from AmEmbassy, Conakry, to the secretary of state, 30 June 1959 (NA).

89. *West Africa,* 28 October 1960.

90. Paper prepared by the Colonial Policy Review Sub-Committee of the Committee on Problems of Dependent Areas, "United States Policy toward Dependent Territories," 26 April 1950, *FRUS, 1952–1954, vol. 3* (1979), 1088.

91. Byroade, "The World's Colonies and Ex-Colonies: A Challenge to America."

92. Navy Department, "Factors Affecting Changes in the Power Position in Areas Bordering the Southern Oceans (Indian Ocean, South Atlantic)," enclosure 1 in memorandum from director, Long Range Objectives Group, "Long-Range Requirements for the

Southern Oceans," Ser. 0079P83, 31 May 1960 (Naval Historical Center, Washington, DC).

93. Eisenhower, *The White House Years,* 572.

94. 745H.00/4–2351, Letter of 23 April 1951 on "Preparedness for War," from E. H. Bourgerie, director, State Department Office of African Affairs, to A. W. Childs, American consul general in Lagos (NA). This was a circular letter sent to other United States missions in Africa as well.

95. Vernon McKay, "The United States, the United Nations, and Africa," *Department of State Bulletin,* 16 February 1953, 268.

96. For example, see Charles C. Alexander, *Holding the Line: The Eisenhower Era, 1952–1961* (Bloomington and London: Indiana University Press, 1975), 5–7; Robert A. Divine, *Second Chance: The Triumph of Internationalism in America during World War II* (New York: Atheneum, 1967), 22; Richard Melanson, "The Foundations of Eisenhower's Foreign Policy: Continuity, Community, and Consensus," in *Reevaluating Eisenhower: American Foreign Policy in the 1950s,* eds. Richard Melanson and David Mayers (Urbana and Chicago: University of Illinois Press, 1987), 50; Rolf Steininger, "John Foster Dulles, the European Community, and the German Question," in *John Foster Dulles and the Diplomacy of the Cold War,* ed. Richard H. Immerman (Princeton, NJ: Princeton University Press, 1990), 79; Pruessen, *John Foster Dulles,* esp. 214–15, 299–307.

97. William Stivers, "Eisenhower and the Middle East," in *Reevaluating Eisenhower,* eds. Melanson and Mayers, 194.

98. Divine, *Second Chance,* 22. Dean Acheson was in this group; see Smith, *Dean Acheson,* passim, but especially, pp. 414–19. So too was Eisenhower; see Alexander, *Holding the Line,* 5–7; Melanson, "The Foundations of Eisenhower's Foreign Policy: Continuity, Community, and Consensus," 50.

99. James Mittleman, *Ideology and Politics in Uganda from Obote to Amin* (Ithaca, NY, and London: Cornell University Press, 1975), 44.

100. Michael Hunt, *Ideology and U.S. Foreign Policy* (New Haven, CT, and London: Yale University Press, 1987), 77–79.

101. Ibid., 162, 165.

102. Address by Henry S. Villard (assistant chief of the Division of Near Eastern Affairs of the State Department), State Department Press Release No. 345, 19 August 1943 (NA).

103. See Policy Information Committee, State Department, "Weekly Review," 21 June 1950 (HSTL); Policy paper prepared by the Bureau of Near Eastern, South Asian, and African Affairs, "Future of Africa," 18 April 1950, *FRUS, 1950, vol. 5* (1978), 1524–38.

104. Acheson, "The Foreign Policy of the United States," 232.

105. By August 1957, Nixon was being referred to as the "father" of a new African policy in top administration circles. See Memorandum of Discussion at the 335th Meeting of the NSC, 22 August 1957, *FRUS, 1955–1957, vol. 18* (1989), 72; also see Eisenhower, *The White House Years,* 573.

106. Memorandum of Discussion at the 432nd Meeting of the NSC, 14 January 1960, *FRUS, 1958–1960, vol. 14* (1992), 75. Nixon had a blatantly racist attitude towards blacks in general (including, of course, Africans). Seymour Hersh has since observed that even during the Nixon presidency (1969–74), there was "an unrelenting stream of anti-black remarks" and contempt for Africa and Africans "from the President" and his top aides, notably National Security Adviser Henry Kissinger and Alexander Haig (an army

colonel, who was Kissinger's military aide). Nixon "repeatedly referred to blacks as 'niggers,' 'jigs,' 'jiga-boos,' and 'jungle bunnies.'" Given this environment, the "NSC staff aides", according to Hersh, "understood what was acceptable behavior and what was not. They would join the laughter at Alexander Haig's antics during the rare staff meetings that dealt with African issues. [Roger] Morris [the NSC staff member in charge of African Affairs] recalls that when he would enter the Situation Room laden with briefing books, "Haig would begin to beat his hands on the table, as if he was pounding a tom-tom. . . .Haig would make Tarzan jokes—'Where's your pet ape?' or, talking about blacks, say 'Henry [Kissinger] can't stand the smell.'"

Apart from Africa, Morris also handled the AID and the UN; in this respect, Hersh observed that "[y]ou couldn't find three subjects less important [to Kissinger] and more the object of ridicule" in the White House. Hersh also found that when, in late 1969, Secretary of State William Rogers "received good press coverage during a trip to Africa, Kissinger had been distraught with jealousy and anxiety. There had been a soothing telephone call from Nixon, also overheard by one of the NSC aides: 'Henry, let's leave the niggers to Bill and we'll take care of the rest of the world.'" See Seymour M. Hersh, *The Price of Power: Kissinger in the Nixon White House* (New York: Summit Books, 1983), 110–11.

107. For example, see Douglas W. Blum, "The Soviet Foreign Policy Belief System: Beliefs, Politics, and Foreign Policy Outcomes," *International Studies Quarterly*, 37, 4 (December 1993); Alexander L. George, "The 'Operational Code': A Neglected Approach to the Study of Political Leaders and Decision-Making," ibid., 13, 2 (June 1969); *Ideas and Foreign Policy: Beliefs, Institutions and Political Change*, eds. Judith Goldstein and Robert O. Keohane (Ithaca, NY: Cornell University Press, 1993); Irving Janis, *Victims of Groupthink: A Psychological Study of Foreign Policy and Fiascoes* (Boston: Houghton Mifflin, 1972).

108. Gary Hess, "Global Expansion and Regional Balances: The Emerging Scholarship on United States Relations with India and Pakistan," *Pacific Historical Review*, 56, 2 (May 1987), 291.

109. See Philip D. Curtin, *The Image of Africa: British Ideas and Action, 1780–1850* (Madison: University of Wisconsin Press, 1964).

110. As late as October 1963, Hugh Trevor-Roper pontificated from his distinguished history chair at Oxford that African history is "the unrewarding gyrations of barbarous tribes in picturesque but irrelevant corners of the globe." See his *The Rise of Christian Europe* (London: Harcourt, Brace and World, 1965), 9.

111. Elliot P. Skinner, "African, Afro-American, White Americans: A Case of Pride and Prejudice," *Freedomways* (Summer 1965), 384.

112. 611.70/2–1756, State Department Instruction CA-6309, "Paper on United States Problems in Africa," 17 February 1956 (NA).

113. See Dennis Hickey and Kenneth C. Wylie, *An Enchanting Darkness: The American Vision of Africa in the Twentieth Century* (East Lansing: Michigan State University Press, 1993). In late 1994, Howard W. French found that "For many Americans, the 'real Africa' is a blurred concatenation of game parks . . . a Disney-field cradle of civilization." See his "An Ignorance of Africa as Vast as the Continent," *New York Times*, 20 November 1994. Also see Schraeder, *United States Foreign Policy Toward Africa*, 5.

114. Rupert Emerson and Martin Kilson, "The American Dilemma in a Changing World: The Rise of Africa and the Negro American," *Daedalus* (Fall 1965), 1061; James H. Meriwether, "The African Connection and the Struggle for Freedom: Africa's Role in Afri-

can-American Life, 1935–1963," Ph.D. dissertation, University of California, Los Angeles (1995), 5–10.

115. Hunt, *Ideology and United States Foreign Policy,* 18, 116, 124.

116. S. Neil MacFarlane, *Superpower Rivalry & 3rd World Radicalism: The Idea of National Liberation* (London & Sydney: Croom Helm, 1985), 5, 7, 199.

117. Hunt, *Ideology and United States Foreign Policy,* 160.

118. Byroade, "The World's Colonies and Ex-Colonies: A Challenge to America."

119. Memorandum of Conversation, "Belgian Congo," 8 October 1958, *FRUS, 1958–1960, vol. 14* (1992), 252.

120. Gordon Bertolin, "United States Economic Interests in Africa: Investments, Trade, and Raw Materials," in *Africa and the United States: Vital Interests,* ed. Jennifer S. Whitaker (New York: New York University Press, 1978), 24.

121. Program of African Studies, Northwestern University, *Africa: A Study Prepared at the Request of the Committee on Foreign Relations, United States Senate, United States Foreign Policy No. 4, October 23, 1959; 86th Congress, 1st session* (Washington, DC: United States Printing Office, 1959), 42.

122. Bertolin, "United States Economic Interests in Africa: Investments, Trade, and Raw Materials," 24. One can understand why the racist enclaves—the Federation of Rhodesia and Nyasaland, and especially apartheid South Africa—had a magnetic pull on United States (and other Western) investors. These were internal colonial economies based on the appropriation of African surplus labor by an entrenched white settler class. In this setting, the African constituted a specific periphery within a system that ensured the reproduction of low wages and thus high returns on investment. Apartheid, in particular, because it was the most elaborate white settler economy, created the most favorable conditions that enhanced this appropriation.

123. This is borne out by their response to the opportunities offered by Ghana's transition to sovereignty. By March 1959, almost a dozen foreign trade missions had been to Ghana, from Britain, Israel, Poland, Czechoslovakia, East Germany, Egypt, the Netherlands, the Soviet Union, West Germany, and Yugoslavia. See "Cocoa for Communists," *West Africa,* 7 February 1959. Americans were not interested in this scramble: it was not until 1960 that a United States trade mission visited Ghana, together with Liberia, Sierra Leone, and Guinea. The mission found that United States businesses had not considered Ghana (and any part of West Africa) as a possible market. It also found that the strong position enjoyed by British goods in Ghana was largely created by the fact that they were tailor-made for the local market, and that similar adaptations were made in packaging and advertising. The report advised United States exporters to advertise, develop contacts, visit Ghana, and even open branch offices there. The mission also found that the prices of United States goods were generally higher than those from Europe and Asia, so that importers were discouraged even from making inquiries. See ibid., 25 June 1960. Earlier, in September 1957, Ghana Finance Minister Komla Gbedemah, had complained to Henry Kearns, the United States assistant secretary of commerce, that the prices of United States goods in Ghana were "exceedingly high in relation to those available from other sources." See 811.05145J/9–2557, Memorandum of Conversation, "Discussion of Commercial and Investment Relations between the United States and Ghana," 25 September 1957 (NA).

124. CIA (ORE-69–49), "Relative United States Security Interest in the European-Mediterranean Area and the Far East," 12 September 1949, PSF, Intelligence File, Box 257 (HSTL).

125. "Objectives and Character of ECA Program in the French Overseas Territories," enclosure in letter from Paul R. Porter, ECA assistant administrator to Assistant Secretary of State George C. McGhee, 11 July 1951, RG 469, Overseas Development Subject Files, 1949–53, Box 15 (Suitland).

126. Paper prepared by the Colonial Policy Review Sub-Committee of the Committee on Problems of Dependent Areas, "United States Policy toward Dependent Territories," 26 April 1950, *FRUS, 1952–1954, vol. 3* (1979), 1088.

127. See Policy Information Committee, State Department, "Weekly Review," 21 June 1950 (HSTL); Policy paper prepared by the Bureau of Near Eastern, South Asian, and African Affairs, "Future of Africa," 18 April 1950, *FRUS, 1950, vol. 5* (1978), 1524–38.

128. 611.70/2–1756, State Department Instruction CA-6309, "Paper on United States Problems in Africa," 17 February 1956 (NA).

129. Airgram from USOM/London, "DOT Program—British African Territories," 31 October 1956, RG 469, N. Euro./Yugo. Division, UK Subject Files, 1948–57, Box 8 (Suitland).

130. NSC 6005, "United States Policy toward West Africa," 29 February 1960 (RG 273, NA). Its amended and final version, NSC 6005/1, contained the portions of NSC 6005 quoted here. See NSC 6005/1, "Statement of United States Policy toward West Africa," 9 April 1960, *FRUS, 1958–1960, vol. 14* (1992), 117–26.

131. For details, see Stephen R. Shalom, *The United States and the Philippines: A Study of Neocolonialism* (Philadelphia: Institute for the Study of Human Issues, 1981).

Notes to Chapter 3

1. Frederick Lugard made his mark as a leading British colonial administrator in Africa. To him belongs the formulation of the 'dual mandate,' a supposedly reciprocal relationship between Europe and Africa. Lugard's premise was that since the Europeans could no longer survive without tropical raw materials and foodstuffs, the responsibility was theirs for the adequate exploitation of the tropics. Africa was according to him "the heritage of mankind" and the colonial powers were there to act as "trustees of civilization." This thinking led to the insistence that Africans could not deny Europeans access to the resources. See Lord Lugard, *The Dual Mandate in British Tropical Africa* (London: Frank Cass, 5th ed. 1965), 42–44, 60–61. It is easy to see the 'dual mandate' for what it really was: a rationalization of the colonial exploitation of Africa's resources. Overall, Lugard's 'dual mandate' has much conceptual similarity to the general pattern of United States policy in Africa in the period 1950–52.

2. George McGhee, *Envoy to the Middle World: Adventures in Diplomacy* (New York: Harper & Row, 1983), 114.

3. Report prepared in the State Department, "Political and Economic Problems of Africa," n.d., *FRUS, 1950, vol. 5* (1978), 1503–09; McGhee, *Envoy to the Middle World*, 115–17.

4. Ibid.

5. 611.70/2–1750, Memorandum, "Panel Discussion on Africa," from NEA—Mr. McGhee to the secretary, 17 February 1950 (NA).

6. Samuel J. Gorlitz, "Economic Situation in Africa (South of the Sahara): Report of

Lourenco Marques Conference," 22 May 1950, Supplement to the Daily Economic Summary, Office Files of Gordon Gray as special assistant to the president, Working Papers: General File, Box 8 (HSTL).

7. Memorandum, Mr. McGhee to the secretary, "Summary of Conclusions and Recommendations Reached at Lourenco Marques Conference," 12 April 1950, Lot 53 D468, Box 9 (NA).

8. Ibid.

9. George C. McGhee, "United States Interests in Africa," *Department of State Bulletin,* 19 June 1950, 999–1003.

10. Ibid.

11. ECA, European Program Division, Dependent Areas Branch, *ECA: Development of Overseas Territories of Marshall Plan: Special Report,* 24 August 1951, 2, 9, RG 469, Overseas Development Subject Files, 1949–53, Box 15 (Suitland).

12. See ECA, "Report on the Application of ECA Assistance to the Development of French West Africa," 31 December 1949, enclosure in Desp. No. 283 from ECA France to ECA Washington, RG 469, Europe: French West Africa 1948–53, Box 2 (Suitland).

13. ECA, European Program Division, Dependent Areas Branch, *ECA: Development of Overseas Territories of Marshall Plan: Special Report,* 24 August 1951, 2, RG 469, Overseas Development Subject Files, 1949–53, Box 15 (Suitland).

14. John E. Orchard, "ECA and the Dependent Territories," *Geographical Review,* 41, 1 (January 1951), 71, 74–75.

15. 811.05145S/10–1750, Outgoing Airgram from the State Department to AmConsulate, Kenya, 6 December 1950 (NA); The State Department, *Point Four: Cooperative Program for Aid in the Development of Economically Underdeveloped Areas,* State Department Publication 3719, Economic Cooperation Series 24 (Washington, DC, January 1950); William Adams Brown, Jr., and Redvers Opie, *American Foreign Assistance* (Washington, DC: The Brookings Institution, 1953), 392–396.

16. Brown and Opie, *American Foreign Assistance,* 74–75.

17. Gabriel Kolko, *Confronting the Third World: United States Foreign Policy, 1945–1980* (New York: Pantheon Books, 1988), 42.

18. Brown and Opie, *American Foreign Assistance,* 393, 396–97.

19. ECA, European Program Division, Dependent Areas Branch, *ECA: Development of Overseas Territories of Marshall Plan: Special Report,* 24 August 1951, 2, RG 469, Overseas Development Subject Files, 1949–53, Box 15 (Suitland).

20. Robert A. Pollard, *Economic Security and the Origins of the Cold War, 1945–1950* (New York: Columbia University Press, 1985), 203–7.

21. Records of the Policy Planning Staff, "Certain Aspects of the European Recovery Problem from the United States Standpoint (Preliminary Report)," 23 July 1947, in *Containment: Documents on American Policy and Strategy, 1945–1950,* eds. Thomas H. Etzold and John Lewis Gaddis (New York: Columbia University Press, 1978), 112–13.

22. Kolko, *Confronting the Third World,* 41–43. Also see Melvyn Leffler, "The United States and the Strategic Dimensions of the Marshall Plan," *Diplomatic History,* 12, 3 (Summer 1988), 278.

23. "Meeting of Advisory Committee on Overseas Territories, Economic Cooperation Administration, Washington, Thursday, July 20, 1950," ECA, Record of Action, ACOT/RA-5, 9 August 1950 in RG 469, Europe Program Division ACUA, 1949–51, Box 3 (Suitland). In January 1951, Allan Smith, acting director, ECA Overseas Territories Divi-

sion, remarked that "[t]he Dependent Overseas Territories have generally been considered by ECA as appendages of European economy or as producers of strategic materials for the U.S. stockpile." See Draft Cable to Washington, "Legislative Presentation of OT Policies," enclosure in Memorandum from Allan Hugh Smith, 22 January 1951, RG 469, Special representative in Europe, Office of the General Consul, Subject Files, 1948–53, Box 47 (Suitland)

24. Draft Cable to Washington, "Legislative Presentation of OT Policies," 22 January 1951, enclosure in Memorandum from Allan Hugh Smith, acting director, Overseas Territories Division, "Overseas Territories in Africa Legislative Presentation," 22 January 1951, RG 469, Special representative in Europe, Office of the General Consul, Subject Files, 1948–53, Box 47 (Suitland).

25. McGhee, "United States Interests in Africa" also Orchard, "ECA and the Dependent Territories."

26. "Africa Area Paper" (July 1950?), Office Files of Gordon Gray as special assistant to the president, Working Papers (General File), Box 8 (HSTL).

27. President's Materials Policy Commission, *Resources for Freedom, vol. 1: A Report to the President* (Washington, DC: United States Government Printing Office, 1952), 1, 59–60.

28. "Objectives and Character of ECA Program in the French Overseas Territories," enclosure in letter from Paul R. Porter, ECA assistant administrator to Assistant Secretary of State George C. McGhee, 11 July 1951, RG 469, Overseas Development Subject Files, 1949–53, Box 15 (Suitland).

29. ECA, European Program Division, Dependent Areas Branch, *ECA: Development of Overseas Territories of Marshall Plan: Special Report,* 24 August 1951, 16, RG 469, Overseas Development Subject Files, 1949–53, Box 15 (Suitland).

30. ECA Document Brief, "ECA Objectives and Program in French Overseas Territories," 6 September 1951, RG 469, Overseas Development Subject Files, 1949–53, Box 15 (Suitland); "Africa Area Paper" (July 1950?), Office Files of Gordon Gray as special assistant to the president, Working Papers (General File), Box 8 (HSTL).

31. ECA, European Program Division, Dependent Areas Branch, *ECA: Development of Overseas Territories of Marshall Plan: Special Report,* 24 August 1951, 3, RG 469, Overseas Development Subject Files, 1949–53, Box 15 (Suitland); also see ECA Document Brief, "ECA Objectives and Program in French Overseas Territories," 6 September 1951, RG 469, Overseas Development Subject Files, 1949–53, Box 15 (Suitland).

32. ECA, "Report on the Application of ECA Assistance to the Development of French West Africa," 31 December 1949, enclosure in Desp. No. 283 from ECA France to ECA, Washington, RG 469, Europe: French West Africa 1948–53, Box 2 (Suitland).

33. "Objectives and Character of ECA Program in the French Overseas Territories," enclosure in letter from Paul R. Porter, ECA assistant administrator to Assistant Secretary of State George C. McGhee, 11 July 1951, RG 469, Overseas Development Subject Files, 1949–53, Box 15 (Suitland).

34. ECA European Program Division/Division of Statistics and Reports, "ECA Special Report: Development of Overseas Territories . . . of Marshall Plan Countries," 24 August 1951, RG 469, Overseas Development Subject Files, 1949–53, Box 15 (Suitland).

35. "Objectives and Character of ECA Program in the French Overseas Territories," enclosure in letter from Paul R. Porter, ECA assistant administrator to Assistant Secretary of State George C. McGhee, 11 July 1951, RG 469, Overseas Development Subject Files, 1949–53, Box 15 (Suitland).

36. Orchard, "ECA and the Dependent Territories," 74.

37. "Objectives and Character of ECA Program in the French Overseas Territories," enclosure in Letter from Paul R. Porter, ECA assistant administrator to Assistant Secretary of State George C. McGhee, 11 July 1951, RG 469, Overseas Development Subject Files, 1949–53, Box 15 (Suitland).

38. ECA, European Program Division, Dependent Areas Branch, *ECA: Development of Overseas Territories of Marshall Plan: Special Report,* 24 August 1951, 10, RG 469, Overseas Development Subject Files, 1949–53, Box 15 (Suitland).

39. 700.5–MSP/5–2951, Memorandum from David M. Clark to Mr. Miller, "Foreign Allocations Policy Statement," 29 May 1951 (NA).

40. "Statement for the Record on the Mutual Security Program in the Dependent Overseas Territories," 17 April 1952, RG 469, special representative in Europe, Office of the Consul General, Subject Files, 1948–53, Box 46 (Suitland).

41. Ibid.

42. Ibid.

43. "Overseas Territories Development Program Budget Presentation Fiscal '54," 4 November 1952, RG 469 N. Euro./Yugo. Division, U.K. Subject Files 1948–57, Box 7 (Suitland).

44. CIA (ORE 46–50), "The Current Situation in British West Africa," 29 September 1950, PSF, Intelligence File, Box 257 (HSTL).

45. Enclosure in Desp. 176 from AmCongen, Dakar, to the State Department, 15 June 1950, RG 469, Dependent Areas Branch, Country Files, (France: French West Africa-Madagascar) 1948–52, Box 13 (Suitland).

46. 870.00TA/7–1850, Memorandum of Conversation, "Visit of Dr. John Orchard, special advisor on Overseas Development to the Special Representative, Paris," 18 July 1950 (NA).

47. 391.1 LO/5–350, Letter from Richard M. Bissell to George C. McGhee, 3 May 1950 (NA).

48. *Economist,* 1 April 1950, 702.

49. Nigeria was then supplying about 95 percent of the world's requirements for columbium, a metal that occurs with tin ore and for which there was a very high worldwide demand. This demand derived from its strategic importance for armaments and industrial projects: it was primarily used in the manufacture of gas turbines and jet engine components; it was also extensively used as a carbide stabilizer in stainless steels, in electrodes for welding stainless steels, and in the manufacture of special alloys and chemical equipment. See 845H.2547/7–2252, Desp. from AmEmbassy, London, to the State Department, "Comment by *Mining Journal* on DMPA Columbium-Tantalum Guaranteed Purchase Program," 22 July 1952. The *Mining Journal* article entitled, "New D.M.P.A. Order Stimulates Columbine Production," was attached as an enclosure to the despatch.

50. Ibid.

51. See Memorandum, Mr. McGhee to the secretary, "Summary of Conclusions and Recommendations Reached at Lourenco Marques Conference," 12 April 1950, Lot 53 D468, Box 9 (NA).

52. See Policy Information Committee, State Department, "Weekly Review," 21 June 1950 (HSTL); Policy paper prepared by the Bureau of Near Eastern, South Asian, and African Affairs, "Future of Africa," 18 April 1950, *FRUS, 1950, vol. 5* (1978), 1524–38.

53. Policy statement prepared in the Bureau of Near Eastern, South Asian, and Afri-

can Affairs, "Regional Policy Statement on Africa South of the Sahara," 29 December 1950, ibid., 1587–97.

54. Ibid.

55. See Memorandum of Conversation prepared in the embassy in the United Kingdom, "Economic Questions Concerning Africa," 20 September 1950, ibid., 1554–1568.

56. Airgram from AmCongen, Dakar, to the secretary of state, 23 April 1949, RG 469, Europe: French West Africa 1948–53, Box 2 (Suitland).

57. 396.1–LO/4–2050, Memorandum of Conversation, "French Plans for the Discussions on Africa at the Foreign Ministers Meeting," 20 April 1950 (NA).

58. 396.1–LO/5–550, Telegram from AmEmbassy, London, to the secretary of state, 5 May 1950 (NA).

59. 740.022/71350, Memorandum from Mr. Bourgerie to Mr. McGhee, 13 July 1950 (NA).

60. Ibid.

61. For example, see 854H.00R/11–350, Desp. from AmConsulate, Lagos, to the State Department, "Visit of Deputy ECA Administrator Curtin," together with enclosure, "Record of a Meeting Held in Government House, Lagos, on the 1st of November, 1950," 3 November 1950 (NA); Memorandum, "UK Interest in Loans for Colonial Development," 20 September 1951; RG 469, UK Subject Files, 1948–57, Box 7; Desp. from AmCongen, Lagos, to the State Department, "Point Four Trainee Program for Nigeria," 24 April 1951; RG 469, Europe: Dependent Areas Branch, 1948–52, Box 24 (both at Suitland).

62. Airgram from ECA special representative in Europe, Paris, to Paris, Brussels, Lisbon, Hague, Rome, 29 August 1952, RG 469, special representative in Europe, Office of the Consul General, Subject Files, 1948–53, Box 46 (Suitland).

63. 845K.25A/2–250, Telegram from AmConsulate, Accra, to the State Department, 2 February 1950 (NA).

64. ECA, "British Colonial Development Policy and the Role of the United States in the DOT's," Confidential Document Brief, 27 February 1951, RG 469, Overseas Development Subject Files, 1949–53, Box 15 (Suitland).

65. Desp. from AmCongen, Lagos, to the State Department, "Attitude of Nigerian Officials Towards ECA," 13 April 1951, RG 469, Europe: Dependent Areas Branch, 1948–52, Box 24 (Suitland).

66. 851T.00R/1–2050, Desp. from AmCongen, Dakar, to the State Department, 20 January 1950; 851T.00R/1–2850, Desp. from Dakar to the State Department, 28 January 1950 (both at NA).

67. Desp. from AmCongen, Dakar, to the State Department, "French Refusal to Grant Licenses for the Importation of American Products into FWA," 31 December 1952, File 510–511, Dakar Consulate General Records, 1950–55, Box 9 (Suitland).

68. 770.00/5–250, Memorandum of Conversation, "Future of Africa," 1–2 May 1950 (NA).

69. 851T.00T.A./1–2150, Desp. from Dakar to the State Department, 21 January 1950 (NA).

70. 851T.00T.A./8–2951, Desp. from AmCongen, Dakar, to the State Department, 29 August 1951 (NA).

71. 851T.2553/2–2550, Desp. from AmCongen, Dakar, to the State Department, "Efforts of French West African Government to Replace American Petroleum Companies in the Petroleum Trade in French West Africa by the Compagnie Française de Distribution

de Petrol d'Afrique," 25 February 1950; 851T.2553/6–2350, Desp. from AmCongen, Dakar, to the State Department, "Efforts of French West African Government to Replace American Petroleum Companies in the Petroleum Trade in French West Africa by the Compagnie Française de Distribution de Petrol d'Afrique," 24 June 1950 (all at NA).

72. 851T.2553/2–2550, Desp. from AmCongen, Dakar, to the State Department, "Efforts of French West African Government to Replace American Petroleum Companies in the Petroleum Trade in French West Africa by the Compagnie Française de Distribution de Petrol d'Afrique," 25 February 1950 (NA).

73. 851T.2553/1–1050, Telegram from the State Department to AmEmbassy, Paris, 10 January 1950 (NA).

74. 851T.2553/10–550, Telegram from AmEmbassy, Paris, to the secretary of state, 5 October, 1950; 870.2553/9–2050, Memorandum of Conversation, "African Petroleum Terminals' Difficulties in Obtaining Approval of French Government to Proceed with Construction of Petroleum Storage and Distribution Facilities at Douala and Conakry," 20 September 1950; 870.2553/10–2050, Memorandum of Conversation, "Latest Developments in APT's Efforts in Paris to Negotiate a Satisfactory Arrangement for Construction and Operation of an Oil Terminal at Douala," 20 October 1950 (all at NA).

75. See David K. Fieldhouse, "The Economic Exploitation of Africa: Some British and French Comparisons," in *France and Britain in Africa: Imperial Rivalry and Colonial Rule,* eds. Prosser Gifford and Wm. Roger Louis (New Haven, CT, and London: Yale University Press, 1971); William J. Foltz, *From French West Africa to the Mali Federation* (New Haven, CT, and London: Yale University Press, 1965), chap. 3.

76. Daniel Yergin, *The Prize: The Epic Quest for Oil, Money and Power* (New York: Simon & Schuster, 1992), 525.

77. See Kolko, *Confronting the Third World,* 111–12.

78. For example, because of its balance of payments crisis, Britain abandoned sterling convertibility on 20 August 1947, after it had been in place for only five weeks. Thereafter, it rebuilt the sterling area as a discriminatory currency zone. In June 1949, Acheson affirmed that section 9 of the Anglo-American Financial Agreement, which disallowed discriminatory import controls by Britain, was no longer applicable. See Alan P. Dobson, *The Politics of the Anglo-American Economic Relationship, 1940–1987* (New York: St. Martin's Press, 1988), 104, 120; Scott Newton, "Britain, the Sterling Area and European Integration, 1945–50," *Journal of Imperial and Commonwealth History,* 13, 3 (May 1985); C. C. S. Newton, "The Sterling Crisis of 1947 and the British Response to the Marshall Plan," *Economic History Review,* 2nd series, 38, 3 (August 1984).

79. McGhee, "United States Interests in Africa."

80. See Policy Information Committee, State Department, "Weekly Review," 21 June 1950 (HSTL).

81. 745K.00/6–2151, Telegram from the State Department to AmConsulate, Accra, 20 June 1951 (NA).

82. On the "Ewe question," see D. E. K. Amenumey, *The Ewe Unification Movement: A Political History* (Accra: Ghana Universities Press, 1989); Benjamin Gerig and Vernon MacKay, "The Ewe Problem: A Case Study in the Operation of the Trusteeship Council," *Department of State Bulletin,* 22 January 1951, 128–37; John Kent, *The Internationalization of Colonialism: Britain, France, and Black Africa, 1939–1956* (Oxford: Clarendon Press, 1992), chap. 9; Kent, "The Ewe Question, 1945–56: French and British Reactions to Nationalism in West Africa," in *Imperialism, The State and the Third World,* ed. Michael Twaddle

268   *Notes to Pages 74–79*

(London and New York: British Academic Press, 1992); Emil J. Sady, *The United Nations and Dependent Peoples* (Washington, DC: The Brookings Institution, 1956), esp. 155–60; Claude E. Welch, Jr., *Dream of Unity: Pan Africanism and Political Unification in West Africa* (Ithaca, NY: Cornell University Press, 1966), chaps. 2–3.

83. See UN Trusteeship Council, *Official Records (TCOR)* Supplement, First Year, 1st session, 1947, 151.

84. Policy Information Committee, State Department, "Weekly Review," 7 June 1950 (HSTL).

85. Gerig and MacKay, "The Ewe Problem," 130.

86. The word, "tribe" and its derivatives ("tribal," "tribalism," etc.) have undisguised pejorative and therefore offensive connotations. *The Oxford Reference Dictionary* (1986), for example, defines "tribe" as "a group of families (especially in a primitive or nomadic culture) living as a community under one or more chiefs." "Ethnic group(s)" and "ethnicity" are preferred to "tribe/tribes" and "tribalism."

87. Gerig and MacKay, "The Ewe Problem," 130.

88. *TC Official Records,* II (First Part), 8 December 1947, 321–36.

89. Trusteeship Council Resolution 14 (II), 15 December 1947.

90. Welch, *Dream of Unity,* 78–79.

91. TC, *Special Report of First Visiting Mission to the Trust Territories of Togoland under British Administration and Togoland under French Administration on the Ewe Problem,* Doc. T/463, 17 February 1950, 34.

92. *TC Official Records,* 6, 20 March 1950, 498–500.

93. See Memorandum of Conversation, "Petition Received by the Trusteeship Council from Ewe Tribesmen [*sic*] in Togoland," 13 October 1947; Memorandum of Conversation, "The Ewe Petitioners to the Trusteeship Council," 3 November, 1947, both in Lot 53 D246, Records of the French Desk, 1941–51, Box 1; 350/6–950, Memorandum, State Department, 19 June 1950 (all at NA).

94. D. E. K. Amenumey, "The General Elections in the 'Autonomous Republic of Togo,' April 1958," *Transactions of the Historical Society of Ghana,* 16, 1 (June 1975), 48–49.

95. UN Doc. T/702, *Joint Observations to the Government of France and the Government of the United Kingdom of Great Britain and Northern Ireland on the Special Report of the Visiting Mission Concerning the Ewe Problem,* 19 June 1950.

96. Memorandum of Conversation, "French Ambassador's Visit to Mr. McGhee," 25 May 1950, Lot 53 D468, 1945–1953, Box 9 (NA).

97. 350/6–850, Telegram from the State Department to USUN, 19 June 1950 (NA).

98. Amenumey, "The General Elections in the 'Autonomous Republic of Togo,' April 1958," 48.

99. Gerig and MacKay, "The Ewe Problem," 136.

100. See State Department Instruction for the United States delegation to the 8th Session of the Trusteeship Council, "The Ewe Problem (Item 17 on the Provisional Agenda)," 12 January, 1951, *FRUS, 1951, vol. 2* (1979), 521—29, esp. 522. For a text of the resolution, see 527–28.

101. See Kent, "The Ewe Question, 1945–56: French and British Reactions to Nationalism in West Africa," 194. Also see Amenumey, *The Ewe Unification Movement,* 95–97; Welch, *Dream of Unity,* 95–96.

102. See State Department Instruction for the United States delegation to the 8th Session of the Trusteeship Council, "The Ewe Problem (Item 17 on the Provisional Agenda),"

12 January, 1951, *FRUS, 1951, vol. 2* (1979), 523.

103. Ibid., 523–27; Gerig and MacKay, "The Ewe Problem,", 131.

104. See enclosure in 745K.00/2–1451, Memorandum of Conversation, "The Ewe Problem," 14 February 1951 (NA); The permanent delegation of the UK at the UN to USUN, "Aide Mémoire—Ewe Problem," 6 February 1951, *FRUS, 1951, vol. 2* (1979), 529–31. For the resolution, see ibid., 537.

105. Minutes of meeting of administering members of the Trusteeship Council, New York, February 16, 1951, "Subject: Meeting of Administering Members to Discuss Ewe Problem," ibid., 532–41.

106. See 350/2–1351, Memorandum of Conversation, "French Proposals Regarding the Ewe Problem," 13 February 1951; 745K.00/2–1451, Memorandum of Conversation, "The Ewe Problem," 14 February 1951; 745K.AWEIGH/2–1951, Memorandum of Conversation, "The Ewe Problem," 19 February 1951; 745K.AWEIGH/2–1951, Memorandum of Conversation, "The Ewe Problem," 19 February 1951; 350/3–151, Memorandum of Conversation, "The Ewe Problem before the Trusteeship Council," 1 March 1951; 350/6–2751, Telegram from USUN to the secretary of state, 27 June 1951 (all at NA).

107. See State Department Instruction for the United States delegation to the 8th Session of the Trusteeship Council, "The Ewe Problem (Item 17 on the Provisional Agenda)," 12 January, 1951, *FRUS, 1951, vol. 2* (1979), 521–29, esp. p. 524.

108. Ibid., 544–45.

109. Ibid., 547.

110. Ibid., 555.

111. Ibid., 558.

112. Ibid., 556.

113. Ibid., 559–60.

114. Ibid., 561–65.

115. Ibid.; 350/3–651, Position to be adopted by the United States delegation to the Trusteeship Council on the Ewe Question, 6 March 1951 (NA).

116. Ibid.

117. *FRUS, 1951, vol. 2* (1979), 564–65; 745K.AWEIGH/3–651, Memorandum of Conversation, "The Ewe Question," 6 March 1951 (NA).

118. The secretary of state to Certain Diplomatic and Consular Offices, 12 April 1951, *FRUS, 1951, vol. 2* (1979), 573–74; 350/4–1251, Airgram from the State Department to Certain American Diplomatic and Consular Officers, 12 April 1951 (NA). It is standard UN procedure to vote on the last resolution on a subject first. After the adoption of the Iraqi–U.S. resolution, the French delegate made a statement on the French abstention and then announced that France desired to withdraw the Anglo–French draft resolution; his British counterpart concurred. See "Editorial Note," *FRUS, 1951, vol. 2* (1979), 572.

119. For the text of the resolution, see *Department of State Bulletin*, 26 March 1951, 509.

120. 350/6–2751, Telegram from USUN to the secretary of state, 27 June 1951 (NA), reproduced in *FRUS, 1951, vol. 2* (1982), 577–78.

121. In reality, the United States, like Britain and France, did not believe in the feasibility of Ewe unification. In October 1952, the State Department asserted: "With regard to unification, it appears that the views of the unificationists in the two Togolands are in a state of flux. In this situation it is difficult and probably unwise to recommend any drastic alteration of the present political status. Furthermore, in considering steps to meet the wishes of certain groups in the two Togolands, it is necessary also to consider the effects

of such actions on the remaining inhabitants of the territories. For example, the interests of the inhabitants of the northern parts of the two territories (where the inhabitants, who form numerical majorities in both territories, have thus far been generally opposed to unification) must certainly be given proper consideration along with the interests of the predominantly Ewe–inhabited southern parts of the territories." See Circular Airgram to Certain American Diplomatic Officers, 18 October 1952, File 350, Accra Consulate, Classified General Records, 1950–52, Box 5 (Suitland).

122. 350/6–2951, Telegram from the State Department to USUN, 29 June 1951 (NA), reproduced in *FRUS, 1951, vol. 2* (1979), 578–79.

123. Minutes of meeting of administering members of the Trusteeship Council, New York, 3 July 1951, ibid., 580. For the detailed redraft, see Annex: "Redraft of Anglo–French Memorandum," ibid., 583–87.

124. Telegram from the secretary of state to the United States representative at the United Nations, 18 July 1951, ibid., 603–4.

125. Telegram from USUN to the secretary of state, 19 July, 1951, ibid., 604.

126. TC Resolution 345 (ix), 24 July 1951.

127. Amenumey, *The Ewe Unification Movement*, 103.

128. Memorandum of Conversation, by the assistant secretary of state for UN Affairs, "Problems Arising at the Tenth Session of the Trusteeship Council," 25 February 1952, *FRUS, 1952–1954, vol. 3* (1979), 1184–85.

129. Memorandum of Conversation, by an adviser of the United States delegation to the Trusteeship Council, 29 February 1952, ibid., 1188. (Francis B. Sayre was the United States representative on the Trusteeship Council from the council's inception in 1946 until 1 June 1952, when he resigned.)

130. See the following by Michael J. Hogan, "The Search for a 'Creative Peace': The United States, European Unity, and the Origins of the Marshall Plan," *Diplomatic History,* 6, 3 (Summer 1982); "Paths to Plenty: Marshall Plan Planners and the Debate over European Integration, 1947–1948," *Pacific Historical Review,* 53, 3 (August 1984); "Revival and Reform: America's Twentieth–Century Search for a New Economic Order Abroad," *Diplomatic History,* 8, 4 (Fall 1984); "American Marshall Planners and the Search for a European Neocapitalism," *American Historical Review,* 90, 1 (February 1985); *The Marshall Plan: America, Britain, and the Reconstruction of Western Europe, 1947–1952* (Cambridge and New York: Cambridge University Press, 1987). Also see Scott Jackson, "Prologue to the Marshall Plan: The Origins of the American Commitment to a European Recovery Program," *Journal of American History,* 65, 4 (March 1979); Leffler, "The United States and the Strategic Dimensions of the Marshall Plan."

131. McGhee, *Envoy to the Middle World,* 128, 123–24.

132. Ibid., 114.

133. Lugard, *The Dual Mandate,* 85.

134. Kolko, *Confronting the Third World,* 41–43.

Notes to Chapter 4

1. Draft Policy Statement prepared by the Bureau of Near Eastern, South Asian, and African Affairs, "Statement of Policy Proposed by the National Security Council on United

States Objectives and Policies with respect to Tropical Africa," *FRUS, 1952–1954, vol. 10* (1983), 98–101. (This paper is undated, but it must have been written before March 1954; see ibid., 98, n. 1.)

2. Airgram from USOM/London, "DOT Program—British African Territories," 31 October 1956, RG 469, N. Euro./Yugo. Division, UK Subject Files, 1948–57, Box 8 (Suitland).

3. NSC 5719, "U.S. Policy Toward Africa South of the Sahara Prior to Calendar Year 1960," 31 July 1957 (RG 273, NA).

4. Briefing memorandum for the official visit of the prime minister of Ghana, 23–26 July 1958, AWF, International Series, Box 15 (DDEL).

5. *Mutual Security Program: Fiscal Year 1958 Estimates—Near East, South Asia and Africa,* No. 175 (author and date of publication not indicated), 164.

6. 611.70/2–1756, State Department Instruction CA-6309, "Paper on United States Problems in Africa," 17 February 1956 (NA). Also see Draft Policy Statement prepared by the Bureau of Near Eastern, South Asian, and African Affairs, "Statement of Policy Proposed by the National Security Council on United States Objectives and Policies with respect to Tropical Africa," *FRUS, 1952–1954, vol. 10* (1983), 98–101. (This paper is undated, but it must have been written before March 1954; see ibid., 98, n. 1.)

7. NIE No. 72–56, "Conditions and Trends in Tropical Africa," 14 August 1956, 335th NSC Meeting, Tab D (RG 273, NA).

8. 611.70/2–1756, State Department Instruction CA-6309, "Paper on United States Problems in Africa," 17 February 1956 (NA).

9. Memorandum, 335th Meeting of the NSC, 22 August 1957, *FRUS, 1955–1957, vol. 18* (1989), 71–74.

10. Dwight D. Eisenhower, *The White House Years: Waging Peace* (Garden City, NY: Doubleday, 1965), 23.

11. Townsend Hoopes, *The Devil and John Foster Dulles: The Diplomacy of the Eisenhower Era* (Boston: Little, Brown, 1973), chaps. 21–22.

12. Eisenhower's diary entry for 28 March 1956. See *The Eisenhower Diaries,* ed. Robert H. Ferrell (New York: W. W. Norton, 1981), 323.

13. The White House, Memorandum for the president, "Near Eastern Policies," 28 March 1956, AWF, DDE Diary Series, Box 13 (DDEL). Through farm subsidies and support prices provided by the government, United States farmers were (and are still) encouraged to overproduce many commodities. This surplus is acquired and held by the government at enormous cost. By February 1956, the government stock of the surplus was over $9 billion. In order to solve this domestic agricultural crisis, Congress passed Public Law 480, the Agricultural Trade and Development Assistance Act, in 1954. PL 480, as the act was better known, authorized the overseas transfer of United States surplus agricultural products through various means—by sale, by barter, and as gifts. Title II, which provided for grants for emergency relief, authorized the release of surplus commodities for free distribution by private United States voluntary agencies engaged in overseas relief programs. Title I—the most important in the foreign aid setting—authorized the sale of the commodities in the local currency of the purchasing country. The currency thus realized could be used in various ways: to help develop new markets for United States agricultural products, to procure materials for the United States strategic stockpile, to pay for United States overseas obligations, and to promote the economic development of the purchasing country. For the latter purpose, three-quarters of such currency was given or loaned back to the country; any

currency that could not be disposed of was held by the United States. By the late 1950s, one-third of all United States foreign aid to the UDCs was in the form of such local currency sales. See Bruce F. Johnston, "Farm Surpluses and Foreign Policy," *World Politics*, 10, 1 (October 1957); Matthew J. Kust, "Economic Development and Agricultural Surpluses," *Foreign Affairs*, 35, 1 (October 1956); Robert M. Stern, "Agricultural Surplus Disposal and U.S. Economic Policies," *World Politics*, 12, 3 (April 1960); David A. Baldwin, *Foreign Aid and American Foreign Policy: A Documentary Analysis* (New York: Frederick A. Praeger, 1966), 40; Jacob J. Kaplan, *The Challenge of Foreign Aid: Policies, Problems, and Possibilities* (New York: Frederick A. Praeger, 1967), 52.

14. Gail E. Meyer, *Egypt and the United States: The Formative Years* (Cranbury, NJ, and London: Associated University Press, 1980), 183–85, 192–94; Matthew F. Holland, *America and Egypt: From Roosevelt to Eisenhower* (Westport, CT, and London: Praeger, 1996), chap. 8; Peter Hahn, *The United States, Great Britain, and Egypt, 1945–1956: Strategy and Diplomacy in the Early Cold War* (Chapel Hill: University of North Carolina Press, 1991), 241.

15. NSC 5820/1, "U.S. Policy Toward the Near East," 4 November 1958 (RG 273, NA). United Arab Republic (UAR) was a union of Egypt and Syria, formed in 1958.

16. Ibid.

17. Memorandum of Discussion at the 452nd Meeting of the NSC, 21 July 1960, *FRUS, 1958–1960, vol. 14* (1992), 339.

18. Memorandum from the director of the Office of Dependent Area Affairs (Gerig) to the assistant secretary of state for International Organization Affairs (Wilcox), "Afro-Asian or Asian-African Concept and its Use by U.S. Officials," 9 May 1957, *FRUS, 1955–1957, vol. 18* (1989) 66–67.

19. State Department Instruction, USIA CA-55, "Activities of the Government of India," 23 July 1954, File 312.2, Dakar Consulate General, Classified General Records 1947–55, Box 3 (Suitland).

20. Attar Chand, *Nonaligned Nations: Challenge of the Eighties* (New Delhi: Selectbook Service Syndicate, 1983), 79. Also see Sisir K. Gupta, "Asian Nonalignment," *Annals of the American Academy of Political and Social Science*, 32 (November 1965).

21. WFM B-2/4, "Means to Combat India's Policy of Neutralism," 30 August 1951, Records of the Council of Foreign Ministers, Washington Foreign Ministers Meeting, September 1951, WFM British Talks 1–56, Box 64 (NA).

22. "India's Neutrality," *Economist*, 24 January 1951, 186–87.

23. H. W. Brands argues that both the Truman and Eisenhower administrations were flexible, indeed accommodative, of neutralism and that they made a scrupulous distinction between "communism" and neutralism: "At a certain level of abstraction," he says, "they *thought* ideologically. With some exceptions, however, they tended to *act* in a remarkably non-ideological fashion." Nonalignment, he says, was opposed by Washington only when it harmed its interests. See Brands, *The Specter of Neutralism: The United States and the Emergence of the Third World, 1947–1960* (New York: Columbia University Press, 1989). The quotation is from p. 9. (Emphasis in original.) It should, however, be obvious enough that the primary evidence from which the position here has been developed does not support Brands' argument.

24. Hoopes, *The Devil and John Foster Dulles*, 316.

25. *New York Times*, 7 June 1956.

26. Secretary Dulles, "The Cost of Peace," *Department of State Bulletin*, 18 June 1956, 999–1000.

27. 511.00/6–2757, State Department Instruction CA-11094, Policy Information Statement (NEA-191), "Talking Point on 'Positive Neutrality' and Nationalism," 27 June 1957 (NA).

28. NSC Memorandum, 25 August 1950, "Discussion at the 456th Meeting of the National Security Council, Thursday, August 18, 1960" (DDEL).

29. See State Department, "The Emergence of Africa: Report to the President by Vice President Nixon on his trip to Africa, February 28–March 21, 1957," 7 April 1957 (S.12:Af8, NA).

30. For example, see NSC 5719, "U.S. Policy toward Africa South of the Sahara Prior to Calendar Year 1960," 31 July 1957; and its later revisions, the last being NSC 5818 of August 1958; *Briefing on Africa (Testimony of J. C. Satterthwaite): Hearings before the Subcommittee on Africa of the Committee on Foreign Affairs, House of Representatives, Eighty-Sixth Congress, 1st Session, March 5 and July 21, 1959* (Washington, DC: United States Government Printing Office, 1959), 9; Hubert Humphrey, "Emergent Africa: Challenge and Response," *Congressional Record—Senate* (2 September 1959); NSC 6005/1, "Statement of U.S. Policy toward West Africa," 9 April 1960, *FRUS, 1958–1960, vol. 14* (1992), 117–26.

31. 611.70/2–1756, State Department Instruction CA-6309, "Paper on United States Problems in Africa," 17 February 1956 (NA).

32. For example, see Michael Clough, *Free at Last? U.S. Policy toward Africa and the End of the Cold War* (New York: Council on Foreign Relations Press, 1992), 1.

33. See Antonio Gramsci, *Selections from the Prison Notebooks of Antonio Gramsci*, trans. Quintin Hoare and Geoffrey Nowell Smith (New York: International Publishers, 1971).

34. Stephen Gill, "Hegemony, Consensus and Trilateralism," *Review of International Studies*, 12, 3 (July 1986), 206.

35. "The Grass Roots Approach," 28 November 1950, Lot 53 D468, Office Files of Assistant Secretary of State George McGhee, 1945–53, Box 10 (NA).

36. NIE 100-7–55, "World Situation and Trends," 1 November 1955, *FRUS, 1955–1957, vol. 19* (1990), 143.

37. Robert E. Elder, *The Foreign Leader Program: Operations in the United States* (Wesport, CT: Greenwood Publishers, 1961), 2.

38. Beginning with the fiscal year 1953 program, the standard length of all foreign leader grants was ninety days. Also from that fiscal year, the maximum rate of per diem expenses for each grantee was raised from $10 to $12. It was from this that they paid for their living expenses (including hotel accommodation and meals) while in the United States. See State Department, Foreign Service Information and Circular No. 86, "Educational Exchange Service—Foreign Leader Program," 28 May 1953, File 321.2, Dakar Consulate General, Classified General Records, 1947–55, Box 3 (Suitland)

39. Ibid.

40. Elder, *The Foreign Leader Program*, 7–8.

41. Ibid., 4.

42. State Department, Foreign Service Information and Circular No. 86, "Educational Exchange Service—Foreign Leader Program," 28 May 1953, File 321.2, Dakar Consulate General, Classified General Records, 1947–55, Box 3 (Suitland)

43. Elder, *The Foreign Leader Program*, 4.

44. State Department, Foreign Service Information and Circular No. 86, "Educa-

tional Exchange Service—Foreign Leader Program," 28 May 1953, File 321.2, Dakar Consulate General, Classified General Records, 1947–55, Box 3 (Suitland).

45. 511.45H3/2–455, Desp. from AmCongen, Lagos, to the State Department, "Educational Exchange: Program Planning for Nigeria," 4 February 1955 (NA). Also excluded were those who held cabinet or ministerial rank in their home governments "since facilities for administration of this program are not adequate to meet the demands of protocol in such cases." See State Department, Foreign Service Information and Circular No. 86, "Educational Exchange Service—Foreign Leader Program," 28 May 1953, File 321.2, Dakar Consulate General, Classified General Records, 1947–55, Box 3 (Suitland).

46. Gramsci, *Selections from the Prison Notebooks*, 5, 12.

47. Walter L. Adamson, *Hegemony and Revolution: A Study of Antonio Gramsci's Political and Cultural Theory* (Berkeley and Los Angeles: University of California Press, 1980), 175.

48. 511.45H3/2–1257, Desp. from AmCongen, Lagos, to the State Department, "Leader Grant Proposal FY 1956 Thompson Oshin Replaced by Richard A. Doherty," 12 February 1957 (NA).

49. 511.45H3/8–2457, Desp. from AmCongen, Lagos, to the State Department, "IES: Nomination of Hon. Ernest N. Egbuna, Speaker, Eastern House of Assembly, FY 58, For Leader Grant," 24 August 1957 (NA).

50. She was also the chairman, Judiciary Committee, Ijebu Divisional Council; member, board of management of the Cooperative Bank of Western Nigeria Limited; executive member, Cooperative Union of Western Nigeria Limited. See 511.45H3/12–856, Desp. from AmCongen, Lagos, to the State Department, "Submission of Nigerian Woman Candidate for Women Leader Program FY 1957," 8 December 1956 (NA).

51. 511.45H3/3–1257, Desp. from AmCongen, Lagos, to the State Department, "IES: Proposed Leader Grant, PL 402, FY 1957," 12 August 1957 (NA).

52. 511.45H3/8–2257, Desp. from AmCongen, Lagos, to the State Department, "Five Leader Grants, Northern Region of Nigeria, FY 58," 22 August 1957 (NA).

53. 511.45H3/9–2857, Desp. from AmCongen, Lagos, to the State Department, "IES: Forwarding of Data on Five Proposed Individual Specialist FY 58," 28 September 1957 (NA).

54. 511.45H3/8–1755, State Department Instruction A-8, "Educational Exchange: Public Law 402 Foreign Leader Program," 17 August 1955 (NA).

55. 511.45H3/8–2257, Desp. from AmCongen, Lagos, to the State Department, "Five Leader Grants, Northern Region of Nigeria, FY 58," 22 August 1957 (NA).

56. 511.45H3/10–1455, State Department Instruction A-23, "Educational Exchange: Public Law 402 Foreign Leader Program," 14 October 1955 (NA).

57. 511.45H3/7–3155, State Department Instruction A-12, "Educational Exchange: PL 402 Foreign Leader Program," 31 July 1956 (NA).

58. 511.45H3/11–3057, Desp. from AmCongen, Lagos, to the State Department, "IES: Forwarding of Data on Proposed Leader Grantee for FY 58," 30 May 1957 (NA).

59. 511.51T3/9–1158, Desp. from AmCongen, Dakar, to the State Department, "Candidate for Foreign Leader Grant under Public Law 402: Mr Gabriel Marie d'Arboussier," 11 September 1958 (NA).

60. 511.51T3/5–2759, Desp. from AmCongen, Dakar, to the State Department, "Leader Grant for Mr. Ernest Boka, Minister of Public Functions, Ivory Coast," 27 May 1959 (NA).

61. 511.51T3/5–2859, Desp. from AmCongen, Dakar, to the State Department, "Educational Exchange: Candidate for FY 1959 Foreign Leader Grant under Public Law 402: Mr. Seydou B. Kouyate," 26 May 1959 (NA).

62. 511.51T3/6–1259, Telegram from AmConsulate, Lome, to the secretary of state, 12 June 1959 (NA).

63. Gramsci, *Selections from the Prison Notebooks,* 181–82.

64. Telegram from AmCongen, Lagos, to the State Department, 7 September 1960, *FRUS, 1958–1960, vol. 14* (1992), 221–22.

65. 611.45H/8–1059, Desp. from AmCongen, Lagos, to the State Department, "Speech by Consul General to 'The Contemporary Society' on 'American Foreign Policy toward Nigeria,' " 10 August 1959 (NA).

66. Paul Conklin, "Nigeria's Youth Speaks Its Mind," *Africa Report,* March 1961.

67. See Colin Legum, *Pan-Africanism: A Short Political Guide* (London: Pall Mall, 1962), 254; *West Africa,* 8 April 1961.

68. Draft Policy Statement prepared by the Bureau of Near Eastern, South, and African Affairs, "Statement of Policy Proposed by the National Security Council on United States Objectives and Policies with Respect to Tropical Africa," (n.d.), *FRUS, 1952–1954, vol. 10* (1983), 100–101. (This paper is undated, but it must have been written before March 1954; see ibid., 98, n. 1.)

69. NIE 70–59, "The Outlook in West Africa through 1960," 16 June 1959, *FRUS, 1958–1960, vol. 14* (1992), 55.

70. Memorandum of Discussion at the 432nd Meeting of the NSC, 14 January 1960, ibid., 75.

71. Gary Hess, "Global Expansion and Regional Balances: The Emerging Scholarship on United States Relations with India and Pakistan," *Pacific Historical Review,* 56, 2 (May 1987), 259.

72. Rupert Emerson, *Africa and United States Policy* (Englewood Cliffs, NJ: Prentice-Hall, 1967), 36.

73. IR 7103, "Africa: A Special Assessment," 3 January 1956 (NA).

74. Senate Committee on Foreign Relations, *Economic Aid and Technical Assistance in Africa: Report of Senator Theodore Francis Green on a Study Mission Pursuant to Senate Resolution. 162, 84th Congress* (Washington, DC: United States Government Printing Office, 1957), 4–7, 14–23.

75. House of Representatives, *Report of the Special Study Mission to Africa, South and East of the Sahara (April 5, 1957), 85th Congress, 1st Session* (Washington, DC: United States Government Printing Office, 1957), 129.

76. Kenneth M. Kauffman and Helena Stalson, "U.S. Assistance to Less Developed Countries, 1956–65," *Foreign Affairs,* 45, 4 (July 1967), 719–20. Also see Agency for International Development, *U.S. Overseas Loans and Grants and Assistance from International Organizations and Loan Authorization, July 1, 1945–September 30, 1960* (Washington, DC: United States Government Printing Office, n.d.).

77. Memorandum for the NSC, "National Security Implications of Future Developments Regarding Africa," 12 July 1960, NSC Meeting Minutes, 456th Meeting, Tab A (RG 273, NA).

78. Program of African Studies, Northwestern University, *Africa: A Study Prepared at the Request of the Committee on Foreign Relations, United States Senate, United States Foreign Policy No. 4, October 23, 1959; 86th Congress, 1st Session* (Washington: United States Printing Office, 1959), 47.

79. Waldermar A. Nielsen, *The Great Powers and Africa* (New York: Praeger Publishers, 1969), 389.

80. Robert A. Pollard, *Economic Security and the Origins of the Cold War, 1945–1950* (New York: Columbia University Press, 1985), 3.

81. Senate Committee on Appropriations, Testimony of Secretary of State Dean Rusk, *Foreign Assistance and Related Appropriations for FY 1966: Hearings . . . 89th Congress, 2nd Session, 1965* (Washington, DC: Government Printing Office, 1965), 94.

82. The International Cooperation Administration (ICA) was the successor to a number of United States foreign aid agencies. The first was the ECA, created in April 1948 to administer the Marshall Plan. At the end of 1951, the ECA was replaced by the Mutual Security Agency (MSA). In June 1953, the Foreign Operations Administration (FOA) centralized in a single organization the foreign aid and related programs that had been administered by the MSA, the Institute of Inter-American Affairs, the Technical Cooperation Administration, the Mutual Defense Assistance Program, and the Yugoslav Emergency Relief Assistance. In 1955, the FOA gave way to the ICA. See William Adams Brown, Jr., and Redvers Opie, *American Foreign Assistance* (Washington, DC: The Brookings Institution, 1953).

83. Airgram from ICA/USOM, London, "FY56 UK DOT Program," 27 September 1956, RG 469, N. Euro./Yugo. Division, UK Subject Files, 1948–57, Box 8 (Suitland).

84. Paper prepared in the Department of Defense, "Some Basic U.S. Interests in Africa," 22 March 1954, *FRUS, 1952–1954, vol. 11* (1983), 106.

85. Program of African Studies, Northwestern University, *Africa: A Study Prepared at the Request of the Committee on Foreign Relations, United States Senate*, 43.

86. Memorandum for the president from Christian A. Herter, "Aid to the Ivory Coast," 5 August 1960, White House Office, Office of the Staff Secretary, International Series, Box 1 (DDEL).

87. Letter (with enclosure) from B. E. L. Timmons, acting director, USOM/Paris, to C. Vaughan Ferguson, Jr., American consul, Dakar, 9 July 1954, File 523.5 in 500 FOA, Dakar Consulate General, General Records, 1951–55, Box 8 (Suitland).

88. 851T.2614/1–1058, Desp. from AmEmbassy, Paris, to the State Department and Other Interested Agencies, "French African Development Projects Looking Toward IBRD Financing," 10 January 1958 (NA).

89. 611.70/4–3058, "Briefing for Mr. Clarence B. Randall on United States Foreign Economic Policy in Africa by the Staff of Amory Houghton, U.S. ambassador, Paris, March 21, 1958, Paris," Tab W of C. B. Randall, "Report to Council on Foreign Economic Policy on U.S. Foreign Economic Policy in Africa, south of the Sahara," vol. 2, April 1958 (NA).

90. Ibid.

91. Airgram from ICA/W to London, Accra, Lagos, Nairobi, Salisbury, Monrovia, "FY 1956 UK DOT Program," 23 September 1955, RG 469, N. Euro/Yugo. Division, UK Subject Files, 1948–57, Box 8 (Suitland).

92. Airgram from USOM/London, "DOT Program—British African Territories," 31 October 1956, RG 469, N. Euro./Yugo. Division, UK Subject Files, 1948–57, Box 8 (Suitland).

93. Incoming Telegram from AmEmbassy, London, to the secretary of state, 14 March 1957, RG 469, N.Euro/Yugo. Division, UK Subject Files, 1948–57, Box 8 (Suitland).

94. 745J.00/4–257, Incoming Telegram from AmEmbassy, London, to the secretary of state, 2 April 1957 (NA). This is not to say that Britain ever intended to surrender its

imperial heritage to the United States or even give it a blank check. In January 1954, Hilton Poynton, Britain's deputy undersecretary of state, assured a group of senior United States aid officials that the Colonial Office desired United States aid in British colonies but only on condition that the United States would act "as a partner." He emphasized that "he did not by any means mean that he thought the Empire should become American, but rather that a certain amount of active interest on the part of the U.S. would benefit not only the British themselves but would be encouraging to the people of the areas concerned." See "U.S. Assistance to British Overseas Territories: Discussion at Luncheon Given by Mr. Lincoln Gordon at United Hunt Club, 26 January 1954," RG 469, N. Euro./Yugo. Division, UK Subject Files, 1948–57, Box 7 (Suitland).

95. Airgram from ICA/USOM London, "FY56 UK DOT Aid Program," 27 September 1956, RG 469, N. Euro./Yugo. Division, UK Subject Files, 1948–57, Box 8 (Suitland).

96. Airgram from USOM/London, "DOT Program—British African Territories," 31 October 1956, RG 469, N. Euro./Yugo. Division, UK Subject Files, 1948–57, Box 8 (Suitland).

97. Ibid.

98. Senate Committee on Foreign Relations, *Economic Aid and Technical Assistance in Africa: Report of Senator Theodore Francis Green*.

99. Airgram from ICA/W to London, Accra, Lagos, Nairobi, Salisbury, Monrovia, "FY 1956 UK DOT Program," 23 September 1955, RG 469, N. Euro/Yugo. Division, UK Subject Files, 1948–57, Box 8 (Suitland).

100. Airgram from USOM, London, "FY56 UK DOT Aid Program," 27 September 1955, RG 469, N. Euro./Yugo. Division, UK Subject Files 1948–57, Box 8 (Suitland).

101. Sherman Adams, *Firsthand Report* (New York: Harper, 1961), 381–95; Raymond A. Bauer, Ithiel de Sola Pool, and Lewis Anthony Dexter, *American Business Policy* (New York: Atherton, 1963), 29; Burton I. Kaufman, *Trade and Aid: Eisenhower's Foreign Economic Policy, 1953–1961* (Baltimore: Johns Hopkins University Press, 1982), 131.

102. See Commission on Foreign Economic Policy, *Report to the President and the Congress, 83rd Congress, 2nd Session,* House Document No. 290 (Washington, DC: United States Government Printing Office, 23 January 1954), 8–9, 16–23. "Communist" gains in Asia, manifested at the time by the increasing French military reverses in Indochina, informed the commission's recommendation that aid be concentrated on Asia. The French were finally defeated in Indochina in mid-1954. (The commission was headed by Clarence Randall, who later became the chairman of Eisenhower's Council on Foreign Economic Policy.)

103. State Department, office of the assistant secretary for economic affairs, "President's Message on United States Foreign Economic Policy," 30 March 1954, File 361.1, Dakar Consulate General, General Records, 1951–55, Box 6 (Suitland).

104. "Africa: Problems of United States Policy," enclosure in 611.70/2–1755, State Department Instruction CA-6309, "Paper on United States Problems in Africa," 17 February 1956 (NA).

105. From FOA/W, "Instructions Concerning Use of FY '54 African DOT Fund" (n.d.), RG 469, N. Euro/Yugo. Division, UK Subject Files, 1948–57, Box 8 (Suitland). Also see the draft of the United States-Ghana technical cooperation agreement, 845J.00TA/3–1557, State Department Instruction A-58, "Technical Cooperation Agreement with Ghana," 1 April 1957 (NA). The draft was a standard State Department document. Ghana

adhered to the agreement on 3 June 1957. Other West African countries adhered to the agreement individually shortly after their independence.

106. State Department Instruction (Joint State-ICA Message), "Establishment of ICA Administrative Positions in Kenya, Nigeria, and the Gold Coast," 8 August 1955, RG 469, N. Euro./Yugo. Division, UK Subject Files, 1948–57, Box 8 (Suitland).

107. Senate Committee on Foreign Relations, *Economic Aid and Technical Assistance in Africa: Report of Senator Theodore Francis Green.*

108. Airgram from FOA/USOM London, "FY1956 BOB (Bureau of Budget) Presentation—UK African OTs," 21 October 1954, RG 469, N. Euro/Yugo. Division, UK Subject Files, 1948–57, Box 8 (Suitland).

109. Memorandum to Council on Foreign Economic Policy, "CFEP 568: United States Foreign Economic Policy for Africa south of the Sahara," 13 June 1958, White House Office, Special Assistant Series, Subject Subseries, Box 3 (DDEL).

110. James K. Penfield, "The Role of the United States in Africa: Our Interests and Operation," *Department of State Bulletin,* 8 June 1959, 842.

111. Memorandum from the assistant secretary of state for African Affairs (Satterthwaite) to the undersecretary of state (Dillon), "United States Assistance to Sub-Sahara Africa," 30 March 1960, *FRUS, 1958–1960, vol. 14* (1992), 99.

112. Memorandum of Conversation, "Meeting with Under Secretary Dillon to discuss U.S. Policy in Sub-Saharan Africa, particularly U.S. Assistance," 7 April 1960, ibid., 111.

113. John D. Montgomery, *Aid to Africa: New Test for U.S. Policy,* Headline Series No. 149 (New York: Foreign Policy Association-World Affairs Center, September/October, 1961), 37.

114. Dana Adams Schmidt, "U.S. Studies Role of Reds in Africa: Experts Find Soviet Bloc's Economic Aid to Guinea is Pattern for Congo," *New York Times,* 21 July 1960.

115. See "Address by the President," *Department of State Bulletin,* 10 October 1960, 551–57.

116. See Memorandum of Conference with the president (and President Sylvanus Olympio), 23 September 1960, and Memorandum of Conversation, "President Olympio's Call on President Eisenhower," 23 September 1960; Memorandum of Conversation, "Conversation with President Nasser," 26 September 1960; Memorandum of Conference with the president (and President Nasser of Egypt, etc.), 28 September 1960; Memorandum of Conference with the president (and Crown Prince Hassan of Morocco, etc.), 27 September 1960; Memorandum of Conference with the president (and Deputy Prime Minister Akilou of Ethiopia), 27 September 1960; Memorandum of Conference with the president (and Prime Minister Macmillan), 28 September 1960. All are in AWF, DDE Diary Series, Box 53 (DDEL). Also, Memorandum of Conference with the president (and Prime Minister Balewa), 8 October 1960, White House Office, International Series, Box 1 (DDEL).

117. Kaufman, *Trade and Aid,* 178.

118. "The New Administration and the Dollar Problem," 30 November 1960, enclosure in letter from Edward M. Bernstein, EMB (Economic Consultants) Ltd., Washington, to Dean Acheson, 2 December 1960, Papers of Dean Acheson (Post-Administration Files), 1960–62, Box 85 (HSTL).

119. "President Outlines Steps to Improve U.S. Balance-of-Payments Position," *Department of State Bulletin,* 5 December 1960, 860–63. Established by the Eisenhower administration in 1957, the DLF provided investment capital for development projects in

the UDCs, through loans and other forms of credit but not grants. In a number of important ways, it differed from the Export-import Bank: its loans were at lower rates, had longer repayment periods, and repayment could be made in local currencies. And generally, the fund was required to attach minimal conditions concerning either the international behavior or the broad economic and social policies of the borrowing country. See MSP, "Development Loan Fund Fiscal Year 1959 Supplemental Estimates," USAID Library, Washington, DC, n.d.

120. "President Outlines Steps to Improve U.S. Balance-of-Payments Position."

121. A creditor country gains by lending to other countries. If country A makes a loan in dollars to country B, the immediate effect is an increase in the amount of A's dollars at B's disposal. The government or citizens of B can spend A's dollars for A's goods and services or the dollars can be exchanged for another currency, say the pound sterling. But no matter the number of intermediate transfers, A's dollars can only be spent for A's goods and services. Thus the ultimate effect of A's foreign lending is to increase A's exports relative to its imports.

122. V. I. Lenin, *Imperialism: The Highest Stage of Capitalism* (Moscow: Foreign Languages Publishing House, 1947), 79–80.

123. 611.70/4–3058, Report to Council on Foreign Economic Policy on U.S. Foreign Economic Policy in Africa, South of the Sahara by Clarence B. Randall, chairman, Council on Foreign Economic Policy, vol. 1, April 1958 (NA).

124. 851T.0000/12–959, Memorandum of Conversation, " 'Pre-reconnaissance' of Aid Possibilities," enclosure in Memorandum from United States mission to the European Communities, Brussels to the State Department, "Call of H. C. Blisson, Assistant to Senegal Prime Minister," 9 December 1959 (NA).

125. Airgram from FOA/USOM London, "FY1956 BOB (Bureau of Budget) Presentation: UK African OTs," 21 October 1954, RG 469, N. Euro/Yugo. Division, UK Subject Files, 1948–57, Box 8 (Suitland).

126. Airgram from ICA/USOM, London, "FY56 UK DOT Program," 27 September 1956, RG 469, N. Euro./Yugo. Division, UK Subject Files, 1948–57, Box 8 (Suitland).

127. "Final Appropriation for Mutual Security Program," 21 July 1952, *FRUS, 1952–1954*, vol. 1 (1983), 514–16.

128. Andrew F. Westwood, *Foreign Aid in a Foreign Policy Framework* (Washington, DC: The Brookings Institution, 1966), 50.

129. Kaufman, *Trade and Aid,* 68–69, 169–75, chap. 11. For a more detailed discussion of the 1957 congressional debate, see H. Field Haviland, Jr., "Foreign Aid and the Policy Process: 1957," *American Political Science Review,* 52, 3 (September 1958).

130. Kaplan, *The Challenge of Foreign Aid,* 49.

131. "United States Policy toward Africa," Conference Document No. 13, attached to Office Memorandum from Mr. Hare to Mrs. Hope, "Summary of African Panel," 7 March 1950, Lot 53 D468, Office Files of Assistant Secretary of George C. McGhee, 1945–53, Box 9 (NA).

132. Memorandum from the assistant secretary of state for Near Eastern, South Asian, and African Affairs (Rountree) to the secretary of state, "Request for Approval of a United States Policy of Cooperation with other Governments in Organizing a Colombo Plan for Africa," *FRUS, 1955–57, vol. 17* (1989), 71.

133. Memorandum, "Discussion at the 456th Meeting of the National Security Council, Thursday, August 18, 1960," 25 August 1960, *FRUS, 1958–1960, vol. 14* (1992), 147–59.

134. Ibid. The exception made for Guinea represented a shift in policy. The Eisenhower administration had initially hoped that Guinea "will continue to look to France as a major source of external financial and technical assistance." See NSC 5818, "Report on Africa South of the Sahara Prior to Calendar Year 1960," 14 January 1959 (RG 273, NA).

135. This mood was depicted in a major study, "The Nature and Problems of Soviet Economic Penetration in Underdeveloped Areas," AWF, Dulles-Herter Series, Box 6 (DDEL). This paper is not dated, but it must have been prepared in 1956–57: on its last page, there is a tabulation of "Credits Extended and under Serious Consideration by Sino-Soviet Bloc to non-Bloc Countries, January 1956." The discomfort with Soviet economic penetration in the UDCs was also the subject of a long telegram that the United States embassy in Moscow sent to Washington in January 1956: see Incoming Telegram from Moscow to the secretary of state, 27 January 1956, AWF, Dulles-Herter Series, Box 6 (DDEL); and Dulles made it the focal point in a speech he gave in Philadelphia a month later: see "Address by John Foster Dulles, Secretary of State before the Philadelphia Bulletin Forum, February 26, 1956," Press Release No. 92 (State Department) Public Services Division Series 5 No. 43 (NA). By 1960, the "Bloc economic offensive" in the UDCs had become a major concern for NATO as well: see Memorandum on NATO's Competence and Objectives in the Economic Field, 4 November 1960, Papers of Dean Acheson (Post-Administration Files), 1960–62, Box 85 (HSTL).

136. Kaufman, *Trade and Aid,* esp. 9, 73, 208, chap. 4. Also see Burton I. Kaufman, "The United States Response to the Soviet Economic Offensive of the 1950s," *Diplomatic History,* 2, 2 (Spring 1978); W. W. Rostow, *Eisenhower, Kennedy, and Foreign Aid* (Austin: University of Texas Press, 1985), 141–46. For contemporary studies, see Hans Heymann, Jr., "Soviet Foreign Aid as a Problem for U.S. Policy," *World Politics,* 12, 4 (July 1960); Stanley J. Zyzniewski, "The Soviet Bloc and the Underdeveloped Countries," ibid., 11 (1958–59).

137. James M. Hagen and Vernon W. Ruttan, "Development Policy under Eisenhower and Kennedy," *Journal of Developing Areas,* 23, 1 (October 1988), 4; also Kaufman, *Trade and Aid,* 71.

138. 511.00/1–758, State Department Instruction to United States diplomatic missions, "Economic Aid to India," 7 January 1958 (NA).

139. See Memorandum from the chairman of the Joint Chiefs of Staff (Twining) to Secretary of Defense Gates, "The Kitona-Banana and Kamina Bases in the Congo," 18 August 1960, *FRUS, 1958–1960, vol. 14* (1992), 425–27. For Dillon's response, see ibid., 427, n. 1.

140. Memorandum from the JCS to Secretary of Defense Gates, "U.S. Interest in Ghana and Guinea," 17 October 1960, ibid., 161.

141. Draft Policy Statement prepared by the Bureau of Near Eastern, South Asian, and African Affairs, "Statement of Policy Proposed by the National Security Council on United States Objectives and Policies with Respect to Tropical Africa," *FRUS, 1952–1954, vol. 11* (1983), 98–101. (This paper is not dated, but it must have been written before March 1954; see ibid., 98, n. 1.)

142. 745J.00/4–2351, Letter of 23 April 1951 on "Preparedness for War," from E. H. Bourgerie, director, State Department Office of African Affairs to A. W. Childs, American consul general in Lagos (NA). This was a circular letter also sent to other United States missions in Africa.

143. Memorandum from the director of the Office of Dependent Area Affairs (Gerig) to the assistant secretary of state for International Organization Affairs (Wilcox), "Afro-

Asian or Asian-African Concept and its Use by U.S. Officials," 9 May 1957, *FRUS, 1955–1957, vol. 18* (1989), 67.

144. "Project Proposal for a Study of Africa in Transition," 22 July 1957, NSC 335th Meeting, Tab D (NA).

145. NSC 5614/1, "Statement of Policy on Tunisia, Morocco, Algeria, October 3, 1956," *FRUS, 1955–1957, vol. 18* (1989), 139, 143; OCB Report, "Progress Report on Tunisia, Morocco and Algeria, November 13, 1957," ibid., 145.

146. Memorandum of Conversation, "First Tripartite [United States, Britain, France] Talks on Africa," 16 April 1959, *FRUS, 1958–1960, vol. 14* (1992), 46.

147. For example, see CIA, "Major U.S. Interests in Africa," 22 March 1954, *FRUS, 1952–1954, vol. 11* (1983), 107; Draft Policy Statement prepared by the Bureau of Near Eastern, South Asian, and African Affairs, "Statement of Policy Proposed by the National Security Council on United States Objectives and Policies with Respect to Tropical Africa", *ibid.*, esp. 99. (This paper is not dated, but it must have been written before March 1954; see ibid., 98, n.1.)

148. Program of African Studies, Northwestern University, *Africa: A Study Prepared at the Request of the Committee on Foreign Relations, United States Senate*, 40.

149. NIE 72–56, "Conditions and Trends in Tropical Africa," 14 August 1956, *FRUS, 1955–1957, vol. 18* (1989), 47.

150. NIE 70–59, "The Outlook in West Africa Through 1960," 16 June 1959, *FRUS, 1958–1960, vol. 14* (1992), 56; NSC 5818, "Statement of U.S. Policy toward Africa South of the Sahara Prior to Calendar Year 1960," ibid., 29. Also see NIE 76–59, "The Outlook in East, Central, and South Africa," 20 October 1959, ibid., 67; 611.70/1–1455, State Department Office Memorandum, from Mr. Utter to Mr. Jernegan, "Internal Security of the AF Area," 14 January 1955 (NA).

151. Montgomery, *Aid to Africa*, 37.

152. Memorandum for the NSC, "National Security Implications of Future Developments Regarding Africa," 12 July 1960, NSC Meeting Minutes, 456th Meeting, Tab A (RG 273, NA).

153. NSC 5719, "U.S. Policy toward Africa South of the Sahara Prior to Calendar Year 1960," 31 July 1957 (RG 273, NA). This objective was retained in later revisions of NSC 5719, the last being NSC 5818 of August 1958.

154. Memorandum of Conference with the president, 1 November 1960, White House Office, International Series, Box 1 (DDEL).

155. Ibid.

Notes to Chapter 5

1. 745K.02/1–2457, Memorandum for the vice president, "United States delegation to the Gold Coast Independence Ceremonies, March 3–10, 1957," 24 January 1957 (NA).

2. 745J.5MSP/10–2059, Telegram from AmEmbassy, Accra, to the secretary of state, 20 October 1959 (NA).

3. *Mutual Security Program: Fiscal Year 1958 Estimates—Near East, South Asia and Africa*, No. 175, p. 189 (author, publisher and date not indicated), RG 469, N. Euro./Yugo. Division, UK Subject Files, 1948–57, Box 8 (Suitland).

4. 645K.60/2–1857, Memorandum for the vice president, "Communist Bloc Activities in West Africa," 18 February 1957 (NA).

5. Panaf Great Lives, *Kwame Nkrumah* (London: Panaf, 1974), 7.

6. Shortly after Ghana's independence, Nkrumah pulled it out of the West African Airways Corporation, the West African Currency Board, the West African Cocoa Research Institute, and the West African Court of Appeal. These institutions, created by the British, could have been strengthened and elaborated upon to foster regional cooperation in West Africa.

7. W. Scott Thompson, *Ghana's Foreign Policy, 1957–1966: Diplomacy, Ideology, and the New State* (Princeton, NJ: Princeton University Press, 1969), 42–43, 96–97.

8. *Report of the Commission of Enquiry into the Disturbances in the Gold Coast, 1948*, Colonial No. 231 (London: HMSO, 1948), paras. 17–20; appendixes 11, 12.

9. The context of this is discussed in chapter 1.

10. *West Africa*, 17 February 1951.

11. John D. Hargreaves, *Decolonization in Africa* (London and New York: Longman, 1988), 120. That must have been the background of Nkrumah's February 1954 announcement that his government would "in future refuse to employ, in certain branches of the Public Service, persons who are proved to its satisfaction to be active communists." The affected departments were administration (including advisory posts in the ministries), education (including mass education and community development), labor, information services, the police, the army, and the Gold Coast commissioner's overseas office. Nkrumah also noted that some people were attending conferences "behind what is generally known as the Iron Curtain," with all expenses paid, and that scholarships were being offered for Gold Coast students to attend conferences and seminars "organized by communist organizations." He promised that the government was "taking measures to deal with this aspect of the matter. "A verbatim transcription of Nkrumah's speech is in 745K.001/2–2654, Desp. from AmCongen, Accra, to the State Department, "Nkrumah's Statement on Communists in Government," 26 February 1954 (NA).

12. 745K.001/6–1153, Desp. from AmConsulate, Accra, to the State Department, "Anti-Communist Measures of Gold Coast Government," 11 June 1953 (NA).

13. The World Federation of Trade Unions (WFTU) had emerged after World War II as the global fusion of all labor unions. But by 1949, the international labor movement had split along Cold War lines: the Western labor federations disaffiliated to form the ICFTU, leaving the WFTU for the "communist" bloc. See Harold K. Jacobson, "Labor, the UN and the Cold War," *International Organization*, 11, 1 (Winter 1957).

14. 845K.062/11–753, Desp. from AmCongen, Accra, to the State Department, "Transmitting Report by Vice Consul Fleming Regarding Meeting between Prime Minister and ICFTU Representative," 7 November 1953; 845K.062/11–353, Telegram from AmCongen, Accra, to the secretary of state, 3 November 1953 (all at NA).

15. Quoted in Douglas G. Anglin, "Ghana, the West, and the Soviet Union," *Canadian Journal of Economics and Political Science*, 24, 2 (May 1958), 160.

16. Ibid.

17. 845K.062/3–554, Desp. from AmCongen, Accra, to the State Department, "Reaffiliation of Gold Coast TUC with International Confederation of Free Trade Unions," 5 March 1954 (NA).

18. 845K.062/11–753, State Department Instruction A-27 to the AmCongen, Accra, "Commendations for Consul Cole and Vice Consuls Sawyer and Fleming," 15 January 1954 (NA).

19. Jitendra Mohan, "Nkrumah and Nkrumahism," in *Socialist Register 1967,* eds. Ralph Miliband and John Saville (New York: Monthly Review Press, 1967), 199.

20. David E. Apter, "Some Economic Factors in the Political Development of the Gold Coast," *Journal of Economic History,* 14, 4 (1954), 421.

21. St. Clair Drake, "Prospects for Democracy in the Gold Coast," *Annals of the American Academy of Political and Social Science,* 306 (July 1956), 86.

22. George Padmore, *Pan-Africanism or Communism?* (London: Dennis Dobson, 1956), 375–76.

23. See Obed Asamoah, "Nkrumah's Foreign Policy, 1951–1966," in *The Life and Work of Kwame Nkrumah,* ed. Kwame Arhin (Trenton, NJ: Africa World Press, 1993), 235; John D. Esseks, "Political Independence and Economic Decolonization: The Case of Ghana under Nkrumah," *Western Political Quarterly,* 24, 1 (March 1971); Thompson, *Ghana's Foreign Policy,* 14, 26–27; Anglin, "Ghana, the West, and the Soviet Union," 158–59.

24. Anglin, "Ghana, the West, and the Soviet Union," 159.

25. Thompson, *Ghana's Foreign Policy,* 14.

26. See Philip Siekman, "Edgar Kaiser's Gamble in Africa," *Fortune,* November 1961, 131.

27. 845J.411/10–957, Telegram from the State Department to AmEmbassy, Accra, 9 October 1957 (NA).

28. 845J.411/10–957, Telegram from the State Department to AmEmbassy, Accra, 9 October 1957 (NA).

29. 845J.411/10–957, Telegram from AmEmbassy, Accra, to the secretary of state, 9 October 1957 (NA).

30. He was in the United States in 1935–44 for his undergraduate and graduate studies at Lincoln University and the University of Pennsylvania respectively. See Kwame Nkrumah, *Autobiography* (London: Thomas Nelson, 1957).

31. 845J.411/10–1057, Telegram from AmEmbassy, Accra, to the secretary of state, 10 October 1957 (NA).

32. Ibid.

33. 845J.411/10–1157, Telegram from AmEmbassy, Accra, to the secretary of state, 11 October 1957 (NA).

34. 845J.411/10–957, Telegram from the State Department to AmEmbassy, Accra, 9 October 1957 (NA).

35. 845J.411/10–1057, Telegram from AmEmbassy, Accra, to the secretary of state, 10 October 1957 (NA).

36. The British file on this—CO 544/1397, "Exchange of Diplomatic Mission between Gold Coast and USSR," PRO, London—contains so little information that it is of no use here.

37. In a telegram issued on 5 March (but for release on the following day) to the United States consul, the State Department announced that the United States had officially recognized Ghana, and that, with the permission of the Ghanaian government, the United States consulate general in Accra was being raised to the status of an embassy. The telegram also announced that the Ghanaian government had been informed that it was welcome to establish an embassy in Washington "as soon as practicable." See 745K.02/3–557, Telegram from the State Department to AmCongen, Accra, 5 March 1957 (NA).

38. 645J.61/3–957, Telegram from AmCongen, Accra, to the secretary of state, 9 March 1957 (NA).

39. 645J.60/3–1857, Telegram from the State Department to AmEmbassy, Accra, and AmEmbassy, London, 18 March 1957 (NA).
40. 645K.61/1–2356, Desp. from AmCongen, Accra, to the State Department, "USSR Likely to Receive Invitation to Gold Coast Independence Celebrations," 23 January 1956 (NA).
41. 645K.61/2–2056, State Department Instruction CA-6355 to the AmCongen, Accra, "Department's Views on Prospect of USSR Establishing Diplomatic Relations with the Gold Coast," 20 February 1956 (NA).
42. 645K.61/2–2157, State Department Instruction A-50 to AmEmbassy, Monrovia, "Possible Liberian Talk with Ghana Officials on Soviet Mission," 21 February 1957 (NA).
43. 645K.61/2–2757, Telegram from AmEmbassy, Monrovia, to the secretary of state, 27 February 1957 (NA).
44. 645K.61/2–2857, Telegram from AmEmbassy, Monrovia, to the secretary of state, 28 February 1957 (NA).
45. 645J.61/3–657, Telegram from AmCongen, Accra, to the State Department, 6 March 1957 (NA). For Nixon's discussions with Nkrumah, see Memorandum of Conversation, "Visit of Vice President Richard M. Nixon," 4 March 1957, TAB B in "Report to the President on the Vice President's Visit to Africa, February 28–March 21, 1957—Detailed Conclusions and Recommendations," 5 April 1957, White House Central Files (Confidential File), Subject Series, Box 100 (DDEL).
46. 645J.61/3–1357, Telegram from AmEmbassy, London, to the secretary of state, 13 March 1957 (NA).
47. 645J.60/3–2157, Telegram from AmEmbassy, London, to the secretary of state, 21 March 1957 (NA).
48. 645J.61/10–3057, Telegram from AmEmbassy, London, to the secretary of state, 30 October 1957 (NA).
49. 645J.61/10–3057, Telegram from the State Department to AmEmbassy, Accra, 1 November 1957 (NA).
50. 645J.61/11–457, Telegram from AmEmbassy, Accra, to the State Department, 4 November 1957 (NA).
51. 645J.61/11–657, Telegram from AmEmbassy, Accra, to the secretary of state, 6 November 1957 (NA).
52. Ibid. The United States did not agree to any limitation on its diplomatic staff in Accra. See 645J.61/11–1857, Telegram from AmEmbassy, Accra, to the secretary of state, 18 November 1957 (NA).
53. 645J.61/1–1558, Telegram from AmEmbassy, London, to the secretary of state, 15 January 1958 (NA).
54. 745J.00/7–2458, Memorandum of Conversation, "Discussion of Ghana's Various Diplomatic Problems, including Exchange of Missions with USSR and Recognition of Communist China," 24 July 1958 (NA).
55. Thompson, *Ghana's Foreign Policy,* 100, 102.
56. 745J.5MSP/4–1957, Desp. from AmEmbassy, Accra, to the State Department, "Aid Discussion with Ghanaian Officials," 19 April 1957 (NA).
57. 745J.5MSP/6–2857, Desp. from AmEmbassy, Accra, to the State Department, "Possible Loan to Ghana under the Mutual Security Program," 28 June 1957 (NA).
58. 845J.00–TA/9–2657, Memorandum of Conversation, "Visit of Ghana's Finance Minister Gbedemah to ICA," 26 September 1957 (NA).

59. 811.05145J/9–2557, Memorandum of Conversation, "Discussion of Commercial and Investment Relations between the United States and Ghana," 25 September 1957 (NA).

60. 845J.00TA/7–2558, Memorandum of Conversation, "U.S. Technical Assistance and Ghana's Five Year Plan," 25 July 1958 (NA).

61. See letter from A. L. Adu, permanent secretary, Ghana's Ministry of External Affairs, to the United States ambassador, Accra, 30 October 1957. This is an enclosure in 745J.5MSP/11–1–57, Desp. from AmEmbassy, Accra, to the State Department and ICA, "Technical Assistance Program in Ghana: Government of Ghana Requests an ICA Survey Team as a Preliminary to the Possible Establishment of a United States Operation Mission," 1 November 1957 (NA).

62. 845J.00–TA/3–2658, Memorandum of Conversation, "ICA Survey Team's Views on Technical Cooperation Program in Ghana," 26 March 1958 (NA).

63. For example, see 745J.5MSP/8–1357, Desp. from AmEmbassy, Accra, to the State Department, "American Economic Aid to Ghana," 13 August 1957; 745J.5MSP/1–859, Desp. from AmEmbassy, Accra, to the State Department, "Ghana's Possible Need for Loan Funds: Conversation with the Minister of Finance," 8 January 1959 (both at NA); Memorandum of Conversation, "Prime Minister Nkrumah's Talk (Second) with the President," 24 July 1958, AWF, International Series, Box 15 (DDEL).

64. Letter from Eisenhower to Nkrumah, 4 March 1958, AWF, International Series, Box 15 (DDEL).

65. Letter from Nkrumah to Eisenhower, 7 March 1958, AWF, International Series, Box 15 (DDEL).

66. 745J.13/9–558, Telegram from the State Department to AmEmbassy, Accra, 5 September 1958 (NA).

67. 845J.4711/3–459, Telegram from the State Department to AmEmbassy, Accra, 4 March 1959 (NA).

68. Tom Mboya, "Impressions of a Visitor to Ghana: European Civil Servants Stay On," *East African Standard,* 2 April 1958.

69. 745J.00/4–258, Desp. from AmConsulate, Nairobi, to the State Department, "Mboya's Article on Ghana," 2 April 1958 (NA).

70. 745J.00/5–1959, State Department Instruction CA-10091, "Ghana and its Influence in Africa," 19 May 1958 (NA).

71. Ibid.

72. *Time,* 4 August 1958, quoted in Thompson, *Ghana's Foreign Policy,* 44.

73. Memorandum for the president, "Official Visit by Prime Minister Nkrumah of Ghana," 19 July 1958, AWF, International Series, Box 15 (DDEL).

74. Robert C. Keith, "The Nkrumah Visit—A Triumphal Return," *Africa Special Report,* August 1958.

75. See Kwame Nkrumah, *I Speak of Freedom: A Statement of African Ideology* (New York: Frederick A. Praeger, 1961), 139–42.

76. 611.45J/7–2558, Telegram from the State Department to AmEmbassy, Accra, 25 July 1958 (NA).

77. Nkrumah, *I Speak of Freedom,* 141–45. The speech was published as "African Prospect," *Foreign Affairs,* 37, 1 (October 1958).

78. Keith, "The Nkrumah Visit—A Triumphal Return." The DLF and the ICA were each authorized to guarantee United States private investments in the UDCs. DLF

guaranties covered up to $100 million and could be extended without limit as to risks covered or nationality of the benefactor, provided that ordinary business risks of equity investment could not be covered. The ICA investment guaranty program covered up to $1 billion of investment in the UDCs by United States citizens and companies against risks of loss arising from appropriation, inconvertibility of exchange, capital, or earnings as well as war damages. By December 1960, the United States had guaranty agreements under the ICA program with forty-nine countries, seven of them in Africa. See Eric Hager, "Some Aspects of Private Foreign Investment," *Department of State Bulletin,* 12 December 1960, 893. (In the article, Hager is simply introduced as "Legal Adviser.")

79. 811.05145J/7–2958, Cablegram from ICA Accra, 29 July 1958; also 811.05145J/7–2658, Cablegram from ICA Accra, 26 July 1958 (both at NA).

80. 811.05145J/9–3058, Desp. from AmEmbassy, Accra, to the State Department, "Signature of Investment Guaranty Agreement with Ghana," 30 September 1958 (NA).

81. 611.45J/7–2558, Telegram from the State Department to AmEmbassy, Accra, 25 July 1958 (NA).

82. 745J.13/8–858, Telegram from AmEmbassy, Accra, to the secretary of state, 8 August 1958; 645J.00/8–1358, Telegram from AmEmbassy, Accra, to the secretary of state, 13 August 1958 (both at NA).

83. Nkrumah, *I Speak of Freedom,* 150.

84. 845J.49/8–3058, Airgram from ICA Accra, "Food Situation in Northern Ghana," 30 August 1958 (NA).

85. 845J.49/9–458, Cablegram from ICA Accra, 4 September 1958 (NA).

86. Ibid.

87. 845J.49/9–1758, Telegram from AmEmbassy, Accra, to the secretary of state, 17 September 1958 (NA).

88. Ibid.

89. 845J.49/10–858, Telegram from the State Department to AmEmbassy, Accra, 8 October 1958 (NA).

90. Nkrumah, *I Speak of Freedom,* 98.

91. (Ghana) Ministry of Information and Broadcasting, "Prime Minister's Speech on Foreign Policy," Press Release No. 632/58, 15 July 1958. The speech is enclosed in 645J.00/7–1958, Desp. from AmEmbassy, Accra, to the State Department, "Prime Minister Makes Foreign Policy Speech," 19 July 1958 (NA). For the distinction between positive neutralism and nonalignment, see Khalid I. Babaa and Cecil V. Crabb, Jr., "Nonalignment as a Diplomatic and Ideological Credo," *Annals of the American Academy of Political and Social Science,* 32 (November 1965).

92. (Ghana) Ministry of Information and Broadcasting, "Prime Minister's Speech on Foreign Policy," Press Release No. 632/58, 15 July 1958. The speech is enclosed in 645J.00/7–1958, Desp. from AmEmbassy, Accra, to the State Department, "Prime Minister Makes Foreign Policy Speech," 19 July 1958 (NA).

93. Ibid.

94. The states involved were Tunisia, Libya, Morocco, Ethiopia, Sudan, Egypt, Liberia, and Ghana. See Alex Quaison-Sackey, *Africa Unbound: Reflections of an African Statesman* (New York: Frederick A. Praeger, 1963), 65–72; Thompson, *Ghana's Foreign Policy,* 31–38.

95. Thompson, *Ghana's Foreign Policy,* 39–41, 58–67.

96. 870–46/6–2158, Memorandum from Joseph Palmer 2nd to Mr. Rountree, "Prime Minister Nkrumah and Pan-Africanism," 21 June 1958 (NA).

97. 645J.76/6–3058, Telegram from AmEmbassy, Monrovia, to the secretary of state, 1 July 1958 (NA).

98. 645J.00/7–1159, Telegram from AmEmbassy, Accra, to the secretary of state, 11 July 1958 (NA).

99. (Ghana) Ministry of Information and Broadcasting, "Prime Minister's Speech on Foreign Policy," Press Release No. 632/58, 15 July 1958. The speech is enclosed in 645J.00/7–1958, Desp. from AmEmbassy, Accra, to the State Department, "Prime Minister Makes Foreign Policy Speech," 19 July 1958 (NA).

100. Anglin, "Ghana, the West, and the Soviet Union," 154, 160.

101. Ibid., 160. Also writing in 1958, Henry Bretton reached the same conclusions in "Current Political Thought in Ghana," *American Political Science Review,* 52, 1 (March 1958).

102. 645J.48/2–1959, Desp. from AmEmbassy, Accra, to the State Department, "Polish and East German Officials Announce Plans to Establish Ties with Ghana," 19 February 1959 (NA).

103. 845J.0060/10–659, Desp. from AmEmbassy, Accra, to the State Department, "Recent Developments in Ghana-Soviet Bloc Economic Relations," 6 October 1959 (NA).

104. 845J.33/10–2759, Telegram from AmEmbassy, Accra, to the secretary of state, 27 October 1959 (NA).

105. 645J.93/10–259, Desp. from AmEmbassy, Accra, to the State Department, "Congratulatory Message to Communist China is Another Indication Ghana May Extend Formal Recognition," 2 October 1959 (NA).

106. 645J.62B/9–2259, Telegram from AmEmbassy, Accra, to the secretary of state, 22 September 1959 (NA).

107. 745J.5/3–2059, Desp. from AmEmbassy, Accra, to the State Department, "Israeli Government to Train Ghana Air Force Personnel," 20 March 1959. Also see 845J.0084A/3–2059, Desp. from AmEmbassy, Conakry, to the State Department, "Israeli-Ghana Economic Cooperation: Guinea-Ghana Relations," 20 March 1959 (both at NA).

108. 611.45J/11–2357, Telegram from AmEmbassy, Accra, to the secretary of state, 23 November 1957 (NA).

109. 611.45J/10–2659, State Department Instruction CA-3588, "Criticism of the United States by the Foreign Minister of Ghana," 26 October 1959 (NA). According to Thompson, the original brief for the Ghanaian mission to the UN was that it should follow Canada on Western issues and India on Soviet bloc issues, "but from the first a tradition of independence developed in the delegation which resulted in a better balanced nonalignment than was evident in Accra during the same period." He found that the mission could exercise this independence because Nkrumah did not follow UN affairs; thus "the delegation became a virtually independent subsystem of Ghana's foreign policy, seldom worrying about Accra's reaction to particular votes." See Thompson, *Ghana's Foreign Policy,* 52–53.

110. 611.45J/10–2659, State Department Instruction CA-3588, "Criticism of the United States by the Foreign Minister of Ghana," 26 October 1959 (NA).

111. 611.45J/10–3059, Telegram from USUN to the secretary of state, 30 October 1959 (NA).

112. 611.45J/11–759, Telegram from the State Department to AmEmbassy, Accra, 27 November 1959 (NA).

113. 611.45J/12–759, Desp. from AmEmbassy, Accra, to the State Department, "Criticism of the United States by the Foreign Minister of Ghana," 7 December 1959 (NA).

114. Ibid.

115. In July 1959, Ghana had protested France's decision to test atomic weapons in the Sahara; and in November 1959, sponsored a UN resolution that condemned the decision. Nonetheless, France carried out the test in February 1960. See Thompson, *Ghana's Foreign Policy,* 98–99.

116. The relevant portion of the proceedings is cited in 611.45J/12–2159, Desp. from AmEmbassy, Accra, to the State Department, "Foreign Minister discusses U.S. Voting in UN During Foreign Policy Debate," 21 December 1959 (NA).

117. 745J.5MSP/3–1659, Desp. from AmEmbassy, Accra, to the State Department, "USIS-USOM Coordination Agreement/Joint Embassy-USIS-USOM Message," 16 March 1959 (NA).

118. 745J.5MSP/10–2059, Telegram for AmEmbassy, Accra, to the secretary of state, 20 October 1959 (NA).

119. NSC 6005, "U.S. Policy toward West Africa," 29 February 1960 (RG 273, NA). Its final and amended version, NSC 6005/1, was adopted by the NSC and received presidential approval as a statement of policy on 9 April 1960. See NSC 6005/1, "Statement of U.S. Policy toward West Africa," 9 April 1960, *FRUS, 1958–1960, vol. 14* (1992), 117–26.

120. Study Mission to Africa, November-December 1960, *Report of Senators Frank Church, Gale W. McGhee, and Frank E. Moss to the Committee on Foreign Relations, Committee on Appropriations, and Committee on Interior and Insular Affairs, United States Senate, February 12, 1961, 87th Congress, 1st Session* (Washington, DC: United States Government Printing Office, 1961), 31.

121. *New York Times,* 24 September 1960.

122. 745J.11/8–1260, Telegram to AmEmbassy, Accra, 12 August 1960, *FRUS, 1958–1960, vol. 14* (1992), 658, n. 1.

123. Telegram from AmEmbassy, Accra, to the State Department, 25 August 1960, ibid., 658–60.

124. Ibid.

125. Ibid.

126. See Thompson, *Ghana's Foreign Policy,* esp. 164–69.

127. "Ghana-Soviet Trade Pact," *West Africa,* 3 September 1960.

128. Thompson, *Ghana's Foreign Policy,* 164, 166.

129. See 870–46/6–2158, Memorandum from Joseph Palmer 2nd to Mr. Rountree, "Prime Minister Nkrumah and Pan-Africanism," 21 June 1958 (NA).

130. NSC 6005, "U.S. Policy toward West Africa," 29 February 1960 (RG 273, NA).

131. What follows is not about the Congo crisis per se; it is a subject that has received and continues to receive due scholarly attention. Nor is it about the Nkrumah/Lumumba relationship and such related issues as the Ghana-Congo-Guinea unification project. The focus here is specifically on the pivotal role played by the Congo crisis in the deterioration of United States relations with Ghana. For this reason, the analysis of the crisis itself is brief and based on secondary sources.

132. Thomas Hodgkin, *Nationalism in Colonial Africa* (London: Frederick Muller, 1956), 48–55.

133. Kanza attended the Congolese University, Lovanium (an affiliate of the Catholic University of Louvain in Belgium). See Thomas Kanza, *Conflict in the Congo: The Rise*

and Fall of Lumumba (Harmondsworth, England: Penguin Books, 1972). During Lumumba's tenure as prime minister, Kanza served as Congolese minister delegate to the UN.

134. See Crawford Young, *Politics in the Congo: Decolonization and Independence* (Princeton, NJ: Princeton University Press, 1965), esp. 94, 296, 312–15.

135. Alan James, *Britain and the Congo Crisis, 1960–63* (London: Macmillan, 1996), 42.

136. The literature on the Congo crisis is vast, but see ibid.; also Young, *Politics in the Congo*, chap. 13; David N. Gibbs, *The Political Economy of Third World Intervention: Mines, Money and U.S. Policy in the Congo Crisis* (Chicago and London: University of Chicago Press, 1991); Catherine Hoskyns, *The Congo since Independence: January 1960–December 1961* (London: Oxford University Press, 1965); Madeleine G. Kalb, *The Congo Cables: The Cold War in Africa—from Eisenhower to Kennedy* (New York: Macmillan, 1982); Kanza, *Conflict in the Congo*; Alan P. Merriam, *Congo: Background of Conflict* (Evanston, IL: Northwestern University Press, 1961); Michael G. Schatzberg, *Mobutu or Chaos? The United States and Zaire, 1960–1990* (Lanham, MD: University Press of America, 1991); Stephen R. Weissman, *American Foreign Policy in the Congo, 1960–1964* (Ithaca, NY, and London: Cornell University Press, 1974). For Nkrumah's account, see Kwame Nkrumah, *Challenge of the Congo* (New York: International Publishers, 1967).

137. James, *Britain and the Congo Crisis,* 42.

138. Weissman, *American Foreign Policy in the Congo,* 64.

139. Carole Collins, "Fatally Flawed Mediation: Cordier and the Congo Crisis of 1960," *Africa Today* (3rd Quarter, 1992), 10.

140. Gibbs, *The Political Economy of Third World Intervention,* 92–95; Richard D. Mahoney, *JFK: Ordeal in Africa* (New York: Oxford University Press, 1983) 38; Jitendra Mohan, "Ghana, the Congo, and the United Nations," *Journal of Modern African Studies,* 7, 3 (1969), 379; Schatzberg, *Mobutu or Chaos?* 38.

141. James, *Britain and the Congo Crisis,* 42–43.

142. Kalb, *The Congo Cables,* xiii.

143. For an overview of this, see Gibbs, *The Political Economy of Third World Intervention,* 92–94; Mahoney, *JFK: Ordeal in Africa,* 38–41, 44–45; Stephen R. Weissman, "CIA Covert Action in Zaire and Angola: Patterns and Consequences," *Political Science Quarterly,* 94, 2 (Summer 1979), 265–68.

144. Memorandum of discussion at the 452nd Meeting of the NSC, 21 July 1960, *FRUS, 1958–1960, vol. 14* (1992), 339.

145. Editorial Note, ibid., 495. Lumumba must have incurred Eisenhower's hostility even before the Congo crisis: during the ceremonies marking the transfer of power from Belgium, he lambasted Belgian paternalism, and he did so in the presence of the Belgian king who was Eisenhower's personal friend. Eisenhower was later to recall: "Things went badly from the start. Even the ceremonies marking independence in the Congo portended ill. With King Baudouin present, the radical and unstable Congolese Prime Minister, Patrice Lumumba, took the occasion to excoriate Belgium for afflicting 'atrocious sufferings' on the Congolese. . . . The President, Mr. Joseph Kasavubu, a man of considerably more moderation, was obviously discomfited and embarrassed." See Dwight D. Eisenhower, *Waging Peace, 1956–1951: The White House Years* (Garden City, NY: Doubleday, 1965), 573.

146. See Telegram from AmEmbassy, Leopoldville, to the State Department, 22 September 1960, *FRUS, 1958–1960, vol. 14* (1992), 501.

147. The United States embassy in Brussels acknowledged that Lumumba's strength

derived from his "adroitness as a politician and propagandist" and his "apparent dominance over Congolese Chamber (but not Senate)." See Telegram from the United States embassy in Belgium to the State Department, 19 July 1960, ibid., 330–31.

148. Collins, "Fatally Flawed Mediation: Cordier and the Congo Crisis of 1960," 15.

149. Ibid., 11, 13, 14.

150. Ibid., 17. Also see James, *Britain and the Congo Crisis*, 70–71; Kalb, *The Congo Cables*, 80–82.

151. In 1984, two former CIA officials publicly disclosed their agency's relationship with Mobutu during the crisis. See William Colby and John Stockwell, panel discussion, "Should the U.S. Fight Secret Wars?" *Harpers*, September 1984.

152. Mohan, "Ghana, the Congo, and the United Nations," 390–91; Gibbs, *The Political Economy of Third World Intervention*, 96.

153. Collins, "Fatally Flawed Mediation: Cordier and the Congo Crisis of 1960," 18.

154. Telegram from AmEmbassy, Leopoldville, to the State Department, Lepoldville, 26 September 1960, *FRUS, 1958–1960, vol. 14* (1992), 505.

155. James, *Britain and the Congo Crisis*, chap. 7.

156. Telegram from USUN to the State Department, 26 August 1960, *FRUS, 1958–1960, vol. 14* (1992), 444, 446.

157. Telegram from USUN to the State Department, 7 September 1960, ibid., 465.

158. Quoted in James, *Britain and the Congo Crisis*, 71.

159. Ibid., 69, 71.

160. Hoskyns, *The Congo since Independence*, 472–73; Weissman, "CIA Covert Action in Zaire and Angola: Patterns and Consequences," 269–70; Collins, "Fatally Flawed Mediation: Cordier and the Congo Crisis of 1960," 16.

161. This interpretation is evident in virtually all the references cited in n. 136 above. In addition, see Nzongola-Ntalaja, "United States Policy toward Zaire"; and Crawford Young, "The Zairean Crisis and American Foreign Policy," both in *African Crisis Areas and U.S. Foreign Policy*, eds.Gerald J. Bender, James Coleman, and Richard L. Sklar (Berkeley and Los Angeles: University of California Press, 1985). David Gibbs has recently dissented from this interpretation. Arguing that Katanga holds the key to understanding United States conduct in the crisis, he insists that Washington supported Tshombe's secession, not because of Cold War dictates, but to defend American corporate interests. In Gibbs' words, "the Eisenhower administration supported Katanga because it had a financial interest in doing so." For good measure, he also emphasizes that United States "interests were synonymous with Belgian interests, and the USA accordingly supported Belgian policy. . . .Belgian interests organized the Katanga secession, and the United States, in turn, supported the secession. . . .The economic perspective explains the Eisenhower policy quite well. See Gibbs, *The Political Economy of Third World Intervention*, 100–101.

True, the Eisenhower administration generally supported the Belgian position on the Congo crisis, but there is evidence that the administration neither welcomed nor endorsed Katanga's secession. For example, see Telegram from the State Department to the consulate at Elisabethville, 16 July 1960, *FRUS, 1958–1960, vol. 14* (1992), 317–18; Memorandum of Conference with President Eisenhower, 19 July 1960, ibid., 328–30; Telegram from the United States embassy in Belgium to the State Department, 19 July 1960, ibid., 330–32; Telegram from the State Department to the United States embassy in France, 19

July 1960, ibid., 333–34; Circular Telegram from the State Department to certain diplomatic missions, 21 July 1960, ibid., 344–45; Telegram from the State Department to USUN, 6 August 1960, ibid., 392–94.

162. Weissman, *American Foreign Policy in the Congo,* 77; Ilungo Kabongo, "The Catastrophe of Belgian Decolonization," in *Decolonization and African Independence: The Transfer of Power, 1960–1980,* eds. Prosser Gifford and Wm. Roger Louis (New Haven, CT, and London: Yale University Press, 1988), 383.

163. Schatzberg, *Mobutu or Chaos?* 14.

164. See Jonathan E. Helmreich, *United States Relations with Belgium and the Congo, 1940–1960* (Newark: University of Delaware Press, 1998).

165. According to Weissman, this "NATO reflex in African policy was partly the result of past [United States] estimates of Europe's strategic and politico-economic importance vis-à-vis Africa." He demonstrates how this "reflex" predisposed the United States to act in deference to Belgium. See his *American Foreign Policy in the Congo,* 43–46. Also see James, *Britain and the Congo Crisis,* 46–47.

166. Senate Select Committee to Study Governmental Operations with Respect to Intelligence Activities, *Interim Report: Alleged Assassination Plots Involving Foreign Leaders, 94th Congress, 1st Session* (Washington, DC: United States Government Printing Office, 20 November 1975), 51. Also see Kalb, *The Congo Cables*; Mahoney, *JFK: Ordeal in Africa,* 40–41, 44–49; Schatzberg, *Mobutu or Chaos?* 21, 25, 85; Andrew Tully, *CIA: The Inside Story* (New York: William Morrow, 1962); Weissman, *American Foreign Policy in the Congo,* esp. chaps. 2 and 3; Weissman, "CIA Covert Action in Zaire and Angola: Patterns and Consequences."

167. Mwelwa C. Musambachime, "The Changing Political Personality of an African Politician: The Case of Patrice Emery Lumumba," *Genève-Afrique,* 25, 2 (1967).

168. Mohan, "Ghana, the Congo, and the United Nations," 371.

169. Thompson, *Ghana's Foreign Policy,* 123–24; Nkrumah, *Challenge of the Congo,* 21.

170. *Correspondence Exchanged between Osagyefo Dr. Kwame Nkrumah . . . and the Leader of the Republic of the Congo on the Congo Situation* (Accra: n.d.) quoted in Mohan, "Ghana, the Congo, and the United Nations," 374, n. 4.

171. In the light of later events, it is instructive that in spite of the Ghanaian pledge and its prompt acceptance by the Congolese, "the Ghanaian Government was nevertheless anxious to avoid *direct* military aid," preferring, instead, to contribute its troops as part of a UN force: "That same day Nkrumah spoke by telephone with Hammarskjold to urge the need for a quick and favorable response to the Congolese request for military assistance and to offer Ghanaian troops for that purpose." See ibid., 374–75. (Emphasis in original.)

172. Telegram from the State Department to AmEmbassy, Accra, 28 April 1960, *FRUS, 1958–1960, vol. 14* (1992), 271.

173. 755A.00/5-160, Telegram from AmEmbassy, Accra, to the secretary of state, 1 May 1960, ibid., 271, n. 2.

174. Telegram from the State Department to AmEmbassy, Accra, 2 August 1960, ibid., 379–80.

175. Telegram from AmEmbassy, Accra, to the State Department, 6 August 1960, ibid., 319.

176. Thompson, *Ghana's Foreign Policy,* 131–32.

177. *New York Times,* 24 September 1960.

178. Ibid.

179. Mohan, "Ghana, the Congo, and the United Nations," 382, 375, 382–83; Thompson, *Ghana's Foreign Policy*, 130.
180. Eisenhower, *The White House Years*, 583.
181. *New York Times*, 24 September 1960.
182. Ibid., 26 September 1960.
183. Ibid., 27 September 1960.
184. For the speech, see Nkrumah, *I Speak of Freedom*, 262–80; *New York Times*, 24 September 1960.
185. Kalb, *The Congo Cables*, 103–4; *The New York Times*, 21 September 1960.
186. *The New York Times*, 21 September 1960.
187. James, *Britain and the Congo Crisis*, 73.
188. See Nkrumah, *I Speak of Freedom*, 262–80; *New York Times*, 24 September 1960.
189. Ibid.
190. *New York Times*, 24 September 1960.
191. Mahoney, *JFK: Ordeal in Africa*, 51.
192. Memorandum of Telephone Conversation between the assistant secretary of state for African Affairs (Satterthwaite) and the Ghanaian representative at the UN (Quaison-Sackey), "Appointment to Call on President Nkrumah," 24 September 1960, *FRUS, 1958–1960, vol. 14* (1992), 663–65. In the course of the conversation, Quaison-Sackey first expressed surprise at Herter's reaction to Nkrumah's speech. He denied any Khrushchev/Nkrumah collusion, saying that he had fixed the time for Nkrumah's speech "several weeks ago." He attributed the Eastern bloc's applause to the fact that the speech was anticolonial in tone. See ibid.
193. Telegram from AmEmbassy, Leopoldville, to the State Department, Léopoldville, 17 August 1960, ibid., 419.
194. Telegram from AmEmbassy, Leopoldville, to the State Department, Lepoldville, 18 September 1960, ibid., 494.
195. Telegram from USUN to the State Department, 19 August 1960, ibid., 433.
196. Nkrumah, *I Speak of Freedom*, 260–61.
197. Eisenhower, *The White House Years*, 583.
198. Quoted in Mahoney, *JFK: Ordeal in Africa*, 50.
199. Memorandum of Conversation, "President Nkrumah's Call on the President," 22 September 1960, *FRUS, 1958–1960, vol. 14* (1992), 661–62.
200. Editorial Note, ibid., 503.
201. Telegram from AmEmbassy, Leopoldville, to the State Department, Lepoldville, 22 September 1960, ibid., 501. UAR stands for the United Arab Republic, a union of Egypt and Syria, formed in 1958. (Joseph Ileo was the president of the Congolese Senate.)
202. Telegram from the Department to USUN, 23 September, 1960, ibid., 502.
203. 770G.00/9–2260, Telegram from the State Department to USUN, 24 September 1960, ibid., 503, n. 3.
204. Telegram from AmEmbassy, Leopoldville, to the State Department, Lepoldville, 26 September 1960, ibid., 504–5.
205. Thus on 6 August 1960, Flake and the United States ambassador to the Congo, Timberlake, met with Nkrumah and secured his agreement that all technical and financial assistance to the Congo should be provided through the UN. See 770G.00/8–660, Telegram from AmEmbassy, Accra, to the secretary of state, 6 August 1960, ibid., 391, n. 1.

206. Nkrumah, *I Speak of Freedom,* chaps. 31–32.
207. *New York Times,* 22 September 1960.
208. Telegram from the embassy to the State Department, 7 October 1960, *FRUS, 1958–1960, vol. 14* (1992), 665–67.
209. Telegram from the State Department to the embassy in Ghana, 13 October 1960, ibid., 667–68.
210. Ibid.
211. Apter, "Some Economic Factors in the Political Development of the Gold Coast," 419.
212. See NSC 6005, "U.S. Policy toward West Africa," 29 February 1960 (RG 273, NA).
213. On this, see the coverage by *New York Times,* 26 September 1960, of the luncheon Herter gave in honor of the chief UN delegates of the 12 African states newly admitted into the UN.
214. Ibid., 23 September 1960.
215. Thompson, *Ghana's Foreign Policy,* 166.
216. Mahoney, *JFK: Ordeal in Africa,* 51.
217. Ibid., 165.
218. Thompson, *Ghana's Foreign Policy,* 167.

Notes to Chapter 6

1. *West Africa,* 16 August 1958.
2. See Rhoda Howard, *Colonialism and Underdevelopment in Ghana* (New York: Africana Publishing Company, 1978).
3. "Commercial Sense in Ghana," *West Africa,* 17 October 1959.
4. Ibid.
5. Tony Killick, "The Possibilities of Economic Control," in *A Study of Contemporary Ghana, vol. 1: The Economy of Ghana,* eds. Walter Birmingham, I. Neustadt, E. N. Omaboe (Evanston, IL: Northwestern University Press, 1966), 412.
6. See David E. Apter, "Some Economic Factors in the Political Development of the Gold Coast," *Journal of Economic History,* 14, 4 (1954).
7. Kwame Nkrumah, *I Speak of Freedom: A Statement of African Ideology* (New York: Frederick A. Praeger, 1961), 86.
8. 845J.2614/9–2557, Memorandum of Conversation, "Courtesy Call by Ghana's Finance Minister, K. A. Gbedemah—Ghana's Economic Development and Assistance Plans Hinge on Decision Regarding Volta Project," 25 September 1957 (NA).
9. See Kenneth W. Grundy, "Nkrumah's Theory of Underdevelopment: An Analysis of Recurrent Themes," *World Politics,* 15, 3 (April 1963).
10. Kwame Nkrumah, *Africa Must Unite* (New York: Frederick A. Praeger, 1963), 167.
11. Kwame Nkrumah, *Neocolonialism: The Last Stage of Imperialism* (New York: International Publishers, 1965), 7.
12. *Report of the Commission of Enquiry into the Disturbances in the Gold Coast, 1948,* Colonial No. 231 (London: HMSO, 1948), paras. 298–303.
13. P. N. Rosenstein-Rodan, "Problems of Industrialization of Eastern and Southeastern Europe," *Economic Journal,* 53, (June-September 1943), 210–11; Albert Hirshman,

The Strategy of Economic Development (New Haven, CT: Yale University Press, 1957); W. A. Lewis, *The Theory of Economic Growth* (London: Allen and Unwin, 1961); W. W. Rostow, *The Stages of Economic Growth: A Non-Communist Manifesto* (Cambridge: Cambridge University Press, 1960). Of particular dramatic effect was Hans Singer's observation that since the 1870s, "the trend of prices has been heavily against sellers of food and raw materials and in favor of the sellers of manufactured articles." See his *International Development: Growth and Change* (New York: McGraw Hill, 1964), 165.

14. Rostow, *The Stages of Economic Growth,* esp. 1–3, 145–67.

15. Quoted in David Hart, *The Volta River Project: A Case Study in Politics and Technology* (Edinburgh: Edinburgh University Press, 1980), 40–41.

16. Kwame Nkrumah, "African Prospect," *Foreign Affairs,* 37, 1 (October 1958), 51.

17. "Foreign Policy for Ghana," *West Africa,* 16 March 1957.

18. See Chief Secretary's Office, "The Volta River Project, 1914–1950: An Account of the Development of the Mining of Bauxite in the Gold Coast and the History of the Volta River Project," Accra, 20 January 1951 (Mss. Afr.s.111, Russell 2/11, Rhodes House Library, Oxford); Robert G. A. Jackson, "The Volta River Project," *Progress: The Unilever Project,* 50, 4 (1964); Emil R. Rado, "The Volta River Project—Retrospect and Prospect," *Economic Bulletin,* 4, 2 (February 1960); the article also appeared in *West Africa,* 20, 27, February; 5, 12 March 1960; "Imperialism and the Volta Dam," ibid., 24, 31 March, 14 April, 1980; Philip Siekman, "Edgar Kaiser's Gamble in Africa," *Fortune,* November 1961, 128–206; David Hart, "The Political Economy of a Development Scheme: The Volta River Project," *International Relations,* 6, 1 (May 1978); Hart, *The Volta River Project: A Case Study in Politics and Technology*; Tony Killick, "The Volta River Project," in *A Study of Contemporary Ghana,* eds. Birmingham, Neustadt, and Omaboe; James Moxon, *Volta: Man's Greatest Lake* (London: Andre Deutsch, 1969); David Rooney, *Kwame Nkrumah: The Political Kingdom in the Third World* (London: I. B. Tauris, 1988), chap. 12.

19. See "Prospect Fair for Aluminum," *West Africa,* 10 November 1960.

20. Government of the Gold Coast, "Report on the Development of the River Volta Basin by Sir William Halcrow and Partners, 15th August, 1951," Alliance House, Caxton Street, Westminster, London.

21. *Volta River Scheme,* Cmd. 8702 (London: HMSO, November 1952).

22. Ibid.

23. Ibid.

24. Ibid.

25. Robert Jackson, an Australian, was the chairman of Ghana Development Corporation and one of Nkrumah's top advisers. He had previously been with the British Treasury, served as an assistant secretary-general of the UN, and been an adviser to the governments of India and Pakistan. See Thompson, *Ghana's Foreign Policy,* 21.

26. The commission's report was in three volumes, but its essentials were in vol. 1, *Report of the Preparatory Commission* (London: HMSO, 1956).

27. In United States dollar terms, the revised estimates called for about $700 million as the cost of the dam and the generating units necessary to produce 100,000 tons of aluminum ingots per annum; eventually this would reach $900 million (plus a 40 to 50 percent inflationary allowance) when the maximum production target of 210,000 tons had been achieved. These dollar figures were given by Robert Jackson himself when he called on the State Department on 11 December 1956. See 845K.2614/12–1156, Memorandum of Conversation, "Survey of Gold Coast Volta River Project" (NA).

28. In return for these financial commitments, the aluminum smelter company was to be under a thirty-year obligation (from the time of initial production) to offer buyers in Britain not less than 75 percent of the metal produced, at a price that would compare favorably with North American prices. Britain would have thus counted on a minimum of 90,000 tons of aluminum a year when output reached 120,000 tons, a saving, according to Thorneycroft, of "some £42 million pounds a year." See C.P. (56) 60, Volta River Aluminum Scheme: Memorandum by the president of the Board of Trade [Peter Thorneycroft], 2 March 1956 (CAB 129/80, PRO, London). (The memorandum has a Board of Trade date of 29 February 1956.)

29. Ibid.

30. Ibid.

31. C.P. (56) 71, Volta River Aluminum Scheme: Memorandum by the secretary of state for the colonies, 7 March 1956 (CAB 129/80, PRO, London).

32. C.M. (56), 20th Conclusions, Conclusions of a Meeting of the Cabinet held at 10 Downing Street, S.W. 1, on Thursday, 8 March 1956, at 11 a.m., Minute Item 5 (CAB 128/30 Part I, PRO, London).

33. See Report by Sir Frank Lee [the permanent secretary of the Board of Trade], chairman of the Official Discussions on Volta River Project, April 1956 in C. P. (56) 105, Volta River Project: Note by the president of the Board of Trade, 26 April 1956 (CAB 129/81, PRO, London).

34. Ibid.

35. Ibid.

36. Ibid. On 17 May 1956, Thorneycroft informed his cabinet colleagues of the meeting between officials of the British and Gold Coast governments as well as the aluminum companies, and reported that "[t]he Gold Coast Minister of Finance had subsequently seen the President of the International Bank, who had undertaken to have the scheme examined. A delay of something between six and twelve months had thus been secured." See C.M. (56), 37th Conclusions, Conclusions of a Meeting of the Cabinet held at 10 Downing Street, S.W. 1, on Thursday, 17 May, 1956, at 11 a.m., Minute Item 6 (CAB 128/30 Part I, PRO, London).

37. 845K.2614/9–656, Desp. from AmEmbassy, London, to the State Department, "Volta River Scheme," 6 September 1956 (NA).

38. *Daily Times* (Lagos) 28 July 1956.

39. 845K.2614/7–3156, Desp. from AmCongen, Accra, to the State Department, "Public Statements Regarding the Volta River Project," 31 July 1956 (NA).

40. See "Rivals for the Volta," *West Africa,* 31 August 1957.

41. See "Production Ahead of Demand," ibid., 30 March 1957.

42. 845K.2614VOLTA/4–550, Outgoing Airgram from the State Department to AmConsulate, Accra, 5 April 1950 (NA).

43. 845K.00R/11–250, Desp. from AmConsulate, Accra, to the State Department, "Visit of Enos Curtis, ECA Official," 2 November 1950 (NA).

44. 845K.2614/10–252, Outgoing Telegram from the State Department to AmConsulate, Accra, and AmEmbassy, London, 7 October 1952 (NA).

45. Kwame Nkrumah, *Autobiography* (London: Thomas Nelson, 1957), chap. 14; Rooney, *Kwame Nkrumah,* 66.

46. 845R.10/1–2253, Letter from L. E. Detwiler to John Foster Dulles, 22 January 1953 (NA).

47. Ibid.

48. Ibid.
49. 845K.2614/3–2553, Desp. from AmConsulate, Accra, to the State Department, "Interview with Prime Minister Concerning the Volta River Project," 25 March 1953 (NA).
50. Ibid.
51. 845K.2614/2–2453, Outgoing Telegram from the State Department to AmConsulate, Accra, 6 March 1953 (NA).
52. 845K.2614/3–2253, Desp. from AmConsulate, Accra, to the State Department, "Interview with Prime Minister Concerning the Volta River Project," 25 March 1953 (NA).
53. 845K.2614/12–1156, Memorandum of Conversation, "Survey of Gold Coast Volta River Project," 11 December 1956 (NA).
54. Memorandum of Conversation, "Visit of Vice President Richard M. Nixon," Tab B in Report to the president on the vice president's Visit to Africa, February 28–March 21, 1957, 5 April 1957, White House Central Files, (Confidential File), Subject Series, Box 100 (DDEL).
55. 845J.2614/5–357, Telegram from AmEmbassy, Accra, to the secretary of state, 17 April 1957 (NA).
56. Nkrumah's letter is attached to 845J.2614/5–257, Memorandum of Conversation, "Kaiser Interest in the Volta River Project (Ghana)," 2 May 1957 (NA).
57. 845J.2614/5–657, Telegram from AmEmbassy, Accra, to the secretary of state, 6 May 1957 (NA).
58. 845J.2614/5–1557, Memorandum of Conversation, "Ghana—Volta River Project and Tema Housing Scheme," 15 May 1957 (NA).
59. 845J.2614/5–257, Memorandum of Conversation, "Kaiser Interest in the Volta River Project (Ghana)," 2 May 1957 (NA).
60. 845J.2614/5–357, Telegram from the State Department to AmEmbassy, Accra, 3 May 1957 (NA).
61. 845J.2614/5–657, Telegram from AmEmbassy, Accra, to the secretary of state, 6 May 1957 (NA).
62. 845J.2614/5–1057, Memorandum of Conversation, "Conversation of Mr. G. van B. Slagle with Deputy Assistant Secretary Joseph Palmer 2nd," 10 May 1957 (NA).
63. Ibid.
64. 845J.2614/5–1557, Memorandum of Conversation, "Ghana—Volta River Project and Tema Housing Scheme," 15 May 1957 (NA).
65. 845J.2614/5–2357, Memorandum of Conversation, "Volta River Scheme," 23 May 1957 (NA).
66. 845J.2614/7–2957, Memorandum of Conversation, "Volta River Project and Ghana's Economic Development Needs; Ghana's Relations with Communist Countries," 29 July 1957 (NA).
67. Ibid.
68. 845J.2614/9–2557, Memorandum of Conversation, "Courtesy Call by Ghana's Finance Minister, K. A. Gbedemah—Ghana's Economic Development and Assistance Plans Hinge on Decision Regarding Volta Project," 25 September 1957 (NA).
69. Siekman, "Edgar Kaiser's Gamble in Africa," 131.
70. Letter from Prime Minister Kwame Nkrumah to President Dwight D. Eisenhower, 17 October 1957, AWF, International Series, Box 15 (DDEL).
71. Letter from President Eisenhower to Prime Minister Kwame Nkrumah, 8 November 1957, AWF, International Series, Box 15 (DDEL).

72. Letter from President Eisenhower to Prime Minister Kwame Nkrumah, 21 November 1957, AWF, International Series, Box 15 (DDEL). I could not locate Nkrumah's letter, but a general sense of what he wrote can be gleaned from 845J.2614/12–2657, Memorandum from William M. Rountree to the acting secretary, "Proposed Reply by President Eisenhower to Letter of November 12 from Prime Minister Kwame Nkrumah of Ghana," 26 December 1957; and 845J.2614/5–658, Memorandum of Conversation, "Status of ICA's Efforts to Determine the Interest of American Aluminum Companies in the Volta River Project," 6 May 1958 (both at NA).

73. 645J.61/11–657, Telegram from the State Department to AmEmbassy, Accra, 7 November 1957 (NA).

74. 845J.2614/4–2457, State Department Instruction CA-8812 to the AmEmbassy, Accra, "IBRD Report to Ghana on the Volta River Project," 24 April 1957 (NA).

75. 845J.2614/12–2657, Memorandum from William M. Rountree to the acting secretary, "Proposed Reply by President Eisenhower to Letter of November 12 from Prime Minister Kwame Nkrumah of Ghana," 26 December 1957 (NA).

76. Letter from Eisenhower to Nkrumah, 3 January 1958, AWF, International Series, Box 15 (DDEL).

77. "Volta's Vicious Cycle," *West Africa,* 1 March 1958.

78. Letter from Nkrumah to Eisenhower, 17 January 1958, AWF, International Series, Box 15 (DDEL).

79. For the letters, see Herter Papers, 1957–61 (Letters M–Z Official–Classified), Box 20 (DDEL).

80. 845J.2614/1–1558, Telegram from AmEmbassy, Accra, to the secretary of state, 15 January 1958 (NA).

81. 845J.2614/2–2458, Memorandum of Conversation, "Volta River Project," 24 February 1958 (NA).

82. Ibid.

83. 845J.2614/3–1858, Telegram from AmEmbassy, Accra, to the secretary of state, 19 March 1958 (NA).

84. 845J.2614/5–558, Memorandum of Conversation, "Interest of Kaiser Aluminum Company in Volta Project," 5 May 1958 (NA).

85. 845J.2614/5–658, Memorandum of Conversation, "Status of ICA's Efforts to Determine the Interest of American Aluminum Companies in the Volta River Project," 6 May 1958 (NA).

86. Ibid.

87. 845J.2614/5–1958, Telegram from the State Department to AmEmbassy, London and AmEmbassy, Accra, 19 May 1958 (NA).

88. 845J.2614/5–2758, Memorandum of Conversation, "Volta River Project—U.S. Position to be Taken in the Secretary's Talks with Prime Minister Nkrumah," 27 May 1958 (NA).

89. Ibid.

90. Siekman, "Edgar Kaiser's Gamble in Africa," 199.

91. 845J.2614/7–1858, Memorandum of Conversation, "Kaiser Interest in the Volta River Project," 18 July 1958 (NA).

92. Ibid.

93. Siekman, "Edgar Kaiser's Gamble in Africa," 199.

94. Memorandum of Conversation, "Prime Minister Nkrumah's Talk (Second) with the President," 24 July 1958, AWF, International Series, Box 15 (DDEL).

95. Ibid.

96. Ibid.

97. On the Ghanaian side were Nkrumah himself; Finance Minister Gbedemah; Trade and Industries Minister Kojo Botsio; A. L. Adu, permanent secretary, Ministry of External Affairs and Defense; Robert Jackson, chairman, Ghana Development Commission; Enoch Okoh, acting secretary to the cabinet; and Amon Nikori, Richard Akwei, and H. R. Amonoo, all of the Ghana embassy in Washington. The United States was represented by Undersecretary of State Herter; Undersecretary of State Douglas Dillon; Assistant Secretary Palmer; C. Vaughan Ferguson, Jr., director, Office of Southern Africa Affairs; William Duggan, international relations officer of Southern Africa Affairs; Robert Ross, Liberia/Nigeria desk officer; and Stuart Van Dyke and Carl Flesher, both of the ICA. See 845J.00/7–2558, Memorandum of Conversation, "Prime Minister Nkrumah's Discussion of Ghana's General Economic Needs," 25 July 1958 (NA).

98. Ibid.

99. Ibid.

100. 845J.2614/7–2558, Memorandum of Conservation, "Ghana's Volta River Project," 25 July 1958 (NA).

101. Ibid.

102. Ibid.

103. Siekman, "Edgar Kaiser's Gamble in Africa," 199; Rooney, *Kwame Nkrumah,* 156.

104. 611.45J/7–2558, Telegram from the State Department to AmEmbassy, Accra, 25 July 1958 (NA).

105. 845J.2614/8–2558, Telegram from the State Department to AmEmbassy, Accra, 25 August 1958 (NA).

106. 845J.2614/9–3058, Desp. from AmEmbassy, Accra, to the State Department, "Visit to Ghana of Edgar F. Kaiser and Chad Calhoun of Kaiser Industries Corporation in Connection with Current Volta River Survey," 30 September 1958 (NA).

107. See Henry J. Kaiser and Company, *Reassessment Report on the Volta River Project for the Government of Ghana* (Oakland, CA: 1959).

108. Ibid.

109. For the minutes of the meeting, see 845J.2614/3–1759, Desp. from AmEmbassy, Accra, to the State Department, "Volta River Project," 17 March 1959; Attachment II to 845J.2614/3–1959, Memorandum of Conversation, "Volta River Project," 19 March 1959 (both at NA).

110. For the minutes of the meeting, see 845J.2614/3–1759, Desp. from AmEmbassy, Accra, to the State Department, "Volta River Project," 17 March 1959; Attachment II to 845J.2614/3–1959, Memorandum of Conversation, "Volta River Project," 19 March 1959 (both at NA).

111. Letter from Nkrumah to Wilson C. Flake, 14 March 1959, enclosure to 845J.2614/3–1759, Desp. from AmEmbassy, Accra, to the State Department, "Volta River Project," 17 March 1959 (NA).

112. 845J.2614/3–1659, Telegram from AmEmbassy, Accra, to the secretary of state, 16 March 1959; also 845J.2614/3–1759, Desp. from AmEmbassy, Accra, to the State Department, "Volta River Project," 17 March 1959 (both at NA).

113. 845J.2614/4–159, Telegram from AmEmbassy, Accra, to the secretary of state, 1 April 1959 (NA).

114. 845J.2614/4–159, Telegram from the State Department to AmEmbassy, Accra, 6 April 1959 (NA).
115. 845J.2614/4–1059, Memorandum of Conversation, "Volta River Project," 10 April 1959 (NA).
116. 845J.2614/4–2059, Memorandum of Conversation, "Volta River Project," 20 April 1959 (NA).
117. 845J.2614/4–2959, Telegram from AmEmbassy, Accra, to the State Department, 29 April 1959 (NA).
118. 845J.2614/4–2959, Telegram from the State Department to AmEmbassy, Accra, 30 April 1959 (NA).
119. Ibid.
120. 845J.2614/5–459, Telegram from AmEmbassy, Accra, to the secretary of state, 4 May 1959 (NA).
121. 845J.2614/4–2959, Telegram from the State Department to AmEmbassy, Accra, 6 May 1959 (NA).
122. For the ambassador's draft, see 845J.2614/5–759, Telegram from AmEmbassy, Accra, to the secretary of state, 7 May 1959; for the department's endorsement, see 845J.2614/4–2959, Telegram from the State Department to AmEmbassy, Accra, 8 May 1959; for a neat copy of the letter, see 845J.2614/5–1359, Desp. from AmEmbassy, Accra, to the State Department, "Volta River Project: Letter from Ambassador to the Prime Minister," 13 May 1959 (all at NA).
123. 845J.2614/5–1159, Memorandum from the embassy of Ghana, Washington, 11 May 1959 (NA).
124. 845J.2614/5–1159, Telegram from the State Department to AmEmbassy, Accra, 11 May 1959; 845J.2614/5–1159, Memorandum of Conversation, "Volta River Project," 11 May 1959 (both at NA).
125. 845J.2614/5–1459, Telegram from AmEmbassy, Accra, to the secretary of state, 14 May 1959 (NA).
126. 845J.2614/5–2859, Memorandum of Conversation, "Volta River Project," 28 May 1959 (NA).
127. Ibid.
128. For example, see 845J.394/5–1859, Telegram from AmEmbassy, Accra, to the secretary of state, 5 May 1959 (NA). In this telegram, Flake urged that Dillon should write to Kaiser stressing the value of the VRP to United States foreign policy and expressing the hope that the company's efforts would be successful.
129. 845J.2614/5–2759, Letter from Acting Secretary Douglas Dillon to Lynn U. Stambaugh, first vice president of Export-Import Bank, 29 May 1959 (NA).
130. 845J.2614/6–859, Memorandum of Conversation, "Volta River Project—Meeting with Kaiser Industries," 8 June 1959 (NA).
131. Ibid.
132. Ibid.
133. 845J.2614/6–1859, Memorandum of Conversation, "Volta River Project," 18 June 1959 (NA).
134. 845J.2614/7–959, Letter from Douglas Dillon to Eugene Black, World Bank president, 9 July 1959 (NA).
135. 845J.2614/8–1059, Letter from the president, Export-Import Bank of Washington, to Douglas Dillon, 10 August 1959 (NA).

136. Ibid.

137. 845J.2614/8–1059, Letter from Acting Secretary Douglas to Samuel C. Waugh, president, Export-Import Bank of Washington, 19 August 1959 (NA).

138. 845J.2614/9–2559, Memorandum of Conversation, "Volta River Project," 25 September 1959 (NA).

139. See 845J.2614/9–1859, Desp. from AmEmbassy, Accra, to the State Department, "Present Status of Negotiations between Kaiser Group and Ghana Government Concerning Volta River Project," 18 September 1959 (NA), and its enclosures. Also relevant is a letter dated 19 September, together with a number of attachments, from Kaiser Industries to Acting Secretary Dillon, informing him of "recent actions and events pertaining to the formation of a Ghana Aluminum Consortium for the purposes of producing primary aluminum in Ghana, utilizing electrical energy form the proposed Volta River Project." The letter has no classification number.

140. 845J.2614/9–1859, Desp. from AmEmbassy, Accra, to the State Department, "Present Status of Negotiations between Kaiser Group and Ghana Government Concerning Volta River Project," 18 September 1959 (NA).

141. Ibid.

142. Ibid.

143. 845J.2614/11–2359, Memorandum of Conversation, "Volta River Project and Guinea Bauxite Deposits," 23 November 1959 (NA).

144. 845J.2614/12–1659, Telegram from AmEmbassy, Accra, to the secretary of state, 16 December 1959 (NA).

145. 845J.2614/12–2259, Memorandum of Conversation, "Volta Project," 22 December 1959 (NA).

146. 845J.2614/12–2459, Telegram from AmEmbassy, Accra, to the secretary of state, 24 December 1959 (NA).

147. Siekman, "Edgar Kaiser's Gamble in Africa," 204.

148. A mill, equivalent to one-tenth of a United States cent, is the unit used in the United States to calculate power payments.

149. Siekman, "Edgar Kaiser's Gamble in Africa," 204.

150. Discussion at the 456th Meeting of the NSC, Thursday, 18 August 1960, AWF, NSC Series, Box 13 (DDEL).

151. Telegram from the State Department to AmEmbassy, Accra, 17 August 1960, White House Office, International Series, Box 7 (DDEL).

152. Memorandum for the president, "Your Appointment with President Nkrumah of Ghana," 21 September 1960, AWF, DDE Diary Series, Box 53 (DDEL).

153. "Imperialism and the Volta Dam," *West Africa*, 24 March 1980.

154. "Prospect on the Volta," ibid., 21 May 1960, front page editorial.

155. "Imperialism and the Volta Dam," ibid., 24 March 1980; Rooney, *Kwame Nkrumah*, 157.

156. Killick, "The Volta River Project," 402–3; Hart, *The Volta River Project*, 62–63; "Imperialism and the Volta Dam," *West Africa*, 24 March 1980.

157. Kaiser and Company, *Reassessment Report*, 1–4.

158. And by 1966, when the dam was completed, the project had pulled Ghana into heavy external debt. All the expectations built around the project are yet to materialize.

159. See Howard, *Colonialism and Underdevelopment in Ghana*, 227; "Imperialism and the Volta Dam, *West Africa*, 24 March 1980.

160. *New York Times,* 22 September 1960; *Economist,* 15 October 1960.

161. See NSC 6005, "U.S. Policy Toward West Africa," 29 February 1960 (RG 273, NA).

162. In 1930–60, the percentage annual rate of growth in production of the principal metals was as follows: lead, 1.4; zinc, 2.4; copper, 3; steel, 3; aluminum, 9. Another way of looking at the matter is to note that world aluminum consumption trebled in the decade 1949 to 1958, from 1.2 million metric tons to 3.1 million. See "Prospect Fair for Aluminum," *West Africa,* 10 November 1960.

163. NSC 6005, "U.S. Policy Toward West Africa," 29 February 1960 (RG 273, NA).

Notes to Chapter 7

1. Program of African Studies, Northwestern University, *Africa: A Study Prepared at the Request of the Committee on Foreign Relations, United States Senate, United States Foreign Policy No. 4, October 23, 1959; 86th Congress, 1st Session* (Washington, DC: United States Government Printing Office, 1959), 1–2.

2. Dwight D. Eisenhower, *The White House Years: Waging Peace* (Garden City, NY: Doubleday, 1965), 572.

3. John H. Morrow, *First American Ambassador to Guinea* (New Brunswick, NJ: Rutgers University Press, 1968), 249–50. (Morrow was the first United States ambassador to Guinea, 30 July 1959 to 3 March 1961.)

4. After World War II, the French were well aware that their claim to world power status derived from their imperial heritage. This spawned what Tony Smith calls a "colonial consensus," the conviction that France had to retain its dependencies at all costs. See his *The French Stake in Algeria, 1954–1962* (Ithaca, NY: Cornell University Press, 1978). A reading of *The Complete War Memoirs of Charles de Gaulle* (New York: Simon and Schuster, 1964) shows that de Gaulle fully subscribed to this consensus.

5. Quoted in William J. Foltz, *From French West Africa to the Mali Federation* (New Haven, CT, and London: Yale University Press, 1965), 88.

6. *West Africa,* 5 July 1958.

7. W. A. E. Skurnik, "France and Fragmentation in West Africa: 1945–1960," *Journal of African History,* 8, 2 (1967), 329; Edward Mortimer, *France and Africans, 1944–1960: A Political History* (London: Faber and Faber, 1969), 311; Alexander Werth, *The de Gaulle Revolution* (London: Robert Hale, 1960), 251.

8. Quoted in Dorothy S. White, *Black Africa and de Gaulle: From the French Empire to Independence* (University Park: Pennsylvania State University Press, 1979), 198.

9. Ibid., 253.

10. Sekou Toure, *Expérience guinéenne et unité africaine* (Paris: Présence africaine, 1959), 79–80. For an English translation of the speech, see O. R. Dathmore and W. Fenser eds., *Africa in Prose* (Harmondsworth, England: Penguin Books, 1969), 177–80.

11. Toure, *Expérience,* 83–84.

12. Charles de Gaulle, *Mémoirs d'Espoir: Le Renouveau, 1958–1962* (Paris: 1970), quoted in Michael Crowder and Donal Cruise O'Brien, "Politics of Decolonization in French West Africa, 1945–1960" in *History of West Africa, vol. 2,* eds. J. F. Ade Ajayi and Michael Crowder (Essex, England: Longman Group, 1987), 768.

13. Mortimer, *France and Africans,* 316.

14. Quoted in Thomas Hodgkin and Ruth Schachter, "French-Speaking West Africa in Transition," *International Conciliation,* 528 (May 1960), 420.

15. From a confidential paper titled "Guinea: Economic Background Highlights" (author and date not given), AWF, International Series, Box 25 (DDEL).

16. Ibid.; Desp. from AmCongen, Dakar, to the State Department, "Instruction from the Department of Commerce, September 2, 1955," 7 October 1955, File 501.801, Dakar Consulate General, Classified Records, 1947–55, Box 4 (Suitland). In these respects, Guinea was not receiving any special attention. Since most of its African empire was poor, France contributed direct budgetary supports to most of its colonies, absorbed the administrative costs of many important services, and cushioned commodity exports with price supports. For an overview of this, see David K. Fieldhouse, "The Economic Exploitation of Africa: Some British and French Comparisons," in *France and Britain in Africa: Imperial Rivalry and Colonial Rule,* eds. Prosser Gifford and Wm. Roger Louis (New Haven, CT, and London: Yale University Press, 1971); Foltz, *From French West Africa to the Mali Federation,* chap. 3; IR No. 7737, "Conditions and Trends in French Tropical Africa, 27 June 1958 (NA).

17. Ruth Schachter Morgenthau, *Political Parties in French-Speaking West Africa* (London: Oxford University Press, 1964), 74; Mortimer, *France and Africans,* 333; Hodgkin and Schachter, "French-Speaking West Africa in Transition," 423.

18. This overdraft figure and its implications were given to the United States consulate general in Dakar by Jean Trouver, the financial adviser of the high commissioner for French West Africa. See 870B.10/10–1758, Incoming Telegram from AmCongen, Dakar, to the secretary of state, 17 October 1958 (NA).

19. On the loan, offered by Ghana in December 1958, see "Ghana-Guinea Union Proposed," *West Africa,* 29 November 1958; "Ghana-Guinea Loan," ibid., 27 December 1958.

20. 611.70B/6–2459, Incoming Telegram from AmEmbassy, Conakry, to the secretary of state, 24 June 1959 (NA).

21. Morrow, *First American Ambassador to Guinea,* 209–11.

22. 611.70B/8–2159, State Department Office Memorandum, "Guinea," 21 August 1959 (NA). Also see "United States Relations with Guinea," enclosure in 611.70B/7–259, Memorandum for the president, "Call of Ambassador John H. Morrow," 2 July 1959 (NA).

23. NSC 5818, "Report on Africa South of the Sahara Prior to Calendar Year 1960," 14 January 1959 (RG 273, NA).

24. Telegram from the State Department to AmEmbassy, Paris, 25 September 1958, *FRUS, 1958–1960, vol. 14* (1992), 670–71.

25. Telegram from AmEmbassy, Paris, to the secretary of state, 27 September 1958, ibid., 671, n. 3.

26. Memorandum of Conversation, "Guinea's Request for Recognition," 4 October 1958, ibid., 671–72.

27. The telegram is filed as an enclosure in 770B.02/10–858, Desp. from AmCongen, Dakar, to the State Department, 8 October 1958 cited in ibid., 674, n. 2.

28. Telegram from AmCongen, Dakar, to the secretary of state, 13 October 1958, ibid., 673, n. 2; 611.70B/10–1758, Outgoing Telegram from the State Department to AmCongen, Dakar, 17 October 1958 (NA). For Toure's letter of 13 October, see 611.70B/10–1458, Outgoing Telegram from the State Department to AmEmbassy, Paris, London, and AmCongen, Dakar, 14 October 1958 (NA).

29. Telegram from the State Department to AmEmbassy, Paris, 14 October 1958, *FRUS, 1958–1960, vol. 14* (1992), 672, n. 1.

30. Telegram from AmEmbassy, Paris, to the State Department, 15 October 1958, ibid., 672–73.

31. Ibid., 675, n. 2.

32. Ibid., 678, n. 1.

33. Memorandum of Conversation, "Guinea," 25 October 1958, ibid., 678–79.

34. In advance of this move, Britain consulted France. The British decision encouraged not only the United States, but Italy and West Germany as well to quickly follow in recognizing Guinea. See "U.K. Recognizes Guinea," *West Africa,* 8 November 1959.

35. Telephone Call to Mr. Elbrick, Papers of John Foster Dulles, Telephone Calls Series, Box 9 (DDEL).

36. Memorandum from Secretary of State Dulles to President Eisenhower, "Recognition of the Republic of Guinea," 31 October 1958, *FRUS, 1958–1960, vol. 14* (1992), 679–80.

37. Letter from Eisenhower to Sekou Toure, 1 November 1960, AWF, International Series, Box 25 (DDEL); 870B.47411/11–158, Outgoing Telegram from the White House to Sekou Toure, 1 November 1958 (NA).

38. Memorandum from Secretary of State Dulles to President Eisenhower, "Recognition of the Republic of Guinea," 31 October 1958, *FRUS, 1958–1960, vol. 14* (1992), 679–80.

39. 645J.70B/10–2858, Incoming Telegram from AmEmbassy, Accra, to the secretary of state, 28 October 1958 (NA).

40. For the letter, see the enclosure in 870B.47411/12–558, "Message to Secretary from Sekou Toure," 5 December 1958 (NA).

41. 320.14/11–2658, Memorandum of Conversation 2 of 2, "Conversation with Mr. Charles Lucet, Minister of the Embassy of France (Discussion of Cameroun and Guinea)," 26 November 1958 (NA).

42. *West Africa,* 13 December 1958; ibid., 20 December 1958.

43. For the letter, see enclosure in 611.70B/1–1459, Desp. from AmCongen, Dakar, to the State Department, "Transmitting Letter to the Secretary from Sekou Toure, President of Guinea," 14 January 1959 (NA).

44. Memorandum of Conversation, "Sixth Tripartite Talk on Africa," 28 April 1959, *FRUS, 1958–1960, vol. 14* (1992), 691, 690.

45. 611.70B/5–1159, Desp. from AmEmbassy, Conakry, to the State Department, "French Charge Comments on Technical Assistance to Guinea," 11 May 1959 (NA).

46. Morrow, *First American Ambassador to Guinea,* 11.

47. 611.70B/12–158, Memorandum of Conversation, "United States Relations with Guinea," 1 December 1958 (NA).

48. Memorandum from J. C. Satterthwaite to Mr. Dillon, "Assistance for the Republic of Guinea," 27 April 1959, enclosure in 870B.00TA/10–659, Memorandum from J. C. Satterthwaite to the secretary, "Circular 175: Technical Assistance Agreement with the Republic of Guinea," 6 October 1959 (NA).

49. 870B.00/5–2759, Incoming Telegram from AmEmbassy, Paris, to secretary of state, 27 May 1959 (NA).

50. See 611.70B/9–159, Desp. from AmEmbassy, Conakry, to the State Department, "The Russian Loan to Guinea: Significance and Implications for the United States Policy," 1 September 1959 (NA).

51. Ibid.

52. Morrow, *First American Ambassador to Guinea*, 73–74.

53. 611.70B/10–2458, Memorandum of Conversation 2 of 2, "Liberian Offer of 'Good Offices' towards Establishment of U.S.-Guinean Relations," 24 October 1958 (NA).

54. See "Industrializing Guinea," *West Africa*, 18 April 1960.

55. Memorandum of Conversation, "Economic Assistance," 18 May 1960, *FRUS, 1958–1960, vol. 14* (1992), 709–10.

56. Also known as the Sahel-Benin Union, the Conseil had the Ivory Coast, Upper Volta, Niger, and Dahomey as its members. The group's moving ideas were those of Houphouet-Boigny: very close links with France, and therefore membership of a French-centered federal community; and opposition to independence.

57. Memorandum of Conversation, "Economic Assistance," 18 May 1960, *FRUS, 1958–1960, vol. 14* (1992), 709–10.

58. Telegram from the State Department to AmEmbassy, Paris, 24 June 1960, ibid., 713–14.

59. Ibid., 714, n. 5.

60. Telegram from the State Department AmEmbassy, Conakry, 21 July 1960, ibid., 714–15. Two days before the proposal was passed on to Conakry, Toure had written to Eisenhower. He described Guinea's huge bauxite and iron ore deposits and discussed the Konkoure dam project, which was being held back because France had withdrawn its guarantee for the World Bank loan. Part of the letter suggested that it was not exclusive to Eisenhower, but rather a circular "appeal to friendly powers that sincerely desire to help us achieve rapid progress on the African Continent and a better future for mankind." See letter from Sekou Toure to Eisenhower, 19 July 1960, AWF, International Series, Box 25 (DDEL). Eisenhower's reply, which followed a month later, stated that the United States was prepared to proceed with the updating survey, if it was acceptable to Guinea. See letter from Eisenhower to Sekou Toure, 15 August 1960, AWF, International Series, Box 25 (DDEL).

61. Memorandum of Conversation, "U.S.-Guinea Relations (One of two)," 12 October 1960, *FRUS, 1958–1960, vol. 14* (1992), 720.

62. Memorandum of Conversation, "Konkoure Dam," 6 October 1960, ibid., 717. Six days after the Toure/Satterthwaite meeting, Herter met Diallo and reiterated the offer to update the hydroelectric survey, stressing that Washington could not make any commitments without adequate analysis of all the problems involved. Memorandum of Conversation, "U.S.-Guinea Relations (One of Two)," 12 October 1960, ibid., 718–21, but especially 719, n. 4.

63. "U.S. Views on Arms Shipments," *West Africa*, 2 May 1959.

64. *New York Times*, 30 April 1959. Toure repeated this in private before Satterthwaite (in June 1959) and before Eisenhower (in October 1959), and neither contradicted him. See 611.70B/6–2459, Incoming Telegram from AmEmbassy, Conakry, to the secretary of state, 24 June 1959 (NA); Memorandum of Conversation, "Guinea," *FRUS, 1958–1960, vol. 14* (1992), 698–702. The State Department confirmed that Guinea made the request through Tubman. "However, the request was not acted upon." See 611.70B/8–2159, Office Memorandum from G. R. Kenny and W. H. Price to Mr. Stephen Brown, "Guinea," 21 August 1959 (NA).

65. Telegram-letter from Sekou Toure to Eisenhower, 8 April 1959, White House Office, International Series, Box 7 (DDEL).

66. Memorandum of Conversation, "Conversation between Mr. Murphy and Mr. Telli Diallo, Appointed Ambassador of the Republic of Guinea," 24 April 1959, *FRUS, 1958–1960, vol. 14* (1992), 685–87.

67. Memorandum for the president by Christian Herter, "Proposed Visit of the President of Guinea," ibid., 687–89.

68. Ibid.; also see Memorandum from the assistant secretary of state for African Affairs (Satterthwaite) to the under secretary of state (Dillon), "Aid to Guinea," 6 October 1959, ibid., 693–97.

69. Memorandum from the assistant secretary of state for African Affairs (Satterthwaite) to the under secretary of state (Dillon), "Aid to Guinea," 6 October 1959, ibid., 693–97.

70. Memorandum for the president, "State Visit by President Sekou Toure of Guinea," 22 October 1959, AWF, International Series, Box 25 (DDEL).

71. Incoming Telegram from AmEmbassy, Conakry, to secretary of state, 4 June 1959, White House Office, International Series, Box 7 (DDEL).

72. "Sekou Toure's Surprises," *West Africa,* 12 March 1960.

73. 870B.00/11-1858, Incoming Telegram from AmEmbassy, Paris, to secretary of state, 18 November 1958 (NA).

74. "The Communists in Guinea," *West Africa,* 16 April 1960.

75. Editorial Note, *FRUS, 1958–1960, vol. 14* (1993), 708.

76. IR No. 8251, "Pro-Soviet Neutralism in Guinea?" 12 April 1960 (NA).

77. On the loan, also see 870B.10/8-2559, Incoming Telegram from AmEmbassy, Conakry, to the secretary of state, 25 August 1959; 870B.10/8-2659, Desp. from AmEmbassy, Conakry, to the State Department, "Announcement of Russian Long-term Loan to Guinea," 26 August 1959; 870B.10/9-159, Desp. From AmEmbassy, Conakry, to the State Department, "Announcement of Further Details of Russian Loan to Guinea," 1 September 1959 (all at NA).

78. Memorandum of Conversation, "U.S.-Guinean Relations (One of Two)," 12 October 1960, *FRUS, 1958–1960, vol. 14* (1992), 719, n. 3.

79. Study Mission to Africa, November–December 1960, *Report of Senators Frank Church, Gale W. McGhee, and Frank E. Moss to the Committee on Foreign Relations, Committee on Appropriations, and Committee on Interior and Insular Affairs, United States Senate, 12 February 1961, 87th Congress, 1st Session* (Washington, DC: United States Government Printing Office, 1961), 40–41.

80. 751T.001/3-751, Incoming Telegram from AmCongen, Dakar, to the State Department, 7 March 1951 (NA).

81. For Toure's biography, see Panaf Great Lives, *Sekou Toure* (London: Panaf, 1978); Claude Rivière, *Guinea: The Mobilization of a People,* trans. Virginia Thompson and Richard Adloff (Ithaca, NY, and London: Cornell University Press, 1977).

82. See Bernard Charles, "Un Parti politique africain: Le Parti démocratique de Guinée," *Revue française de sciences politiques,* 12, 2 (June 1962); Immanuel Wallerstein, "The Political Ideology of the PDG," *Présence africaine,* 40, 1 (1962); Ladipo Adamolekun, *Sekou Touré's Guinea: An Experiment in Nation Building* (London: Methuen & Co., 1976), 6–13; Thomas Hodgkin, *African Political Parties* (Harmondsworth, England: Penguin Books, 1961), esp. 156, 163; Rivière, *Guinea: The Mobilization of a People,* chap. 3; Panaf Great Lives, *Sekou Toure,* chap. 6.

83. "As M. Sekou Toure Sees It," *Economist,* 23 July 1960.

84. Memorandum of Conversation, "Guinea," *FRUS, 1958–1960, vol. 14* (1992), 698–702.

85. Memorandum from the assistant secretary of state for African Affairs (Satterthwaite) to the under secretary of state (Dillon), "Aid to Guinea," 6 October 1959, ibid., 693–97.

86. Morrow, *First American Ambassador to Guinea,* 24–25.

87. 870B.053/4–959, Memorandum of Conversation, "Comments on Guinea," 9 April 1959 (NA).

88. Morrow, *First American Ambassador to Guinea,* 198, 233, 82.

89. Telegram from AmEmbassy, Conakry, to the State Department, 20 December 1960, *FRUS, 1958–1960, vol. 14* (1992), 722–23.

90. Morrow, *First American Ambassador to Guinea,* 216.

91. Message from President Toure to President Eisenhower, 7 August 1960, *FRUS, 1958–1960, vol. 14* (1992), 395.

92. Telegram from the State Department to AmEmbassy, Conakry, 15 August 1960, ibid., 411.

93. Ibid., 416, n. 1. Scheyven's request was a sequel to messages Lumumba had sent to Hammarskjold. Citing the Security Council resolution of 14 July, which had authorized the secretary-general to provide the Congolese government with military assistance and to do so in consultation with the Congolese authorities, Lumumba asked that the UN "place all its resources at the disposal of my Government," and that Congolese troops take over the task of guarding all airfields in the Congo from UN troops, that Congolese troops and those from the African contingents in the Congo be sent to Katanga, that aircraft be provided to the Congo government for the purpose of restoring order, that the Katanga rebels be disarmed and their weapons be put at the disposal of the Congo government, and that all non-African troops be withdrawn from Katanga. On 15 August, Lumumba informed Hammarskjold that the Congo government had lost confidence in the secretary-general and requested that the Security Council should send observers from African and Asian countries to ensure the application of its resolutions. See ibid., 412–13.

94. Telegram from the State Department to USUN, 16 August 1960, ibid., 414.

95. Telegram from USUN to the State Department, 26 August 1960, ibid., 445.

96. Memorandum of Conversation, "Congo," ibid., 515.

97. Telegram from Sekou Toure to Eisenhower, 20 November 1960, AWF, International Series, Box 25 (DDEL).

98. Letter from Eisenhower to Sekou Toure, 25 November 1960 in Outgoing Telegram from State Department to AmEmbassy, Conakry, 26 November 1960, AWF, International Series, Box 25 (DDEL).

99. Morrow, *First American Ambassador to Guinea,* 216–21.

100. Telegram from AmCongen, Lagos, to the State Department, 7 September 1960, *FRUS, 1958–1960, vol. 14* (1992), 221.

101. 611.70B/10–2158, Incoming Telegram from AmEmbassy, Monrovia, to the secretary of state, 21 October 1958 (NA).

102. *New York Times,* 30 April 1959.

Notes to Chapter 8

1. John H. Morrow, *First American Ambassador to Guinea* (New Brunswick, NJ: Rutgers University Press, 1968), 28–29.

2. 611.70B/6–3059, Incoming Airgram from AmEmbassy, Conakry, to the secretary of state, 30 June 1959 (NA).

3. 811.05145H/6–1659, Incoming Telegram from AmConsulate, Abidjan, to the secretary of state, 16 June 1959 (NA).

4. 745H.5–MSP/8–1059, Desp. from AmCongen, Lagos, to the State Department, "Call on Acting Prime Minister of Western Region," 10 August 1959 (NA).

5. *New York Times,* 28 July 1960.

6. Program of African Studies, Northwestern University, *Africa: A Study Prepared at the Request of the Committee on Foreign Relations, United States Senate, United States Foreign Policy No. 4, October 23, 1959; 86th Congress, 1st Session* (Washington DC: United States Government Printing Office, 1959), 1, 7, 2, 13, 12.

7. Study Mission to Africa, November–December 1960, *Report of Senators Frank Church, Gale W. McGhee, and Frank E. Moss to the Committee on Foreign Relations, Committee on Appropriations, and Committee on Interior and Insular Affairs, United States Senate, February 12, 1961, 87th Congress, 1st Session* (Washington, DC: United States Government Printing Office, 1961), 3–6.

8. For the speeches, see "Remarks of Senator John F. Kennedy, Fourth Annual Rockhurst Day Banquet of Rockhurst College, Kansas City, Missouri, Saturday, June 2, 1956," *Congressional Record—Senate,* 6 June 1956; "Facing Facts on Algeria," Speeches of Hon. John F. Kennedy of Massachusetts in the Senate of the United States, Tuesday, 2 July 1957 (Washington, DC: United States Government Printing Office, 1957).

9. Arthur M. Schlesinger, Jr., *A Thousand Days: John F. Kennedy in the White House* (Boston: Houghton Mifflin, 1965), 554.

10. Richard D. Mahoney, *JFK: Ordeal in Africa* (New York: Oxford University Press, 1983), 30–31.

11. State Department, "The Emergence of Africa: Report to the President by Vice President Nixon on his trip to Africa, February 28–March 21, 1957," 7 April 1957 (S.12:Af8, NA).

12. Study Mission to Africa, November–December 1960, *Report of Senators Frank Church, Gale W. McGhee, and Frank E. Moss,* 3–6.

13. Letter from Myer Feldman, Deputy Special Counsel to the President to Mrs. Ave L. Rawdon (Reedsville, PA), 12 May 1961, White House Central File, Box 237 (John F. Kennedy Library, Boston).

14. Brenda G. Plummer, *Rising Wind: Black Americans and U.S. Foreign Affairs, 1935–1960* (Chapel Hill: University of North Carolina Press, 1996); Penny M. Von Eschen, *Race against Empire: Black Americans and Anticolonialism, 1935–1957* (Ithaca, NY: Cornell University Press, 1997).

15. Milton Morris, "Black Americans and the Foreign Policy Process: The Case of Africa," *Western Political Quarterly,* 25, 3 (September 1972).

16. James L. Roark, "American Black Leaders: The Response to Colonialism and the Cold War, 1943–1953," *African Historical Studies,* 4, 2 (1971).

17. Elliot P. Skinner, "African, Afro-American, White Americans: A Case of Pride and Prejudice," *Freedomways* (Summer 1965), 391, 387.

18. Alfred O. Hero, Jr., "American Negroes and U.S. Foreign Policy: 1937–1967," *Conflict Resolution,* 12, 2 (June 1969).

19. James H. Meriwether, "The African Connection and the Struggle for Freedom: Africa's Role in African-American Life, 1935–1963," Ph.D. dissertation, University of California, Los Angeles (1995), 5–17.

20. As Francis Kornegay and Chris Landsberg have recently observed, Africa remains—as it has always been—the backwater of United States foreign policy. Consequently, "[w]ithin the federal bureaucracy, rarely is Africa credited with the type of relevant appoint-

ments of officials, white as well as black, who have the expertise, political sensitivity and consciousness to move Africa off the bottom of the foreign policy totem-pole." The "major responsibility" for this continuing neglect of Africa, Kornegay and Landsberg contend, "rests with the African-American leadership for whom one suspects Africa is no more of a priority than it is for the white political establishment. Interestingly enough, as the Congressional Black Caucus has expanded within the US House of Representatives, its engagement with Africa as a priority Black focus has shrunk." (Kornegay and Landsberg concede that African-Americans are still "on the margins in the formulation of US policy toward Africa"). See Francis Kornegay and Chris Landsberg, "Overcoming White Foreign Affairs Dominance in South Africa and America," *Africa Insight* (January 2000), 37.

21. Department of State, "The Emergence of Africa: Report to the President by Vice President Nixon on His Trip to Africa, February 28–March 21, 1957," 7 April 1957 (S.12:Af8, NA).

22. The Justice Department's brief in the landmark *Brown v. Board of Education* case—by which the Supreme Court, on 17 May 1954, outlawed legal segregation in public schools—explained that "it is in the context of the present world struggle between freedom and tyranny that the problem of racial discrimination must be viewed. . . .Racial discrimination furnishes grist for the Communist propaganda mills, and it raises doubt among friendly nations as to the intensity of our devotion to the democratic faith." The same argument was made in the brief of the secretary of state: "The segregation of school children on a racial basis is one of the practices in the United States which has been singled out for hostile foreign comment in the United Nations and elsewhere. Other people cannot understand how such a practice can exist in a country which professes to be a staunch supporter of freedom, justice, and democracy." Quoted in Rupert Emerson and Martin Kilson, "The American Dilemma in a Changing World: The Rise of Africa and the Negro American," *Daedalus* (Fall 1965), 1073.

23. Ibid., esp. 1072–73.

24. Telegram from USUN to the secretary of state, 9 November 1960, White House Office, Office of the Staff Secretary, International Series, Box 1 (DDEL).

25. Memorandum of Conference with the President (and Prime Minister Harold Macmillan), 27 September 1960, AWF, DDE Diary Series, Box 53 (DDEL).

26. Skinner, "African, Afro-American, White American: A Case of Pride and Prejudice," 391, 387, 385–86.

27. Ibid., 390.

28. Ibid., 388.

29. Ibid., 387–88.

30. Alfred O. Hero, Jr., *The Southerner and World Affairs* (Baton Rouge: Louisiana State University Press, 1965), 530.

31. Skinner, "African, Afro-American, White American: A Case of Pride and Prejudice," 391. (Emphasis in original.)

32. David J. Garrow, *Bearing the Cross: Martin Luther King, Jr., and the Southern Christian Leadership Conference* (New York: William Morrow and Co., 1986), 91.

33. Memorandum from the JCS to Secretary of Defense Gates, "U.S. Interests in Ghana and Guinea," 17 October 1960, *FRUS, 1958–1960, vol. 14* (1992), 161.

34. Dana Adams Schmidt, "U.S. Studies Role of Reds in Africa: Experts Find Soviet Bloc's Economic Aid to Guinea is Pattern for Congo," *New York Times,* 21 July 1960.

35. IR No. 8251, "Pro-Soviet Neutralism in Guinea?" State Department Bureau of Intelligence and Research, 12 April 1960 (NA).

36. Memorandum for the NSC, "National Security Implications of Future Developments Regarding Africa," 12 July 1960, NSC Meeting Minutes, 456th Meeting, Tab A (RG 273, NA).

37. George McGhee, *Envoy to the Middle World: Adventures in Diplomacy* (New York: Harper & Row, 1983), 116.

38. Memorandum prepared in the State Department Office of African Affairs, "The United States in Africa South of the Sahara," 4 August 1955, *FRUS, 1955–1957, vol. 18* (1989), 13–22.

39. Ibid.

40. 611.70/10–3155, Desp. from AmEmbassy, Monrovia, to the State Department, "Comments on the Paper on United States in Africa South of the Sahara," 31 October 1955 (NA).

41. In January 1959, the OCB reported that "[w]here it appears feasible and useful to do so, the U.S. has continued its exchange of views with the metropolitan governments and their colonial officials and, with *greater discretion*, with local [African] government officials." See NSC, 5818, "Report on Africa South of the Sahara Prior to Calendar Year 1960," 14 January 1959, RG 273 (NA). (Emphasis added.)

42. "Project Proposal for a Study of Africa in Transition," 22 July 1957, NSC 335th Meeting, Tab D, RG 273 (NA).

43. Dana Adams Schmidt, "U.S. Still Seeking an African Policy," *New York Times*, 2 February 1959.

44. Program of African Studies, Northwestern University, *Africa: A Study Prepared at the Request of the Committee on Foreign Relations, United States Senate*, 1, 7, 2, 13, 12.

45. Morrow, *First American Ambassador to Guinea*, 23, 28.

46. 845M.00–TA/7–1059, Outgoing Airgram from the State Department to AmConsulate, Freetown, 10 July 1959 (NA).

47. George V. Allen (assistant secretary of state for Near Eastern, South Asian, and African Affairs), "United States Foreign Policy in Africa," State Department Press Release No. 206, 20 April 1956 (NA).

48. Joseph Palmer 2nd (deputy assistant secretary of state for African Affairs), "The Problems and Prospects of Sub-Saharan Africa: A United States Point of View," *Department of State Bulletin*, 9 December 1957, 930–33.

49. See the following by Ronald Robinson: "Non-European Foundations of European Imperialism: Sketch for a Theory of Collaboration," in *Studies in the Theory of Imperialism*, eds. Roger Owen and Bob Sutcliffe (London: Longman, 1972); "Imperial Theory and the Question of Imperialism after Empire," *Journal of Imperial and Commonwealth History*, 12, 2 (January 1984); and "The Excentric Idea of Imperialism, with or without Empire," in *Imperialism and After: Continuities and Discontinuities*, eds. Wolfgang J. Mommsen and Jürgen Osterhammel (London: Allen & Unwin, 1986).

50. See the excerpts from the address by Holmes to the 13th American Assembly held in New York in May 1958, in *Africa Special Report* (May 1958).

51. NSC 5719, "U.S. Policy Toward Africa South of the Sahara Prior to Calendar Year 1960," 31 July 1957 (RG 273, NA); also NSC 5719/1, "Statement of US Policy Toward Africa South of the Sahara Prior to Calendar Year 1960," 23 August 1957, *FRUS, 1955–1957, vol. 18* (1989), 76–87.

52. Ibid.

53. Memorandum of Conversation, "First Tripartite Talks on Africa," 16 April 1959, *FRUS, 1958–1960, vol. 14* (1992), 47.

54. CIA (ORE 79–49), "U.S. Security and the British Dollar Problem," 31 August 1949, PSF, Intelligence File, Box 257 (HSTL).

55. H. W. Brands, "India and Pakistan in American Strategic Planning, 1947–54: The Commonwealth as Collaborator," *Journal of Imperial and Commonwealth History,* 15, 1 (October 1986). Robert McMahon also found that during the same period, Washington opted to defer to "Britain's leadership" in the region. In McMahon's words, "Citing Britain's historic ties to South Asia and the continuing connection through the British Commonwealth, every major American policy formulation of the late 1940s advised that the United States follow Great Britain's lead on all substantive matters relating to the Indian subcontinent." See his *The Cold War on the Periphery: The United States, India, and Pakistan* (New York: Columbia University Press, 1994), 18–19.

56. Walter LaFeber, "Roosevelt, Churchill, and Indochina: 1942–45," *American Historical Review,* 80, 5 (December 1975), 1280.

57. Report by the Policy Planning Staff, "Résumé of World Situation," 6 November 1947, *FRUS, 1947, vol. 1* (1973), 772–77.

58. Discussion at the 456th Meeting of the NSC, Thursday, 18 August 1960, AWF, NSC Series, Box 13 (DDEL).

BIBLIOGRAPHY

Newspapers, UN Documents, State Department Publications, Archival Records

Newspapers and Weekly Magazines

Africa Report/Africa Special Report
Daily Times (Lagos)
East African Standard
Economist
Life
New York Herald Tribune
New York Times
Washington Post
West Africa

United Nations Documents (available at the Robarts Library, University of Toronto)

UN Trusteeship Council, *Official Records (TCOR)* Supplement, First Year, 1st session, 1947.
TC Official Records, II (First Part), 8 December 1947.
TC, *Special Report of First Visiting Mission to the Trust Territories of Togoland under British Administration and Togoland under French Administration on the Ewe Problem,* Doc. T/463, 17 February 1950.
TC Official Records, 6, 20 March 1950.
UN Doc. T/702, *Joint Observations to the Government of France and the Government of the United Kingdom of Great Britain and Northern Ireland on the Special Report of the Visiting Mission Concerning the Ewe Problem,* 19 June 1950.
General Assembly Records (15th session), 947th Plenary Meeting, 14 December 1960.

The Gold Coast: Official Documents

Gold Coast: Report to His Excellency The Governor by the Committee on Constitutional Reform 1949, Colonial No. 248 (Accra: 1949).
Chief Secretary's Office, "The Volta River Project, 1914–1950: An Account of the Devel-

opment of the Mining of Bauxite in the Gold Coast and the History of the Volta River Project," Accra, 20 January, 1951 (Mss. Afr.s.111, Russell 2/11, Rhodes House Library, Oxford).

Government of the Gold Coast, "Report on the Development of the River Volta Basin by Sir William Halcrow and Partners, 15th August, 1951," Alliance House, Caxton Street, Westminster, London.

British Government Reports

Report of the Commission of Enquiry into the Disturbances in the Gold Coast, 1948, Colonial No. 231(London: HMSO, 1948).

Statement by His Majesty's Government on the Report of the Commission of Enquiry into the Disturbances in the Gold Coast 1948, Colonial No. 232 (London: HMSO, 1948).

Statement by His Majesty's Government on the Report of the Committee on Constitutional Reform 1949, Colonial No. 250 (14 October 1949).

Volta River Scheme, Cmd. 8702 (London: HMSO, November 1952).

Report of the Preparatory Commission 3 volumes (London: HMSO, 1956).

Report of the Advisory (Monckton) Commission on the Review of the Constitution of Rhodesia and Nyasaland, Cmd. 1148 (London: HMSO, October 1960).

United States State Department Publications

Byroade, Henry A. "The World's Colonies and Ex-Colonies: A Challenge to America." *Department of State Bulletin* (16 November 1953), 655–60.

Dulles, John F. "The Moral Initiative." *Department of State Bulletin* (30 November 1953), 741–44.

———. "The Cost of Peace." *Department of State Bulletin* (18 June 1956), 999–1000.

Eisenhower, Dwight D. "Address by the President." *Department of State Bulletin* (10 October 1960), 551–57.

———. "President Outlines Steps to Improve U.S. Balance-of-Payments Position." *Department of State Bulletin* (5 December 1960), 860–63.

Gerig, Benjamin, and Vernon MacKay. "The Ewe Problem: A Case Study in the Operation of the Trusteeship Council." *Department of State Bulletin* (22 January 1951), 128–37.

Hager, Eric. "Some Aspects of Private Foreign Investment." *Department of State Bulletin* (12 December 1960), 890–94.

Hull, Cordell. "The War and Human Freedom." *Department of State Bulletin* (25 July 1942), 639–47.

McGhee, George C. "Africa's Role in the Free World Today." *Department of State Bulletin* (16 July 1951), 97–101.

———. "United States Interests in Africa." *Department of State Bulletin* (19 June 1950), 999–1003.

McKay, Vernon. "The United States, the United Nations, and Africa." *Department of State Bulletin* (16 February 1953), 267–73.

Palmer 2nd, Joseph. "The Problems and Prospects of Sub-Saharan Africa: A United States Point of View." *Department of State Bulletin* (9 December 1957), 930–33.

Penfield, James K. "The Role of the United States in Africa: Our Interests and Operation." *Department of State Bulletin* (8 June 1959), 841–49.
The State Department. *Point Four: Cooperative Program for Aid in the Development of Economically Underdeveloped Areas,* State Department Publication 3719, Economic Cooperation Series 24. Washington, DC. January 1950.
Foreign Relations of the United States (*FRUS*) (Washington, DC: United States Government Printing Office) is published by the State Department; the publication dates of particular volumes are in brackets.
FRUS: The Conferences at Cairo and Teheran, 1943 (1961)
FRUS, 1945, vol. 1: General—The United Nations (1967)FRUS, 1947, vol. 1 (1973)
FRUS, 1948, vol. 1 (1976)
FRUS, 1950, vol. 5 (1978)
FRUS, 1951, vol. 2 (1979)
FRUS 1952–1954, vol. 3 (1979)
FRUS, 1952–1954, vol. 10 (1983)
FRUS, 1952–1954, vol. 11 (1983)
FRUS, 1955–1957, vol. 17 (1989)
FRUS, 1955–1957, vol. 18 (1989)
FRUS, 1955–1957, vol. 19 (1990)
FRUS, 1958–1960, vol. 14 (1992)
FRUS, 1961–1963, vol. 13 (1994)

Miscellaneous United States Government Papers/Reports

President's Materials Policy Commission. *Resources for Freedom, vol. 1: A Report to the President.* Washington, DC: United States Government Printing Office, 1952.
Mutual Security Program: Fiscal Year 1958 Estimates—Near East, South Asia and Africa, No. 175 (author and date of publication not indicated).
Agency for International Development. *U.S. Overseas Loans and Grants and Assistance from International Organizations and Loan Authorization, July 1, 1945–September 30, 1960* Washington, DC: United States Government Printing Office, n.d.
OSS/State Department Intelligence and Research Reports Part 13: *Africa, 1941–61.* Washington, DC: Union of America Publications Inc., 1980.

Congressional Papers/Reports

Commission on Foreign Economic Policy. *Report to the President and the Congress, 83rd Congress, 2nd Session,* House Document No. 290. Washington, DC: United States Government Printing Office, 23 January 1954.
"Remarks of Senator John F. Kennedy, Fourth Annual Rockhurst Day Banquet of Rockhurst College, Kansas City, Missouri, Saturday, June 2, 1956," *Congressional Record—Senate,* 6 June 1956.
"Facing Facts on Algeria," Speeches of Hon. John F. Kennedy of Massachusetts in the Senate of the United States, Tuesday, 2 July 1957. Washington, DC: United States Government Printing Office, 1957.
Senate Committee on Foreign Relations. *Economic Aid and Technical Assistance in Africa:*

Report of Senator Theodore Francis Green on a Study Mission Pursuant to Senate Resolution 162, 84th Congress. Washington, DC: United States Government Printing Office, 1957.
House of Representatives. *Report of the Special Study Mission to Africa, South and East of the Sahara (April 5, 1957), 85th Congress, 1st Session.* Washington, DC: United States Government Printing Office, October 1957.
House of Representatives. *Briefing on Africa (Testimony of J. C. Satterthwaite): Hearings before the Subcommittee on Africa of the Committee on Foreign Affairs, 86th Congress, 1st Session, March 5 and July 21, 1959.* Washington, DC: United States Government Printing Office, 1959.
Hubert Humphrey, "Emergent Africa: Challenge and Response," *Congressional Record—Senate,* 2 September 1959.
Program of African Studies, Northwestern University. *Africa: A Study Prepared at the Request of the Committee on Foreign Relations, United States Senate, United States Foreign Policy No. 4, October 23, 1959; 86th Congress, 1st Session.* Washington, DC: United States Government Printing Office, 1959.
Morse, Wayne. "The United States in the United Nations, 1960: A Turning Point." *Supplementary Report to the Committee on Foreign Relations, United States Senate, 87th Congress, 1st Session.* Washington, DC: United States Government Printing Office, 1961.
Study Mission to Africa, November–December 1960. *Report of Senators Frank Church, Gale W. McGhee, and Frank E. Moss to the Committee on Foreign Relations, Committee on Appropriations, and Committee on Interior and Insular Affairs, United States Senate, February 12, 1961, 87th Congress, 1st Session.* Washington, DC: United States Government Printing Office, 1961.
Senate Committee on Appropriations. Testimony of Secretary of State Dean Rusk. *Foreign Assistance and Related Appropriations for FY 1966: Hearings . . . 89th Congress, 2nd Session, 1965.* Washington, DC: United States Government Printing Office, 1965.
Senate Select Committee to Study Governmental Operations with Respect to Intelligence Activities, *Interim Report: Alleged Assassination Plots Involving Foreign Leaders, 94th Congress, 1st Session.* Washington, DC: United States Government Printing Office, 20 November 1975.

The Public Record Office, London

CO 583/287/30, A. B. Cohen to Sir J. Macpherson, 12 June 1948.
CO 583/287/5/30453/4, Sir J. Macpherson to A. B. Cohen, 28 June 1948.
CAB 129\24, CP (48)36, Memorandum by colonial secretary, "United Nations General Assembly, 1947: The Colonial Question," 30 June 1948.
CO 537/7136, Confidential Desp. from the British ambassador in Washington (Oliver Franks) to the secretary of state for foreign affairs, 14 January 1950.
CO 936/317, no. 13, "Notes on Colonialism for Washington Talks": Note prepared in the Colonial Office for use by Sir W. Churchill and Mr. Eden, June 1954.
C.P. (56) 60, Volta River Aluminium Scheme: Memorandum by the president of the Board of Trade [Peter Thorneycroft], 2 March 1956 (CAB 129/80).
C.P. (56) 71, Volta River Aluminium Scheme: Memorandum by the secretary of state for the colonies, 7 March 1956 (CAB 129/80).
C.M. (56), 20th Conclusions, Conclusions of a Meeting of the Cabinet held at 10 Down-

ing Street, S.W. 1, on Thursday, 8 March 1956, at 11 a.m., Minute Item 5 (CAB 128/30 Part I.
Report by Sir Frank Lee [the permanent secretary of the Board of Trade], chairman of the Official Discussions on Volta River Project, April 1956 in C. P. (56) 105, Volta River Project: Note by the president of the Board of Trade, 26 April 1956 (CAB 129/81).
C.M. (56), 37th Conclusions, Conclusions of a Meeting of the Cabinet held at 10 Downing Street, S.W. 1, on Thursday, 17 May, 1956, at 11 a.m., Minute Item 6 (CAB 128/30 Part I.

Naval Historical Center, Washington, DC

Navy Department, "Factors Affecting Changes in the Power Position in Areas Bordering the Southern Oceans (Indian Ocean, South Atlantic)," enclosure 1 in memorandum from director, Long Range Objectives Group, "Long-Range Requirements for the Southern Oceans," Ser. 0079P83, 31 May 1960.

National Archives, Washington, DC (NA)

Record Group (RG) 59, General Records of the State Department
RG 273, Records of the National Security Council

National Archives Reference Branch, Suitland, Maryland

File FWA-12.1 Projects
RG 84, Consulate Files
RG 286, Records of the Agency for International Development and Predecessor Agencies
RG 469, Records of the U.S. Foreign Assistance Agencies, 1948–61

Harry S. Truman Library, Independence, Missouri (HSTL)

Naval Aide Files
Office Files of Gordon Gray as special assistant to the president
President's Secretary's File (PSF)
White House Confidential File

Dwight David Eisenhower Library, Abilene, Kansas (DDEL)

Christian A. Herter Papers
White House Central Files
White House Office Files
Ann Whitman Files (AWF)

John F. Kennedy Library, Boston

White House Central File, Box 237

Books, Journal Articles, etc.

Acheson, Dean. "Fifty Years After." *Yale Review*, 51, 1 (October 1961): 1–10.

———. "The Foreign Policy of the United States." *Arkansas Law Review and Bar Association Journal*, 18, 3 (Fall 1964): 225–234.

———. *Grapes from Thorns*. New York: W. W. Norton, 1972.

———. *Power and Diplomacy*. Cambridge: Harvard University Press, 1959.

Adamolekun, Ladipo. *Sekou Touré's Guinea: An Experiment in Nation Building*. London: Methuen & Co., 1976.

Adams, Sherman. *Firsthand Report*. New York: Harper, 1961.

Adamson, Walter L. *Hegemony and Revolution: A Study of Antonio Gramsci's Political and Cultural Theory*. Berkeley and Los Angeles: University of California Press, 1980.

Albertini, Rudolf von. *Decolonization: The Administration and Future of the Colonies, 1919–1960*, trans. Francisca Garvie. New York: Doubleday, 1971.

Alexander, Charles C. *Holding the Line: The Eisenhower Era, 1952–1961*. Bloomington and London: Indiana University Press, 1975.

Allman, Jean Marie. *The Quills of the Porcupine: Asante Nationalism in an Emergent Ghana*. Madison: University of Wisconsin Press, 1993.

———. "The Youngmen and the Porcupine: Class, Nationalism and Asante's Struggle for Self-Determination, 1954–57." *Journal of African History*, 31, 2 (1990): 263–79.

Aluko, Olajide. "Politics of Decolonization in British West Africa, 1945–1960." In *History of West Africa, vol. 2*, eds. J. F. Ade Ajayi and Michael Crowder. Essex, England: Longman Group UK, 1987: 693–735.

Ambrose, Stephen E. *Eisenhower, vol. 2: The President*. New York: Simon & Schuster, 1984.

Amenumey, D. E. K. *The Ewe Unification Movement: A Political History*. Accra: Ghana Universities Press, 1989.

———. "The General Elections in the 'Autonomous Republic of Togo,' April 1958." *Transactions of the Historical Society of Ghana*, 16, 1 (June 1975): 47–65.

Anglin, Douglas G. "Ghana, the West, and the Soviet Union." *Canadian Journal of Economics and Political Science*, 24, 2 (May 1958): 152–65.

Apter, David E. *Ghana in Transition*. 2nd rev. ed. Princeton: Princeton University Press, 1972.

———. *The Politics of Modernization*. Chicago and London: University of Chicago Press, 1965.

———. "Some Economic Factors in the Political Development of the Gold Coast." *Journal of Economic History*, 14, 4 (1954): 409–27.

Arden-Clarke, Charles. "Eight Years of Transition in Ghana." *African Affairs*, 56, 226 (January 1958): 29–36.

Asamoah, Obed. "Nkrumah's Foreign Policy, 1951–1966." In *The Life and Work of Kwame Nkrumah*, ed. Kwame Arhin. Trenton, NJ: Africa World Press, 1993: 231–247.

Austin, Dennis. *Ghana Observed: Essays on the Politics of a West African Republic*. Manchester: Manchester University Press, 1976.

———. *Politics in Ghana, 1946–1960*. London: Oxford University Press, 1964.

Awolowo, Obafemi. *AWO: The Autobiography of Chief Obafemi Awolowo*. Cambridge: Cambridge University Press, 1960.

———. *Path to Nigerian Freedom*. London: Faber & Faber, 1947.

Babaa, Khalid I., and Cecil V. Crabb, Jr. "Nonalignment as a Diplomatic and Ideological

Credo." *Annals of the American Academy of Political and Social Science,* 32 (November 1965): 6–17.

Baldwin, David A. *Foreign Aid and American Foreign Policy: A Documentary Analysis.* New York: Frederick A. Praeger, 1966.

Barry, Boubacar. "Neocolonialism and Dependence in Senegal, 1960–1980." In *Decolonization and African Independence: The Transfer of Power, 1960–1980,* eds. Prosser Gifford and Wm. Roger Louis. New Haven, CT, and London: Yale University Press, 1988: 593–662.

Bauer, Raymond A., Ithiel de Sola Pool, and Lewis Anthony Dexter. *American Business Policy.* New York: Atherton, 1963.

Berg, Elliot J. "The Economic Basis of Political Choice in French West Africa." *American Political Science Review,* 54, 2 (June 1960): 391–405.

Bertolin, Gordon. "U.S. Economic Interests in Africa: Investments, Trade, and Raw Materials." In *Africa and the United States: Vital Interests,* ed. Jennifer S. Whitaker. New York: New York University Press, 1978: 21–59.

Bills, Scott L. *Empire and Cold War: The Roots of U.S.-Third World Antagonism, 1945–47.* New York: St. Martin's Press, 1990.

Birmingham, W. B. "An Index of Real Wages of the Unskilled Labourer in Accra." *Economic Bulletin of Ghana,* 4, 3 (1960): 1–12.

Blum, Douglas W. "The Soviet Foreign Policy Belief System: Beliefs, Politics, and Foreign Policy Outcomes." *International Studies Quarterly,* 37, 4 (December 1993): 373–94.

Blundell, Michael. *So Rough a Wind.* London: Weidenfeld and Nicolson, 1964.

Bourret, F. M. *Ghana: The Road to Independence, 1919–1957.* Stanford, CA: Stanford University Press, 1960.

Brands, H. W. "India and Pakistan in American Strategic Planning, 1947–54: The Commonwealth as Collaborator." *Journal of Imperial and Commonwealth History,* 15, 1 (October 1986): 41–54.

———. *The Specter of Neutralism: The United States and the Emergence of the Third World 1947–1960.* New York: Columbia University Press, 1989.

Bretton, Henry. "Current Political Thought in Ghana." *American Political Science Review,* 52, 1 (March 1958): 46–63.

Brinkley, Douglas. *Dean Acheson: The Cold War Years, 1953–71.* New Haven, CT, and London: Yale University Press, 1992.

Brinkley, Douglas and G. E. Thomas. "Dean Acheson's Opposition to African Liberation." *TransAfrican Forum,* 5, 4 (Summer 1988): 63–81.

Brown, Jr., William Adams, and Redvers Opie. *American Foreign Assistance.* Washington, DC: The Brookings Institution, 1953.

Bustin, Edouard. "The Limits of French Intervention in Africa: A Study in Applied Neo-Colonialism." Working Paper No. 54, African Studies Center, Boston University (1982).

Catroux, Georges. "The French Union: Concept, Reality and Prospects." *International Conciliation,* 494 (November 1953): 195–295.

Chand, Attar. *Nonaligned Nations: Challenge of the Eighties.* New Delhi: Selectbook Service Syndicate, 1983.

Charles, Bernard. "Un Parti politique africain: Le Parti démocratique de Guinée." *Revue française de sciences politiques,* 12, 2 (June 1962): 312–59.

Chipman, John. *French Power in Africa.* Oxford: Basil Blackwell, 1989.

Clough, Michael. *Free at Last? U.S. Policy toward Africa and the End of the Cold War.* New York: Council on Foreign Relations Press, 1992.
Cohen, Andrew. *British Policy in Changing Africa.* London: Routledge & Kegan Paul, 1959.
Colby, William and John Stockwell, panel discussion, "Should the U.S. Fight Secret Wars?" *Harpers,* September 1984.
Coleman, James S. *Nigeria: Background to Nationalism.* Second printing. Berkeley and Los Angeles: University of California Press, 1960.
Collins, Carole. "Fatally Flawed Mediation: Cordier and the Congo Crisis of 1960." *Africa Today* (3rd Quarter, 1992): 5–22.
Crowder, Michael. "Independence as a Goal in French West African Politics: 1944–60." In *French-Speaking Africa: The Search for Identity,* ed. William H. Lewis. New York: Walker, 1965: 15–41.
Crowder, Michael and Donal Cruise O'Brien. "Politics of Decolonization in French West Africa, 1945–1960." In *History of West Africa, vol. 2,* eds. J. F. Ade Ajayi and Michael Crowder, Essex, England: Longman Group, 1987: 736–73.
Curtin, Philip D. *The Image of Africa: British Ideas and Action, 1780–1850.* Madison: University of Wisconsin Press, 1964.
Darwin, J. G. "In Search of Decolonization." *History,* 73, 237 (February 1988): 55–62.
Darwin, John. *Britain and Decolonization: The Retreat from Empire in the Postwar World.* London: Macmillan, 1988.
Dathmore, O. R. and W. Fenser, eds. *Africa in Prose.* Harmondsworth, England: Penguin Books, 1969.
Davidson, Basil. *Black Star: A View of the Life and Times of Kwame Nkrumah.* London: Allen Lane, 1973.
de Gaulle, Charles. *The Complete War Memoirs of Charles de Gaulle.* New York: Simon and Schuster, 1964.
Divine, Robert A. *Second Chance: The Triumph of Internationalism in America during World War II.* New York: Atheneum, 1967.
Dobson, Alan P. *The Politics of the Anglo-American Economic Relationship, 1940–1987.* New York: St. Martin's Press, 1988.
Drake, St. Clair. "Prospects for Democracy in the Gold Coast." *Annals of the American Academy of Political and Social Science,* 306 (July 1956): 78–87.
Dulles, Foster Rhea, and Gerald E. Ridinger. "The Anticolonial Policies of Franklin D. Roosevelt." *Political Science Quarterly,* 70, 1 (March 1955): 1–18.
Eisenhower, Dwight D. *The White House Years: Waging Peace.* Garden City, NY: Doubleday, 1965.
Elder, Robert E. *The Foreign Leader Program: Operations in the United States.* Wesport, CT: Greenwood Publishers, 1961.
Emerson, Rupert. *Africa and United States Policy.* Englewood Cliffs, NJ: Prentice-Hall, 1967.
———. *From Empire to Nation: The Rise to Self-Assertion of Asian and African Peoples.* Cambridge, MA: Harvard University Press, 1960.
Emerson, Rupert and Martin Kilson. "The American Dilemma in a Changing World: The Rise of Africa and the Negro American." *Daedalus* (Fall 1965): 1055–84.
Eschen, Penny M. Von. *Race against Empire: Black Americans and Anticolonialism, 1935–1957.* Ithaca, NY: Cornell University Press, 1997.
Esseks, John D. "Political Independence and Economic Decolonization: The Case of Ghana under Nkrumah." *Western Political Quarterly,* 24, 1 (March 1971): 59–64.

Etzold, Thomas H., and John Lewis Gaddis, eds. *Containment: Documents on American Policy and Strategy, 1945–1950.* New York: Columbia University Press, 1978.

Ezera, Kalu. *Constitutional Developments in Nigeria.* Cambridge: Cambridge University Press, 1960.

Fanon, Frantz. *The Wretched of the Earth.* New York: Grove Press, 1963.

Ferrell, Robert H., ed. *The Eisenhower Diaries.* New York: W. W. Norton, 1981.

Fieldhouse, David K. "The Economic Exploitation of Africa: Some British and French Comparisons." In *France and Britain in Africa: Imperial Rivalry and Colonial Rule,* eds. Prosser Gifford and Wm. Roger Louis. New Haven, CT, and London: Yale University Press, 1971: 593–662.

Fitch, Bob, and Mary Oppenheimer. *Ghana: The End of an Illusion.* New York and London: Monthly Review Press, 1966.

Foltz, William J. *From French West Africa to the Mali Federation.* New Haven, CT, and London: Yale University Press, 1965.

Frieden, Jeffrey A. "The Economics of Intervention: American Overseas Investments and Relations with Underdeveloped Areas, 1890–1950." *Comparative Studies in Society and History,* 31, 1 (January 1989): 55–80.

Frimpong, Kofi. "The Joint Provincial Council of Paramount Chiefs and the Politics of Independence, 1946–58." *Transactions of the Historical Society of Ghana,* 1, 14 (June 1973): 79–91.

Funk, Arthur L. *Charles de Gaulle: The Crucial Years, 1943–1944.* Norman: University of Oklahoma Press, 1959.

Gallagher, John, and Ronald Robinson. "The Imperialism of Free Trade." *Economic History Review,* 6, 1 (1953): 1–15.

Garrow, David J. *Bearing the Cross: Martin Luther King, Jr., and the Southern Christian Leadership Conference.* New York: William Morrow and Co., 1986.

George, Alexander L. "The 'Operational Code': A Neglected Approach to the Study of Political Leaders and Decision-Making." *International Studies Quarterly,* 13, 2 (June 1969): 190–222.

Gibbs, David N. *The Political Economy of Third World Intervention: Mines, Money and U.S. Policy in the Congo Crisis.* Chicago and London: University of Chicago Press, 1991.

Gill, Stephen. "Hegemony, Consensus and Trilateralism." *Review of International Studies,* 12, 3 (July 1986): 205–22.

Goldstein, Judith, and Robert O. Keohane, eds. *Ideas and Foreign Policy: Beliefs, Institutions and Political Change.* Ithaca, NY: Cornell University Press, 1993.

Gramsci, Antonio. *Selections from the Prison Notebooks of Antonio Gramsci,* trans. Quintin Hoare and Geoffrey Nowell Smith. New York: International Publishers, 1971.

Grundy, Kenneth W. "Nkrumah's Theory of Underdevelopment: An Analysis of Recurrent Themes." *World Politics,* 15, 3 (April 1963): 438–54.

Gupta, Sisir K. "Asian Nonalignment." *Annals of the American Academy of Political and Social Science,* 32 (November 1965): 44–51.

Hagen, James M., and Vernon W. Ruttan. "Development Policy under Eisenhower and Kennedy." *Journal of Developing Areas,* 23, 1 (October 1988): 1–30.

Hahn, Peter. *The United States, Great Britain, and Egypt, 1945–1956: Strategy and Diplomacy in the Early Cold War.* Chapel Hill: University of North Carolina Press, 1991.

Hargreaves, John D. *Decolonization in Africa.* London and New York: Longman, 1988.

Hart, David. "The Political Economy of a Development Scheme: The Volta River Project."

International Relations, 6, 1 (May 1978): 245–56.

———. *The Volta River Project: A Case Study in Politics and Technology.* Edinburgh: Edinburgh University Press, 1980.

Haviland, Jr., H. Field. "Foreign Aid and the Policy Process: 1957." *American Political Science Review,* 52, 3 (September 1958): 689–724.

Hayter, Teresa. "French Aid to Africa: Its Scope and Achievements." *International Affairs,* 41, 2 (April 1965): 236–51.

Helmreich, Jonathan E. *United States Relations with Belgium and the Congo, 1940–1960.* Newark: University of Delaware Press, 1998.

Hero Jr., Alfred O. "American Negroes and U.S. Foreign Policy: 1937–1967." *Conflict Resolution,* 12, 2 (June 1969): 220–51.

———. *The Southerner and World Affairs.* Baton Rouge: Louisiana State University Press, 1965.

Hersh, Seymour M. *The Price of Power: Kissinger in the Nixon White House.* New York: Summit Books, 1983.

Herskovits, Jean. "Subsaharan Africa: The Lowest Priority." In *The Dynamics of World Power: A Documentary History of United States Foreign Policy 1945–1973, vol. 5,* ed. Albert M. Schlesinger, Jr. New York: Chelsea House, 1973: 539–709.

Hess, Gary. "Global Expansion and Regional Balances: The Emerging Scholarship on United States Relations with India and Pakistan." *Pacific Historical Review,* 56, 2 (May 1987): 259–95.

Heymann Jr., Hans. "Soviet Foreign Aid as a Problem for U.S. Policy." *World Politics,* 12, 4 (July 1960): 525–40.

Hickey, Dennis, and Kenneth C. Wylie. *An Enchanting Darkness: The American Vision of Africa in the Twentieth Century.* East Lansing: Michigan State University Press, 1993.

Hill, Polly. *The Gold Coast Cocoa Farmer: A Preliminary Survey.* London: Oxford University Press, 1956.

Hirshman, Albert. *The Strategy of Economic Development.* New Haven, CT: Yale University Press, 1957.

Hodgkin, Thomas. *African Political Parties.* Harmondsworth, England: Penguin Books, 1961. ———. *Nationalism in Colonial Africa.* London: Frederick Muller, 1956.

Hodgkin, Thomas and Ruth Schachter. "French-Speaking West Africa in Transition." *International Conciliation,* 528 (May 1960): 375–429.

Hogan, Michael J. "American Marshall Planners and the Search for a European Neocapitalism." *American Historical Review,* 90, 1 (February 1985): 44–72.

———. *The Marshall Plan: America, Britain, and the Reconstruction of Western Europe, 1947–1952.* Cambridge and New York: Cambridge University Press, 1987.

———. "Paths to Plenty: Marshall Plan Planners and the Debate over European Integration, 1947–1948." *Pacific Historical Review,* 53, 3 (August 1984): 337–65.

———. "Revival and Reform: America's Twentieth-Century Search for a New Economic Order Abroad." *Diplomatic History,* 8, 4 (Fall 1984): 287–310.

———. "The Search for a 'Creative Peace': The United States, European Unity, and the Origins of the Marshall Plan." *Diplomatic History,* 6, 3 (Summer 1982): 267–85.

Holland, Matthew F. *America and Egypt: From Roosevelt to Eisenhower.* Westport, CT, and London: Praeger, 1996.

Hoopes, Townsend. *The Devil and John Foster Dulles: The Diplomacy of the Eisenhower Era.* Boston: Little, Brown, 1973.

Hopkins, A. G. *An Economic History of West Africa.* London: Longman, 1973.
Hoskyns, Catherine. *The Congo since Independence: January 1960–December 1961.* London: Oxford University Press, 1965.
Houphouet-Boigny, Felix. "Black Africa and the French Union." *Foreign Affairs,* 35, 34 (July 1957): 593–99.
Howard, Rhoda. *Colonialism and Underdevelopment in Ghana.* New York: Africana Publishing Company, 1978.
Hull, Cordell. *The Memoirs of Cordell Hull, vol. 2.* New York: The Macmillan Press, 1948.
Hunt, Michael. *Ideology and U.S. Foreign Policy.* New Haven, CT, and London: Yale University Press, 1987.
Iweriebor, Ehiedu E. G. *Radical Politics in Nigeria, 1945–1950.* Zaria, Nigeria: Ahmadu Bello University Press, 1996.
Jackson, Robert G. A. "The Volta River Project." *Progress: The Unilever Project,* 50, 4 (1964): 146–61.
Jackson, Scott. "Prologue to the Marshall Plan: The Origins of the American Commitment to a European Recovery Program." *Journal of American History,* 65, 4 (March 1979): 1043–68.
Jacobson, Harold K. "Labor, the UN and the Cold War." *International Organization,* 11, 1 (Winter 1957), 55–67.
James, Alan. *Britain and the Congo Crisis, 1960–63.* London: Macmillan, 1996.
Janis, Irving. *Victims of Groupthink: A Psychological Study of Foreign Policy and Fiascoes.* Boston: Houghton Mifflin, 1972.
Jeffries, Richard. *Class, Power and Ideology in Ghana: The Railwaymen of Sekondi.* Cambridge: Cambridge University Press, 1978.
Johnston, Bruce F. "Farm Surpluses and Foreign Policy." *World Politics,* 10, 1 (October 1957): 1–23.
Joseph, Richard. "The Gaullist Legacy: Patterns of French Neo-Colonialism." *Review of African Political Economy,* 6 (May–August 1976): 4–13.
Kabongo, Ilungo. "The Catastrophe of Belgian Decolonization." In *Decolonization and African Independence: The Transfer of Power, 1960–1980,* eds. Prosser Gifford and Wm. Roger Louis. New Haven, CT, and London: Yale University Press, 1988: 381–400.
Kaiser, Henry J., and Company. *Reassessment Report on the Volta River Project for the Government of Ghana.* Oakland, CA: 1959.
Kalb, Madeleine G. *The Congo Cables: The Cold War in Africa—From Eisenhower to Kennedy.* New York: Macmillan, 1982.
Kanza, Thomas. *Conflict in the Congo: The Rise and Fall of Lumumba.* Harmondsworth, England: Penguin Books, 1972.
Kaplan, Jacob J. *The Challenge of Foreign Aid: Policies, Problems, and Possibilities.* New York: Frederick A. Praeger, 1967.
Kauffman, Kenneth M., and Helena Stalson. "U.S. Assistance to Less Developed Countries, 1956–65." *Foreign Affairs,* 45, 4 (July 1967): 715–25.
Kaufman, Burton I. *Trade and Aid: Eisenhower's Foreign Economic Policy, 1953–1961.* Baltimore: Johns Hopkins University Press, 1982.
———. "The United States Response to the Soviet Economic Offensive of the 1950s." *Diplomatic History,* 2, 2 (Spring 1978): 153–65.
Keith, A. B. *Responsible Government in the Dominions, vol. 1.* London: Oxford University Press, 1928.

Keith, Robert C. "The Nkrumah Visit: A Triumphal Return." *Africa Special Report* (August 1958): 1–7.

Kent, John. "The Ewe Question, 1945–56: French and British Reactions to Nationalism in West Africa." In Michael Twaddle, ed. *Imperialism, the State and the Third World.* London and New York: British Academic Press, 1992: 183–206.

———. *The Internationalization of Colonialism: Britain, France, and Black Africa, 1939–1956.* Oxford: Clarendon Press, 1992.

Killick, Tony. "The Possibilities of Economic Control." In *A Study of Contemporary Ghana, vol. 1: The Economy of Ghana,* eds. Walter Birmingham, I. Neustadt, E. N. Omaboe. Evanston: Northwestern University Press, 1966: 411–38.

———. "The Volta River Project." In *A Study of Contemporary Ghana, vol. 1: The Economy of Ghana,* eds. Walter Birmingham, I. Neustadt, E. N. Omaboe. Evanston: Northwestern University Press, 1966: 391–410.

Kilson, Martin." African Political Change and the Modernization Process." *Journal of Modern African Studies,* 1, 4 (December 1963): 425–40.

———. "Nationalism and Social Classes in British West Africa." *Journal of Politics,* 20, 2 (May 1958): 368–87.

———. *Political Change in West Africa: A Study of the Modernization Process in Sierra Leone.* New York: Atheneum, 1969.

Kimble, David. *A Political History of Ghana: The Rise of Gold Coast Nationalism.* Oxford: Clarendon Press, 1963.

Kitchen, Helen. "Still on Safari in Africa." In *Centerstage: American Diplomacy Since World War II,* ed. L. Carl Brown. New York and London: Holmes & Meier, 1990: 171–92.

Kolko, Gabriel. *Confronting the Third World: United States Foreign Policy, 1945–1980.* New York: Pantheon Books, 1988.

Kornegay, Francis, and Chris Landsberg, "Overcoming White Foreign Affairs Dominance in South Africa and America," *Africa Insight* (January 2000): 33–37.

Kust, Matthew J. "Economic Development and Agricultural Surpluses." *Foreign Affairs,* 35, 1 (October 1956): 105–15.

LaFeber, Walter. "Roosevelt, Churchill, and Indochina: 1942–45." *American Historical Review,* 80, 5 (December 1975): 1277–95.

Langer, William L. *Our Vichy Gamble.* New York: Alfred A. Knopf, 1947.

Langer, William L., and S. Everett Gleason. *The Undeclared War, 1940–1941.* New York: Harper Publishers, 1953.

———. *The Challenge of Isolation, 1937–1940.* New York: Harper & Bros., 1952.

Lee, J. M. *Colonial Government and Good Government: A Study of the Ideas Expressed by the British Official Classes in Planning Decolonization 1939–1964.* Oxford: Clarendon Press, 1967.

Leffler, Melvyn. "The United States and the Strategic Dimensions of the Marshall Plan." *Diplomatic History,* 12, 3 (Summer 1988): 227–306.

Legum, Colin. *Pan-Africanism: A Short Political Guide.* London: Pall Mall, 1962.

Lenin, V. I. *Imperialism: The Highest Stage of Capitalism.* Moscow: Foreign Languages Publishing House, 1947.

Lewis, W. A. *The Theory of Economic Growth.* London: Allen and Unwin, 1961.

Leys, Colin. *Underdevelopment in Kenya: The Political Economy of Neo-Colonialism 1964–1971.* Berkeley and Los Angeles: University of California Press, 1974.

Louis, Wm. Roger. *The British Empire in the Middle East 1945–1951: Arab Nationalism, the United States, and Postwar Imperialism.* New York: Oxford University Press, 1984.

———. *Imperialism at Bay, 1941–1945: The United States and the Decolonization of the British Empire.* New York: Oxford University Press, 1977.

Louis, Wm. Roger, and Ronald Robinson, "The United States and the Liquidation of British Empire in Tropical Africa, 1941–1951." In *The Transfer of Power in Africa: Decolonization 1940–1960,* eds. Prosser Gifford and Wm. Roger Louis. New Haven, CT: Yale University Press, 1982: 31–55.

Lugard, Frederick. *The Dual Mandate in British Tropical Africa.* 5th ed. London: Frank Cass, 1965.

MacFarlane, S. Neil. *Superpower Rivalry & 3rd World Radicalism: The Idea of National Liberation.* London and Sydney: Croom Helm, 1985.

Mahoney, Richard D. *JFK: Ordeal in Africa.* New York: Oxford University Press, 1983.

Marshall, Judith. "The State of Ambivalence: Right and Left Options in Ghana." *Review of African Political Economy,* 5 (1976): 49–62.

Martin, Guy. "The Historical, Economic, and Political Bases of France's African Policy." *Journal of Modern African Studies,* 23, 2 (June 1985): 189–208.

McGhee, George. *Envoy to the Middle World: Adventures in Diplomacy.* New York: Harper & Row, 1983.

McMahon, Robert. *The Cold War on the Periphery: The United States, India, and Pakistan.* New York: Columbia University Press, 1994.

Melanson, Richard. "The Foundations of Eisenhower's Foreign Policy: Continuity, Community, and Consensus." In *Reevaluating Eisenhower: American Foreign Policy in the 1950s,* eds. Richard Melanson and David Mayers. Urbana and Chicago: University of Illinois Press, 1987: 31–64.

Meriwether, James H. "The African Connection and the Struggle for Freedom: Africa's Role in African-American Life, 1935–1963." Ph.D. dissertation, University of California, Los Angeles (1995).

Merriam, Alan P. *Congo: Background of Conflict.* Evanston, IL: Northwestern University Press, 1961.

Meyer, Gail E. *Egypt and the United States: The Formative Years.* Cranbury, NJ, and London: Associated University Press, 1980.

Mittleman, James. *Ideology and Politics in Uganda from Obote to Amin.* Ithaca, NY, and London: Cornell University Press, 1975.

Mohan, Jitendra. "Ghana, the Congo, and the United Nations." *Journal of Modern African Studies,* 7, 3 (1969): 369–406.

———. "Nkrumah and Nkrumahism." In *The Socialist Register 1967,* eds. Ralph Miliband and John Saville. New York: Monthly Review Press, 1967: 191–228.

Montgomery, John D. *Aid to Africa: New Test for U.S. Policy* Headline Series No. 149. New York: Foreign Policy Association-World Affairs Center, September/October, 1961.

Morgan, D. J. *The Official History of Colonial Development, vol. 5: Guidance towards Self-Government in British Colonies, 1941–1971.* London: Macmillan Press, 1980.

Morgenthau, Ruth Schachter. *Political Parties in French-Speaking West Africa.* London: Oxford University Press, 1964.

Morris, Milton, D. "Black Americans and the Foreign Policy Process: The Case of Africa." *Western Political Quarterly,* 25, 3 (September 1972): 451–63.

Morrow, John H. *First American Ambassador to Guinea.* New Brunswick, NJ: Rutgers University Press, 1968.
Mortimer, Edward. *France and Africans, 1944–1960: A Political History.* London: Faber and Faber, 1969.
Moxon, James. *Volta: Man's Greatest Lake.* London: Andre Deutsch, 1969.
Musambachime, Mwelwa C. "The Changing Political Personality of an African Politician: The Case of Patrice Emery Lumumba." *Genève-Afrique,* 25, 2 (1967): 61–78.
Newton, C. C. S. "The Sterling Crisis of 1947 and the British Response to the Marshall Plan." *Economic History Review,* 2nd series, 38, 3 (August 1984): 391–408.
Newton, Scott. "Britain, the Sterling Area and European Integration, 1945–50." *Journal of Imperial and Commonwealth History,* 13, 3 (May 1985): 163–82.
Nielsen, Waldermar A. *The Great Powers and Africa.* New York: Praeger Publishers, 1969.
Nkrumah, Kwame. *Africa Must Unite.* New York: Frederick A. Praeger, 1963.
———. "African Prospect." *Foreign Affairs,* 37, 1 (October 1958): 45–53.
———. *Autobiography.* London: Thomas Nelson, 1957.
———. *Challenge of the Congo.* New York: International Publishers, 1967.
———. *I Speak of Freedom: A Statement of African Ideology.* New York: Frederick A. Praeger, 1961.
———. *Neocolonialism: The Last Stage of Imperialism.* New York: International Publishers, 1965.
Noer, Thomas J. "'Non-Benign Neglect': The United States and Black Africa in the Twentieth Century." In *American Foreign Relations: A Historiographical Review,* eds. Gerald K. Haines and J. Samuel Walker. Westport, CT: Greenwood Press, 1981: 271–92.
Nwaubani, Ebere. "Getting behind a Myth: The British Labour Party and Decolonization in Africa, 1945–1951." *Australian Journal of Politics and History,* 39, 2 (1993): 197–217.
Nzongola-Ntalaja. "United States Policy toward Zaire." In *African Crisis Areas and U.S. Foreign Policy,* eds. Gerald J. Bender, James Coleman, and Richard L. Sklar. Berkeley and Los Angeles: University of California Press, 1985: 225–38.
Olusanya, Gabriel O. *The Second World War and Politics in Nigeria, 1939–1953.* Lagos, Nigeria: University of Lagos and Evans, 1973.
———. "The Zikist Movement: A Study in Political Radicalism, 1946–50." *Journal of Modern African Studies,* 4, 3 (November 1966): 323–33.
Onimode, Bade. *Imperialism and Underdevelopment in Nigeria: Dialectics of Mass Poverty.* London: Macmillan and Zed, 1983.
Orchard, John E. "ECA and the Dependent Territories." *Geographical Review,* 41, 1 (January 1951): 66–87.
Osadebay, Dennis. *Building a Nation.* Ibadan, Nigeria: Macmillan, 1978.
Padmore, George. *Pan-Africanism or Communism?* London: Dennis Dobson, 1956.
Panaf Great Lives. *Kwame Nkrumah.* London: Panaf, 1974.
Panaf Great Lives. *Sekou Toure.* London: Panaf, 1978.
Plummer, Brenda G. *Rising Wind: Black Americans and U.S. Foreign Affairs, 1935–1960.* Chapel Hill: University of North Carolina Press, 1996.
Pollard, Robert A. *Economic Security and the Origins of the Cold War, 1945–1950.* New York: Columbia University Press, 1985.
Price, J. H. *Political Institutions of West Africa.* London: Hutchinson, 1966.
Pruessen, Ronald W. *John Foster Dulles: The Road to Power.* New York: The Free Press; London: Collier Macmillan, 1982.

Quaison-Sackey, Alex. *Africa Unbound: Reflections of an African Statesman.* New York: Frederick A. Praeger, 1963.
Rado, Emil R. "The Volta River Project: Retrospect and Prospect." *Economic Bulletin,* 4, 2 (February 1960): 20–30.
Range, Willard. *Franklin D. Roosevelt's World Order.* Athens: University of Georgia Press, 1959.
Rathbone, Richard, ed. *British Documents on the End of Empire: Ghana,* 2 vols. London: HMSO, 1992.
Ray, Deborah Wing. "The Takoradi Route: Roosevelt's Prewar Venture beyond the Western Hemisphere." *Journal of American History,* 62, 2 (September 1975): 340–58.
Rivière, Claude. *Guinea: The Mobilization of a People,* trans. Virginia Thompson and Richard Adloff. Ithaca and London: Cornell University Press, 1977.
Roark, James L. "American Black Leaders: The Response to Colonialism and the Cold War, 1943–1953." *African Historical Studies,* 4, 2 (1971): 253–70.
Robinson, Ronald. "The Excentric Idea of Imperialism, with or without Empire." In *Imperialism and After: Continuities and Discontinuities,* eds. Wolfgang J. Mommsen and Jürgen Osterhammel. London: Allen & Unwin, 1986: 267–324.
———. "Imperial Theory and the Question of Imperialism after Empire." *Journal of Imperial and Commonwealth History,* 12, 2 (January 1984): 42–54.
———. "Non-European Foundations of European Imperialism: Sketch for a Theory of Collaboration." In *Studies in the Theory of Imperialism,* eds. Roger Owen and Bob Sutcliffe, London: Longman, 1972: 117–40.
Rooney, David. *Kwame Nkrumah: The Political Kingdom in the Third World.* London: I. B. Tauris, 1988.
Roosevelt, Elliot. *As He Saw It.* New York: Duell, Sloan and Pearce, 1946.
Rosenman, Samuel I., comp. *The Public Papers and Addresses of Franklin D. Roosevelt, vol. 11, 1942.* New York: Russell and Russell, 1969.
———, comp. *The Public Papers and Addresses of Franklin D. Roosevelt, vol. 12, 1943.* New York: Russell and Russell, 1969.
Rosenstein-Rodan, P. N. "Problems of Industrialization of Eastern and Southeastern Europe." *Economic Journal,* 53, 210–11 (June–September 1943): 202–11.
Rostow, W. W. *Eisenhower, Kennedy, and Foreign Aid.* Austin: University of Texas Press, 1985.
———. *The Stages of Economic Growth: A Non-Communist Manifesto.* Cambridge: Cambridge University Press, 1960.
Sady, Emil J. *The United Nations and Dependent Peoples.* Washington, DC: The Brookings Institution, 1956.
Saloway, Reginald. "The New Gold Coast." *International Affairs,* 31, 4 (October 1955): 469–76.
Sbrega, John J. "The Anticolonial Policies of Franklin D. Roosevelt: A Reappraisal." *Political Science Quarterly,* 101, 1 (1986): 65–84.
Schatzberg, Michael G. *Mobutu or Chaos? The United States and Zaire, 1960–1990.* Lanham, MD: University Press of America, 1991.
Schlesinger, Jr., Arthur M. *A Thousand Days: John F. Kennedy in the White House.* Boston: Houghton Mifflin, 1965.
Schraeder, Peter J. *United States Foreign Policy toward Africa: Incrementalism, Crisis and Change.* New York: Cambridge University Press, 1994.

Shalom, Stephen R. *The United States and the Philippines: A Study of Neocolonialism.* Philadelphia: Institute for the Study of Human Issues, 1981.
Shils, Edward. "Political Development in the New States (I)." *Comparative Studies in Society and History,* 2, 3 (April 1960): 265–93.
———. "Political Development in the New States (II)." *Comparative Studies in Society and History,* 2, 4 (July 1960): 379–411.
Siekman, Philip. "Edgar Kaiser's Gamble in Africa." *Fortune* (November 1961): 128–31.
Singer, Hans. *International Development: Growth and Change.* New York: McGraw Hill, 1964.
Skinner, Elliot P. "African, Afro-American, White Americans: A Case of Pride and Prejudice." *Freedomways* (Summer 1965): 380–95.
Sklar, Richard L. *Nigerian Political Parties: Power in an Emergent African Nation.* Princeton, NJ: Princeton University Press, 1970.
Skurnik, W. A. E. "France and Fragmentation in West Africa: 1945–1960." *Journal of African History,* 8, 2 (1967): 317–33.
Smith, Gaddis. *Dean Acheson.* New York: Cooper Square Publishers, 1972.
Smith, Tony. *The French Stake in Algeria, 1954–1962.* Ithaca, NY: Cornell University Press, 1978.
Steininger, Rolf. "John Foster Dulles, the European Community, and the German Question." In *John Foster Dulles and the Diplomacy of the Cold War,* ed. Richard H. Immerman. Princeton, NJ: Princeton University Press, 1990: 79–108.
Stern, Robert M. "Agricultural Surplus Disposal and U.S. Economic Policies." *World Politics,* 12, 3 (April 1960): 422–33.
Stivers, William. "Eisenhower and the Middle East." In *Reevaluating Eisenhower: American Foreign Policy in the 1950s,* eds. Richard Melanson and David Mayers. Urbana and Chicago: University of Illinois Press, 1987: 192–219.
Thompson, W. Scott. *Ghana's Foreign Policy, 1957–1966: Diplomacy, Ideology, and the New State.* Princeton, NJ: Princeton University Press, 1969.
Thorne, Christopher. "Indonesia and Anglo-American Relations, 1942–1945." *Pacific Historical Review,* 45, 1 (February 1976): 73–96.
Toure, Sekou. *Expérience guinéenne et unité africaine.* Paris: Présence africaine, 1959.
Trevor-Roper, Hugh. *The Rise of Christian Europe.* London: Harcourt, Brace and World, 1965.
Truman, Harry S. *Memoirs, vol. 1: Year of Decisions.* Garden City, NY: Doubleday, 1955.
Tully, Andrew. *CIA: The Inside Story.* New York: William Morrow, 1962.
Venkataramani, M. S. "The United States, the Colonial Issue, and the Atlantic Charter Hoax." *International Studies* (Delhi), 13, 1 (January–March 1974):1–5.
Wallerstein, Immanuel. "Elites in French-speaking West Africa: The Social Basis of Ideas." *Journal of Modern African Studies,* 3, 1 (May 1965): 1–23.
———. *The Stages of Economic Growth: A Non-Communist Manifesto.* Cambridge: Cambridge University Press, 1960.
Wasserman, Gary. *Politics of Decolonization: Kenya Europeans and the Land Issue, 1960–1965.* Cambridge: Cambridge University Press, 1976.
Wasson, Thomas C. "The Mystery of Dakar: An Enigma Resolved." *American Foreign Service Journal,* 20, 4 (April 1943): 169–218.
Watt, D. Cameron. *Succeeding John Bull: America in Britain's Place, 1900–1975.* Cambridge: Cambridge University Press, 1984.

Weissman, Stephen R. *American Foreign Policy in the Congo, 1960–1964.* Ithaca, NY, and London: Cornell University Press, 1974.

———. "CIA Covert Action in Zaire and Angola: Patterns and Consequences." *Political Science Quarterly,* 94, 2 (Summer 1979): 263–86.

Welch, Jr., Claude E. *Dream of Unity: Pan Africanism and Political Unification in West Africa.* Ithaca, NY: Cornell University Press, 1966.

Werth, Alexander. *The de Gaulle Revolution.* London: Robert Hale, 1960.

Westwood, Andrew F. *Foreign Aid in a Foreign Policy Framework.* Washington, DC: The Brookings Institution, 1966.

White, Dorothy S. *Black Africa and de Gaulle: From the French Empire to Independence.* University Park: Pennsylvania State University Press, 1979.

Wight, Martin. *The Development of the Legislative Council, 1606–1945.* London: Faber & Faber, 1946.

Wilson, H. S. *African Decolonization.* London: Edward Arnold, 1994.

Yansane, Aguibo Y. *Decolonization in West African States with French Colonial Legacy—Comparison and Contrast: Development in Guinea, the Ivory Coast and Senegal (1945–1980).* Cambridge, MA: Schenkman Publishing, 1984.

Yergin, Daniel. *The Prize: The Epic Quest for Oil, Money and Power.* New York: Simon & Schuster, 1992.

Young, Crawford. *Politics in the Congo: Decolonization and Independence.* Princeton, NJ: Princeton University Press, 1965.

———. "The Zairean Crisis and American Foreign Policy." In *African Crisis Areas and U.S. Foreign Policy,* eds. Gerald J. Bender, James Coleman, and Richard L. Sklar. Berkeley and Los Angeles: University of California Press, 1985: 209–24.

Zyzniewski, Stanley J. "The Soviet Bloc and the Underdeveloped Countries." *World Politics,* 11 (1958–59): 378–98.

INDEX

Acheson, Dean
  opposition to independence for European colonies in Africa, 37–38, 49, 232
  on the Volta River Project, 174
Adamafia, Tawia (Ghanaian labor leader), 145
Adekogbe, Elizabeth (Foreign Leader Program grantee), 96
Adeniyi, Jonathan (Foreign Leader Program grantee), 96
Adjei, Ajo (Ghanaian diplomat), 121, 141–43
Adu, A. L. (Ghanaian diplomat), 125
African Studies Program, Northwestern University
  study on Africa for the United States Senate, 99, 101, 205, 230, 232, 240
Akosombo, 189, 203
Akpom, E. N. (Foreign Leader Program grantee), 96
Akran, Claudius (deputy premier, Western Nigeria), 229
All African Peoples' Conference
  on neocolonialism, 22, 98
  1958 conference in Accra, 138
  Lumumba at, 150
Allen, George (United States assistant secretary of state), 43, 241
All-Ewe Conference, 75–78
Aluminum Company of America (ALCOA), 199–200
Aluminum of Canada (ALCAN), 166, 173, 175, 176, 178, 181, 183, 184, 196, 198, 199
Amachree, Godfrey Kio Jaja (Foreign Leader Program grantee), 96
Amegee, Paul (Foreign Leader Program grantee), 97
Aminu, Muhammadu (Foreign Leader Program grantee), 96
Arden-Clarke, Charles (last colonial governor of the Gold Coast), 13, 15
Aribisala, Theophilus (Foreign Leader Program grantee), 96
Aswan Dam, 89, 203
Awokoya, Stephen Oluwole (Foreign Leader Program grantee), 96
Awolowo, Obafemi, xv, 17

Balewa, Abubakar Tafawa (prime minister, Nigeria) 97, 108, 227
Ball, George (United States undersecretary of state), 28
Bello, Ayo (Foreign Leader Program grantee), 96
Bing, Geoffrey (attorney general, Ghana), 123
Bissel, Richard, Jr., 67
Blisson, Henry Claude (personal assistant to prime minister of Senegal), 110

Boka, Ernest (Foreign Leader Program grantee), 97
Bond, Horace M. (president, Lincoln University)
  involvement in the Volta River Project, 174–75
Bonne, Nii Kwabena (Ghanaian chief and businessman)
  organization of boycott of imported goods, 4, 9
Botsio, Kojo (minister for trade and industries, Ghana)
  on neocolonialism, 22
  in talks on possible United States economic assistance to Ghana, 129
  meeting on Volta River Project, 188
Bourgerie, Elmer (director, United States State Department Office of African Affairs), 47, 70
Braithwaite, Talabi A. (Foreign Leader Program grantee), 96
Brezhnev, Leonid
  visit to Guinea and Ghana, 162
British Aluminum Company (BAC), 164, 173, 175, 181, 183, 196, 198
Bureau of African Affairs, xviii, 237
Burns, Alan (Britain's representative at the Trusteeship Council), 80–81, 83
Byroade, Henry (United States assistant secretary of state), 36, 38, 46

Cabell, Charles (CIA deputy director)
  the relationship between Islam and "communism," 88
Central Intelligence Agency
  successor to the Office of Strategic Services, 29
  ranking areas of strategic importance, 30
  on independence of European colonies, 35
  importance of "industrial-military power," 53
  importance of Africa's raw materials, 66
  British role in United States global power, 244
  involvement in the Congo, 290 n. 151
Chapman, Daniel (Ghanian diplomat), 191, 193–95
Churchill, Winston
  correspondence with Eisenhower on independence for European colonies, 38–40, 257 n. 54
Comité de l'Unité, 78–80
Compagnie Française de Distribution des Pétroles en Afrique, 72
Confédération Générale du Travail (Guinea), 221
The Congo crisis
  background and course, 146–47
  objectives of the Congolese government, 147–48, 306 n. 93
  UN position, 149–50
  United States objectives and attitude, 150, 157–59, 290–91 n. 161
  Eisenhower-Nkrumah correspondence, 151–52
  Eisenhower-Nkrumah meeting, 157
  United States-Ghana breach, 144, 153–54, 159–60
  Ghana's objectives, 153, 157, 159 (see also Nkrumah's speech at the UN)
  Nkrumah's speech at the UN, 153, 154–55
  United States resentment of Ghana's role, 156–60
  influence on Ghana's foreign policy, 162

330 Index

The Congo crisis *(continued)*
   Eisenhower-Toure correspondence, 223–25
   Toure-Satterthwaite meeting, 224
   See also Lumumba
Convention Peoples' Party
   formation, 10–11
   Positive Action, 12
   purge of Marxists, 122
   See also Gold Coast, Nkrumah
Cordier, Andrew (UN special representative in the Congo), 148–49
Coussey, J. Henley, 6 *See also* Gold Coast
Creech Jones, Arthur (Britain's secretary of state for the colonies)
   observations on the Coussey report, 6–7
   evaluation of United States position on colonial independence, 35

Dakar
   strategic importance for the United States, 29–30
Danquah, J. B., 10, 12, 250 n. 38
d'Arboussier, Gabriel (Foreign Leader Program grantee), 97
Decolonization
   assumed United States influence on Britain, xv-xvi
   application of modernization theory, 1–2
   nationalist interpretation, 1–2
   Britain's co-optation strategy, 17–18
   French decolonization, 18–22
   redefinition, xix, 25–27
   dependency interpretation, 17, 23–24
Defense Materials Procurement Agency, 68
de Gaulle, Charles, 19, 29, 206–09, 226
Detwiler, Louis
   interest in the Volta River Project, 174–76

Development Loan Fund (DLF), 109, 116, 129, 130, 181, 187, 193–94, 195, 196, 201, 278–89 n. 119, 285–86 n. 78
Dia, Mamadou (prime minister of Senegal), 110
Diagne, Blaise, 22
Diallo, Telli (Sekou Toure's personal emissary to the United States), 214–18
Dillon, Douglas (United States undersecretary of state)
   speech in support of French position in North Africa, 43
   nonalignment by African countries, 92–93
   United States economic policy in Africa, 107, 112–13
   strategic insignificance of Africa, 112–14
   meeting on aid to Mali, 116–17
   possible United States economic assistance to Ghana, 129–31
   meetings on Volta River Project, 187–88, 193–97
   meeting on the Konkoure hydroelectric project, 216–17
Diori, Hamani (prime minister, Niger), 229
Doherty, Richard (Foreign Leader Program grantee), 96
Douathe, Gallin (ambassador of the Central African Republic to the United States), 235
dual mandate, 85, 262 n. 1 *See also* Lugard
Dulles, Allen (CIA director)
   on Soviet-Egyptian influence in Africa, 90
   on Lumumba, 148, 158
   on Soviet influence in Guinea, 219
Dulles, John Foster
   his position on colonial (and

African independence), 40–42, 52
on nonalignment," 91–92, 272 n. 23
the importance of Ghana's independence, 119
on the Volta River Project, 175
recognition of Guinea, 213–14

Economic Cooperation Administration (ECA), xviii, 59–64, 84, 173, 276 n. 82
Eden, Anthony, 41
Egbuna, Ernest Nwanolue (Foreign Leader Program grantee), 96
Egypt
United States concern on influence in Africa, 88–90
See also Nasser
Eisenhower, Dwight David
his administration's position on African independence, 38–45, 205–06, 246–47 n. 9
private correspondence on colonial independence, 38–40, 257 n. 57
briefing concerning Nkrumah's first official visit, 87, 133
on the relationship between Islam and "communism," 88
on Nasser, 89
on nonalignment, 91–92
economic philosophy, 105
his administration's economic programs in Africa, 99–113
meeting on aid to Mali, 116–17
congratulatory message to Nkrumah, 130–31
Ejiwuno, T. O. (Foreign Leader Program grantee), 96
Esua, Eyo (Foreign Leader Program grantee), 96
European Economic Community, 102, 110, 123

The "Ewe Question" at the United Nations
background, 74–75
United States, British, and French alliance on, 75–84
United States position, 269–70 n. 121
Export-Import Bank, 174, 178, 185, 196–98, 201
Ex-servicemen
demonstrations in Accra, 3, 5

Flake, William (United States ambassador to Ghana)
handling of Gbedemah's orange juice incident, 124–25
on the establishment of Ghana/Soviet diplomatic relations, 125–26
on possible United States economic assistance to Ghana, 129
assessment of Nkrumah's foreign policy, 136
meeting with Ajo Adjei, 142–43
explanation of Ghana's foreign policy, 144–45
meeting with Nkrumah, 159–60
on Volta River Project, 190–94, 200
admission of Guinea into the UN, 214
Foreign Leader Program, 94–97 *See also* hegemonic socialization
Foreign Operations Administration, 101, 106, 276 n. 82
French Community
underlying concepts, 19
1958 referendum on, 20–21, 209
United States support, 40, 226
relevance in United States policy in Africa, 110, 112
constitutional proposals and provisions, 207, 209
French Constitution (1946), 249 n. 34, 255–56 n. 35

332 Index

Gbedemah, Komla (minister of finance, Ghana)
  formation of Convention Peoples' Party, 10
  organizing for 1951 Gold Coast elections, 13
  the Howard Johnson restaurant orange juice incident, 124–25, 180, 234
  in talks on possible United States economic assistance to Ghana, 129
  assessment by Tom Mboya, 131
  meetings on Volta River Project, 164, 180, 187–88, 201
Gerig, Benjamin (United States State Department), 90
Ghana
  United States intention to assist, 119
  United States objectives in, 120
  cultivating United States friendship, 120–28
  Soviet diplomatic representation, 125
  relations with Eastern Europe, 140
  relations with Israel, 140–41
  dependence on cocoa, 123, 160–61, 163, 165
  See also Gold Coast, Nkrumah
Gold Coast
  Coussey report, 6
  1948 riots, xviii, 3–5
  1946 constitution, 3, 248 n. 11, 250 n. 38
  1950 constitution (and its wider impact), 7–8
  1951 elections, 13
  background to 1954 constitution, 14
  1954 elections and constitution, 14
  1956 elections, 15

  See also Ghana, Nkrumah, and Watson Commission
Gramsci, Antonio, 94, 96, 97
Green, Francis (United States senator), 36, 37, 99, 104, 106, 232
Grunther, Alfred (supreme commander of the Allied Forces in Europe)
  Eisenhower's letter on independence for European colonies, 39–40
Guinea
  independence and French response, 210–11
  United States response to Guinea's independence, 211–23
  recognition by the United States, 214
  admission into the UN, 214–15
  diplomatic relations with the United States, 215
  Czech military assistance, 218–19
  United States assessment of Soviet influence, 220–21
  neutralism, 223
  See also Sekou Toure

Hammarskjold, Dag, 224
  hostility towards Lumumba, 149–50, 153
  support by Ghana, 154
  criticism by the Soviet Union, 154
Hammerton, Albert (International Confederation of Free Trade Unions)
  concern about "communist" infiltration into the Gold Coast labor movement, 121–22
Harding, Warren (United States president)
  Ewe petition to, 74
hegemonic socialization, 93–98 See also Foreign Leader Program

Herskovits, Melville, 99 *See also* African Studies Program, Northwestern University
Herter, Christian (United States secretary of state), 162
  "communist" threat in Africa, 88
  on difficulties posed by the French in Africa, 101
  congratulatory message to Nkrumah, 131
  breach with Ghana (Nkrumah), 144, 153
  criticism of Nikita Khrushchev, 152
  meeting with Nkrumah on the Congo, 157
  meeting on Volta River Project, 187
  racial discrimination against Nigerian diplomats, 235
Hickerson, John (United States assistant secretary for UN affairs), 36
Houphouet-Boigny, Felix, 21–22, 207, 304 n. 56
Hull, Cordell
  on Dakar, 29
  on United States and colonial independence, 32–33
Humphrey, George (United States secretary of the Treasury), 108

India
  United States concern on India and nonalignment in Africa, 88, 90–93
  strategic importance to the United States, 113–14
indirect rule
  impact on the constitutional development of British Africa, 2–3
  definition, 248 n. 7
internal self-government
  following the 1950 Gold Coast constitution, 7
  in British colonial practice, 251 n. 66
International Confederation of Free Trade Unions, 121–22, 164
International Cooperation Administration (ICA), 109–10, 130, 179, 183, 276 n. 82
  criticisms of Eisenhower's economic programs in Africa, 101–04, 109–10
  "Buy American" policy, 109
  talks on possible United States economic assistance to Ghana, 129
  food crisis in Ghana, 135–36
  mission to Guinea, 215–16
  guarantee of overseas American private investment, 285–86 n. 78
International Materials Policy (William Paley) Commission, 62

Jackson, Robert (economic adviser to Nkrumah), 169, 176, 188, 294 n.25
Joint Chiefs of Staff
  ranking of areas of strategic importance, 30, 53
  importance of Congo's Kitona airfield and the "western bulge" of Africa, 114
  Soviet influence in Guinea, 237

Kaiser (Henry J. Kaiser Company), 173, 178, 179, 184, 185, 188, 189, 190, 198, 201–03
Kaiser, Edgar 184, 186, 188, 189, 190, 198–99
Kanza, Thomas 147
Kasavubu, Joseph 147–48, 155, 158, 225

334   Index

Katsina, H. M. (Foreign Leader Program grantee), 96
Kennan, George, 30–31, 245
Kennedy, John F., 225, 231
Khrushchev, Nikita 156, 157
   meeting with Ghana's labor leaders; economic assistance for Ghana, 145–46
   response to request from the Congolese government, 147–48
   criticism of Dag Hammarskjold, 154
   meeting with Nkrumah, 154, 162
   appreciation of Nkrumah's UN speech, 156
Konkoure hydroelectric project (in Guinea), 173, 216–18, 304 n. 60
Kouyate, Seydou B. (Foreign Leader Program grantee), 97

League of Nations Permanent Mandates Commission
   Ewe petition to, 74
Leith, Fraser
   interest in the Volta River Project, 175–79
Lennox-Boyd, Alan, 103, 171–72
Lodge, Henry (United States representative at the UN), 42
Loi Cadre, 249 n. 34
Lord Home, 235
Lord Perth, 103
Lord Swinton, 28
Lourenço Marques conference of United States consular officials in Africa, 57–58, 68
Lugard, Frederick
   the dual mandate, 84, 262 n. 1
Lumumba, Patrice
   objectives in the Congo crisis, 147–48
   United States antipathy, 148–50, 156, 158, 289 n. 145
   UN antipathy, 149–50

   influence of Nkrumah, 150–51
   support by Nkrumah, 155
   death, 162
   support by Sekou Toure, 223–25
   See also the Congo Crisis
Luther King, Martin, Jr., 231, 236
Lyttleton, Oliver (Britain's secretary of state for the colonies), 14

Macmillan, Harold, 45
Macpherson, John (colonial governor of Nigeria), 8
Margai, Milton (prime minister of Sierra Leone), 16
Markham, James (secretary of Ghana's Pan-African Office), 123
Mboya, Tom (Kenyan nationalist)
   criticism of United States policy, 45, 229–30
   assessment of Ghana, 131
McGhee, George (United States assistant secretary of state)
   support of the European position in Africa, pp. 36–37
   attempt at formulating policy for Africa, 56–59, 239
   the Truman administration's relationship with European powers in Africa, 84
McKay, Vernon (United States State Department), 48
Mendes-France, Pierre, 39
Mobutu, Joseph, 149, 155
Morrow, John (United States ambassador to Guinea), 206, 211, 215, 216, 222–23, 225, 229, 240
Morse, Wayne (United States senator)
   criticism of United States abstention from UN declaration on independence, 44
Mutual Security Agency, 59, 64–65, 84, 174, 180, 276 n. 82

Nasser, Gamal Abdel
  United States policy towards, 89–90
  meeting with Nkrumah, 139
  See also Egypt
National Intelligence Estimate, xviii, 88, 94, 98, 246 n. 7,
National Security Council
  first paper on Africa, xviii, 239–40
  malleability of Africans, 87
  "communism," nonalignment, and Egypt's Arab nationalism, 88
  policy towards Egypt, 89–90
  containing Egypt's influence in Africa, 90
  nonalignment by African countries, 92–93
  on the size of United States economic assistance to Africa, 99
  United States to play secondary role to the Europeans in Africa, 112
  strategic insignificance of Africa, 115
  containing Soviet influence in Africa, 116
  on Ghana, 142, 144, 204
  on Guinea, 211
  accommodation of Soviet influence in Africa, 238
  decolonization-as-neocolonialism: United States policy in Africa, 55, 239–43
Navy Department
  implications of African independence, 46
Nehru, Jawaharlal, 41, 91
neocolonialism
  as the outcome of decolonization/independence, 22–25, 55, 239–43
  United States in the Philippines, 55
Nigeria
  1946 constitution, 3
  impact of constitutional proposals in the Gold Coast, 8
  1951 constitution, 8
  nature of anticolonialism, 16
  Zikist Movement, 17
Nixon, Richard
  racial stereotyping Africans, 50, 259–60 n. 106
  "communist" threat in Africa, 88, 93
  briefing on Soviet interest in Africa, 120
  meeting with William Tolbert, 126–27
  report of his visit to Africa, 232, 234
Nkrumah, Kwame, 5
  the 1948 Accra riots, 9–10
  co-optation by Britain, 17–18
  Positive Action, 11–13, 250 n. 51
  Tactical Action, 13–14
  criticism of United States policy, 45
  his personality, 119
  cultivating United States friendship, 120–28
  anticommunism and pro-West orientation, 120–24, 125–28, 133–34, 139–40, 282 n. 11
  handling of Gbedemah's orange juice incident, 124–25
  first official visit to the United States, 132–34
  reorientation of foreign policy (1958), 136–38
  economic philosophy, 164
  sponsorship of Guinea's admission into the UN, 214
  See also the Congo Crisis, Ghana, the Gold Coast, and the Volta River Project
nonalignment
  identification with "communism," 88
  India's policy, 91

nonalignment *(continued)*
  United States concern about India's policy, 90–91
  Eisenhower on, 91–92, 272 n. 23
  Dulles on, 92
  United States and nonalignment by African countries, 92–93
  Ghana's policy, 137, 139–40

Ocran, Turkson (Ghanaian labor leader), 121–22
Office of Strategic Services
  plan for United States invasion of West Africa, 29
  United States support for European empires as part of the strategy to contain the Soviet Union, 33–34
Okotie-Eboh, Festus Sam (Foreign Leader Program grantee), 96
Okulaja, Amos (Foreign Leader Program grantee), 96
Olympio, Sylvanus, 75–78
Orchard, John (top ECA official), 61, 66
Osadebay, Dennis (Nigerian politician), 16
Oyono, Ferdinand (Cameroonian representative at the UN), 235

Padmore, George, 45, 123
Palmer, Joseph, 2nd (United States deputy assistant secretary of state), 178–79, 241
Pam, B. R. (Foreign Leader Program grantee), 96
panel on the formulation of United States policy for Africa, 56–57
Parti Démocratique de Guinée, 20, 208, 209 *See also* Sekou Toure
Penfield, James (United States deputy assistant secretary of state), 107, 216
Point IV, 59–61, 84

Public Law 480, 129, 135–36, 271–72 n. 13

Quaisson-Sackey, Alex (Ghanaian diplomat), 154–56

Randall, Clarence (chairman, Eisenhower's presidential Council on Foreign Economic Policy), 106–07, 109, 232
Roosevelt, Franklin D.
  on the importance of Dakar, 30–31
  anticolonialism: a reassessment, 32–33
  on international supervisory roles for the major powers, 245
Rountree, William (United States assistant secretary of state)
  advocating a "Colombo Plan" for Africa, 111–12
Rusk, Dean, 100

Salazar, Antonio de Oliveira, 28
Saloway, Reginald (Gold Coast colonial secretary), 11–12
Satterthwaite, Joseph (United States assistant secretary of state), 107, 154, 211, 215, 218, 222, 232, 293 n. 192
self-government
  impact of indirect rule, 3
  in British colonial practice, 249 n. 33
Senators' report on 1960 visit to Africa, 32, 146, 221, 230
Senghor, Leopold, 21, 22, 207
Slagle, G. van B.
  interest in the Volta River Project, 177–79
sub-Saharan Africa (Africa south of the Sahara)
  geographical definition in United States diplomacy, xvii

strategic insignificance in United
States diplomacy, 28, 30, 53,
112–17, 245
neglect by private American
business interests, 53–54, 261 n.
123
Soviet (Cold War) factor in United
States policy, 88, 93, 113–17,
237–38
evaluation of the African-American
factor in United States policy,
233–34, 307–08 n. 20
Suez Crisis, 89
Sule, Yusuf Maitama (Foreign Leader
Program grantee), 96
Sutherland, Bill (Gbedemah's personal
assistant), 124–25

Takoradi-Chad air route, 28–29
Tettegah, John (Ghanaian labor
leader), 145
Timberlake, Clare (United States
ambassador to the Congo), 149,
156, 158–59
Togoland
as a League of Nations mandate and
a UN trust territory, 74
See also All-Ewe Conference, the
"Ewe Question" at the United
Nations, and Olympio
Tolbert, William (vice president of
Liberia), 126–27
Toure, Sekou, 214, 218, 226
advocating partnership with France,
19–20
advocates independence, 20, 208–
10
criticism of United States policy, 45,
229
on United States recognition of
Guinea, 212–13
request for English language
teachers, 216

official visit to Washington, 218–
19, 222
biography, 221–22
See also Guinea, Parti Démocratique
de Guinée
Trade Union Congress (the Gold
Coast), 12, 121
Tripartite (Britain, France, United
States) foreign ministers'
meetings, 49, 54, 68, 70, 74, 243
Truman, Harry S.
his administration's position on
African independence, 34–38
importance of Africa's raw materials,
59–66, 68
relationship with European powers
in Africa, 84
See also Acheson, "Ewe Question,"
and McGhee
Tshombe, Moïse, 147
Tubman, William, 120, 126, 138–39,
218

United American Management
Corporation
interest in the Volta River Project,
174–75
United Gold Coast Convention, 9–10
UN General Assembly
Declaration on the Granting of
Independence to Colonial
Countries and Peoples, 45
Fourth Committee involvement in
Togoland affairs, 79, 83
United States
attitude towards African
independence, 32–45, 255 n. 29
support for European
neocolonialism in Africa, xix,
54–55, 238–45
ideological (including racial)
underpinnings of foreign policy,
48–52, 228

United States *(continued)*
  belief in malleability of Africans, 56, 86–87
  cultivating Ghana's friendship, 128–36, 283 n. 37
  breach with Ghana, 144, 146, 153–54, 159–62
  the African factor on racial crisis, 234
  European power as component of United States global hegemony, 244–45
United States Congress
  neglect of Africa, xvii-xviii, 232–33
  congressional hostility to aid-giving and its impact on policy in Africa, 110–12
United States Investment Guaranty Program, 134, 285–86 n. 78
United States Operations Mission, 54, 87, 104

Villard, Henry (United States State Department), 49
Volta River Project, 130, 136, 163
  influence on Ghana's foreign policy, 123
  justification for, 163–65, 186–87
  British White Paper (including, proposals and financial estimates), 164–68
  the Preparatory Commission's Report and its aftermath, 168–73
  Nixon-Nkrumah meeting, 177
  Eisenhower-Nkrumah letters and meetings, 181, 182, 183, 186–87, 189, 191, 192–93
  World Bank study, 182, 195, 197, 200–01
  involvement of ICA, 184–86, 188
  Kaiser study, 189–90, 192, 197, 197–98
  Nkrumah-Kaiser meetings, 188, 190, 199–200
  Volta Aluminum Company (VALCO), 198–203
  loan commitments, 201

Wadsworth, James (United States representative at the UN), 45
Watson, Aiken, 5
Watson Commission (into the 1948 Gold Coast riots)
  members, 5, 249 n. 24
  causes of the riots, 5, 248 n. 19
  recommendations for constitutional change, 5–6
  on Nkrumah's anticommunism, 121
  on industrialization, 165
  See also Ex-servicemen, Gold Coast
Webb, James (United States acting secretary of state), 80
Wigny, Pierre (Belgian foreign minister), 52
Woode, Anthony (Ghanian labor leader), 121–22
World Bank, 108, 171, 172, 175, 179, 182, 187, 193, 196, 198, 201
World Federation of Trade Unions, 122

Zik (Nnamdi Azikiwe), 8, 250 n. 36

WITHDRAWN